应用型本科院校"十二五"规划教材/旅游类

2011年黑龙江省高等教育教学改革重点项目阶段性成果

英语导游培训用书

# Practical English for Tour Guides

# 实用导游英语

主 编 崔玉范 李家春
副主编 张 微 刘 巍 牟晓一

哈尔滨工业大学出版社
HARBIN INSTITUTE OF TECHNOLOGY PRESS

## 内容提要

本书是针对应用型本科院校和高等职业技术学院培养涉外导游应用型、职业性人才而编写的,突出英语导游职业能力的培养和训练。全书以旅游业现实需求和职业能力培养为目标,突出黑龙江省旅游特色,汇集英语导游服务情景对话、旅游英语应用文写作、黑龙江省主要城市和景点的中英文导游词,有利于提高导游后备人才的口语、写作能力和相关知识储备,是黑龙江省英语导游考试和导游英语学习的必备教材。

图书在版编目(CIP)数据

实用导游英语/崔玉范,李家春主编.
—哈尔滨:哈尔滨工业大学出版社,2013.8
ISBN 978-7-5603-4107-1

Ⅰ.①实… Ⅱ.①崔… ②李… Ⅲ.①导游-英语-高等学校-教材 Ⅳ.①H31

中国版本图书馆 CIP 数据核字(2013)第 122231 号

| | |
|---|---|
| 策划编辑 | 杜 燕 赵文斌 |
| 责任编辑 | 李广鑫 |
| 出版发行 | 哈尔滨工业大学出版社 |
| 社　　址 | 哈尔滨市南岗区复华四道街10号 邮编150006 |
| 传　　真 | 0451-86414749 |
| 网　　址 | http://hitpress.hit.edu.cn |
| 印　　刷 | 黑龙江省委党校印刷厂 |
| 开　　本 | 787mm×960mm 1/16 印张18.5 字数420千字 |
| 版　　次 | 2013年8月第1版 2013年8月第1次印刷 |
| 书　　号 | ISBN 978-7-5603-4107-1 |
| 定　　价 | 36.00元 |

(如因印装质量问题影响阅读,我社负责调换)

# 《应用型本科院校"十二五"规划教材》编委会

**主　任**　修朋月　竺培国

**副主任**　王玉文　吕其诚　线恒录　李敬来

**委　员**　（按姓氏笔画排序）

　　　　　丁福庆　于长福　马志民　王庄严　王建华

　　　　　王德章　刘金祺　刘宝华　刘通学　刘福荣

　　　　　关晓冬　李云波　杨玉顺　吴知丰　张幸刚

　　　　　陈江波　林　艳　林文华　周方圆　姜思政

　　　　　庹　莉　韩毓洁　臧玉英

# 序

哈尔滨工业大学出版社策划的《应用型本科院校"十二五"规划教材》即将付梓,诚可贺也。

该系列教材卷帙浩繁,凡百余种,涉及众多学科门类,定位准确,内容新颖,体系完整,实用性强,突出实践能力培养。不仅便于教师教学和学生学习,而且满足就业市场对应用型人才的迫切需求。

应用型本科院校的人才培养目标是面对现代社会生产、建设、管理、服务等一线岗位,培养能直接从事实际工作、解决具体问题、维持工作有效运行的高等应用型人才。应用型本科与研究型本科和高职高专院校在人才培养上有着明显的区别,其培养的人才特征是:①就业导向与社会需求高度吻合;②扎实的理论基础和过硬的实践能力紧密结合;③具备良好的人文素质和科学技术素质;④富于面对职业应用的创新精神。因此,应用型本科院校只有着力培养"进入角色快、业务水平高、动手能力强、综合素质好"的人才,才能在激烈的就业市场竞争中站稳脚跟。

目前国内应用型本科院校所采用的教材往往只是对理论性较强的本科院校教材的简单删减,针对性、应用性不够突出,因材施教的目的难以达到。因此亟须既有一定的理论深度又注重实践能力培养的系列教材,以满足应用型本科院校教学目标、培养方向和办学特色的需要。

哈尔滨工业大学出版社出版的《应用型本科院校"十二五"规划教材》,在选题设计思路上认真贯彻教育部关于培养适应地方、区域经济和社会发展需要的"本科应用型高级专门人才"精神,根据黑龙江省委书记吉炳轩同志提出的关于加强应用型本科院校建设的意见,在应用型本科试点院校成功经验总结的基础上,特邀请黑龙江省9所知名的应用型本科院校的专家、学者联合编写。

本系列教材突出与办学定位、教学目标的一致性和适应性,既严格遵照学科体系的知识构成和教材编写的一般规律,又针对应用型本科人才培养目标及与之相适应的教学特点,精心设计写作体例,科学安排知识内容,围绕应用讲授理论,做到"基础知识够用、实践技能实用、专业理论管用"。同时注意适当融入新理论、新技术、新工艺、新成果,并且制作了与本书配套的PPT多媒体教学课件,形成立体化教材,供教师参考使用。

《应用型本科院校"十二五"规划教材》的编辑出版,是适应"科教兴国"战略对复合型、应用型人才的需求,是推动相对滞后的应用型本科院校教材建设的一种有益尝试,在应用型创新人才培养方面是一件具有开创意义的工作,为应用型人才的培养提供了及时、可靠、坚实的保证。

希望本系列教材在使用过程中,通过编者、作者和读者的共同努力,厚积薄发、推陈出新、细上加细、精益求精,不断丰富、不断完善、不断创新,力争成为同类教材中的精品。

# 前　言

近年来,中国旅游业国际地位显著提升,现已成为世界上第三大旅游目的地国家,出境旅游消费跃居全球第三位。这些促使我们重视旅游人才的培养尤其是优秀的涉外导游人员的培养。

《实用导游英语》是针对应用型本科大学和高等职业技术学院培养涉外导游应用型、职业性人才而编写的教材,突出英语导游职业能力的培养和训练。本书以旅游业现实需求和职业能力分析为依据,由3个部分组成。

第1部分为英语导游服务情景对话,共有10个单元,按照导游服务的顺序及过程从迎客与车上讲解、登记入住、行程安排、室内观光、酒店用餐、购买纪念品、投诉处理及送客等场景,提供了常见与必备的情景对话,并且配备了大量的相关专业词汇、句型及练习,力图使学习者能够熟练掌握相关场景知识和沟通技巧,以提升英语口语水平。

第2部分为旅游英语应用文写作,共有10个单元,内容包括常用的旅游广告类宣传资料,国际旅游合同与协议,旅游行程、报价及最终确认,预订表格,登记表格内容及填写,预订确认函、邀请函及回复,以及通知等文体的写作范文。该部分内容可以使学生熟悉旅游业的常用文本,提高旅游常用文的写作能力,进而增强其就业的竞争能力。

第3部分为黑龙江省主要城市和景点的中英文导游词。通过中英文的对比阅读及学习,读者可以丰富导游知识并提高翻译能力。

在本书的编写过程中,为了适应旅游行业需求,并发展地方教育特色,特邀请旅游业内资深人士、具有国外留学经历的旅游专业人员、应用英语专业教师等参与本书的编撰工作,并经美国学者审校。本书编写过程中充分地征求了在职英语导游和翻译的意见,内容经过仔细斟酌、科学建构,并慎重选材,力图突显以下特点:

**1. 以旅游服务的实际工作需求与流程为导向**

在本书第1部分的场景对话和第2部分的应用文写作的各单元次序安排上完全依据旅游服务的实际工作流程。例如,情景对话从接团、带团到送团逐步进行。其中各单元对话内容,也遵从实际的旅游场景。例如"路线介绍"这一单元,要求学生完成英语导游及领队需要完成的"设计路线""向游客介绍路线"和"根据游客意见更改/制定新路线"3个任务。此外,在应用文写作部分,从宣传旅游景点及饭店、签订旅游合同和协议、确定旅游路线与价格到填写预订单、确认预订信函、登记、通知等,无一不是遵照旅行社对游客的实际服务工作过程。这有利于旅游英语课程与其他旅游专业课程的有效结合。

**2. 突出黑龙江省旅游特色**

根据调查，目前大部分旅游英语教材缺乏针对地方特色的教学内容，其教材的内容更倾向于选取国内的主要旅游城市的景点采用情景对话或景点介绍的方式，而针对黑龙江省旅游的英文资料又大多只是泛泛的景点介绍词。因此，此教材的出版，既可以满足黑龙江省旅游职业人才培养的需要，又可以满足黑龙江旅游行业从业人员的需求。本书的各部分学习内容及练习尽量关注黑龙江省本地资源。例如，在情景对话中，所选用的景点路线、酒店或宾馆、购物环节等均采用黑龙江省的旅游景点。在写作环节中，旅游宣传资料、合同协议等也以哈尔滨的必游景点为主。在导游介绍词中所涉及的景点均为黑龙江省的主要城市和著名旅游景点。由于黑龙江省英语导游考试所涉及的景点均包括在内，所以该教材可以作为英语导游考试的参考教材。

此外，本教材以学习者的英语口语沟通能力需求为目的，力图打破以知识传授为主要特征的传统英语课程教学模式，将教学中心转变为以工作任务为核心的项目课程模式，让学生通过完成具体项目来培养和训练自己的英语沟通能力，并发展职业能力。因此，建议教师在教学中应该采取不同于传统英语教学的教学理念和教学方法，例如采用"以学生职业需求培养为中心"的教学理念以及导游英语工作坊的方法，模拟真实工作场景，给学生提供更真实的情景体验和切身的过程指导。

本书主要由黑龙江大学应用外语学院老师负责编写，主要编写人员有：崔玉范、李家春任本书主编，其中，崔玉范拟定编写大纲和统稿、负责本教材整体编排与设计等工作，并撰写第3部分的景点介绍，共计10万字；李家春负责本书口语1～5单元和写作部分11～15单元内容的编写，以及第3部分的部分内容编写，撰写字数为15万字以上。张微负责本书口语6～10单元和写作部分16～20单元和第3部分的部分内容编写，撰写字数为15万字以上。哈尔滨商业大学的刘巍和黑龙江东方学院的牟晓一老师承担了本书的资料收集和校对工作，黑龙江大学的应用外语学院翻译研究生孙再玲、高丽娟承担了资料搜集和文字初译工作。

本书在编写过程中，得到了同行业朋友们的热忱支持，并提供了大量相关资料，在此一并表示感谢！尽管我们在编写该教材的过程中作出了很多努力，但由于能力和条件限制，疏漏和不足之处在所难免，恳请同行及读者在使用教材过程中给予关注，并将改进意见反馈给我们，以便改进完善。

本书受到2011年黑龙江省高等教育教学改革重点项目基金资助，以及黑龙江省旅游培训中心的鼎力协助，特此致谢！

编　者

2013年5月

# Contents

## Part One  Oral Practice ......... 1
Unit 1  Meeting and Transferring ......... 1
Unit 2  Arriving at the Hotel ......... 8
Unit 3  Itinerary Planning ......... 14
Unit 4  City Sightseeing ......... 20
Unit 5  Restaurant Service ......... 25
Unit 6  Shopping ......... 30
Unit 7  Dealing with Complaints ......... 36
Unit 8  Handling Accidents ......... 42
Unit 9  Checking out ......... 47
Unit 10  Sending off the Tour Group ......... 52

## Part Two  Practical Writing ......... 60
Unit 11  Advertisements and Promotion Materials ......... 60
Unit 12  Travel Agreements and Contracts ......... 67
Unit 13  Itinerary, Quotation and Final Confirmation ......... 72
Unit 14  Reservation Form and Confirmation Letter ......... 79
Unit 15  Registration Form ......... 87
Unit 16  Notices ......... 94
Unit 17  Memorandum ......... 97
Unit 18  Letter of Invitation and Reply ......... 101
Unit 19  Letter of Complaint and Reply ......... 105
Unit 20  Resumes in Tourism Industry ......... 110

## Part Three  Cities and Attractions in Heilongjiang Province ......... 114
1. Heilongjiang Province ......... 114
2. The City of Harbin ......... 122
3. The City of Qiqihar ......... 129
4. The City of Mudanjiang ......... 133
5. The City of Jiamusi ......... 136
6. Mohe County ......... 140
7. Songhua River and Sun Island ......... 143
8. Heilongjiang Norcheast Tiger Park ......... 153

9. The Zhongyang Street ……………………………………………………… 157
10. Jile Temple (The Temple of Ultimate Bliss) …………………………… 162
11. Stalin Park & Flood Control Monument ………………………………… 168
12. Yabuli Ski Resort …………………………………………………………… 170
13. The Zhaolin Park and Harbin Ice Lantern Show ……………………… 176
14. The Jingpo Lake Scenic Area …………………………………………… 179
15. Wudalianchi World Geopark ……………………………………………… 182
16. Sino-Russian Border Lake—Lake Xingkai ……………………………… 185
17. Qiqihar Zhalong Nature Reserve ………………………………………… 188
18. Mudanjiang Snow Village—Snow World in China ……………………… 198
19. Wanyan Aguda Mausoleum ………………………………………………… 199
20. History Museum of the Upper Capital of the Jin Dynasty in Acheng …… 200
21. Site of Huiningfu, the Upper Capital of the Jin Dynasty in Acheng …… 200
22. Yagou Moya Stone Carving Statues of the Jin Dynasty ……………… 201
23. Ice and Snow Sculpture World of Harbin ……………………………… 202
24. Daqing Grassland Racetrack in Daqing ………………………………… 204
25. Uhomill Scenic Spot in Daqing …………………………………………… 204
26. Harbin Huatian Wujimi Ski Resort ……………………………………… 205
27. Harbin Moon Bay Ski Resort ……………………………………………… 206
28. Jihua Longevity Mountain Ski Resort …………………………………… 206
29. Langxiang Rock Monkey Mountain Ski Resort ………………………… 207
30. The Longzhu Ski Resort in Double-Dragon Mountain ………………… 208
31. The Riyuexia Ski Resort in Tieli ………………………………………… 208
32. The Wofuo Mountain Ski Resort ………………………………………… 209
33. The Amota Tourist Resort in Daqing …………………………………… 210
34. The Shoushan Tourist Resort in Daqing ………………………………… 210
35. The Oroqen Folklore Tour ………………………………………………… 211
36. The Jiejinkou Hezhen Village ……………………………………………… 212
37. Meilisi Daur Hala Village in Qiqihar …………………………………… 213
38. Site of Longquanfu, the Upper Capital of the Bohai State …………… 213
39. The Dalizi Site ……………………………………………………………… 215
40. Heilongjiang Provincial Museum ………………………………………… 215
41. The Site of Ancient Cemetery in Hengshan …………………………… 216
42. Ruins of Puyulu Ancient City (Jin Dynasty) …………………………… 217

43. Yanzhigou Gold Mine in Mohe County ……… 218
44. Site of Ancient Human Beings of Daziyang Mountain in Songling District ……… 219
45. Site of Shibazhan Ancient Human Beings in Tahe County ……… 219
46. The Former Residence of Xiao Hong ……… 220
47. "Northern First Rafting"—Rafting On Balan River ……… 221
48. Rafting On Fenglin River ……… 221
49. Rafting On Jinsha River in Meixi District ……… 222
50. Rafting On Xiangshui River ……… 222
51. Rafting on Zhan River in Xunke County ……… 223
52. Rafting on Yongcui River ……… 223
53. Baliwan National Forest Park ……… 224
54. Longevity Mountain National Forest Park ……… 224
55. Xinlin Virgin Forest Park of "Beauty Pines" on Greater Khingan Mountains ……… 225
56. Liangshui Nature Reserve in Dailing District ……… 226
57. The Virgin Forests Park in Fangzheng County ……… 226
58. Fenglin Nature Reserve in Wuying District ……… 227
59. The Fenghuang (Phoenix) Mountain Forests Park ……… 228
60. Harbin Northern Forest Zoo ……… 229
61. The Heilongjiang Forest Botanical Garden ……… 229
62. Huzhong National Nature Reserve ……… 230
63. Langxiang Garden in the Forest ……… 231
64. Meihuashan National Forest Park ……… 232
65. The Mudanfeng (Peony Peak) National Forest Park ……… 232
66. Sandaoguan National Forest Park ……… 233
67. Linhaiqishi National Forest Park ……… 234
68. Taoshan National Forest Park ……… 234
69. Taoshan Hunting Ground ……… 235
70. Weihushan National Forest Park ……… 236
71. Chinese Woodcarving Park in the City of Woods ……… 236
72. The Lianhua (Lotus) Lake Scenic Area in Fangzheng County ……… 236
73. The Great White Mountain in Huzhong ……… 237
74. Baleng River Scenic Resort in Jidong County ……… 238
75. Unicorn Mountain Scenic Resort in Jixi City ……… 238
76. Tianci Lake (The Heaven-sent Lake) ……… 239

77. Toulong Mountain Scenic Spot in Tieli City ································ 239
78. Wogui Mountain (Crouching Turtle Mountain) ······························ 240
79. Wusuli River ······························································· 240
80. Cuibei Wetland Nature Reserve ············································ 241
81. Sanjiang Wetland Nature Reserve ·········································· 242
82. Songfeng Mountain in Acheng District ····································· 242
83. Guogeli Street ····························································· 243
84. Dragon Tower—The Highest Steel Tower in Asia ···························· 244
85. Hengdaohezi Amur Tiger Garden ··········································· 245
86. Jingpo Lake Lava Tunnel Scenery ·········································· 245
87. Shuangfeng Snow Town ···················································· 246
88. Erke Mountain ····························································· 247
89. Shedong Mountain Scenic Spot in Qiqihar ·································· 248
90. Jiayin Dinosaur National Geological Park ·································· 249
91. Maolangou National Forest Park ············································ 250
92. Stone Forest Scenic Area ·················································· 251
93. The Dinosaur Museum of Lesser Khingan Mountains ························ 251
94. Wuying National Forest Park in Yichun City ······························· 252
95. Pukui Mosque ····························································· 253
96. Jinshantun Orthodox Church ··············································· 254
97. Mahayana Temple in Qiqihar ··············································· 254
98. The Huamei Western-style Restaurant ······································ 255
99. The Modern Hotel in Harbin ··············································· 256

**Appendix** ······································································ 260
Ⅰ. Folk Arts ································································· 260
Ⅱ. Ethnic Culture ···························································· 263

**REFERENCES** ································································ 279

# Part One  Oral Practice

## Unit 1  Meeting and Transferring

### Word and Expressions

| | |
|---|---|
| local guide | 地方陪同导游,简称地陪 |
| tour leader | 领队 |
| China International Travel Service | 中国国际旅行社 |
| Youth Travel Service | 青年旅行社 |
| branch | 分部,分社 |
| fascinating | 精彩的,激动人心的 |
| parking lot | 停车场 |
| Shangri-la | 香格里拉饭店 |
| delayed flight | 延误航班 |
| terminal building | 候机大厅 |
| information desk | 问讯处 |
| baggage claim area | 行李认领区 |
| arrival platform | 下客站台 |
| berth/bunk | 火车铺位 |

## Useful Sentences

1. You must be our long-expected guests, Mr. John Denver from the U. S.
2. Allow me to introduce myself.
3. I am Han Meimei from Youth Travel Service, Harbin branch.
4. Very nice/glad/pleased to meet you.
5. I'm delighted to meet you at last.
6. How was your journey?
7. I hope you've had a pleasant flight/trip.
8. I hope you'll have a pleasant/enjoyable stay here.
9. You must be very tired after such a long trip.
10. May I help you with your baggage/luggage?
11. Now shall we go and collect your luggage?
12. I'll be happy if I can help with anything.
13. Is there anything I can do for you?
14. You have a group of 25, right?
15. I wonder if everyone is on the bus.
16. Ladies and gentlemen, attention, please.
17. May I have your attention please?
18. I would like to introduce you to Mr. Zhang.
19. This is Mr. Deng, our driver, who has had 10 years of driving experience.
20. We'll do everything possible to make your visit a pleasant experience.
21. If you have any problem or suggestion, please don't hesitate to let us know.
22. Please do remember the plate number of our bus.

## Situational Conversations

Listen to the dialogues for the first time. Then practice the dialogues by reading each of them aloud with your partner. Read through each at least twice, changing your role each time.

### Meeting the Guests at the Airport

[Scene] *In the airport lobby, a young tour guide from the Youth Travel Service, is greeting a tourist group from the United States headed by tour leader.*

(A: local guide    B: tour leader)

A: Excuse me! Are you Mr. White from Los Angeles?

B: Yes, I'm Jacky White.

A: Nice to meet you, Mr. White. I'm Han Meimei, your tour guide from the Youth Travel Service. Just call me Han.

B: Nice to meet you, too.

A: (Han Meimei shakes hands with Mr. White and other guests.) Welcome to China! And welcome to Harbin!

B: We're so glad you've come to meet us at the airport, Han.

A: Did you have a good trip, Mr. White?

B: Yes, quite pleasant. But we feel a little bit tired after the long flight.

A: Yes, you must. You all need a good rest first.

B: Nevertheless we are all excited that we've finally arrived in the country that we have been wishing to see for years.

A: You will have plenty of time to see all the fascinating places in Harbin. Is everyone in the group here?

B: Yes, a party of ten. We have five ladies and five gentlemen.

A: Good. Can we go now? Shall I help you with your luggage, Mr. White?

B: No, thanks. I can manage.

A: Please follow me, ladies and gentlemen! The shuttle bus is just waiting in the parking lot.

B: That's fine. Hurry up, guys!

A: This way, please.

[Scene] *At the airport, the local guide is waiting for a tour group from Canada. The following dialogue is between the local guide and the tour leader.*

(A: local guide    B: tour leader)

A: Excuse me. Are you Mr. Brown from Canada?

B: Yes, I am. Are you our local guide here?

A: Yes. My name is Lily. Welcome to Harbin.

B: Thank you.

A: How was your trip?

B: Pretty good. People were chatting all the way. They are getting off the plane now.

A: No hurry. But can I check the luggage first?

B: Of course. Here you are. There are 18 pieces altogether.

A: Good. Is everybody here now?

B: Let me check. Yes, everyone is here.

A: Before we move, could you tell the guests to follow my flag since it's so crowded here?

B: Sure. You go ahead and we will follow you.

## Meeting the Guest at the Railway Station

[Scene] *The local guide is waiting for the group led by the tour leader at Harbin Railway Station. She has a flag in her hand. The train has arrived and the passengers are just coming out.*

(A: local guide    B: tour leader)

A: Excuse me, sir. But are you Mr. Smith?

B: Yes, I am.

A: How do you do, Mr. Smith?

B: How do you do? I guess you must be Lily, our local guide.

A: Yes, Mr. Smith. Welcome to Harbin. I am Lily from China International Travel Service, Harbin branch.

B: Glad to meet you.

A: Glad to meet you, too. You have a group of 25, right?

B: Yes, everyone of the group is here.

A: How many pieces of luggage do you have?

B: 48 and here they are. Shall we take them to the bus?

A: No, you needn't. I'll ask the porter to take care of them.

B: Thank you very much.

A: Ladies and gentlemen, attention, please. Our bus is waiting outside. Now please follow me to the bus.

(After they get on the bus, Lily counts the tourists. And then they will head for the hotel.)

A: May I have your attention please? I wonder if everyone is on the bus.

B: Sorry, but Jenny is not on. Ah, here she comes.

A: Since everybody is on the bus, shall we go now?

B: Great.

[Scene] *The local guide, Mr. Han, is waiting for the group led by the tour leader at Harbin Railway Station. The train has arrived and the passengers are just coming out.*

(A: local guide    B: tour leader)

A: Excuse me, Sir. Are you Mr. Kennedy?

B: Yes, I am. So you are our local guide?
A: Yes, I will be your guide. My name is Han. How was your trip?
B: It's good. We enjoyed it.
A: Is everybody here in your group?
B: No, there are some people in the washroom. Let's wait for a moment. (waiting) Now everybody is here.
A: So we can move all the luggage to the coach. Everybody, listen. Please check your luggage and move them into the coach.
B: Han, you can go ahead leading the way. We will follow your flag.
A: Everybody, please follow me.
B: Please follow Han and get out of the station. Watch the flag please.
A: Our coach is waiting in the parking lot. Please remember the number of our coach—45891. Please try to remember it, in case you lose your way.

## On-the-way Introduction

[Scene] *The local tour guide, Lily, is taking the tour group from the airport to the hotel. The bus is ready to start. Mr. Brown is the tour leader.*
(A: local guide   B: tour leader   C: tourist)
A: Good afternoon, ladies and gentlemen. Are we all on the bus?
B: Just a moment, please. Mrs. Johnson is not here yet.
A: Where is she?
B: There she comes.
C: I'm sorry. Am I the last one?
A: Yes, but that's all right. I guess you must be attracted by the beauty of the airport, aren't you?
C: Well, yes! But now I'm ready to go.
A: OK. Ladies and gentlemen, on behalf of China International Travel Service and our driver, I would like to extend our warmest welcome to you. Welcome to Harbin! Welcome to the capital of Heilongjiang! Mr. Zhang, our driver, has 10 years of driving experience, and my name is Lily. During your stay in this city, Mr. Zhang and I will be at your service. We'll do everything possible to make your visit a pleasant experience. If you have any problem or request, please do not hesitate to let us know. Now, we are heading for our hotel, Shangri-la Hotel, a five-star hotel, located in Daoli District. It takes about 40 minutes' drive to get there. So please relax yourselves while I'm giving you some general information about this city.
B: That's great.

A: Harbin stands at the northeast of China and is very famous for its snow and ice culture.

B: Right. I've heard of the Snow and Ice World before and saw it once on TV. It was really fascinating. We are looking forward to seeing it tomorrow.

A: Tomorrow comes very soon. And here is our hotel. If you have any special interests, please don't hesitate to let us know. Our job is to smooth your way, care for your welfare, answer any question you have and assist you in whatever way we can. We will try to do our very best to make your stay a pleasant one. We really appreciate your understanding and cooperation. I hope you will enjoy your stay in my city.

[Scene] *Zhu Wei, the guide, met the tour group at the airport and they are driving to the hotel. The coach is about to start.*

(A: tour guide    B: tourist)

A: Is everybody on the bus?

B: Yes, I think so.

A: Shall we go now?

B: Yes, please.

A: (to all the tourists in the coach) Welcome to China, ladies and gentlemen. Let me introduce my team to you first. My name is Zhu Wei. I am a tour guide from China International Travel Service. I'll be with you for your trip in Harbin. This is Mr. Fang, our driver. We will do our best to make your trip more enjoyable and memorable. I hope you will have a very pleasant stay here in Harbin. Thank you very much! Now, we are driving straight to the hotel, the Swan Hotel.

B: Well, how far is it to the hotel?

A: It'll take us about one hour. It's one of the best four-star hotels in the city. There is warm and efficient service with extensive leisure facilities. I hope you will enjoy your stay there.

B: That's great.

A: Next, I'd like to introduce something about this city. Harbin is the capital of Heilongjiang province. It is a pleasant place to visit as well as to do business, shop, dine, or be entertained. There're many famous scenic spots and historical sites in Harbin, such as the St. Sophia Church, the Jile Temple, and so on.

B: We are really longing for a visit.

A: You must be tired after the long trip. I'm afraid you need a good rest first. We will always inform you in advance when we meet to go somewhere and when we will have our meals. It's very important that you always try to be on time. To make sure that we don't have any problems, I'd like to remind you of the time difference. While you are traveling in China, you will always use Bei-

jing Standard Time. Right now it is September 12 and the current time is 3:10 p. m. Please adjust your watches now, so that we can avoid any confusion later on.
B: That's very kind of you. Oh, look, what a big square!
A: Yes, it is Mother Square. It is quite famous in the local area. Well, here we are. This is the hotel. Let's get off and go to the reception desk.
B: OK.

# Your Turn

**Work in pairs. Make up your own conversations according to the situations given below.**
【Situation A】
You are at the airport to meet a tour group of 25 people. The tour leader is Mr. Black. Several groups have arrived. Find Mr. Black, greet him and his group and show them to the bus according to the working procedure.
【Situation B】
You just met a group of 10 American guests who came from Shanghai to Harbin by train. You are on the way from the train station to Shangri-la Hotel where they are going to stay. Express your welcome to them and introduce to them what you see on the way.
【Situation C】
You are an English tour guide who is meeting an American tour group at the airport in Harbin. On the way to the hotel, you are supposed:
☐ to make a welcome speech
☐ to say something about the hotel
☐ to brief on the city
☐ to explain the scene along the way
Discuss with your partner, and then speak it by yourself.

# Unit 2   Arriving at the Hotel

## Words and Expressions

| | |
|---|---|
| deluxe | 豪华的,华丽的 |
| presidential | 总统的 |
| confirm | 确认 |
| suite | (一套)家具,套房 |
| delegation | 代表团 |
| namelist | 名单 |
| well-prepared | 准备充分的 |
| voucher | 凭证,[美]优惠购货券 |
| single room | 单人房 |
| be equipped with | 装备 |
| feel like doing sth. | 喜欢做某事 |
| air-conditioner | 空调 |
| registration forms | 登记表 |
| be about to | 打算,将要 |
| well-known | 知名的 |
| in the center of | 在……中心 |
| large-scale | 大规模的 |
| derive from | 从……中分离 |
| a glimpse of | 一瞥 |
| according to | 根据 |
| transfer to | 转移 |
| consist of | 由……组成 |
| be made up of | 由……构成 |
| sightseeing travel | 观光旅行 |
| arrival and departure time | 抵离时间 |
| go through the formalities | 办手续 |

| | |
|---|---|
| one bill for all | 合单结账 |
| store the valuables | 储存贵重物品 |
| foreign currency exchange | 外币兑换 |
| the information desk | 问讯部 |
| duty manager | 值班经理 |
| front office cashier | 前台收银员 |
| currency exchange limit | 兑换限额 |
| type of accommodation desired | 要求的住宿类型 |
| cash in advance | 预付现金 |
| cash payment departure on | 离店现付 |
| automated bill | 自动开账单 |
| ambulatory room | 残疾人专用房 |
| hold mail | 留交邮件 |
| basement car park | 地下停车场 |

## Useful Sentences

1. May I help you?
2. We'd like to check in.
3. Do you have reservations?
4. A moment, please.
5. Here is the namelist with the group visa.
6. Here are the vouchers for your breakfast buffet.
7. Wish you a nice stay here.
8. This is Hu Hong, the tour guide of China Youth Travel Agency.
9. I'd like to reserve a room in Guangzhou.
10. What kind of room would you like to reserve?
11. How long would you stay here?
12. Is there anything else I can do for you?
13. There would be some discount when the hotel is not very busy.
14. Just call me when you have other questions.

## Situational Conversations

**Listen to the dialogues for the first time. Then practice the dialogues by reading each of them aloud with your partner. Read through each at least twice, changing your role each time.**

## Hotel Room Reservation

[Scene] *The tour guide Hu Hong of China Youth Travel Agency is helping the client reserve a hotel room.*
(G:guide    C:client)

G: This is Hu Hong, the tour guide of China Youth Travel Agency. Can I help you?

C: This is John Smith from London. I'd like to reserve a room in Guangzhou. Will you please arrange it for me?

G: It's my pleasure. What kind of room would you like to reserve? We have singles, doubles, suites of different styles, deluxe ones.

C: A British suite, please.

G: OK. How long would you stay here?

C: Three days from the third to the fifth of March.

G: Now, Mr. Smith, let's check the information. You'd like to reserve a British suite for three days from the third to the fifth of March. Is that so?

C: Yes, exactly.

G: Is there anything else I can do for you?

C: Can you give some idea about the price for the hotel?

G: Well, it's about 1 000 RMB for one day. And there would be some discount when the hotel is not very busy.

C: OK. I see. Thank you for the information.

G: Thank you for calling. We look forward to seeing you. Just call me when you have other questions.

C: Thank you. Bye!

G: Good bye.

## Group Check-in

[Scene] *The guide and his tour group come to the reception desk of the hotel. They have made a reservation through the travel service. A receptionist attends them.*
(R:receptionist    G:tour guide    T:tourist    L:tour leader)

R: Good afternoon! Welcome to our hotel.
G: Good afternoon! I'd like to have two suites and ten single rooms, please.
R: Have you made a reservation?
G: Yes. We have booked them for our tour group from the United States. I'm Wang Hai. I'm from China International Travel Service.
R: Oh, I'm sorry. There is no reservation from your service.
G: I'm sure we have made a reservation. Could you check again a reservation for Friday for the tour group from the United States?
R: All right. Let me cheek again. Ah, yes, two suites and ten single rooms from China International Travel Service.
T: Do the rooms have a bath? I feel like taking a bath right now.
R: Yes, every room is equipped with a bathroom, a telephone and an air-conditioner.
T: That's good!
R: Can I see your passports, please?
L: Yes, these are our passports.
R: Thank you. Here are your passports. Please fill in these registration forms.
L: The registration forms are finished. Shall we have our keys to the rooms?
R: Of course. Here are the keys to your rooms. Your rooms are on the third floor. The bellboy will take you to your rooms.
L: Thanks!
G: I guess you must be tired after a long trip. If there's nothing else you want, I will be leaving. I will meet you at the lobby on the ground floor at seven o'clock tomorrow morning for your breakfast. You can take a good rest tonight.
L: I don't think there is anything else. You have been very considerate. Thank you very much.
G: You are welcome. Enjoy your stay. See you tomorrow.
L: See you tomorrow.

## Checking in

[Scene] *The tour guide is helping a group of foreign visitors to check in at a hotel in Shanghai. The reception clerk receives the tour guide.*
(C: clerk    G: guide)
C: Good morning, madam. May I help you?
G: Yes, please. We'd like to check in.
C: Do you have reservations?

G: Yes. The Shanghai Youth Travel Agency has booked 15 rooms for us.

C: Would you please tell me the name of your group?

G: The Sino-German Friendship Bridge Delegation.

C: A moment, please.

(*The clerk looks up the computer*)

C: Yes, 15 twin rooms for four nights.

G: Yes, exactly. Here is the namelist with the group visa.

C: Thank you. You are well-prepared. Here are the keys to the rooms. Do you need morning call service?

G: Yes, please make it at 7:00 a.m. for tomorrow morning and 8:00 a.m. for the rest of the days.

C: Here are the vouchers for your breakfast buffet. The breakfast will be served at the dining hall on the second floor from 7:00 to 9:00 a.m.

G: Thank you.

C: Thank you and wish you a nice stay here.

## Money Exchange

[Scene] *A tourist is buying some foreign currency at the bank with the help of a bank clerk.*

(A: bank clerk    B: tourist)

A: May I help you, sir?

B: Yes, I'm here to buy some foreign currency.

A: What kind of currency do you want?

B: I'd like to change some RMB into South Korean won.

A: OK. How much would you like to change?

B: 1 000 RMB yuan worth of South Korean won. What is the exchange rate of the RMB yuan into the South Korean won today?

A: The South Korean won price of a RMB yuan is 126 today.

B: All right. Then I'd like to change 1 000 RMB.

A: Would you please show your passport?

B: Certainly. Here you are.

A: Very well, please sign your name on this memo, would you?

B: Sure. Is that all?

A: Yes, sir. Here is 126 000 South Korean won. Please take care of the exchange memo. You may need it for converting your unspent South Korean won back into RMB.

B: Thanks a lot.

Part One  Oral Practice

## Your Turn

**Work in pairs. Make up your own conversations according to the situations given below.**

【Situation A】A Chinese tour guide makes a group reservation for 28 guests to stay in New York for two days.

【Situation B】A French travel agency asks a Chinese tour guide to reserve a room for Mr. Steve to stay in Nanjing for three days.

【Situation C】Wu Fei, a tour guide of Rainbow Travel Agency is receiving the phone. Eleanor Swan is a foreign guest who wants to make a reservation through Rainbow Travel Agency. They are having a conversation about the reservation.

Guide:
☐ Upon receiving the call, greet Eleanor Swan and make a self-introduction.
☐ Offer help.
☐ Tell the different kinds of rooms and their respective prices.
☐ Ask the kind of room Eleanor Swan would like to reserve.
☐ Ask the date Eleanor Swan would like to stay.
☐ Ask to check the information.
☐ Say good-bye and express good wishes.

Client:
☐ Greet the guide and gives a self-introduction.
☐ Ask to reserve a room.
☐ Ask the different prices of different rooms.
☐ Ask to reserve a double-room with a bath.
☐ Tell the date he/she would stay.
☐ Confirm the information with guide.
☐ Express thanks.

# Unit 3  Itinerary Planning

## Words and Expressions

| | |
|---|---|
| itinerary | 路线 |
| accompany | 陪同 |
| pedestrian | 步行的 |
| memorial | 纪念碑 |
| sightseeing | 观光 |
| vehicle | 交通工具,车辆 |
| crystal | 水晶 |
| be settled | 安排好了 |
| lake cruise | 坐船游湖 |
| tourist boom | 旅游热 |
| tourist ghetto | 度假村 |
| theme park | 主题游乐公园 |
| departure | 出发 |
| tentative | 暂定的 |
| city tour | 城市游 |
| package tour/trip | 包价旅游 |
| sightseeing trip | 观光旅游 |
| conducted/guided tour | 有导游的旅游 |
| family group | 家庭旅游团 |
| optional tour | 选择性旅游 |
| as your request | 按照您的要求 |
| historical relics | 历史遗迹 |

## Useful Sentences

1. Hello everybody, can everyone hear me?
2. I'd like to say something about tomorrow's arrangement.

3. The tour starts at 9 o'clock tomorrow morning and lasts about two hours.
4. We'll meet outside the hotel entrance at about ten to nine.
5. There are some sightseeing vehicles available here and there.
6. The tour will end at the Crystal Teahouse in the main square.
7. Shall we have a discussion on the itinerary?
8. Have you got anything special in mind that you would like to see?
9. This is the tentative plan I've worked out. Would you please go over the details?
10. Perhaps you would like visit the old part of Hangzhou?
11. It might be a good idea to...
12. For the afternoon, we will tour to...
13. It's all up to you.
14. Please read/check it to see if there is a need of any change.
15. We have a number of places that are worth visiting.
16. I think we'd better make it 10:30, in case we get caught in the traffic.
17. Wouldn't it be better to...?
18. I think you will find ... interesting.

## Situational Conversations

**Listen to the dialogues for the first time. Then practice the dialogues by reading each of them aloud with your partner. Read through each at least twice, changing your role each time.**

### Discussing the Itinerary

[Scene] *Mr. Li knocks on the door of Mr. Kent's room in the hotel. He is going to talk with him about the itinerary.*

(A: guide    B: tour leader)

A: Good morning, Mr. Kent.
B: Good morning, Mr. Li. Sit down, please.
A: Thank you. Let's talk about the itinerary for this trip.
B: Fine. Our group received a copy of the itinerary from your travel service before we left for China. I'd like to know if there've been any change.
A: Hardly any change.
B: Can you be specific please?
A: Certainly. The general plan includes the sightseeing in Beijing for three days, then we will go to

the Imperial Summer Resort of Chengde. After we return to Beijing, we'll leave for other places.

B: Where are we going first?

A: We'll go to Beidaihe first and then to Northeast China.

B: And then?

A: We'll follow the itinerary we sent you the last time.

B: We'll leave everything up to you, then.

A: The itinerary covers so many places. I'm afraid you'll be exhausted.

B: Never mind. Everybody in this group is physically fit.

A: Have a good time on the trip, then.

B: Thank you for everything you've done for us. Just wonderful.

A: My pleasure. If there should be any changes, I'll let you know in time.

B: That's fine.

A: I'm afraid I must be off. Good-bye.

【Scene】*The tour guide Lily is talking about the itinerary with the tourist Mr. Brown.*
(A: tour guide    B: tourist)

A: Good morning, Mr. Brown. Sorry to disturb you, but I come to talk about the itinerary.

B: OK. Please come in and sit down.

A: Thank you.

B: We received a copy of the itinerary from your travel agency before we came. I wonder if there's any change.

A: No. There's not any change. But shall I confirm it to make sure that everything is perfect?

B: Good. Let's go it over again.

A: OK. First you will stay four days in Harbin. During your stay in Harbin, you will tour around the city, visit Jin Dynasty Museum, the Ice and Snow World, the Sun Island, and go shopping. Then you will leave Harbin for Dalian by air. From Dalian you will go to Weihai by boat.

B: How long will the cruise take us?

A: Six hours. I'm sure you will enjoy the beautiful river scenery.

B: I'm looking forward to it.

A: After spending two days in Weihai, you will visit Qingdao where a lot more excitements are waiting for you.

B: We'll stay in Qingdao for 5 days, right?

A: Yes. And then you'll leave Qingdao for home by air. The whole trip will last half a month. I hope you are well prepared for this long trip.

B: No problem. Everybody is healthy and strong.
A: Well. If there should be any change, please let me know in advance.
B: OK. Thank you very much for such a full and interesting itinerary.
A: My pleasure.

## Itinerary Arrangement

[Scene] *Mr. and Mrs. Brown want to have a city tour to Shenzhen, Guangzhou and Zhuhai. They ask a travel agency for the information.*

(C: travel clerk    T: tourist)

C: Good morning!
T: Good morning!
C: What can I do for you?
T: My wife and I want to see the places of interest in Shenzhen, Guangzhou and Zhuhai. Can you arrange a tour for us?
C: How long would you like to stay in these cities?
T: Well, three days.
C: There is a three-day package tour. You will have 3 full days in the cities. It is a general tour of the cities. The itinerary includes the places of interest such as Window of the World, China Folk Culture Village, Chen Clan Ancestral Temple, Southern Yue Tomb, and Gongbei Market.
T: That sounds good. How much is the tour?
C: 2 000 yuan for each person.
T: What does it include?
C: It includes your airfare, your hotel accommodations and the meals.
T: Could we have you make all the necessary plane, hotel, and tour reservations?
C: Yes, we could do that for you.

[Scene] *The tour guide is talking about the itinerary with the tourist.*

(A: tour guide    B: tourist)

A: I've made a plan for the following days. Please go it over and see if there are any places you are interested in.
B: But I have an itinerary provided by the travel agency in the USA. They have listed the places I am supposed to visit.
A: May I see the list, please?
B: Here you are. But I'm sure you know much better than those people in the USA. I will follow

your suggestion.

A: Thank you. According to my plan, the first day, that's tomorrow, we will visit Heilongjiang Provincial Museum. Then I'll show you Guogeli Street. Before lunch, we will go to the Indian-style Street where our lunch is reserved.

B: That sounds very attractive.

A: The morning is a bit tight but the afternoon will be relaxing. We will go to see the Botanical Garden before visiting a souvenir shop.

B: Yes. I would like to buy some souvenirs.

A: The next day will be long. We will visit the Erlong Mountain.

B: That would be tough. Can I climb the mountain?

A: It's all up to you.

B: What will we do on the third day?

A: I'll take you to a big and famous temple, the Jile Temple. After lunch, we'll have to leave for the airport.

B: Everything sounds great. Thank you very much.

A: You're welcome. See you tomorrow at 8 o'clock.

## Your Turn

## Role-play

Act out the following dialogues.

**【Situation A】** Make an itinerary plan around the city Hangzhou to include Lingyin Temple and the West Lake with your partner.

**Tour guide:**
☐ Greet the guests.
☐ Say the next day they'll visit Lingyin Temple and the West Lake.
☐ Tell the time and place to meet.
☐ Tell the time to the two places respectively and how long the tour lasts.
☐ Tell the things to prepare according to the weather.
☐ Say the lunch will be taken in a snack bar.
☐ Say they would go by coach.
☐ Tell the time to return the hotel.

☐Thanks for attention and wishes them a nice tour.

**Guest(s):**

☐Greet the guide.

☐Agree warmly for longing for the famous places.

☐Ask the time and place to meet.

☐Ask how long the tour will last.

☐Ask what to prepare.

☐Ask where to have lunch.

☐Ask how they would go to the two places.

☐Ask when they would go back to the hotel.

☐Thanks for the information.

**【Situation B】** Make a conversation about an itinerary plan with your partner. You can choose different cities or areas, but you should include at least two scenic spots.

# Unit 4　City Sightseeing

## Words and Expressions

| | |
|---|---|
| approach | 走近 |
| establish | 确立,建立 |
| title | 称呼 |
| assign | 分配 |
| deposit | 押金 |
| cardholder | 持卡人 |
| validity | 有效 |
| receipt | 收据 |
| cashier | 收银员 |
| eye contact | 目光接触 |
| foreign escorted tour | 国外派导游的旅游团 |
| final itinerary | 最终旅行路线 |
| full appointment | 全项委托 |
| best-selling China-tours | 最畅销的中国旅行路线 |
| entertainments and diversions | 娱乐与消遣 |
| on-shore visit | 上岸参观 |
| estimated time of arrival | 预计抵达时间 |
| travel arrangements | 旅行安排 |
| mini destination area | 中途小目的地 |
| sightseeing tour | 观光旅行 |
| selected itinerary | 精选路线 |
| add-ons | 附加旅游项目 |

Part One  Oral Practice

## Useful Sentences

1. Are you ready to start?
2. Here we are at the entrance of park.
3. The whole trip takes about three hours.
4. According to our schedule, today we're going to visit the botanical garden.
5. Let's move on.
6. Please meet at 11:00 by the gate.
7. Would you please wait for a moment? I am going to buy the tickets.
8. You can take some time to walk around, please be back to the bus at a quarter to 4 o'clock.

## Situational Conversations

Listen to the dialogues for the first time. Then practice the dialogues by reading each of them aloud with your partner. Read through each at least twice, changing your role each time.

### At the Museum

[Scene] *The tour guide is introducing the museum to the tourist.*
(A: guide    B: tourist)

A: Now, we are arriving at the provincial integrated museum. Have you ever been here before?
B: No, this is my fist time in Harbin, so it's my first time to visit this museum.
A: Well, OK! It is my pleasure to be your guide. It was built in 1906. Its architecture belongs to a Baroque style. Its vermilion roof and yellow walls make it look very extravagant.
B: So it is a very impressive museum.
A: Yes, it is. The museum is the center of research, exhibiting Heilongjiang history, cultural heritage, flora and fauna, art and science.
B: Oh, I can't wait to see it! Does it look the same as when it was first completed?
A: Well, it was first used as a department store named "Moscow Market". On June 12, 1928, it was turned into a museum. It was not until August 1954 that it took its present name. The horizontal inscribed board over the main entrance has the calligraphy of a late famous Chinese archaeologist—Guo Moruo. Heilongjiang Museum has a large collection of historical relics, arts and animal and plant samples, numbering over 100 000 pieces.

B: Oh, I see.

A: With fast development of society, more and more museums are free of visiting, and this museum is no exception.

B: It sounds good! These cultural relics are really rare and precious. It's worthwhile to appreciate it.

A: Yes. As you enter the hall, you will see the first part of the museum, historical relics. There are over 2 000 relics here. There are stone tools used by pre-historical people over ten thousand years ago. There are relics for the Neolithic period, reflecting people's fishing, hunting and farming activities. Many are well preserved and some arrow heads and stone objects still shine brightly.

B: Are these Bronze mirrors?

A: Yes. Bronze mirrors are a special collection in our museum. A double fish bronze mirror was excavated in Achen, Heilongjiang Province. It measures 43 millimeters and weighs 12.4 kilograms. Its mirror surface still shines and two carps on the back look like real ones. This mirror is thought to be the biggest bronze mirror excavated in China.

B: Wow, it is really wonderful. You have told me so much, thank you very much.

## At the Sophia Church

[Scene] *The tour guide is introducing the Snow and Ice World to the tourist.*

(A: guide    B: tourist)

A: Good morning, Mr. Smith. According to our travelling schedule, today we're going to visit St. Sophia Orthodox Cathedral. Now, we are standing on the ground of the Church.

B: Wow, it's really a stately structure.

A: Yes. St. Sophia Orthodox Cathedral is one of the most magnificent structures in Harbin. It was built in 1907 after the completion of the Trans-Siberian Railway in 1903, which connected Vladivostok to northeast China.

B: How splendid! Can you tell me more about it?

A: Of course. The Russian No.4 Army Division arrived in this region just after Russia's loss to the Japanese in the Russo-Japanese War (1904–1905). St. Sophia Church was built and completed of timber in March, 1907 as part of a plan to reconsolidate the confidence of the army by building an imposing spiritual symbol. In 1921, Harbin had a population of 300 000, including 100 000 Russians. The church was expanded and renovated from September 23, 1923, when a ceremony was held to celebrate the laying of the cornerstone, to its completion on November 25, 1932, after nine years. The present day St. Sophia Church was hailed as a monumental work of art and the largest Orthodox Church in the Far East.

B: I see.

A: The church is located on the corner of Toulong Street (Toulong Jie) and Zhaolin Street (Zhaolin jie). It stands at 53.3 meters (175 ft) tall, occupies an area of 721 square meters (0.18 acres), and is the perfect example of Neo-Byzantine architecture. The main structure is laid out like a cross with the main hall topped with a huge green tipped dome. Under the bright sun, the church and the square area it lies on looks quite like the Red Square in Moscow. On top of the church, there are six crosses. However, the cross of the Orthodox Church is quite different from that of other Christian churches. There is a slanting beam under the normal cross. All the crosses have a golden color. Together with green domes, they offer a distinct contrast to the blue sky, making the church august and elegant. At the front gate, you can find a bell tower with seven bells. The biggest bell is 1.42 meters in diameter and weighs 1.8 tons. Each bell has a special tune. During special holidays, they struck beautiful tunes and its sound could be heard more than 50 kilometers away.

B: Oh, I'm deeply attracted by its interesting history and its charming sight.

A: Today the church is used as an architecture museum in Harbin. Please follow me into the church and find out the beauty of the varying styles of Harbin architecture.

## In the Snow and Ice World

**[Scene]** *The tour guide is introducing the Snow and Ice World to the tourist.*

(A: guide    B: tourist)

A: Now, we are at our first stop—the Snow and Ice World.

B: Wow, It's the place in my dream.

A: Yes, it is very beautiful. Harbin Ice and Snow World covers an area of 400 000 square meters. Its ice consumption is about 120 000 cubic meters and snow consumption nearly 100 000 cubic meters. Over 2 000 ice-and-snow art works will be on shown this year and its entertainment items are more than 30, all these figures reach a maximum among the ice-and-snow arts record. The skillful craftsmen here carve out a series of impressive icy architecture each year with their wit and handicraft.

B: Can you list that about 30 entertainment items?

A: Of course. It includes skiing, sliding on the ice, driving motor on the snow ground, playing on the slide, playing football on the snow ground, icy rock climbing, ice hockey shooting, playing color golf on the snow ground (practice item), experiencing in space. Among them, the most exciting game is the huge slide—over 200 meters long. Besides, there are other fantastic performances shown in succession every night, namely, the north-characteristic animal performance, the Russian amorous singing and dancing, ballet on the ice, disco on the ice, fireworks performances, films shown on the snow screen, etc.

B: It sounds exciting. I can't wait to take part in them.

A: Yes. The splendid Ice and Snow Land—it aims at making the activity in this area more colorful and impressive by mixing all kinds of performances and celebrations with cartoon ice sculptures which follows the organization pattern of Disney series.

B: Wonderful! I'd like to take some picture there.

A: Yeah, let's go.

## Free Activity

【Scene】*The tour guide accompanied a tourist to the hospital. The guide is talking about the tourist's sickness with the doctor.*

(A: guide    B: doctor)

A: My friend, Mr. Yu, has a sore throat and his chest hurts.

B: How long has he has been like this?

A: Two or three days now.

B: I think he has got the flu. There's a lot of it going around.

A: What do you think he ought to do?

B: It's nothing serious. Get this prescription filled and go straight to bed for a day or two.

# Your Turn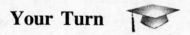

**Work in pairs. Make up your own conversations according to the situations given below.**

【Situation A】You are taking a Canadian group and having a tour to Zhongyang Street. Explain what you can see there to your guests.

【Situation B】Some foreigners from an English spoken country have come to your college and they want to look around your campus. Show them around as a guide.

# Unit 5　Restaurant Service

## Words and Expressions

| | |
|---|---|
| appointment | 约会 |
| confirmation | 确认 |
| expect | 期望 |
| inform | 通知 |
| postpone | 推迟 |
| occupy | 占用 |
| delicious | 美味可口的 |
| waitress | 女服务员 |
| booth | 小室 |
| grill | 烧烤 |
| fully booked | 满座 |
| book a seat | 订座 |
| look forward to | 期待 |
| be still available | 有座 |
| a table for two | 两人桌 |
| make an appointment with sb. | 与某人约会 |
| speciality | 特色菜 |
| vegetable | 蔬菜 |
| smoked | 熏制的 |
| recommend | 推荐 |
| chef | 厨师长 |
| voucher | 代金券 |
| signature | 签名 |

## Useful Sentences

1. Do you have a reservation?
2. Do you prefer a smoking or nonsmoking area?
3. We'll be expecting you.
4. Would you like a table in the main restaurant or in a private room, sir?
5. By the way, we can only keep your table till 8:00 p.m., since that will be a peak season.
6. I'd like to book a banquet in a private room at 6:00 p.m. the day after tomorrow.
7. How much for food per person? The minimum charge for a private room is 100 yuan per person.
8. Would you like to order now?
9. What would you like to have?
10. What are your chef's specialities?
11. Well, same right now. Here is the money.
12. I'm afraid the travel agent requires your signature.
13. I'm sorry. We will do our best to improve our service.

## Situational Conversations

Listen to the dialogues for the first time. Then practice the dialogues by reading each of them aloud with your partner. Read through each at least twice, changing your role each time.

### Booking a Table

[Scene] *The guest is talking to the operator to book a table.*
(A: operator    B: guest)

B: I would like to reserve a table for dinner tonight.

A: Yes, sir. For how many persons, please?

B: A party of ten.

A: At what time can we expect you?

B: At 6:30. I want to start earlier because we have other activities after dinner.

A: OK. Would you like a table in a private room?

B: Sure. A private room is facing the sea.

A: Let me check. Yes, a table for 10 at 6:30 in the Peony Room. This room faces the sea. May I

have your name and telephone number, please?
B: It's a Wang Ning and my phone number is 130-1234-5678.
A: Yes, Mr. Wang. We look forward to meeting you.


【Scene】*A guest is talking with the operator to reserve a table.*
(A: operator　　B: guest)
A: Hello! Holiday Restaurant. May I help you?
B: What time do you open this evening?
A: We open at 5:00 p.m..
B: I see I like to reserve a table for two.
A: Yes, sir. What time would you like your table, sir?
B: 7:00 p.m.
A: Fine! I'll reserve a table for two at 7 p.m.. May I have your name, please?
B: John Smith.
A: Thank you, Mr. Smith.
B: Oh, any chance of a table by the window?
A: No problem.
B: Good. Thank you very much.
A: It's a pleasure. Goodbye.
B: Goodbye.

## Taking Orders

【Scene】*The waiter is taking orders from the guest.*
(A: guest　　B: waiter)
A: I'd like to taste some local dishes. What would you recommend?
B: That's fine. You must try this dish.
A: Could you tell me how this thing is cooked?
B: It's fish steamed and served with our special sauce.
A: Is it good?
B: Sure. It's a most popular dish.
A: I think I'll try it, and give me some green salad together.
B: We have two dressings for salad. Which one would you like?
A: What kind do you have?
B: We have French and Thousand Island.

A: Make it Thousand Island.

[Scene] *The waiter is taking orders from the guest.*

(A: guest    B: waiter)

A: Are you ready to order now, sir?

B: Yes.

A: Would you like an appetizer?

B: Yes. I'd like a crab.

A: Would you like some soup first?

B: Very well.

A: What kind of soup would you like?

B: I want egg soup.

A: Have you decided on anything?

B: I'd like to have some meat.

A: How about stewed-fried steamed pork?

B: No, thank you.

A: Are you interested in today's special?

B: What is it?

A: Twice cooked spicy pork slices.

B: OK. Let me try it.

A: Anything else?

B: No, thank you.

# Paying Bills

[Scene] *The guest is paying bills in the restaurant.*

(A: waiter    B: guest)

A: Are you through with your meal?

B: Yes, we are. Could we have the check, please?

A: There you go. I can take care of it here when you're ready.

B: Do you accept checks?

A: No, I'm sorry we don't. We accept credit card and cash.

B: Well, I don't have any cash with me. I'll have to put in on credit.

A: Thank you. I will be right back. Do you need any to-go boxes? I'd be glad to bring you some when I come back.

B: Yes, we do. Thank you.

【Scene】*The guest is paying bills to the waiter.*
(G: guest    W: waiter)
G: Can I use this voucher to pay for my meal?
W: Certainly, sir. But I'm afraid it will not cover the cost of the meal. Would you mind paying the extra in cash, please?
G: Not at all. How much is the voucher worth?
W: It is worth $200 and your bill comes to $280. The difference is $80, please.
G: Here you are.
W: Thank you, sir. Could you sign the voucher here, please?
G: Why do I have to sign?
W: I'm afraid the travel agent requires your signature.
G: I see. Here you are.
W: Thank you, sir. Hope to see you again soon.

# Your Turn

Make a dialogue according to the following situations.
【Situation A】You are an operator. Mr. Smith is booking a table in your restaurant. Unfortunately, there is no available one. Therefore, Mr. Smith gets angry about it. How will you deal with this problem?
【Situation B】You are a waiter. Mr. Smith is a guest in your restaurant. After his meal, he wants to pay for his meal in credit card. But your restaurant can only accept cash. You are asked to help Mr. Smith.

# Unit 6　　Shopping

## Words and Expressions

| | |
|---|---|
| feather | 羽毛 |
| mural | 壁画 |
| wrap | 包 |
| arts and crafts | 工艺 |
| fan | 扇子 |
| separately | 分离地 |
| tapestry | 挂毯 |
| pure | 纯的 |
| patchwork | 拼缝物 |
| assure | 使相信 |
| traditional | 传统的 |
| sandalwood | 檀香 |
| fragrant | 芳香的 |
| china | 瓷器 |
| paper-cut | 剪纸 |
| loose change | 零钱 |
| souvenir | 纪念品 |
| salesclerk | 店员 |

## Useful Sentences

1. Everything for summer is 20% off.
2. I'm looking for some local products for my family. Can you recommend something special?
3. Would you like to have a souvenir from China?

4. I can assure you this is the best price you can get for a mural like this.
5. I'll have it wrapped for you.
6. Can you show me some traditional Chinese arts and crafts?
7. Please show me this one?
8. How do you like this pattern?
9. You'd better try on both feet and see whether the shoes are comfortable to wear.
10. Sorry, but we can't make any reduction.
11. The price is a bit high.
12. You're so kind. But we don't accept tips. This is your 10 yuan change. Thank you.
13. Do you have loose change, two yuan, please?
14. Here is the change. Thank you for coming. Goodbye.

## Situational Conversations

**Listen to the dialogues for the first time. Then practice the dialogues by reading each of them aloud with your partner. Read through each at least twice, changing your role each time.**

### At the Souvenir Shop

[Scene] *A shop assistant is serving a tourist at the souvenir shop.*

(A: shop assistant    B: tourist)

A: Good morning, madam. Can I help you?
B: Yes, thank you. I'm especially interested in traditional Chinese paintings. Do you have any good ones?
A: Yes, we do. Do you prefer landscape or figure painting?
B: That one with beautiful lady seems good.
A: You've made a good choice. The lady's name is Xishi, she was one of the most famous of the four beauties in ancient China.
B: It's really very nice. How much is it?
A: 270 yuan.
B: I'll take it. By the way, one of my friend likes porcelain wares very much. Could you recommend some to me?
A: (Points to a set of blue and white porcelain tea set) This china tea set is unusual, it is made in Jingdezhen, the capital of porcelain.
B: It is extremely beautiful. I'm sure he will like it. How much do I owe you?

A: Two hundred and seventy yuan for the painting, three hundred and fifty for the tea set. That's 620 yuan in all. Can I get you anything else?

B: That's all, thank you. Here is 700 yuan.

A: Here's the change. Thank you, madam. Have a nice trip.

【Scene】*A shop assistant is serving a tourist at the souvenir shop.*
(A: shop assistant    B: tourist)

A: What can I do for you?

B: I want to buy some handicrafts as souvenirs for my family and relatives.

A: We have quite a wide variety of handicrafts here. What do you have in mind?

B: I'd like something typical Chinese, but not very expensive. What is your suggestion?

A: You don't want anything too heavy, do you?

B: Yes. I want something light and easy to carry.

A: What about some chopsticks? They will be a good present.

B: Can you show me some?

A: Of course. This way, please.

B: Oh, they are really beautiful. But I'm afraid they're quite a bit expensive.

A: About how much are you planning to spend?

B: No more than one hundred yuan.

A: Oh, in that case, this one is OK.

B: Oh! It's perfect. I think I'll take it. Would you wrap it, please?

A: OK. Wait for a moment, please.

## At the Shopping Center

【Scene】*A salesclerk is serving a customer at the shopping center.*
(C: customer    S: salesclerk)

S: Hello, madam. Can I help you?

C: I'm looking for a sweater.

S: What size are you looking for?

C: Well, I'm looking for size ten but you don't have it.

S: How about this one? I think it looks terrific on you.

C: Yes. I like the color. Can I try it on?

S: Sure. The fitting-room is on your left.

C: It fits well. I like it much. What do you think?
S: You look pretty in red.
C: Oh it's my favorite. How much is it?
S: $36.88.
C: Okay. I'll take it. Thank you very much for your help.
S: You're welcome.

【Scene】*A salesclerk is serving a customer at the shopping center.*
(C: customer    S: salesclerk)
C: That China-gown of Tang Dynasty style is so beautiful. Would you show it to me, please?
S: Absolutely. Here it is.
C: Could I try it on?
S: Please do. The fitting-room is over there.
C: It feels a little tight around the waist. Do you have a bigger one?
S: I'm sorry. We don't have this color in your size. We have some green ones in your size. Would you please have a look at this green one?
C: Yes. How much does it cost?
S: It's priced at 488 yuan.
C: It's too expensive. Can you come down a bit?
S: I'm sorry. We sell according to the price tag an there's no room for bargaining.
C: Let me think it over. Well, I'll have it. Here is the money. Thank you.
S: Here is the charge. Please wait a minute. I'll wrap it up for you. Goodbye.

## Antiques and Traditional Chinese Painting

【Scene】*A foreign tourist is shopping with the aid of a shop assistant.*
(A: shop assistant    B: tourist)
A: Good morning! What can I do for you?
B: I'd like to buy some souvenirs of this trip to China. But I don't know what to buy. Would you mind doing me a favor?
A: Certainly. I suggest you take something closely related to our ancient civilization.
B: That's a good idea! What then?
A: Have you ever heard of "cloisonne"? It's a famous art craft from Beijing. The history of the craft can be traced back to the reign of Jingtai in the Ming Dynasty.
B: I see. How much does an medium-sized cloisonne vase cost?

A: 1 200 yuan.

B: Okay. I'll take it.

A: What else would you like, sir?

B: I'm especially interested in traditional Chinese paintings. Do you have any good ones?

A: Yeah, we do.

B: Could you tell me the difference between Western oil paintings and Chinese ink paintings?

A: Sure, madam. Briefly speaking, oil paintings are created by colors and brush touches while traditional Chinese paintings are by lines and strokes.

B: I see. Those ancient Chinese paintings are an important part of your national culture, aren't they?

A: Yeah. How do you like the reproduction of the famous painting?

B: Oh, very much. How much does it cost?

A: 160 yuan.

B: The price is reasonable. I'll take it.

## Payments

[Scene] *A customer is going to pay his bill in cash to a salesclerk.*

(C: customer    S: salesclerk)

S: Is there anything else I may show you?

C: No. That's enough. How much, please?

S: Let me see: 15 yuan for the paper-cut, 26 yuan for the masks, 35 yuan for the wooden doll and 46 yuan for the clay doll. That comes to 122 yuan.

C: Here are 200 yuan notes.

S: Here is your charge, 78 yuan. Please count it.

C: OK. Thank you very much.

S: My pleasure. Welcome here again.

C: I will. Goodbye.

S: Goodbye.

[Scene] *A customer is paying for his bill by credit card with the help of a salesclerk.*

(C: customer    S: salesclerk)

C: Waiter. We'd like to check the bill, please.

S: Yes, sir. Here is your bill. How would you like to pay for it? Cash or charge?

C: Do you accept credit cards?

S: Yes. We can accept it.
C: Charge, please. Put it on my American Express. But I have the VIP card of this shopping mall. Shall I have discount?
S: Sure. It comes to $300, with 10% discount.
C: Here is my credit card.
S: Wait a minute, please.
C: OK.

## Your Turn

Work in pairs. Make up your own conversations according to the situations given below.

**〖Situation A〗** You are working as a shopping guide. Now a couple of American just came into your shopping center and coming to get your help. Greet them and help them properly.

**〖Situation B〗** The tour leader of a group of 30 British has just finished the check-in and is ready to walk around to buy something typical in your shopping mall. You are a salesclerk on duty. Work with the tour leader and do your job in a good manner.

# Unit 7  Dealing with Complaints

## Words and Expressions

| | |
|---|---|
| shower | 淋浴 |
| fix | 修理 |
| pillow | 枕头 |
| in a mess | 乱七八糟 |
| inconvenience | 麻烦 |
| incident | 事件,事变 |
| assignment | 任务 |
| emergency | 紧急事件,突发事件 |
| amazing | 令人惊异的 |
| due to | 归因于 |
| clear away | 消散 |
| kill the time | 打发时间 |
| lamb | 羔羊 |
| inedible | 不能吃的 |
| fatty | 油腻的 |
| oily | 油腻的 |
| recommendation | 推荐 |
| discount | 折扣 |
| roast duck | 烤鸭 |

## Useful Sentences

1. What's up?
2. I will call the waiter to deal with it.

3. I've told them to make a change for you.
4. They promised to serve you in less than 5 minutes.
5. They give us a 15% discount.
6. The staff here told me that the flight had been delayed due to the foggy weather.
7. The weather report said that the fog will be cleared away in 2 hours.
8. I'm afraid so.
9. Why don't we kill the time by looking around the shops and stores here?
10. Maybe you will find something amazing!
11. Well, actually, nothing is right in my room.
12. I'll have it fixed immediately.
13. The pillow is dirty, and the room is in a mess.

## Situational Conversations

**Listen to the dialogues for the first time. Then practice the dialogues by reading each of them aloud with your partner. Read through each at least twice, changing your role each time.**

### Complaining about Food and Service

[Scene] *A foreign tourist is complaining to the waiter in a restaurant about the service.*
(A: foreign tourist    B: waiter)

A: Waiter, I want to have a word with you.
B: Yes, sir. Is everything to your satisfaction?
A: Satisfaction? I don't know how you can think of such a word. No, far from that.
B: I wonder if you could give me another word?
A: We've been kept waiting here for almost half an hour and we don't know how long we'll have to wait before you can bring us the first dish.
B: I'm sorry about that. We have more guests than usual today. Furthermore, one of our waiters didn't feel well just an hour ago and asked for leave. But I'll see to it at once. Do you mind if I ask the wine steward to serve you some drink first?
A: Oh, one moment, please. I have to say that the table cloth is in a disgrace. Look, it's covered with soup stains. It seems that it has been here for ages.
B: Oh, I'm sorry, sir. It should have been changed before. Excuse me, I'll be with you in a minute.

[Scene] *A foreign tourist is complaining to the guide in a restaurant about the food.*

(A: the foreign tourist    B: the guide)

A: Look, the food in this restaurant is so terrible!

B: What's up?

A: I hate to say, but this leg of lamb is inedible. It is so fatty. And the roast duck is too oily. In fact, it's the worst I've ever eaten!

B: Mm. It did like what you say. I will call the waiter to deal with it.

(*Several minutes later*)

B: OK, I've told them to make a change for you.

A: Will I wait for a long time?

B: No need, they promised to serve you in less than 5 minutes.

A: I also want to order a soup. What's your recommendation?

B: I heard that the egg and vegetable soup here is quite delicious.

A: Really? That's good. Could you please order one for me?

B: No problem!

(*After meal*)

A: Can we have a discount for this?

B: Of course, they give us a 15% discount.

A: You are so nice!

B: You are welcome.

## Complaining about Room and Service

[Scene] *Mr. Brown, together with his wife, has stayed one night at the hotel. Now he is complaining to the tour guide, Mr. Wang, about the room conditions. He demands to move to a quiet room.*

(A: Mr. Wang    B: Mr. Brown)

A: Is everything all right, Mr. Brown?

B: Well, actually, nothing is right in my room.

A: What seems to be the problem, Mr. Brown? How can I help you?

B: You can help me by putting my bathroom right. It's in a terrible condition. When I took the shower, there's no cold water at all. I almost got burnt! Shouldn't the hotel know the condition of the shower before we checked in?

A: I'm terribly sorry to hear that. I'll have it fixed immediately.

B: That's not all. The pillow is dirty, and the room is in a mess.

A: I sincerely apologize for this inconvenience, Mr. Brown. The hotel is rather short-staffed at present.

B: To be frank, I'm not happy with this room for some other reasons. This room faces the street. It is rather noisy. I can't fall asleep at night. Could you change it for a quiet room? It doesn't have to be on the same floor.

A: No problem, Mr. Brown, I'll talk to the receptionist.

(*After contacting the Front Office*)

A: Well, Mr. Brown, could you move to room 401? It doesn't face the street, and now it's ready for you. In the meantime I'll send up a porter to help you with your luggage.

B: Thank you. You are very helpful. We are lucky to have you as our local guide.

A: It's my pleasure, Mr. Brown. Just get hold of me whenever you need any help.

【Scene】*A tourist is complaining about the service of the hotel to her tour guide.*
(A: guide    B: tourist)

B: Sir, I've got something to complain.

A: Yes?

B: I'm afraid the room attendant did not properly clean my room.

A: I'm awfully sorry, Madam. Let me call the housekeeping and have it done right away.

B: There is dust on the chest of drawers.

A: Please let me apologize for this. I'll see to it that a room attendant is to dust it immediately.

B: And there's another problem. The window of my bedroom will not close properly.

A: All right. I'll ask the repairman of the hotel to fix it right away. Are there any other problems, Madam?

B: Yes. I think the linen hasn't been changed for three days.

A: I will talk to the manager of the hotel and make sure that this does not happen again.

B: That's very kind of you.

A: Please do not hesitate to let me know if you have any further problems.

B: Well, I think I've complained enough for today.

A: You are right to complain, Madam. We want to make your stay as comfortable as possible.

B: I must say that everyone has been very nice to me.

A: By the way, both the room attendant and the repairman will be right up.

B: Very well. Thank you very much.

A: You are very welcome, Madam.

## A Delayed Flight

**【Scene】** *In the airport lobby, Zhang Hua, a young tour guide from the China Travel Service, is explaining to John Smith about the delayed flight that he will take.*

(J: John Smith　　Z: Zhang Hua)

J: Excuse me, did flight number FU88024 arrive in? I have been waiting here for an hour. And it should be arrived at half an hour ago. What's happened?

Z: I don't know, but I will ask the reception desk for it.

(*Several minutes later*)

Z: The staff here told me that the flight had been delayed due to the foggy weather.

J: Oh, it's terrible. Did they say when exactly will the flight arrive in?

Z: The weather report said that the fog will be cleared away in 2 hours.

J: That's to say we have to wait for another 90 minutes?

Z: I'm afraid so.

J: It's quite a long time to be here waiting the flight.

Z: Why don't we kill the time by looking around the shops and stores here? Maybe you will find something amazing!

J: That's a good idea! Is there any antique shop around here?

Z: Yes, it just around the corner over there. And it offers a large variety of antiques including coins, pottery and traditional Chinese paintings. What do you want to buy?

J: I just want to have a look around there.

Z: OK, let's go!

# Your Turn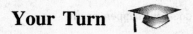

## Role-play

Act out the following dialogues.

**【Situation A】** You are escorting Mr. Black to have dinner in a restaurant. Mr. Black isn't satisfied with the food. You are asked to help Mr. Black to solve the problem.

Mr. Black:

☐ Complain about the food.

☐ Give vivid descriptions.

☐ Ask for the serving time.
☐ Ask for discount.
☐ Give thanks to the guide.
You:
☐ Ask for what happened.
☐ Promise that you will help Mr. Black to solve it.
☐ Say that the problem has solved.
☐ Tell the serving time.
☐ Tell the percentage of discount.

**[Situation B]** At the restaurant, a foreign business traveler is complaining about the bad service and asking for your help.

**[Situation C]** Mr. Black, a tourist, is now complaining about the delayed flight to the tour guide at the airport.

Mr. Black:
☐ Complain to the tour guide.
☐ Ask about the arriving time.
☐ Show anxiety.
☐ Ask if there are some other thing can do.
☐ Suggest to go to visit the nearest souvenir shop.

Tour guide:
☐ Promise to ask for the reason.
☐ Give the reason why it's delayed.
☐ Give the possible time when the flight will come.
☐ Suggest to look around for killing the time.
☐ Show the nearest souvenir shop to Mr. Black.

**[Situation D]** At the bus station, a foreign business traveler is complaining about the delayed bus to the tour guide.

# Unit 8　Handling Accidents

## Words and Expressions

| | |
|---|---|
| missing | 不见的,缺少的 |
| emergency | 紧急情况 |
| misplace | 把……放错地方 |
| ruin | 毁坏 |
| provisional | 临时的 |
| regulation | 规则,规章 |
| primary | 主要的 |
| accordance | 一致 |
| coordinate | 调整,整理 |
| supervise | 监督,管理 |
| ensure | 保证,确保 |
| property | 财产,所有物 |
| enquiry | 询问 |
| en route | 在途中 |
| appoint | 任命,委任 |

## Useful Sentences

1. My luggage seems to be missing.
2. Could I see your luggage claim card?
3. May I have your full name?
4. Well, Mr. Smith, your luggage seems to have been misplaced.
5. I'm terribly sorry. We'll get in touch with the airline and try our best to get them back as soon as

possible.
6. My vacation is ruined!
7. I've been left behind, and what is worse, I've lost my way.
8. Can you describe the place where you are?
9. You can ask for help when necessary.
10. Could see your luggage claim check?
11. Try to get hold of me whenever you need my help.
12. Please let me apologize for this.
13. Please do not hesitate to contact us again if you have any further problems.
14. Let me get a representative from the airline to speak with you.
15. What seems to be the problem, Mr. Smith? How can I help you?
16. I am sorry to hear that. There must have been a mistake.
17. This was entirely due to our error. Please accept our sincere apologies for the inconvenience.
18. This type of slip-up will never occur on your future tours.
19. There is one more thing.
20. I can certainly understand that you're upset about losing your luggage.

## Situational Conversations

**Listen to the dialogues for the first time. Then practice the dialogues by reading each of them aloud with your partner. Read through each at least twice, changing your role each time.**

### Missing Luggage or Belongs

[Scene] *A tourist's luggage is missing, and now the tour guide is handling the emergency.*

(A: tourist    B: tour guide)

A: Excuse me, is this all the luggage?
B: Yes, I think so.
A: My luggage seems to be missing.
B: How many pieces do you have?
A: Two. A large red backpack and a small dark blue suitcase.
B: Could I see your luggage claim card?
A: Yes, here you are.
B: May I have your full name?
A: John Smith.

B: Just a moment. I'll check immediately. Well, Mr. Smith, your luggage seems to have been misplaced.

A: What am I supposed to do?

B: I'm terribly sorry. We'll get in touch with the airline and try our best to get them back as soon as possible. Please fill out this claim form with your card number.

A: OK. What will happen if you can't find them?

B: Well, Mr. Smith, I do not work for the airline. Let me get a clerk from the airline. He or she can answer your questions more completely.

A: My vacation is ruined! I'm sure I'll never see my luggage again!

B: Please, Mr. Smith, let's talk to an airline official.

A: All right. Let's do it right now.

[Scene] Mrs. Brown just came back to her room. Suddenly, she found her ring and credit card missing. Now she is complaining to her tour guide, Mr. Li.

(A: Mr. Li    B: Mrs. Brown)

A: Good morning, Mrs. Brown. Is there anything wrong?

B: Yes. My credit card and a ring are missing in my room.

A: I'm very sorry to hear that. Where did you put them yesterday?

B: On the table in my room.

A: Did you lock the door when you went out?

B: Yes, I locked the door. When I came back, they were gone. It must be one of the staff. I only want my things back, and fast!

A: Well, I can totally understand your feeling now. I'll do everything I can to help you. If they are really stolen, we shall call the police.

B: What do you mean if they are stolen? I told you they were!

A: Calm down, Mrs. Brown. I think first we'll have our staff look through your room in case they are really there.

B: I hope so.

## A Lost Tourist

[Scene] Lily is leading her tourists to a scenic spot when she receives a phone call from a tourist, Mr. Zhang, who has been left behind and lost his way.

(A: Mr. Zhang    B: Lily)

A: Hello? Is that Lily?

Part One　Oral Practice

B: Yes, speaking.
A: This is Zhang Hua. I've been left behind, and what is worse, I've lost my way.
B: Don't worry. Can you describe the place where you are?
A: There is a pavilion here. It's called Perceiving the Spring Pavilion.
B: I see. You've taken the wrong way. Now, you've got to turn back, walk straight till you arrive at a bus station. Then turn left and go about 500 meters and then you'll find us at the parking lot.
A: Oh, it'll take a long time.
B: Not very long, Mr. Zhang. I think it will take you 10 minutes. You can ask for help when necessary.
A: OK. Thank you.
B: You're welcome. Bye.
A: Bye.

[Scene] *A young local guide is going to take the tour group to the next stop, but one of the tourist is on the bus.*
(A: tour leader　　B: local guide)
A: Is everybody on the bus?
B: No, Mrs. Tang, the old lady isn't here.
A: Do you know where she is?
B: I have no idea. Ten minutes ago, I saw her walking around in a souvenir store.
A: She must have lost her way.
B: We have to find her now.
A: You had better take our group to the next stop. I will try to look for her.
B: OK, if you encounter some problems, please let me know.
A: Could you repeat your mobile phone number?
B: My phone number is 138...
A: When I find her, I will inform you immediately.
B: Keep in touch.
A: Sure. Take good care of our group members...
A: Hello, this is Sandy speaking. I have already found Mrs. Tang.
B: Wonderful news! Where are you?
A: We are now on the Jingwei Street. What about your next stop?
B: Our next stop is the Dragon Tower.
A: How can we get to the Dragon Tower?
B: You'd better take a taxi. We are almost arriving there.

A: OK. See you then.
B: See you.

## Calling the First Aid Center

[Scene] *A foreign visitor is suffering from a cute appendicitis. Now the tour guide is calling the first aid center for help.*

(T: tour guide    H: hospital receiver    D: doctor)

T: Is this the Friendship Hospital? Please send an ambulance to 68 Hunan Road.
H: Is it urgent?
T: Yes, it is. I think the patient is suffering from the appendicitis. He may die if not treated in time.
H: All right, we'll come right away. (after a while...)
H: Where's the patient?
T: He's in the room. He's very ill.
H: Don't worry. We'll put him in the stretcher.
D: Carry him into the emergency ward. Here we are.
T: I'm his guide. What's the trouble with him, doctor?
D: He had appendicitis, but is all right now that it was removed. He'll have to rest for a few weeks to recover.
T: May I send food for him?
D: No, outside food is not permitted.
T: When could I take care of him?
D: Our nurse can take good care of him.

## Your Turn

[Situation A] It is in mid-October on the day before the West Lake International Firework Festival. Bars have been set up around the lake to protect the viewers. You have an elderly group going to a boat ride on the lake. Seeing the obstacle, the group starts complaining. Discuss among yourselves and see how you would handle this situation.

[Situation B] You are taking a big group to visit Jile Temple. You told them to follow you closely in case they got lost. But when you come back after visiting the Temple, an old couple comes to you angrily to complain that they did not see the Temple because they did not follow you for you were walking too fast for them. Try your best to solve this problem.

# Unit 9　Checking out

## Words and Expressions

| | |
|---|---|
| check out | 办理退房手续 |
| settle | 决定,确定 |
| account | 账目,账户 |
| counsel | 建议,劝告 |
| managerial | 管理的 |
| retail | 零售的 |
| commission | 佣金 |
| industry principal | 业主 |
| tour operator | 旅游经营商 |
| terminal | 终端 |
| access | 入口,进入 |
| overbook | 超额预订 |
| generate | 产生 |
| currency exchange | 货币兑换 |
| bill | 账单 |
| receipt | 收据 |
| invoice | 发票 |
| change | 零钱 |
| service charge | 服务费 |
| advance deposit | 预付金 |
| in cash | 用现金付款 |
| credit card | 信用卡 |

## Useful Sentences

1. I'd like to settle my bill now.
2. I'd like to check out, please.
3. Can I get your name and room number, please?
4. Have you used any hotel services during your stay here?
5. Yes, I sent a fax to America yesterday afternoon.
6. You have paid an advance deposit of RMB 2 500, haven't you?
7. Please have a check.
8. One moment, please and I'll get the bill ready.
9. Sorry to have kept you waiting.
10. Four nights at $50 each. That makes a total of $200.
11. Your bills total 910 yuan.
12. Please sign your name on the print.
13. How would you like to pay your bill?
14. Can I pay by credit card?
15. We hope you'll come again. Have a nice trip.

## Situational Conversations

Listen to the dialogues for the first time. Then practice the dialogues by reading each of them aloud with your partner. Read through each at least twice, changing your role each time.

### Paying the Hotel Bill in Cash

[Scene] *A guest wishes to pay his hotel bill in cash.*
(S: staff    G: guest)

S: Good morning, sir. May I help you?

G: We are leaving today, and I'd like to pay my bill now.

S: Certainly, sir. Oh, by the way, I'd like to tell you that the check out time is 12:00 noon. Can I get your name and room number, please?

G: John Walker. Room 5006.

S: Yes, Mr. John Walker. You checked in three days ago in the afternoon on June 19, didn't you?

G: Yes.
S: And when are you leaving?
G: Right after lunch.
S: So you'll check out before 12:00?
G: Yes, exactly.
S: Just a moment, please. I'll print the bill for you. Sorry to have kept you waiting. Here you are. This is your bill, RMB 1 980, including 10 percent service charge. Please check it.
G: OK. Oh, that's right.
S: You have paid an advance deposit of RMB 2 500, haven't you?
G: Yes, here is the receipt.
S: Thank you. This is your invoice and your change, RMB 520. Count it, please.
G: That's quite all right. Goodbye.
S: We hope you'll enjoy your trip, Mr. Walker. Goodbye.

## Paying with Credit Card

[Scene] *A guest comes to the Front Desk to check out by credit card.*
(S: staff    G: guest)
S: Good morning, sir. Can I help you?
G: I'd like to check out, please.
S: May I know your name and room number, sir?
G: I'm Mr. John Rich, Room 1508.
S: Yes. Have you used any other hotel services this morning?
G: No, I haven't used any services and I paid cash for my breakfast.
S: Fine. I need to check the folio. Three nights at RMB 500 each, and your bill totals RMB 1 500. Here you are. Have a check, please.
G: Correct. But I don't have enough cash for it. Can I pay by my credit card?
S: Certainly, we do accept some major credit cards. What card do you have?
G: Visa Card.
S: Fine. Let me take an imprint of it.
G: Here it is.
S: Thanks. Just wait a moment. Please sign your name on the print, Mr. Rich.
G: OK. Here you are.
S: Thank you. Please take your credit card and keep the receipt.

## Paying with a Traveler's Check

[Scene] *A guest pays his bill in his traveler's check.*
(S: staff    G: guest)

S: Good morning. Can I help you, sir?

G: I'd like to check out. The name is Alan Dick.

S: Excuse me, were you in Room 2816?

G: That's right. May I see the bill?

S: One moment, please, and I'll get the bill ready... It totals RMB 5 020. Here you are. Please have a check.

G: OK. Does this include service and tax?

S: Yes, that's everything. We charge you for the rate of the room, room service, laundry and drinks. Is that all right, Mr. Dick?

G: Yes, I don't see there is any problem with it.

S: How would you like to pay your bill?

G: By my traveler's check, if that's OK.

S: That'll do nicely. Thank you.

G: Can you tell me the exchange rate of US dollars for traveler's checks?

S: It's RMB 720 against 100 US dollars. May I see your passport, please?

G: Here you are.

S: Please sign your name on the traveler's check and sign again on the memo.

G: OK.

S: Here is your invoice. And this is the exchange memo.

G: Thank you. Goodbye.

S: We hope you'll come again, Mr. Dick. Have a nice trip. Goodbye.

## Your Turn

## Role-play

Act out the following dialogues.

[Situation A] The guest is at the Front Desk and the receptionist receives him. The guest wants to check out.

Part One  Oral Practice

The receptionist:
☐ Greet the guest.
☐ Ask the guest's name and room number.
☐ Ask if the guest has used any other service.
☐ Let the guest wait.
☐ Prepare the guest's bill and tell the guest the total number.
☐ Tell that the guest has paid a deposit.
☐ Give the guest his change and invoice.
☐ Hope that the guests will have a good journey.

The guest:
☐ Greet the receptionist.
☐ Want to settle the bill.
☐ Tell his name and room number.
☐ Say that there is no other service used.
☐ Check the bill.
☐ Give the receptionist the receipt of the deposit.
☐ Check the change.
☐ Say goodbye to the receptionist.

【Situation B】Mr. Clarke checks out at the Cashier's. The clerk asks the guest to exchange his US dollars into RMB.

# Unit 10  Sending off the Tour Group

## Words and Expressions

| | |
|---|---|
| farewell | 告别 |
| impression | 印象 |
| unforgettable | 难忘的 |
| gratitude | 感激 |
| cooperation | 合作,协作 |
| punctual | 准时的 |
| occasion | 场合 |
| attentive | 专注的,留心的 |
| bid farewell to | 告辞,辞行 |
| applause | 鼓掌 |
| the boarding pass | 登机牌 |
| claim | 领取 |
| opportunity | 机会,时机 |
| a great deal of | 许多,好多 |
| add | 补充说 |
| distant | 远的 |
| memory | 记忆,记忆力 |
| observe | 观察,察看 |
| beyond | 超过 |
| recognition | 识别 |
| meanwhile | 同时,其间 |
| humble | 卑下的,低微的,谦逊的 |
| coach | 旅游大巴车 |
| accompany | 陪同 |

## Part One　Oral Practice

| | |
|---|---|
| sincerely | 真诚地 |
| comment | 评论 |
| tour group | 旅游团 |
| more or less | 或多或少 |
| say goodbye (to) | 向某人告别 |
| all the way | 全程 |
| on behalf of | 代表 |
| sweet sorrow | 喜忧参半 |
| give sb. a big hand | 喝彩 |
| cart | 手推车 |
| lobby | 大厅 |
| boarding pass | 登机牌 |
| interpret | 讲解 |
| luggage claim card | 行李牌 |
| security-check | 安全检查 |
| group visa | 团队签证 |
| distinguished | 令人尊敬的 |
| witness | 见证 |
| symbol | 象征 |
| occur | 发生 |
| economy | 经济 |
| fragrance | 香味 |
| seashore | 海滨 |
| handicraft | 手工艺品 |
| promote | 改善,提高,促进 |
| strengthen | 增强,增进 |
| Confucius | 孔子 |
| build up | 建立 |
| send one's best regards to | 把……的祝福带给…… |

## Useful Sentences

1. Are you sure nothing is left behind?

2. It seems as if it were only yesterday when I went to meet you at the airport.
3. Well, you know, before we came here, our knowledge about China mainly came from books and TV programs.
4. Now, I'd like to express my gratitude to you on behalf of our members.
5. First of all, I wish to thank you all for the understanding and cooperation you have given us in the past fifteen days.
6. You have been very punctual on all occasions, which made things a lot easier for our work.
7. Parting is such sweet sorrow. It is happy to meet, sorry to depart, and happy to meet again.
8. Let's give Miss Linda a warm applause to thank her for her service.
9. Your current visit to Shanghai is drawing to a close.
10. It is a good banquet that does not end.
11. I hope you have enjoyed all your stay.
12. Bon voyage!
13. Could you fill out this form of evaluation for me?
14. I'd like to express our heartfelt gratitude to you for your efforts and excellent services.
15. Here we are at the airport.
16. Would you please wait for me for a few seconds?
17. Take your time.
18. It's time for us to say goodbye to each other.
19. Thank you for all your kindness.
20. Hope to see you soon.
21. A happy journey home.
22. We would thank you again for your great patience, cooperation and understanding, which have made our job easier.
23. The tour couldn't have been that successful without your support.
23. There is nothing more delightful than to meet friends afar.
24. I would like to welcome you back.

## Situational Conversations

Listen to the dialogues for the first time. Then practice the dialogues by reading each of them aloud with your partner. Read through each at least twice, changing your role each time.

### (1) See You Again Soon

【Scene】 *It is August 15. The tour group getting on the coach is leaving for the airport in the morning.*
(L: Liu Hua—tour guide    M: Michael Wong—tour leader)

L: Hello, Mr. Wong, ladies and gentlemen, your current visit to Shanghai is drawing to a close. I would like to say a few words before you leave. There is an old Chinese saying, "It is a good banquet that does not end". I think you can more or less guess the meaning of it. I really hate to do this, but the time has come for us to say goodbye. It has been a wonderful experience for me to accompany you all the way. I hope you have enjoyed all your stay. If there's anything that you are not satisfied with me, please do tell me so that I can do better in the future. And here, I'd like to take this opportunity to thank you all for your understanding, cooperation and support. I hope to see you again in the future and to be your guide. I sincerely hope that you'll come to visit China again. Bon voyage!

M: Thank you, Miss Liu. You did a great job. We all had a very wonderful time. Let's give Miss Liu a big hand.

(*Applause and cheers*)

L: Thank you. Before you leave, could you fill out this form of evaluation for me? The comments and suggestions that you provide will be very valuable to help plan future tours.

(*Liu Hua collects the forms.*)

M: Thank you very much, Miss Liu. On behalf of the whole group, I'd like to express our heartfelt gratitude to you for your efforts and excellent services. We certainly have had a wonderful time in the past 5 days and will always remember this unforgettable journey. I believe, there will be further cooperation between us.

L: I suppose we have to, parting is such sweet sorrow. Hope to meet you again. Have a pleasant trip!

M: Thank you!

## (2) Seeing the Guest off at the Airport

**[Scene]** *Now, Miss Linda, the local guide, is making farewell at the airport to an American tour group.*
(L: Miss Linda　　G: tour guide)

L: Here we are at the airport. I would like to say something to our guests. Could you translate for me?

G: My pleasure.

L: Ladies and gentlemen, time flies fast. Now, you're leaving. I wish to say goodbye to everyone. First of all, I wish to thank you all for the understanding and cooperation you have given us in the past fifteen days. You have been very punctual on all occasions, which made things a lot easier for our work. You have been very attentive when we had anything to tell you. Also, you have been kind enough to offer us suggestions on how to better our guiding service. I'd like to add that you are the best group we've ever been with. Fifteen days ago, we met as strangers; today, we bid farewell to each other as friends. I hope you'll take back happy memories of your visit to America. Parting is such sweet sorrow. It is happy to meet, sorry to depart, and happy to meet again. I wish to see you again in the future and to be your guide again. Once again, thank you for your cooperation and support.

G: (*To the guests*) Let's give Miss Linda a warm applause to thank her for her service.

L: Thank you. Would you please wait for me for a few seconds? I am going to get the boarding passes and luggage claim cards for you!

G: OK, don't worry.

(*Miss Linda comes back.*)

L: Sorry to keep you waiting. Here are your tickets, boarding passes and luggage claim cards. Please check them.

G: Thank you very much.

L: Shall we go for the security check now?

G: OK. Let's go.

L: Here we are. These are the airport security personnel. Now, please get ready your plane ticket, group visa and boarding pass.

G: Thank you for your help.

L: It's my duty. Have a wonderful time back home.

## (3) Seeing the Guest off at the Train Station

**[Scene]** *A local guide is helping a tourist to check in at the Train Station*
(A: tourist　　B: local guide)

A: Shall we go on board right now?

B: Yes, let's go on board to avoid the last minute rush.

A: Is everyone here? Yes. OK. Let's move on to the ticket control.

B: Where is the ticket control for going to Hangzhou?

A: Over there, at Gate 3. Please give your ticket to the staff and wait to get the tickets punched.

B: To which platform are we going?

A: Platform 3. I will accompany you there.

B: Thank you.

A: Here we are. Platform 3. The car is just ahead. Car 6. Please get on.

B: It's a nice car. My berth is there.

A: Would you like to put your luggage on the rack or under the berth?

B: On the rack, please. Thank you.

A: Good. Is there anything else I can do for you?

B: No, thank you. You have been a great help. Thank you, indeed.

A: It's my pleasure. The train starts in a few minutes. It's time for us to say goodbye. I have to leave now. Have a nice journey.

B: Goodbye, Mr. Lin. Thank you for your help

## (4) Bidding Farewell

[Scene] *Lily, the local guide, is helping an American tour group to their car. And she is saying farewell outside the hotel.*

(L: Lily    T: tour guide)

L: Is all your luggage here?

T: I guess so.

L: Are you sure nothing is left behind?

T: Yeah, I am quite sure.

L: Good. Let's set off for the airport.

T: Why not?

L: How time flies! You've been in China for half a month. It seems as if it were only yesterday when I went to meet you at the airport. And now you're leaving.

T: Yeah, it has been a wonderful experience for us.

L: And what's your impression of China now?

T: Well, you know, before we came here, our knowledge about China mainly came from books and TV programs. But now it made a very deep impression on us. I think I have a much better un-

derstanding of Chinese culture now.

L: I'm glad you have enjoyed your stay in China.

T: The souvenirs we bought here will always remind us of our unforgettable trip to China. And you have been a great help to us along the way. Now, I'd like to express my gratitude to you on behalf of our members.

L: It's the least I can do for you. And it's a great pleasure for me to be your guide. Oh, here we are at the airport.

【Scene】*A tour guide is bidding farewell to a tourist who is leaving for his country.*
(A: tourist    B: guide)

B: Are you sure there is nothing left?

A: Yeah, I am sure. What is the departure time of my flight?

B: It is 11 o'clock this morning.

A: Then, we don't have to be in a hurry.

B: Well, I think we should start earlier. It may take some time on the way. There are always many traffic jams in this city. Besides, we'd better arrive at the airport one hour before the plane takes off so that we may have time to go through the customs.

A: In that case, let's go a little bit earlier.

B: It's a pity you're leaving. I hope you'll come to China again.

A: I will. Before I came, my knowledge about China mainly came from the travel books and TV programs, many of which were quite stereotyped. After a trip in China, I've got a better understanding of China and Chinese culture, and I'm quite happy about the trip.

B: I'm glad you have enjoyed your stay in China.

A: You've been very considerate and helpful along the way. I'd like to express my heart-felt gratitude to you.

B: It has been a pleasure to help you.

A: Everything I've seen here has left a deep impression on me. I will never forget my stay here in China. Thank you again for all the trouble you have taken. You are a very good guide.

B: Thank you for your appreciation. Have a pleasant journey home.

# Your Turn

Act out the following dialogues.

【Situation A】A tour guide is bidding farewell to a tour group who is leaving for his country.

Part One  Oral Practice

Before the guests leave, there are a large number of matters a tour guide must attend to:
☐ Ask the bellman to collect together the baggage which needs checking.
☐ Check the amount of the baggage and whether they are locked or damaged with the tour leader.
☐ Help the tourists to check out, reminds them to take their own items including their travel certificates, and warns them to take care of their valuables.
☐ Ask the tourists to check whether there is something for the local guide to deal with for them after their departure.
☐ Stand beside the door of the coach, and assist the tourists to get on.
☐ Count the number of the tourists again, and confirm that no tourists' items are forgotten, then asks the driver to start.

【Situation B】British Tour is now on the way to the airport. The tour guide is now bidding a farewell to her guests. They all feel regretful at parting because they all had a memorial experience.

【Situation C】You are an English tour guide who is saying goodbye to an American tour group at the airport. Mr. David is the tourist.
Tour guide:
☐ Ask to gather the baggage.
☐ Help check in.
☐ Remind to put the passport, credit card and travelers check in the suitcase so as to go through the security check.
☐ Tell that the airport tax is included in the air ticket.
☐ Express great honor to serve Mr. Davidson.
☐ Hope that Mr. Davidson enjoys his trip home.
☐ Welcome him to China again. Mr. Davidson:
☐ Thank to accompany to the airport.
☐ Ask about the airport tax.
☐ Thank for all having been done for him.
☐ Appreciate every minute of his stay here.
☐ Wish everything goes well.

【Situation D】The tourists are checking in at the airport with the local guide. With his help, the tourists go through the formalities required. Then they bid farewell at the security check.

# Part Two    Practical Writing

## Unit 11    Advertisements and Promotion Materials

## Learning Objectives

**Having read this unit, you will be able to**
◆ be familiar with the formats of tourism promotion materials
◆ know how to organize promotion materials
◆ write similar promotion materials by yourself

## Samples

1. **China International Travel Service**

> **CITS** provides best quality group tours for visitors all over the world, including China Supreme Tours, Tibet Group Tours, Shangri-La Group Tours, and China Prime Tours. Join in our best-selected group tours with a favorable price as well as enjoy warm friendships right now!
>
> **Contact Us**
> **E-mail**: citshrb@163.com        **Tel**: +86451-55513555
> **Company Address**: Room 311, No. 8 Shanghai Street, Daoli District, Harbin, China 150001
> **Office Hours**: Monday ~ Friday, 9:00 to 17:00 (GMT+0800)

2. **Sinoway Hotel**

## For Refined Luxury and Outstanding Service

  Relax amidst the elegantsettings, enjoy the fine food, or make use of our superb recreational facilities, from working out at the gymnasium to languishing beside the indoor swimming pool. The warm hospitality and gracious service you receive from the 274-room Sinoway Hotel in Nangang District, Harbin's business center.

**For reservation:**
**Sinoway Hotel**
**Address:** No. 2 Yiyuan Street, Nangang District, Harbin, Heilongjiang, China 150001
**Tel:** 0451-86291111
**Fax:** 0451-53670262
**Website:** http://www.sinowayhotel.com

### 3. Holiday Inn, Harbin

## Holiday Inn, Harbin

Strategically located in downtown Harbin, our hotel offers a fresh, comfortable and uncomplicated accommodation choice to travelers who value time and money. The smart simplicity concept makes the hotel a smart choice for the visitors to Harbin.

**For reservation:**
**Address:** No. 443 Xinyang Road, Daoli District, Harbin, P. R. China 150076
**Tel:** (86451) 5556 62222    8428 1776
**Fax:** (86451) 5556 62221
**Website:** www.wandaholidayexpress.com
**E-mail:** whe@ wandaholidayexpress.com

## 4. Harbin Railway International Travel Agency

Harbin Tours:

Harbin is the capital of Heilongjiang province, with a population of 5.3 million and covering an area of 18 000 square kilometers.

Located in eastern Songnen plain, it is a wonderland with low hills and shallow valleys. The well-known Songhua River quietly crosses by. It has a semi-humid climate with an annual average temperature of 3.5 degree Celsius, rainfall of 530 millimeters and a frost-free period of 140 days. Its mineral resources are coal, copper, lead and zinc, etc.

**Contact us:**
**Address:** No. 8 Tielu Street, Nangang District, Harbin, Heilongjiang Province, China
**Tel:** 0085-451-53616721 53616092           **E-mail:** liuboying681@hotmail.com
**Fax:** 0086-451-53616721 53616092          **MSN:** liuboying681@hotmail.com

Harbin Guide: Scenery | Hotels | Car or coach | Special Food | English speaking guide | Other special services

## 5. Shangri-La Hotel (Brochure in Picture)

You wake from slumber feeling relaxed and at home. The goose down pillows have been the perfect indulgence in your spacious bed. You're in Shangri-La Hotel, Harbin.

Excitement takes over as you anticipate your adventure in the days ahead. You go over to the windows and draw the drapes. The Ice City greets you. In the distance, the beautiful Songhua River glitters like a jewel in the morning sun.

Swiftly you get dressed and head downstairs for a hearty breakfast. You decide on casual dining at the Coffee Garden, reserving Shang Palace's Cantonese and Heilongjiang fine cuisine for later.

*Along the serene Songhua River*

Nearby Stalin Park is first on your agenda. Situated along the Songhua River, it boasts vibrant flowerbeds, manicured lawns and intricate art sculptures. Harbin's natural beauty is evident from the get-go.

Around the city, buildings are embellished with spires and cupolas. Many remain untouched since the Russian Revolution. This blend of Asian and European architectural features speaks of Harbin's history and close proximity to Russia. Just like Shangri-La Hotel, Harbin, the city's unique charm is undeniable.

The cold winters here make the famous Harbin Ice and Snow Festival a reality. Dramatic ice sculptures and life-sized constructs amaze visitors day and night.

Tomorrow, you will soak in more of the city's delightful offerings. For now, a refreshing swim in the hotel's heated pool shall precede dinner.

Welcome to Shangri-La Hotel, Harbin, where the feeling is always warm.

**Phone**
(86 451) 8785 8888 ext 6408

**Fax**
(86 451) 8462 1777

**Email**
reservations.shar@shangri-la.com

**Location**
555 You Yi Road, Harbin, 150018, China

**Check-in / Check-out**
Check-in: 2pm
Check-out: 12noon

Horizon Club guests enjoy late check-out till 6pm.

**Payment**
We accept the following cards:
American Express, Diners Club, JCB, MasterCard, Visa

**Useful Information**
▸ Hotel Fact Sheet
▸ Safety Features Fact Sheets

# Simulate and Create

1. **Write an ad according to the idea given below and express your desire to attract more guests to your hotel.**
   ◇ winter special
   ◇ from January 15 to March 15 at only RMB 288
   ◇ located in central Harbin just minutes away from the railway station
   ◇ 400 superbly-appointed guest rooms
   ◇ subject to 15% service charge

2. **Write an ad according to the idea given below, trying to attract more guests to your travel**

**agency.**
- ◇ a package tour to Seoul
- ◇ a week, RMB 2980
- ◇ a 25 percent discount before April 16

**3. Appreciate the following travel ads and try to design a brand new one with local features.**

# Unit 12   Travel Agreements and Contracts

## Learning Objectives

**Having read this unit, you will be able to**
- be familiar with the formats of travel agreements and contracts
- know how to sign travel agreements and contracts
- understand similar agreements and contracts by yourself

## Samples

In general, the international travel contract or agreement is composed of following elements:
① Title
② Signing date
③ Execution period
④ Information of the two parties of the contract
⑤ Signature and seal of two parties

## 1. Harbin Kanghui International Travel Services

TOUR CO-OPERATION AGREEMENT BETWEEN
KANGHUI INTERNATIONAL TRAVEL SERVICES ("KTS")

Contact Name: Wang Jun
Telephone: 13946123752
Fax: 0451-87582669
E-mail: sales@KTS.COM
Address: No. 15 Songhua River Street, Nangang District, Harbin, P. R. China 150001

AND
Y Tour Company, LTD ("YTC")

Contact Name: Jay Brown
Telephone: 617-878-55555
Fax: 617-878-66666
E-mail: sales@YTC.COM
Address: 55 Blueberry Street, Boston, Massachusetts 02111 USA

CONTRACT DATES: Jan 1, 2009 ~ Dec 31, 2010

XTS Signature:
YTC Signature:
Dated: ××××.×.×

\* General terms and conditions.

The general terms and conditions is to list all the specific requirements between the two contracting parties.

①The rates set forth in this agreement, including Addendum A annexed hereto, are quoted in USD and are inclusive of any and all: (Ⅰ) taxes; (Ⅱ) driver's expenses; (Ⅲ) tolls; (Ⅳ) parking fees. Any cost to be paid with the respect to accommodations and/or meals for drivers or guides will be listed separately.

②All vehicles shall be no more than 5 years old, and shall be air-conditioned, equipped with toilet facilities, microphones and stereo/video equipments, and otherwise in good condition.

③All the staff appearances, including drivers and guides, must be dressed appropriately and take the direction of YTC's local representative.

④KTS will not subcontract any of the service to be performed under this agreement to other suppliers without prior written approval of YTC, which approval may be withheld by YTC.

⑤Signs bearing the name "YTC" will be provided by YTC, and displayed for the guests.

⑥All the service work must be well prepared by KTS no later than 30 days prior to the arrival of guests.

\* Payment terms.

The payment terms is an important component in the contract. The international remittance procedure is more complicated than domestic and requires more detailed information. And it can also be specified of the requirement on receiving and sending bills and remittance confirmation.

① STS will invoice YTC by fax upon the arrival of YTC tour guests.

② YTC should confirm and pay each invoice no later than 10 days after receipt.

③ The invoice from STS shall identify the relevant tour group by reference to its respective code, and not solely by the relevant date of arrival or the service to be provided.

④ Contacts.

## 2. Songhua River International Travel Services of Heilongjiang Province

SONGHUA RIVER INTERNATIONAL TRAVEL SERVICES("STS")
Contact Name: Mr. Li Nan
Telephone: 400-696-6007
Fax: 0451-87282698
MSN: zwcxy188@hotmail.com
Financial Contact: Ms. Li Mei

Y Tour Company, LTD("YTC")
Contact Name: Mr. Jay Brown
Telephone: 617-878-55555
Fax: 617-878-66666
E-mail: sales@YTC.COM
Financial Contact: Mrs. Mary Melvyn

\* Force majeure.

Force majeure is simple but an integral part of a contract. It can well prevent all parties' interest from unnecessary loss or dispute. It means an unavoidable event or incident and decisions made by a country or public organization that causes or allows a contract to be changed or cancelled.

# Exercises

### 1. Translate the following English sentences into Chinese.

(1) Force majeure is simple but is an integral part of a contract.

(2) The invoice from XTS shall identify the relevant tour group by reference to its respective code, and not solely by the relevant date of arrival or the service to be provided.

## 2. Translate the following Chinese sentences into English.
(1) 司机和导游的住宿费及餐费另计。
(2) 不可抗力原因而不能或延迟履行合同的,乙方不负有违约责任。

## 3. Writing
(1) Write a complete international travel contract or agreement, includes: over, general terms and conditions, payment terms and force majeure.
(2) Draft a short contract with a local hotel for room accommodations in the following year in your capacity as a local travel agency manager.

# Unit 13   Itinerary, Quotation and Final Confirmation

## Learning Objectives

**Having read this unit, you will be able to**
- be familiar with the process of your tour
- know how to prepare your tour
- make an itinerary by yourself

## Samples

### 1. Travel Itinerary

**Example 1**

| |
|---|
| 1 Day Beijing Forbidden City and Hutong Tour Program for Mr. Daniel Keen |
| Day 01             Beijing |
| 08:00              Hotel pick up at the lobby by your ESP guide and air-conditioned coach |
| 09:00 ~ 12:30      Tour in the Forbidden City—The biggest royal place in the world |
| 12:30 ~ 14:00      Lunch at local restaurant for flavor |
| 15:00 ~ 17:00      Hutong tour in Shichahai region by tricycles to learn the old Beijing life style |
| 18:00              Transfer back to Hotel, tour ends. Dinner on your own |

**Example 2**

| | | |
|---|---|---|
| 3 Days Tour Program in Kunming for Mr. Daniel Keen | | |
| Day 01 | Kunming | (—/—/—) |
| FRI | Arrival in Kunming (your own ticket). Meet your guide at airport and transfer to hotel. The capital of Yunnan province, Kunming is one of China's noted historical and cultural cities. The city is located in central Yunnan at the elevation of 1894 meters above sea level and is praised as the city of eternal spring. | |
| | Rest of day at leisure | |
| | Lunch and dinner at leisure | |
| | Overnight at 4-star Hotel | |
| Day 02 | Kunming | (B/L/—) |
| SAT | Buffet breakfast at hotel | |
| | Drive along the new express way to the Stone Forest. The Stone Forest is 75 kilometers from Kunming and is accessible by a bus ride of 70 minutes. The Stone Forest belongs to the typical Karst geomorphology, it consists of innumerable bizarre-shaped ancient limestone cliffs and peaks created by wind and water erosion some 200 million years ago, and this area is praised as the "First Wonder under Heaven" | |
| | Drive back to Kunming by the old road, visit a village en route | |
| | Visit the Flower and Bird Market. The market, along with old houses that are well kept in its immediate neighborhood, is now under Kunming's protection plan as the Old Town Quarter. Besides flowers and birds, the market offers also state of art samples of traditional Chinese arts, wooden sculptures, bronzeware, China knots, and more | |
| | Lunch at local restaurant, dinner at leisure | |
| | Overnight at 4-star Hotel | |
| Day 03 | Kunming–Beijing Departure | |
| SUN | Buffet breakfast at hotel | |
| | Transfer to airport for morning departure flight | |
| | Tour ends | |

## 2. Travel Quotation

### Example 1

| | |
|---|---|
| 1 Day Beijing Forbidden City and Hutong Tour for Mr. Daniel Keen | |
| Day 01 | Beijing |
| 08:00 | Hotel pick up at the lobby by your ESP guide and air-conditioned coach |
| 09:00 ~ 12:30 | Tour in the Forbidden City—the biggest royal place in the world |
| 12:30 ~ 14:00 | Lunch at local restaurant |
| 15:00 ~ 17:00 | Hutong tour in Shichahai region by tricycles to learn the old Beijing life style |
| 18:00 | Transfer back to Hotel, tour ends. Dinner on your own |

**Quotation**

| | |
|---|---|
| Profession ESP Guide Fee | USD 10 per person |
| Meals | USD 10 per person |
| Vehicle rental | USD 80 per person |
| Entrance Fee | USD 30 per person |
| Totally | USD 130 per person |

**Including**

The lunch as mentioned in the program

Sightseeing tour with local English-speaking guide

All entrance fees + sightseeing as indicated

All transfers and land transportation by private air-conditioned coach

**Excluding**

Any accommodation

Any airfare or tax or fuel surcharge

Any dinner, other meal, drinks and personal expenses

Tips to the guide and driver

Any program other than mentioned in our program

## Example 2

| | | |
|---|---|---|
| 3 Days Program in Kunming for Mr. Daniel Keen | | |
| Day 01<br>FRI | Kunming (1894 meters) arrival | (—/—/—) |

Arrival in Kunming (your own ticket). Meet your guide at airport and transfer to hotel

The capital of Yunnan Province, Kunming is one of China's noted historical and cultural cities. The city is located in central Yunnan at the elevation of 1894 meters above sea level and is praised as the city of eternal spring

Rest of day at leisure/Lunch and dinner at leisure/Overnight at 4-star Hotel

| | | |
|---|---|---|
| Day 02<br>SAT | Kunming | (B/L/—) |

Buffet breakfast at hotel

Drive along the new express way to the Stone Forest. The Stone Forest is 75 kilometers from Kunming and is accessible by a bus ride of 70 minutes The Stone Forest belongs to the typical Karst geomorphology, it consists of innumerable bizarre-shaped ancient limestone cliffs and peaks created by wind and water erosion some 200 million years ago, and this area is praised as the "First Wonder under Heaven"

Drive back to Kunming by the old road, visit a village en route

Visit the Flower and Bird Market. The market, along with old houses that are well kept in its immediate neighborhood, is now under Kunming's protection plan as the Old Town Quarter. Besides flowers and birds, the market offers also state of art samples of traditional Chinese arts, wooden sculptures, bronzeware, China knots, and more

Lunch at local restaurant/Dinner at leisure/Overnight at 4-star Hotel

| | | |
|---|---|---|
| Day03<br>SUN | Kunming-Beijing Departure | (B/—/—) |

Buffet breakfast at hotel/Transfer to airport for morning departure flight

Tour ends

**Quotation**

| | | | |
|---|---|---|---|
| Profession ESP Guide Fee | USD 25 per person | Meals | USD 10 per person |
| Vehicle rental | USD 100 per person | Entrance fee | USD 20 per person |
| Hotel rate | USD 100 per person | Airfare | USD 200 per person |

> Totally USD 455 per person
> 
> **Including**
> 
> Accommodation in sharing twin room at specified hotels with daily breakfast
> 
> All lunch as mentioned in the program
> 
> Sightseeing tour with local English-speaking guide
> 
> All entrance fees+sightseeing as indicated
> 
> All transfers and land transportation by private air-conditioned coach
> 
> Airfares Kunming/Beijing with Tax & Fuel Surcharge
> 
> **Excluding**
> 
> Arrival flight to Kunming with Tax & Fuel surcharge
> 
> All dinners, other meals, drinks and personal expenses
> 
> Tips to the guide and driver, any program other than mentioned in our program

3. **Final confirmation of the travel program**

Example

Voucher

For 3 Days Program in Kunming for Mr. Daniel Keen 2 persons

From XTS

Accommodation (1 king-size room with extra bed incl. Daily BF)

3rd Oct. to 5th Oct. 2 nights at Kunming Hotel

Address:52 Dongfeng Road East, Kunming, Yunnan 650011, PRC

Tel: 86 871 316 2063

Train & Airplane

| Departure | Date | Train or Airline | Train or Flight No. | Time |
| --- | --- | --- | --- | --- |
| Kunming Airport | 5th Oct. | China Eastern Air | MU5715 | 8:50 |

| | | |
|---|---|---|
| Day 01 | Kunming(1894 meters) arrival | (—/—/—) |
| FRI | | |

Arrival in Kunming (your own ticket). Meet your guide at airport and transfer to hotel. The capital of Yunnan Province, Kunming is one of China's noted historical and cultural cities. The city is located in central Yunnan at the elevation of 1894 meters above sea level and is praised as the city of eternal spring

Rest of day at leisure

Lunch and dinner at leisure

Overnight at Kunming Hotel

| | | |
|---|---|---|
| Day 02 | Kunming | (B/L/—) |
| SAT | | |

Buffet breakfast at hotel

Drive along the new express way to the Stone Forest. The Stone Forest is 75 kilometers from Kunming and is accessible by a bus ride of 70 minutes. The Stone Forest belongs to the typical Karst geomorphology, it consists of innumerable bizarre-shaped ancient limestone cliffs and peaks created by wind and water erosion some 200 million years ago, and this area is praised as the "First Wonder under Heaven"

Drive back to Kunming by the old road, visit a village en route

Visit the Flower and Bird Market. The market, along with old houses that are well kept in its immediate neighborhood, is now under Kunming's protection plan as the Old Town Quarter. Besides flowers and birds, the market offers also state of art samples of traditional Chinese arts, wooden sculptures, bronzeware, China knots, and more.

Lunch at local restaurant, dinner at leisure

Overnight at Kunming Hotel

| | | |
|---|---|---|
| Day 03 | Kunming   Beijing Departure | (B/—/—) |
| SUN | | |

Buffet breakfast at hotel

Transfer to airport for morning departure flight

Tour ends

Tour Cost    USD 455 per person

**Including**

Accommodation in sharing twin room at specified hotels with daily breakfast

All lunch as mentioned in the program

Sightseeing tour with local English-speaking guide

All entrance fees + sightseeing as indicated

All transfers and land transportation by private coach air-condition

Airfares Kunming/Beijing with Tax & Fuel Surcharge

**Excluding**

Arrival flight to Kunming with Tax & Fuel Surcharge

All dinners, other meals, drinks and personal expenses

Tips to the guide and driver

Any program other than mentioned in our program

BON VOYAGE

We Wish You a Very Pleasant Journey

You may contact any time if there is an emergency during your journey.

Mr. Wang Jun

Tel：86-10-12345678

---

Booked, paid and confirmed by:
X TRAVEL SERVICES("XTS")
Address:No. 1 East Chang'an Street, Beijing, 100006, PRC
Telephone:86-10-12345678
Fax：86-10-23456789
E-mail：sales@ XTS. COM

---

# Exercises

**1. Translate the following English sentences into Chinese.**

(1) Meet your guide at the airport and transfer to the Hotel.
(2) Accommodation in sharing twin room at specified hotels with daily breakfast

**2. Translate the following Chinese sentences into English.**

(1)如果您在旅行中出现任何紧急情况,请随时与我们联系。
(2)行程包含所有机场专车接送和陆地交通费用(空调旅游车)。

**3. Writing.**

(1) List the important factors in drafting itineraries.
(2) Draft a 10-day itinerary in China covering Beijing, Xi'an, Chengdu, Kunming and Guilin for a forthcoming USA group which is little informed about these destinations.

# Unit 14　Reservation Form and Confirmation Letter

## Learning Objectives

**Having read this unit, you will be able to**
- be familiar with the formats of Reservation Form and Confirmation Letter
- master the basic information involved in the Reservation Form and Confirmation Letter
- find ways to improve your writing skills about Reservation Form and Confirmation Letter

## Samples

### 1. China Tour Reservation

### Step Ⅰ Basic information

| | |
|---|---|
| Name: | ( * Required same as your passport) |
| Gender: | ☐ male ☐ female |
| Age: | |
| Street Address: | |
| City: | |
| State or Province | |
| Country: | --Please Select--　( * Required ) |
| Zip Code or Postal Code: | ( * Recommended) |
| E-mail: | ( * Required ) |
| Alternate E-mail Address: | ( * Recommended) |
| Phone/Cell Number: | ( * Required ) |
| Fax Number: | ( * Recommended) |

## Step II My Tour Requests

| | | |
|---|---|---|
| Total person (s) traveling : | | person (s) traveling ( * Required ) |
| Including child (ren) : | | child (ren) |
| Estimated travel date : | From       To | ( * Required ) |
| Length of traveling days : | | days |
| Which city or cities of China are you planning to visit? | | city (cities) |
| Start city : | | ( * Required ) |
| Estimated budget : | | US$ /per person |
| Planning itinerary : | ◉ Yes, I have my arrangement<br>◯ no idea | |
| Your planned itinerary | | |

## Step III I would also like to have following services

| | | |
|---|---|---|
| Booking air ticket: | From       To | |
| Reserve Hotel (Stars) | stars Hotel | Room(s) |
| provide English-speaking guide | ◉ yes<br>◯ no | |
| The relationship between travel mate and me is: | family ▼ | |
| Interest in | seashore ▼ | |
| Other requirements | | |

submit                                              Reset

## How to book the tour

(1) You can book the tour on-line or by filling the Reservation Form.
(2) You will receive our confirmation E-mail within two working days. Your reservation is done then.
(3) Our tour guide will contact you the night before the tour to inform you the time to pick you up in the next morning, or if you are not in the hotel, the guide will leave a message in your room to inform you the time to pick you up.
(4) Enjoy your tour with our guide.

## Contact us

For your tour request or more information, please contact our tour operator:
Tel: (86) 25-66708104
Fax: (86) 25-66708105
Emergency Call (Mobile): (86) 15062227277 (24 hours)
Office Hours: 9:00 a.m. ~ 18:00 p.m. (GMT+0800) Monday ~ Friday
E-mail: webmaster-chinafun@hotmail.com
MSN: webmaster-chinafun@hotmail.com or wanghuili2000@hotmail.com
ICP:06036925
Add: Zhujiang Road, Nanjing, China

## 2. Hotel Reservation Application Form

| DATE APPLIED<br>May 22, 2012 | RESERVATION APPLICATION | | *NEW BOOKING   CANCELLATION<br>AMENDMENT   ON WAITING   LIST |
|---|---|---|---|
| GUEST NAME:<br>John Paley<br><br>COMPANY:<br>General Motors<br><br>TITLE:<br>Sales manager | ARRIVAL<br>5/22/2012<br>MONTH/DATE/YEAR | | DEPARTURE<br>6/4/2012<br>MONTH/DATE/YEAR |
| | TRANSPORTATION ARRANGEMENT<br>SINGLE TRIP | | ROUND TRIP |
| | FLIGHT<br>ETA:8:00 a.m. May 22 | | ETD: 11:30 June 4 |
| TYPE OF ACCOMMODATION REQUIRED<br>Single room with bath | | RATE<br>SPECIAL DISCOUNT<br>*CORPORATE DISCOUNT<br>TRAVEL AGENT DISCOUNT<br>AIRLINE DISCOUNT | |
| PERSON<br>One | | | |
| FIRM/TRAVEL AGENT<br>Pacific Travel Agency | | PAYMENT INSTRUCTIONS<br>ROOM            *ALL EXPENSES<br>GUEST ACCOUNT   TRANSFER | |
| NAME OF APPLICANT<br>John Paley | A/C NO<br>2123994000323 | | |
| PHONE NUMBER<br>001-446-238-6837 | FAX NUMBER<br>001-446-237-7856 | | |
| | | REMARKS<br>SPECIAL RM RT APPROVED BY | |
| RECEIVED BY<br>Tom Lily | RECONFIRMED BY<br>Kem Jude | | |
| VIP APPROVED BY | CIP APPROVED BY | | |
| Please note that reservations are held until 6 p. m. unless arrival details are notified | | | |

## 3. Confirmation Letter

  *Confirmation letter is very important in order to make a people sure that their request is obtained and being handled. Below there is a sample of the confirmation of booking of the hotel room that informs the client about the situation of the arrangements he made before the arrival to the hotel.*

Diana Samuel
388 Kreidon hills
2299 Barcelona, Spain

14 May 2010

Brian Kruger
388 Velers str
877 Berlin, Germany

Subject: Confirmation of booking in hotel

Dear Mr. Kruger,
This is the confirmation letter on your request dated 12 May 2010. We are pleased to inform you that we reserved for you single room with the garden view in our hotel with the breakfast in the morning as per your request. Al the facilities are included. During the stay in our hotel you can use gym, spa and pool area (the charges are included in fees for the room).

Below there is a picture of the room reserved. Please, review it and let us know if you want to change your reservation or have special requirements that we can meet.

Kindly inform us whether you need someone to meet you in the airport, we can provide with this service as well.
For further requires, please contact us.

Thank you in advance. We are looking forward to meeting you here.

Sincerely,
Diana Samuel

## 4. Reservation Confirmation

**EASTERN PEARL HOTEL**

ADDR:MINISTRIES ROAD,JUBA,SOUTH SUDAN
TEL: +249 (0) 913 568 243 (Glen Lv)
　　　+249 (0) 911 914 005 (Antony)

**RESERVATION CONFIRMATION**

Dear Mr. Ben,
　　Thank you for choosing to stay with us at Eastern Pearl Hotel. We are pleased to confirm your reservation as follows:

| | |
|---|---|
| Guest Name: | Mr. Chaka Ben |
| Arrival Date | October 20, 2011 |
| Departure Date: | October 24, 2011 |
| Number of Guest: | 1 |
| Accommodation: | Deluxe Single |
| Rate per Night: | $ 180 (full board) |

　　Should you require an early check-in, please make your request as soon as possible. Rates are quoted in SOUTH SUDAN funds and subject to application state and local taxes. If you find it necessary to cancel this reservation, our hotel requires notification by 4:00 p.m. the day before your arrival to avoid a charge for one night's room rate.
　　Whatever we can do to make your visit extra special, call us at +249 0913 568 243. You have been taken to our pre-arrival checklist from where we'll assist you with advance reservations for airport transfers.
　　We are looking forward to your coming to Eastern Pearl Hotel.

Sincerely,

Glen Lv
Hotel Reception

## Simulate and Create

(1) Design a hotel reservation form and fill in the form according to the Situational Conversations of Unit 2 Arriving at the Hotel.
(2) Write a confirmation letter based on the reservation you got from question one.
(3) Nowadays making a reservation through the internet is becoming more and more popular. Try to make a reservation in one of the hotels by logging on the internet.

## Announcement

| Title | Publish Time |
|---|---|

## Introduction

Sinoway hotel is situated in the center of the prosperous businss district of harbin. Within easy access to the railway station. The stylish design reflects the perfect blend of art and architecture, where you with always feel at home thanks to che ambience and cham of personalizeds –star hotel senice, where the word over make it their choice to conduct businss.

## Search Order

Booking #
Or Email
Or Mobile

[Search]

## Online Reservation

Check in

Check out

Rooms | Adults | Children
1 | 1 | 0

Currency | Room
USD | All Room

Package

[Booking]

## Contact Us

Add: No.2 YiYuan Street, Harbin, Heilongjiang, China.
Tel: 0451-86291111

## Facilities

◇ Room Services:
Suite, Standard
◇ Restaurant Services:
Chinese Restaurant, western Restaurant, Bar

# Unit 15  Registration Form

## Learning Objectives

**Having read this unit, you will be able to**
- master the basic words and expressions about room reservation and registration
- knowhow to fill in the Registration Form
- design similar Registration Forms by yourself

## Samples

### 1. Registration Form of Temporary Residence for Group

Name of group          Date: Year  Mon  Day  Till  Mon  Day

| Room No. | Name in full | Sex | Date of birth | Occupation | Nationality | Passport No. |
|---|---|---|---|---|---|---|
|  |  |  |  |  |  |  |
|  |  |  |  |  |  |  |
|  |  |  |  |  |  |  |
|  |  |  |  |  |  |  |
|  |  |  |  |  |  |  |
|  |  |  |  |  |  |  |
|  |  |  |  |  |  |  |
| Where from and to | | | | | | |
| Remarks | | | | | | |

Hotel:                                    Agency:

## 2. Group Registration

**Example 1**

# GROUP REGISTRATION

RESV. NO. _____

MKT. _____

GROUP NAME：      TOUR LEADER NO：

ARRIVE     DEPART     CARRIER     ETD：

| DATE | | | | | |
|---|---|---|---|---|---|
| MORNING CALL | / | / | / | / | / |
| BAGGAGE DOWN | | | | | |
| BREAKFAST | | | | | |

ROOM#

CHECKED IN BY                        CHECKED BY

| AGENCY | NO OF PAX | | NO OF ROOMS | | SIGNATURE |
|---|---|---|---|---|---|
| VHR# | ADULT | | TWN | | |
| | 2~5AG | | SGL | | |
| | 6~11AG | | EXB | | |

| GUIDE AGENCY | NO OF GUIDE | | GUIDE RM NO | | SIGNATURE |
|---|---|---|---|---|---|
| | NG | | | | |
| | LG | | | | |
| | DRIVER | | | | |

**Example 2**

## A Form of Tour Group Information

## IN-HOUSE GROUP INFORMATION

Group Name: American Professor Sightseeing Group
Arrival Date: June 11, 2011
ETA: 10:00 a.m. June 11        ETD: 10:25 a.m. June 21
Name Of Agent: Sun Travel Agency   Tel: 0898-32111155
Group Code: 0281
Departure Date: June 21, 2011
Nationality: The United States
Contact Person: Lu Baoguo

| TYPE | No. OF RMS | ROOM NUMBER | No. OF PAX |
|---|---|---|---|
| SK | 1 | 203 | 2211 |
| ST | 2 | 301 302 | 2230 2231 |
| DK | 2 | 204 205 | 2217 2218 |
| DT | 2 | 207 208 | 2280 2290 |
| JS. | 3 | 101 102 103 | 2274 2275 2276 |
| TOTAL | 10 | | |

## MEAL REQUIREMENT

| DATE | TIME | BREAKFAST | LUNCH | DINNER | VENUE | REMARKS |
|---|---|---|---|---|---|---|
| 11$^{th}$ | 12:00 | | 20 | 20 | 2$^{nd}$ Dining Room | |
| 12$^{th}$ ~ 13$^{th}$ | | | | | | |
| | | | | | | |
| | | | | | | |
| | | | | | | |

## WAKE-UP CALLS

| DATE | | | | | | | |
|---|---|---|---|---|---|---|---|
| TIME | | | | | | | |

RECEPTIONIST:
NATIONAL GUIDE:

White copy: Front Desk　　Blue copy: Concierge　　Green copy: Housekeeper
Pink copy: Operator　　　Yellow copy: F&B Dept

## 3. Registration Form of Temporary Residence for Foreigner

# (IN BLOCK LETTERS)

| Name: | surname | first name | middle name |
|---|---|---|---|
| Nationality | Sex | Date of birth | Occupation |
| Visa or travel Document No. | Date of validity | | |
| Object of stay | | Date of entry | |
| Where from & to | | Arrival Date | |
| Received by | | Departure Date | |
| Address | | Guest Signature | |
| ON CHECKING OUT MY ACCOUNT WILL BE SETTLED BY<br>□CASH<br>□COMPANY<br>□CREDIT CARD<br>□AGENTS<br>□RATE | | PLEASE NOTE<br>①Check out time is 12:00 noon<br>②Safe deposit boxes areavailable at cashier counter at no charge<br>③Room rate not including beverage in your room<br>④Please return your room key to the cashier counter after check out | |

**CLERK SIGNATURE**　　　　　　**Room No.**

## 4. Registration Form of Temporary Residence

**Please write in block letters**

| Surname: Levy | First Name: Logan | Sex: Male |
|---|---|---|
| Other Name: | Nationality: U.S.A | Date of Birth: July 3, 1959 |
| Certificate No.: 287129 | Type of Certificate: Passport | Expiry Date: March 1, 2016 |
| Type of Visa: FI Valid Visa Date: March 1. 2013 Port of Entry: Beijing Date of Entry: Oct. 2 ||||
| Arrival Date: Oct. 2　Arrival Time: 9:00 a.m.　Departure Date: Oct. 10　Departure Time: 7 a.m. ||||
| Next Destination: Tianjin　Flight No. CY3135　Departure Time: 8:15 a.m.　Company ||||
| Permanent Address: No. 206 Jackson Street, New York ||||

| Room No.: 1208 | Folio No.: 302 | Booking Source:<br>Travel Agency | Room Rate:<br>$120/night |
|---|---|---|---|

| My account will be settled by:<br>Cash<br>＊Credit card<br>Voucher<br>Company account | Please Note:<br>①I will bear all my expenses in the hotel<br>②Safe deposit boxes are available in the guestroom<br>③The hotel will not be liable for any items left unattended<br>④Check out time is 12:00 noon ||
|---|---|---|

| My | room charges<br>F&B charges<br>＊all charges | will be settled by Mr./Mrs. Logan Levy | Signature<br>Guest<br>Receptionist<br>Du Xiaoling |
|---|---|---|---|

## 5. Registration Form (Computer)

| ROOM NUMBER | |
|---|---|
| RATE | |
| ARRIVAL DATE | |
| DEPARTURE DATE | |

If there is any change in the information presented above, please notify front desk clerk. CHECK-OUT TIME: 12 NOON.

| ACCOUNT NUMBER | ARRIVAL DATE | DEPARTURE DATE | ARRIVAL TIME | NO, OF ROOMS | ROOM TYPE |
|---|---|---|---|---|---|
| | | | | | |
| DAILY RATE | NO. OF GUESTS | ADVANCE DEPARTURE | ROOM NO. | PACKAGE PLAN | |
| SURNAME | | | FIRST NAME | | |
| CURRENT RESIDENCE/COMPANY ADDRESS | | | PASSPORT NO. DATE/PLACE OF ISSUE | | |
| | | | NATIONALITY | DATE OF BIRTH | |
| COMPANY/CONVENTION | | | OCCUPATION | | |
| NEXT DESTINATION | | NAME OF HOTEL | | CHECK OUT TIME 12 NOON | |
| METHOD OF PAYMENT EXPIRY DATE | ☐ CASH  ☐ VISA  ☐ MASTER CARD  ☐ AMEX  ☐ DINERS CLUB  ☐ CARTE BLANCHE  ☐ VOUCHER  ☐ COMPANY ACCOUNT  ☐ OTHER | | | | |
| IMPORTANT: ①Guests are requested under Hotel Licensing Regulation to produce their passports to the Hotel Clerk or Receptionist ②The hotel liability for valuables is governed by Innkeepers Act. Guests are advised to read the notice at the Reception Desk | | | CREDIT CARD/VOUCHER NO. | | |
| | | | SIGNATURE | | |

## Simulate and Create

1. **Please fill in a registration form at the hotel on the following basis:**

◇the number of the tourists is 13
◇the arrival and departure dates is from May 24$^{th}$ to 28$^{th}$
◇the price is 198 RMB per night
◇add some information if necessary

2. **Suppose you are the receptionist in the hotel serving the guest named Mr. Chaka Ben (Reservation Confirmation, UNIT 5). Try to fill out a registration form according to the confirmation letter he received.**

# Unit 16  Notices

## Learning Objectives

**Having read this unit, you will be able to**
- be familiar with the formats of you tour
- know how to write an notice
- understand similar notice by yourself

## Samples

### Warning

May 3, 2011

  Because of the large number of tourists during these days, the top of Mount Maor has become too crowded. We therefore advice our tourists to pay great attention to your safety. If anything unusual happened, please call the following telephone number.

Mount Maor Administrative Committee
Tel: 0451-6625768

## Christmas Party

A Christmas Party
will be held in the lobby
at 8 p.m. on Wednesday, the 25t" December 2011
All the tourists please do not be late. See you!

T.Rosa
Manager

## Notice

Because of the bad weather tomorrow, we have to visit Zhongyang Street instead of climbing Mountain Maor. Please contact us if you have any problem!

July 12, 2011

×× Travel Agency
Tel: 0451-6668888

## Notice

Dec. 12, 2010

There will be a banquet tonight here. We hope you all can attend it. If you have other schedule, please let us know!

XX Travel Agency
Tel: 0451-1234567

# Exercises

Write a notice according to the information given.

1. 兆麟公园内部正在部分装修,有运料的进出车辆,可能会给游客带来不便,请大家谅解,并请大家注意安全。
2. 你们原计划明天去太阳岛游览,但由于一些原因,改为去极乐寺参观,为此给大家带来的不便,请大家谅解。

# Unit 17   Memorandum

## Learning Objectives

**Having read this unit, you will be able to**
- be familiar with the formats and contents of memorandum
- know how to write memorandum with correct format and sufficient information
- write similar promotion materials by yourself

## Samples

**Example 1**

# MEMORANDUM

From: Olive HR Manager  　　　To: All staff
Date: 12$^{th}$ June, 2009　　　Subject: Appointment of Francisco

　　Here we announce the appointment of Mrs. Francisco as our new Sales Manager of the Headquarter. She will be starting her job next Monday morning. There will be a small welcome party by 9:00 that day so everyone please be on time.

　　Olive HR Manager

**Example 2**

# MEMORANDUM

To: Records Section
From: P. Steelpes, Career Planning
Subject: Request for Paid Education Leave
Date: May 22, 2005

　　In response to your request for one year of paid education leave to take a degree in English literature, I have to inform you that we cannot authorize this leave.

　　While we appreciate your desire to improve your knowledge, we feel that English literature is not directly related to your present position and to the goals of this organization.

　　I am aware of your great interest in literature, and I would like to point out that you could gain advantage to apply for leave without pay.

　　If you need another information on the above, do not hesitate to keep touch with me at any time.

　　P. Steelpes

## Example 3

To: David Green, Chief of Operations
From: Tony Party, Supervisor
Subject: Comments on the "Punch-in" System
Date: March 22, 2005

    This is further to your memo dated March. 20, 2004, in which you proposed that employees adopt the "punch-in" system.

    I fully agree with you that we must increase productivity. As far as your proposal that if the "punch-in" system is adopted, we would have a tighter control over the employees is concerned. However, I don't think so. I personally think that, to accomplish this, we should give the employees more incentives to work faster. I feel that if we (the supervisors) could meet with you, we could discuss different possiblilities to create such incentiveness.

    Your consideration of this suggestion would be appreciated.

## Example 4

To: All staff
From: Managing Director
Subject: Study tour of management consultants
Date: 15$^{th}$ June, 2011

    In view of the problems of organization and communications following the rapid growth of our company in recent years, the board of directors has decided to engage a firm of management consultants to study the organization of our company, propose necessary changes, define the responsibilities of all management staff, and suggest improved means of communication.

**Example 5**

> To: Alexander Hallman, Sales Manager
> From: Ralph Huxley, Marketing Representative
> Subject: Request for a systems engineer
> Date: 19 December 2011
> 
>     This is to request you to send a systems engineer from the Chicago office to help me make a large sale to Dombey & Sons, a local company I have visited several times. I understand this is an unusual practice, but this is a special situation. If the said engineer could come to Birmingham and accompany me on my next visit to the firm, I am quite sure that I make the sale. Please act promptly.

# Exercises

(1) You are Secretary to the Managing Director, who asks you now to draft a memo to be sent to all staff, announcing the decision. He is particularly anxious that all staff should understand what is about to be done, so that unnecessary fears will not arise.

(2) Directions: You are the president of a company. Write a memo to Percy Shelley, the vice-president on the employees training on computer:

①The need to train the employees.
②Detailed information.
③Ask him to write a plan.

# Unit 18    Letter of Invitation and Reply

## Learning Objectives

Having read this unit, you will be able to
- be familiar with the formats and contents of letter of invitation and reply
- know how to write memorandum with correct format and sufficient information
- write similar promotion materials by yourself

## Samples

**Example 1    Formal Invitation Letter**

> Mr. and Mrs. Wang Dawei
> Request the pleasure of
> Mr. and Mrs. John Oliver
> The presence at Beijing Opera
> On Saturday, September 6$^{mth}$
> At seven p. m.
> Peace Theater
> 
> R. S. V. P.                    Telephone: 010-62665572

**Example 2   Informal Invitation Letter**

Dear Mr. and Mrs. Johnson,

　　Will you please go with us to see a farewell performance of Tom Walker on Sunday, August 20, at 7:30 p.m. at Cape of Good Hope Theater? It has been a long time since we met in Shanghai last year. We do hope you will find it possible to go with us.

Sincerely yours,
Mary Zhang

**Example 3   Invitation Letter**

Dear Sir or Madam,

　　Under the support of World Tourism Organization, China National Tourism Administration and the Government of Heilongjiang Province, the 5$^{th}$ International Tourism and World Heritage Travel Expo and International Tourism Industry Investment Fair 2012 will be held on October 13～15, 2012 (Thursday to Saturday) at the Conference Center (Hall A) in Harbin, China.

　　This international and professional Expo aims to seek for the buyers of the tourism products and to seek for the investors in the tourism industry investment. It is an exchange platform of the information in tourism industry, capital and resource.

　　Harbin is a political, economical and cultural center of Heilongjiang Province and has got the name of "Eastern Paris" for its rich tradition and vigorous modernity. We are the professional chambers of commerce in the tourism industry of Harbin. Our members cover both professional travel agencies for inbound travel and outbound travel and facilities such as hotels and etc. With the fast development of tourism industry in past years, we have been increasing the co-operations with the tourism industry both in domestic and abroad.

　　We and our member organizations sincerely invite you to participate as an exhibitor in the 5$^{th}$ International Tourism and World Heritage Travel Expo and International Tourism Industry Investment Fair 2012. We will deeply converse and explore the opportunities for cooperation with you during the Expo.

Sincerely yours
×××

## Example 4  Invitation Letter

Dear Mr. /Ms. ,

We should like to invite your corporation to attend the 2012 International Fair which will be held from August 29 to September 4 at the Conference Center (Hall A) in Harbin, China. Full details oh the fair will be sent in a week.

We look forward to hearing from you soon, and hope that you will be able to attend.

Yours faithfully,

×××

## Example 5  Positive reply

Dear Mr. /Ms. ,

Thank you for your letter of June 28 inviting our corporation to participate in the 2012 International Fair. We are very pleased to accept and will plan to display our electrical appliances as we did in previous years.

Mr. Li will be in your city from July 2 to 7 to make specific arrangements and would very much appreciate your assistance.

Yours faithfully,

×××

## Example 6  Negative reply

Dear Mr. /Ms. ,

Thank you very much for your invitation to attend the 2012 International Fair. As we are going to open a repair shop in your city at that time, we are sorry that we shall not be able to go.

We hope to see you on some future occasion.

Yours faithfully,

×××

# Exercises

(1) Please write a short invitation letter for Mr. Paul Smith to invite Mr. Li Lei of X Travel Service to attend the International Business Negotiation Fair which will be held from 20$^{th}$ to 24$^{th}$ May in Harbin.

(2) Please write a short letter for Mr. Li Lei for acceptance of the invitation and express thanks to Mr. Paul Smith.

(3) Please write a short letter for Mr. Li Lei for being unable to accept the invitation due to previous engagement to Mr. Paul Smith.

(4) Translate the following English into Chinese.

①We should like to invite your corporation to attend the 2012 International Business Negotiation Fair, which will be held from Mar. 29 to Apr. 4 in Harbin.

②Thank you for your letter of 22$^{nd}$ Dec. inviting our corporation to participate in the 2012 International Business Negotiation Fair.

## Unit 19  Letter of Complaint and Reply

## Learning Objectives

**Having read this unit, you will be able to**
- be familiar with the formats and contents of letter of complaint and reply
- know how to write letter of complaint with correct format and sufficient information
- write similar materials by yourself

## Samples

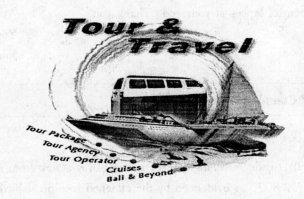

## Example 1  Letter of Complaint

Dear Sir,

I am pained to inform you that my travel plans have been jeopardized, on account of carelessness shown by your staff booking the tickets. I had requested your manager, Mr. Wang, to book an airline ticket for Guangzhou by Southern Airline for $9^{th}$ September. Today to my horror, I was delivered a ticket for the $11^{th}$ of September that is of no use to me.

I have to be in Guangzhou on $10^{th}$ morning to attend a seminar in which I am presenting a paper. It was on account of this, I had booked my ticket one day in advance, as I did not want to risk getting a waitlisted ticket. I am hereby returning the ticket and would like you to immediately arrange for a confirmed ticket, for $9^{th}$ by Southern Airline or any other suitable flight. I shall expect an immediate response, confirming the status of my ticket by today evening. This is imperative, for I have to confirm my travel plan to my host. Besides I have to make other necessary arrangements that I am unable to do now.

Meanwhile you should investigate as to how this happened and ensure that does not recur in future. This would be in your own business interest, so that clients like me do not suffer inconvenience on account of lapses at your end. Thank you.

Yours truly,<br>John Brown

## Example 2  Letter of Complaint

Dear Sir/Madam,

On September 28, while in Shanghai, my suitcase was stolen from my room. The suitcase has a value of ¥2 800, as evidenced by the attached receipt. I have reviewed the contract which I signed when booking my trip and concluded that your company has responsibility for replacing or paying for items stolen while on a trip. Therefore, I would like to have a full refund of ¥2 800 as soon as possible. Thank you for your attention to this matter and I look forward to hearing from you.

Sincerely yours,<br>Penny Catherin

## Example 3  Letter of Complaint

Dear Sir/Madam,

On January 3, while returning to the restaurant, I was seriously injured when while climbing the steps with ice and snow. Obviously, were it not for your company's negligence in failing to ensure that the steps were safe, I would not have been injured. Instead, I have suffered injured ankles. I have attached /will supply when received a copy of my medical and pharmacy bills. I would like your company to pay for these expenses, as I would not have been injured if the steps had been cleaned in time. I have reviewed the contract which I signed when booking the tour and have concluded that your company has responsibility to pay for these injuries. Therefore, I expect full payment as soon as possible for my medical care and expenses, including my pharmacy bills. Thank you for your attention to this matter; I look forward to hearing from you.

Faithfully yours,<br>×××

## Example 4  Letle of lomplant

Dear Sir/Madam,

I recently booked a tour/trip through your company to Beijing. The trip was scheduled for July 24. I paid a deposit of 1 000 yuan RMB to go on the tour and agreed to pay 2 000 yuan RMB later. Attached are copies of receipts showing that payment was made in full for the tour.

On July 26, while in Beijing, my purse was stolen from my bag. The purse has a value of 1 500 yuan RMB, as evidenced by the attached receipt. I have reviewed the contract which I signed when booking my tour and concluded that your company has responsibility for replacing or paying for items stolen while on a tour. Therefore, I would like to have a full refund of 1 500 as soon as possible. Thank you for your attention to this matter; I look forward to hearing from you.

Yours truly,<br>×××

## Example 5　Reply to Letter of Complaint

Dear Mr. Jackson,

　　I am very sorry to know from your letter of December 3 that the room you stayed was not clean enough. And I learned that what you said is really the case.

　　When I received your letter, I sent one of our assistant managers to look into the matter.

　　He said that they had rearranged the beds in your room just a few minutes before you went in and they did not clean it thoroughly.

　　I am very sorry for that and I promise you that there will be no such troubles any more. Welcome you to my hotel again. I enclose a check for $100 as our apologies.

Sincerely yours,

K. Lever

General manager

## Example 6　Reply to Letter of Complaint

Dear Mrs. Mc Evoy,

　　Thank you for your letter of 6$^{th}$ July.

　　I am very sorry to know that there was no ticket for your request date. I apologize to you for the inconvenience it made. I enclose a complete refund of your money.

　　With apologies.

Yours sincerely,

H. J. Hardson

Manager

# Exercises

## 1. Directions

You are a tour guide of China Youth Travel Agency. One of your clients has lost his suitcase due to carelessness of the hotel stuff. The client is very anxious and angry. Now please write a complaint letter to the restaurant in the name of the client.

## 2. Directions

You are thedirector of a travel company. You have received a complaint letter as illustrated in Example 1. Write a reply letter to this client, using proper tone and right style.

# Unit 20　Resumes in Tourism Industry

## Learning Objectives

Having read this unit, you will be able to
- be familiar with the formats of tourism resume
- know how to write a resume

# Samples

**Example 1**

## Li Hong

lihong@ email. com

| Permanent Contact Information | Campus Contact Information |
|---|---|
| 846 Elk Street | 123 Main Street |
| Lipton, South Carolina 46789 | Madison, Alabama 35758 |
| (555)555-5555 | (222)222-2222 |

## OBJECTIVE

Willing to be a tour guide that will help me gain working knowledge of my field of study.

## EDUCATION

Pursuing Bachelors of Tourism Management
University of Alabama in Huntsville
Huntsville, Alabama
Expected Graduation, May 2012
GPA 3.64

## EXPERIENCE

Hardees Restaurant
Cashier
Madison, Alabama
February 2009 ~ Present

- Greeted customers, took orders, collected money, served food
- Closed out register at the end of each shift and reported sales
- Cleaned dining area and restrooms
- Be a temporary guide in Tangwanghe Travel Agency of Yichun city

## OTHER SKILLS

- C++
- CET4
- CET6
- TEM4
- TEM8

**Example 2**

| Name | Wang Chenyu | Date of Birth | 1988.10 |
|---|---|---|---|
| Nationality | Han | Date of Graduation | 2012.06 |
| Gender | Male | Educational Background | Bachelor degree |
| Major | Tourism English | Native Place | Shandong Province |
| Job Intention | Tour guide | | |
| Interests and hobbies | Reading, Sports, Tour, Playing Computer Games | | |
| Experience | A part-time tour guide in Heihe travel agency in 2009<br>A part-time tour guide in Daqing travel agency in 2010<br>A part-time tour guide in Mudanjiang travel agency in 2011 | | |
| Computer Level | C++ | | |
| Languages Known | Excellent English written and verbal communication skills | | |
| Self Evaluation | Able to work under high pressure and time limitation.<br>Highly-motivated and reliable person with excellent health and pleasant personality.<br>The main qualities required are preparedness to work hard, ability to learn, ambition and good health.<br>A team player with good people management and communication skills.<br>Having positive work attitude and being willing and able to work diligently without supervision. | | |

## Example 3

| Name | Liu Xu |
|---|---|
| Gender | female |
| Birthday | September, 4$^{th}$, 1989 |
| Nationality | China |
| Health condition | Good |
| Graduating from | China University of Mine and Technology |
| Major | Tourism English |
| Ways for Contacting | |
| Tel | 13012345678 |
| Email | liuxu123@163.com |
| Address | Class 3 in Xuhai College of China University of Mine and Technology |
| Post Code | 221008 |
| Job Objective | A job related to tourism English major |
| Personal Skills | |
| English | Having a good command for both spoken and written English |
| Computer | common |
| Standard Chinese | Grade 2 |
| Self-Evaluation | |

  I work well with a multi-cultural and diverse work force and with pleasant personality. With strong determination to succeed and strong leadership. Good presentation skills. Ability to deal with personnel at all levels effectively. Positive attitude and active mind. Willing to learn and progress and with strong career-ambition.

# Exercises

(1) Write a resume of your own.
(2) Write a resume according to the information given below.
  基本情况:王丽,女,南京人,1970年6月生,已婚。
  学历情况:1998年获得博士学位,1995年获得硕士学位,1992年获得学士学位。
  工作经历:1998年10月~1999年5月,海天旅游公司市场部经理
      1999年6月至今,碧海国际旅行社总经理

# Part Three  Cities and Attractions in Heilongjiang Province

### 1. Heilongjiang Province

Good Morning/afternoon, ladies and gentlemen. Welcome to Heilongjiang province. I'm ×××, your tour guide. I'm so delighted to spend the wonderful time with you in Heilongjiang. This is An Quan, the best driver of our travel agency, who will provide us traffic service. Mr. An and I will be with you for the entire trip. On the behalf of of our travel agency, and 38.25 million people in Heilongjiang Province, I would like to extend my warm welcome to you again. We will exert ourselves to provide you safe, healthy and high-quality services. I wish you a pleasant stay in Heilongjiang. Have a smooth journey!

It is only 40-minute ride from the airport to the hotel we've arranged for you. During the period, I will give you a brief introduction to Heilongjiang province.

Situated in the central part of Northeast Asian region, Heilongjiang province, also referred to as Hei, is named after the largest river running in the north province, Heilong River (also Amur River). Heilongjiang province is a bond between Northeast China, Russia and Eastern Europe; it is also the main land route from Asia and the Pacific Rim to the European continent. The boundary line on land and water area between Russia and Heilongjiang province is 3 038 kilometers. The province borders on five states and districts of Russia and it has been richly endowed by nature of the border trade and border tourism.

Located in the farthest north of China, Heilongjiang province is where the sun first shines in China each new day. Its northern most point is Mohe whose latitude is over 53. Because it is the nearest place to the Arctic Circle (66° 33′), the appearance of polar day and polar night will separately occur in summer solstice and in winter solstice, thus, Mohe County is also called "the Chinese Arctic Pole". Heixiazi Island (or Bolshoy Ussuriysky Island) is located in the east of Heilongjiang Province, many travelers would like to visit Arctic Village in Mohe County on summer solstice and winter solstice to enjoy where the sun first shines in China each new day, so it is also named "the Chinese East Pole". Heilongjiang province borders Inner Mongolia to the west, Jilin Province to the south. The Heilongjiang River and the Wusuli River run between Heilongjiang province and Russia. Because the boundary line sharing with Russia is 3 045 kilometers (1 892 miles) long, Heilongjiang Province gets the superiority on frontier trade and tourism.

Heilongjiang is divided into thirteen prefecture-level divisions, consisting of twelve prefecture-level cities, one sub-provincial city. Heilongjiang is a multiracial province, and its total population is 38.25 million. Besides the Han nationality, there are another 53 ethnic minorities, including Manchu, Mongol, Korean, Hui, Daur, Oroqen, Hezhen, Ewenki, Xibe, Kyrgyz as the top 10 long-time residents.

Heilongjiang province covers an area of 454 000 sq. km, accounting for 4.7% of the nation's total area, which is the sixth largest province in area (the top five provinces are as follows: Xin Jiang, Tibet, Inner Mongolia, Qinghai, and Sichuan). It ranks the nation's first place in land use and soil quality. Its arable land amounts to 11 838 000 hectare, accounting for 10 percent of the country's total farmland. Songnen Plain and Sanjiang Plain are respectively the main agricultural and pastoral areas and the major commodity grain base. With the expanse of flatland and wide areas of fertile black soil, Heilongjiang is one of China's major commodity grain (e.g. soy bean, wheat, corn, potato, and rice) and cash crops (e.g. Beet, flax, and cured tobacco) growers.

The grassland area of the province is 4 330 000 hectares, with excellent and nutrient grass, suitable for the development of animal husbandry. Songnen grassland is one of the three big meadows for sheep in the world.

A humid continental climate predominates in the Heilongjiang province. Under the control of the Mongolian plateau climate, in winter the weather is arid and bitter, and northwest wind prevails; in summer the weather is hot and rainy, and southeast wind prevails; in spring and autumn, the climate is changeable. The annual average temperature is 5℃ to -4℃, the annual average rainfall is 400 to 700 millimeters, and the frost-free season lasts 130~150 days.

Heilongjiang is a land of varied topography. The province's topography is higher in the northwest, north and the southeast, and lower in the northeast and southwest. Characteristics of topography can be summarized as hills, water, grass, and cropland. Mountainous areas account for 53.2% of the province gross areas. In its northwestern part, there is the Greater Hinggan Mountains, also called "the Green Great Wall", and in the north, the Lesser Hinggan Mountains, known as "the hometown of Korean Pine". In the southeastern part, there are the ridges of Zhangguangcai Mountains, Laoye Mountains and the Wanda Mountains. The province's forest area amounts to 20 070 000 hectares and the forest cover is 43.6%. Heilongjiang is also an important source of lumber for China. There are many important forms of lumber produced in Heilongjiang, including Korean Pine, larch, Mongolian Pine, Fraxinus mandshurica, Phellodendron amurense, and Juglans mandshurica. Among the wild economic plants, food plants are the most widely distributed and stored in Heilongjiang, such as bracken, Osmunda japonica, Heracleum moellendorffii, and so on.

Heilongjiang province is rich in water resource. As a result, numerous rivers and lakes, as well as bogs, are scattered throughout the whole province. The major river systems of the province are Heilong River (also Amur River), Songhua River, Wusuli River (also Ussuri River), Nengjiang River and Suifen River. The relative larger lakes include Khanka Lake, Jingbo Lake, Lianhuan Lake and Wudalianchi. There are 1918 rivers and the drainage area of them is over 50 square kilometers in the province.

Heilongjiang province boasts the rich natural resources. There are 131 kinds of mineral resources discovered, including petroleum, graphite, sillimanite, basalt, marble, boess, pozzuolana as well as potash feldspar, which are the largest in China. In addition, the electrical power and fuel gas play important roles in China. The coal reserve ranks the No. 1 among the three provinces in the northeast of china.

Heilongjiang province is also affluent in wild animals and domestic products. The province is home to 476 species of wide animals. Of the wide animals, 5 kinds (including the Siberian tiger, leopard, sable, wolverine, and sika deer) are under first-class national protection and 11 kinds (including red deer, Asiatic black bear, snow hare, etc.) are under second-class national protection. Of the wide birds, 12 kinds (including Red-crowned Crane, white crane, bustard, white badger, mergus squamatus, etc.) are under first-class national protection and 56 kinds (whooper swan, tetrastes bonasia, mandarin duck, etc) are under second-class national protection. Due to the rich water resources, Heilongjiang produces many kinds of fish, including salmon, white fish, white Amur bream, Jihua, Aohua, mandarin fish, Zheluo, Black Amur Bream, Leuciscus, Tongluo, and Huluo. Moreover, there are more than 1 000 kinds of domestic products, among which the Three Ancestral Treasures(wild ginseng, mink fur, deer velvet antler) enjoy a high reputation. In addition, there are still a great deal of famous products in the nation, such as acanthopanax, black fungus, hericium erinaceus, wildness hazel-mushroom, bear gall, red sausage, Candy Boozy and agate artware.

Heilongjiang is the traditional base of industry for the People's Republic of China. It has a solid industrial foundation and has formed the industrial development pattern composed of such ten preponderant industries as heavy machinery, petrochemical industry, coal power, chemical industry, automobile, aircraft, dairy food, soybean processing, medicament, paper manufacture, and high-technology. The extractive industry is an important part of the Heilongjiang economy. It has one giant oilfield(Daqing Field), two forest regions(the Greater Khingan Range and Yichun), and four coal mine regions(Jixi, Hegang, Shuangyashan, Qitaihe). Heilongjiang companies are active in all major fields, but are particular strong in machinery industry, including one heavy machinery company (China First Heavy Industry), three major power companies (Harbin Electronic Machinery Company Limited, Harbin Boiler Company Limited, and Harbin Turbine Company Limited). In addition, Heilongjiang province boasts a great deal of famous large-scale companies, such as Heilongjiang Agriculture Company Limited, Harbin Pharmaceutical Group Holding Co., Ltd, Hafei Aviation Industry Co., Ltd., Harbin Beer Group, Longdian Group and etc. And some industrial products' outputs rank the first in China, including crude oil, lumber, large-scale power generation equipment, heavy-duty machinery, linen, edible vegetable oil, dairy products, beer, and hard board.

Heilongjiang has abundant and unique tourist resources with clear seasonal distinction. It impresses visitors with original, simple, rough, natural and miraculous appeal, which is an ideal place for returning to nature and enjoying the leisure resort. The World Tourist Organization was so impressed by its beautiful scenery that it named Heilongjiang the "Cool Province"; that is, the vigor world in spring, the cool world in summer, the colorful world in autumn, and the ice and snow world in winter. The tourism resource of Heilongjiang province has eight major features as follows:

Ice and snow: Thanks to the abundant snowfall, long winter for ski, good snow condition and moderate mountain slope, Heilongjiang province is an ideal destination for ski tours. In 1998, the Heilongjiang International Ski Festival was first held, which opened up the Heilongjiang ski tourism market. Harbin, nicknamed "Ice City", is the capital of Heilongjiang province, which is the birthplace of the Chinese snow and ice art. In here, the ice carving and the snow carving has reached the world-class level. Snow Town is situated in southeastern Heilongjiang province. Snow Town is regarded as a dreamlike paradise in winter. In winter the snow here can reach up to two metres. The red lanterns, paper-cutting pasted on panes, red Fu character and the various snow houses form a unique landscape in the snow town. Numerous huge forests, snowy lands and rimes provide abundant resources for traveling in the province.

Forest: Heilongjiang ranks the first among all China's provinces in afforested area, and the forests here feature verdant, majesty, and rough, which are the distinctive characters of the Cold Temperate Zone Forest. There are more than 100 species of trees, including Korean pine, white birch, and other species. The combination of the arbor-shrub-grass forms a natural oxygen bar and a green ecological barrier. The Korean pine forest in YIchun Fenglin Nature Reserve has been regarded as a member of the World Network of Biosphere Reserves by UNESCO, and the Tangwang National Park in Yichun is the first national park in China.

Heilongjing is the province with the most forest parks, boasting ninety-seven national or provincial forest parks. In autumn, the forest is like a colorful oil painting: the red maple leaves, the dark green pines, the pure white birches and some other trees. The forest is decorated with these multi-colors, becoming a "Colorful Mountain".

Wetland: With a total wetland area of 4 340 000 hectare, Heilongjiang province ranks the first among all China's provinces in wetland tourism resource. The main wetlands are widely distributed in Sanjiang Plain, Songnen Plain, the Greater Hinggan Mountains and the lesser Hinggan Mountains. There are four wetlands listed in the List of Wetlands of International Importance, including San Jiang National Natural Reserve, Xingkai Lake National Natural Reserve, Honghe Reserve National Natural Reserve, and Zhalong that is known as "the Paradise of Birds" and "the Hometown of the Red-Crowned Crane".

Boundary River: Heilongjiang river is the longest boundary river in the world, and the Sino-Russian border section of the Heilongjiang river is about 1 890 kilometers. Heilongjiang, like an Innocent girl, is impressed with the simple, natural, and pristine beauty. When you take a look at the river afar, you will find yourself carried away in involuntary admiration by its magnificent and majestic scenery.

Lake: Heilongjiang province is dotted with lakes. Xingkai Lake is the largest boundary lake in Asia, also known as "Northern Emerald". Lianhuan Lake is the natural Waterfowl hunting areas. It is located in Daqing which is reputed as "a hundred-Lake City". Lake Jingpo is the largest barrier lake in China, also a world geopark and well-known tourist destination. Due to its marvelous beauty, it is also named "the Northern Peal" and "the Northern West Lake".

Lava: Situated in the west of Heilongjiang province, Wusalianchi World Geopark is the largest volcanic landscape. It is named "Natural Museum of Volcano" and "An Open Textbook on Volcano" by domestic and foreign geologists. The mineral water here, rich in iron, silicon, calcium carbonate and magnesium, is famous across the world, renowned as "The World's Three Cold Springs". The mineral water here is also known for its special medical care function, good for rehabilitation and recuperation as well as the health of human body.

Oilfield: Daqing boasts the largest oilfield in China, and it is an important petrochemical production base. In addition, there are several industrial tourism destinations, such as the Museum of Oilfield History, the Memorial Hall for the Iron Man, etc. If you come here, you will be fueled by the iron man spirit. The iron man, named Wang Jinxi, a petroleum worker on the Daqing Oilfield, was honored as a national hero due to his contributions to the petroleum industry of China.

Farmland: The area of technical reclamation totals 54 300 kilometers. There are totally over 110 agricultural and pastoral fields. When you come here, you will be attracted by those rare tourism resources, such as the endless farmland, the Mechanical production jobs, the modern processing line of agricultural and pasture products and high-tech agricultural demonstration zone.

In addition, Heilongjiang province has many historic sites and some tourism resource of local customs. Of the historic sites, it has Ang'angxi Site, Xinkailiu Site, Sanggyeong Yongcheonbu Site,

Capital of Balhae, Shangjing Huiningfu Site, Capital of the Jin Dynasty and some others. Of the local customs, different ethnic minorities have different customs, lifestyles and cultures: the Manchu farmers, the Hezhe fishmen, the Oroqen hunters, and the Daur shepherds. If you are interested in their unique festivals, life styles and manual dress and adornment, it must be a great experience to have a close encounter with them.

Heilongjiang is still rich in Red Tourism resources, such as "The Anti-Japanese War in Jiang Qiao" " the Site of Anti-Japanese Union" and "the Place where the World War ended".

The cultural undertakings in Heilongjiang province features nationality and locality. For example, the Longjiang opera, one of the youngest operas in China, is characterized by strong black soil art style. Harbin Summer Music Concert is another characteristic culture. The first concert was held in 1961, and now it has been renowned both home and aboard.

There is an old saying that, "What you hear about may be false, but what you see is true." You will see the beautiful scenery by yourselves. Now we have reached the hotel, and please get off with your personal belongings. Later, you can take the room card and your luggage at the hotel lobby, and then you will take a rest. We will meet at 12:00 in the Chinese dinner hall on the first floor, and you will start your trip after lunch.

## 黑龙江省概况

游客朋友们大家好,欢迎来黑龙江观光旅游。我是你们的导游员×××,很高兴与大家一起度过在黑龙江的美好时光。为我们提供交通服务的是我们社最优秀的驾驶员,他姓安名全。在这几天的行程中将由我和安全师傅为大家提供服务。在此,我代表他和我们旅行社全体员工以及3 825万龙江人民再次向你们表示热烈的欢迎!我们将尽全力为你们提供安全、健康、优质的服务,并预祝大家旅途愉快,一切顺利!

从机场到我们下榻的酒店大约要40分钟的路程。在此期间,我向大家简要介绍一下黑龙江省的基本概况,为大家的金玉之旅抛上一块砖。

黑龙江省,简称黑,因境内最大的河流黑龙江而得名。它位于东北亚地区的中心,是中国东北从陆路通往俄罗斯和东欧的窗口,也是亚洲及太平洋地区陆路通向欧洲大陆的重要通道。与俄罗斯之间的陆地、水域边界线长3 038公里,与俄罗斯五个州、区相接壤,有得天独厚的边境贸易和边境旅游优势。

黑龙江省是我国位置最北、纬度最高、太阳升起最早的省份。最北端在漠河一带,纬度超过了53°,它是中国最接近北极圈(66°31′)的地方,农历夏至时和冬至时,在这里可以看到北极圈的极昼极夜现象,因此被称为"中国的北极"。东端位置在抚远县东乌苏里江和黑龙江汇流处的黑瞎子岛,是我国太阳升起最早的地方,因此有中国"东极"之称。东部隔黑龙江、乌苏里江与俄罗斯相望。西部与内蒙古毗邻。南部与吉林省接壤。

黑龙江省目前现辖13个地级市,其中12个省辖市,1个行政公署,64个县(市),省会为哈尔滨市。总人口3 825万,黑龙江省是一个多民族聚居的省份。除汉族外,还有53个少数民族分布,其中满、蒙古、朝鲜、回、达斡尔、鄂伦春、赫哲、鄂温克、锡伯和柯尔克孜族是黑龙江省10个世居、久居的少数民族。

黑龙江省土地总面积45.4万平方公里,占全国土地总面积的4.7%。仅次于新疆、西藏、内蒙古、青海、四川,居全国第六位,有效利用面积居全国首位。黑龙江省土地条件居全国之首,总耕地面积和可开发的土地后备资源均占全国十分之一以上,人均耕地和农民人均经营耕地是全国平均水平的3倍左右。全省现有耕地1 183.8万公顷,土壤有机质含量高于全国其他地区,黑土、黑钙土和草甸土等占耕地的60%以上,是世界著名的三大黑土带之一。黑龙江省盛产大豆、小麦、玉米、马铃薯、水稻等粮食作物以及甜菜、亚麻、烤烟等经济作物。松嫩平原是黑龙江省主要农牧区和湿地旅游区。三江平原已成为黑龙江省主要商品粮基地之一和农业旅游、湿地旅游观光带。

全省草原面积约433万公顷,草质优良,营养价值高,适于发展畜牧业,其中松嫩草场是世界三大羊草地之一。

气候为温带大陆性季风气候。冬季受蒙古高原气候控制,盛行西北风,寒冷干燥;夏季盛行东南风,高温多雨;春秋两季气候多变。全省年平均气温多在5℃~-4℃之间,降水量400~700毫米,无霜期130~150天。

黑龙江省地势北高东低,地形复杂多样。地形特点可概括为五山、一水、一草、三分田。山地面积占全省总面积的53.2%。大兴安岭山地,被称为"绿色长城"。小兴安岭山地,被誉为红松的故乡。东南部山地,包括张广才岭、老爷岭和完达山等山地。全省森林面积2 007万公顷,森林覆盖率达43.6%,森林资源面积、木材总蓄积量和木材产量均居全国首位,是国家最重要的国有林区和最大的木材生产基地。在木材植物中有全国十分珍贵的红松、落叶松、樟子松、水曲柳、黄菠萝、核桃揪等。食用植物是本省野生经济植物中分布较多、贮量较大的一类,其中以蕨菜、蒺菜、老山芹等产量为最大。

黑龙江省是中国水资源较为丰富的省份,主要有黑龙江、松花江、乌苏里江、嫩江和绥芬河五大水系,有兴凯湖、镜泊湖、连环湖和五大连池4处较大湖泊及星罗棋布的泡沼。全省流域面积在50平方公里以上的河流有1 918条。

黑龙江省物产资源丰富,全省已发现各类矿产131种,保有储量位居全国首位的有10种,即石油、石墨、矽线石、铸石玄武岩、岩棉用玄武岩、水泥用大理岩、颜料黄土、火山灰、玻璃用大理岩和钾长石;除此之外,电力和燃气也占有重要地位。煤炭储量居东北三省第一位。

野生动物和土产山产资源丰富。黑龙江省野生动物共476种,属国家一级保护的兽类有东北虎、豹、紫貂、貂熊、梅花鹿5种,鸟类有丹顶鹤、白鹤、大鸨、白鹳、中华秋沙鸭等12种;属国家二级保护的兽类有马鹿、黑熊、雪兔等11种,鸟类有大天鹅、花尾榛鸡、鸳鸯等56种。鸟类中久负盛名的"飞龙"即是分布在全省的花尾榛鸡。著名水产有大马哈鱼、大白鱼、"三花"

(蝙花、吉花、鳖花)、"五罗"(哲罗、法罗、雅罗、同罗、胡罗)等。土产山产资源有 1 000 多个品种,最著名的是东北三宝(野山参、貂皮、鹿茸),此外刺五加、黑木耳、猴头蘑、榛蘑、熊胆、秋林里道斯香肠和酒心糖果、玛瑙工艺品等在国内享有极高的声誉。

黑龙江省是新中国工业的摇篮,工业基础雄厚,门类比较齐全,是中国重要的重工业基地之一。现已形成重大装备、石化、煤电、化工、汽车和飞机、乳品、大豆加工、医药、造纸、高新技术十大优势产业。在采掘工业方面有一大油田(大庆油田)、两大林区(大兴安岭林区和伊春林区)、四大煤矿(鸡西、鹤岗、双鸭山、七台河);在机械工业方面有一大重型(中国第一重型机械集团)、三大动力(哈尔滨电机厂有限责任公司、哈尔滨锅炉厂有限责任公司、哈尔滨汽轮机厂有限责任公司)。此外,黑龙江北大荒农垦集团、哈药集团、哈航空工业集团、哈啤集团、龙电集团等都是著名的大型企业集团。主要工业品中,原油、木材、大型发电设备、微型轻型汽车、重型机床、亚麻布、食用植物油、乳制品、啤酒、人造板等产量居全国前列。

黑龙江省旅游资源丰富独特,尤以原始、古朴、粗犷、自然与神奇见长,是人们崇尚自然、回归自然、休闲度假的理想之地,它四季分明,气候宜人。世界旅游组织认为:黑龙江是中国旅游的 Cool 省,即春季活力世界,夏季清凉世界,秋季多彩世界,冬季冰雪世界。呈现出"八大"旅游资源特色——

大冰雪:黑龙江省降雪充沛,雪期长,雪质好,山体坡度适中,非常适合滑雪旅游活动。1998 年,黑龙江省率先举办了中国黑龙江省国际滑雪节,开拓了滑雪旅游市场。"冰城"哈尔滨荟萃了世界一流的冰雕和雪雕艺术精华,使之成为我国冰雪艺术的摇篮。"中国雪乡"——大海林双峰旅游区,景区被深达 2 米的大雪覆盖,高挂的红灯笼以及窗花、红福字和错落有致、形态各异的雪屋构成了雪乡独有的景观。全省众多的林海雪原与冰河树挂等景观,构成了黑龙江极具魅力的冰雪旅游资源。

大森林:黑龙江省森林面积居全国之首,具有苍阔、雄伟、粗犷等寒温带森林的鲜明个性。高大挺拔的原始红松林,亭亭玉立的白桦林,奇特的高山偃松,以及百余种针、阔叶树种,乔、灌、草结合的多层植被,形成了天然的氧吧和绿色生态屏障,其中,伊春丰林自然保护区的红松母树林,被联合国教科文组织列为世界生物圈网络成员,伊春汤旺河国家公园是中国首个国家公园。

黑龙江省有国家级和省级森林公园 97 个,是拥有森林公园最多的省份。秋季枫树的鲜红、松树的浓绿、桦树的洁白及其他树木呈现的多种色彩把林海变成了"五花山",置身其中,仿佛游走在无框的油画之中。

大湿地:黑龙江省有全国面积最大的湿地旅游资源,湿地总面积 434 万公顷,主要分布在三江平原、松嫩平原和大、小兴安岭。其中扎龙、三江、兴凯湖、洪河等四处湿地被列入《国际重要湿地名录》。其中扎龙湿地被誉为"鸟的天堂""丹顶鹤的故乡"。

大界江:黑龙江是世界上最长的界江,中俄界江段长 1 890 公里。黑龙江就像一位没有浓妆打扮的少女,给人一种淳朴自然的原始美。远望黑龙江,大气磅礴,自然壮阔。

大湖泊:黑龙江省湖泊星罗棋布。兴凯湖堪称亚洲最大的界湖,有"北方绿宝石"之称。大庆市有"百湖之城"的美誉,其中连环湖是天然的水禽狩猎场。镜泊湖是我国最大的山地堰塞湖,也是世界地质公园和全国知名的旅游胜地。奇、美、秀、绝的镜泊湖又被誉为"塞北明珠"和"北国西湖"。

大熔岩:位于黑龙江省西部的五大连池是世界地质公园,是中国最大的火山地貌景观。被国内外地质学家称为"打开的地质教科书",有天然火山地质博物馆之称。与火山成因有密切联系的五大连池碳酸冷矿泉,是世界三大冷泉之一,具有独特的保健疗效。

大油田:大庆是全国最大的油田和重要的石油化工生产基地,也是工业旅游的重要品牌。油田历史博物馆、铁人纪念馆等工业旅游景点,可以让您感受到"铁人精神"的内涵。

大农场:技术垦区面积5.43万平方公里,横跨小兴安岭南麓、松嫩平原和三江平原,有110多个农牧场。一望无际的大农田,大机械生产作业,现代化的农牧产品加工生产线、高科技农业示范园等都是难得的旅游资源。

除此以外,历史遗迹和民俗风情旅游资源也很多:黑龙江省保留着人类历史悠久的文化遗存,如昂昂溪遗址和新开流遗址、唐代渤海国上京龙泉府遗址、金代上京会宁府遗址。以农耕为主的满族、朝鲜族,以捕鱼为生的赫哲族,以狩猎为生的鄂伦春族和以牧业为主的蒙古族、达斡尔族,这些民族保留着北方少数民族所特有的民俗风情,成为黑龙江省重要的民俗旅游资源。

黑龙江省还有"江桥抗战""抗联遗址""二战终结地"等丰富的红色旅游资源。全省边境口岸众多,对俄旅游成为热点,年入出境旅游者超过百万人次。

黑龙江省文化事业具有鲜明民族特色与地方特色。广大群众所喜爱的龙江剧是具有浓郁黑土艺术风格的我国最年轻的戏曲剧种之一。1961年始办的"哈尔滨之夏"音乐会蜚声海内外。

好了,游客朋友们,俗话说:"耳听为虚,眼见为实。"大家来到这里不是听我讲的,主要是来看的。请大家带好随身物品,随我下车,我们到大堂取房卡和行李,然后进房间稍事休息,12点准时在一楼中餐厅集合,用餐后开始你们的龙江之旅。

## 2. The City of Harbin

Good morning/afternoon, ladies and gentlemen. I am Bai Xue, your tour guide, and you can simply call me Xiao Xue. This is our driver Mr. An. Confucius, our ancient great philosopher once said: "What a great joy it is to have friends from afar!" On behalf of CITS (China International Travel Service), I'd like to extend our warm welcome to all of you. We will try our best to provide the good service for you. If you have any request, don't hesitate to tell us. We are open to any suggestion and advice.

Dear friends, it will take about 30 minutes from the airport to the hotel. Right now I'd like to take a minute to familiarize you with Harbin.

Located in the northeast of China, Harbin sits on the bank of Songhua River, bringing beauty and richness. Its latitude has a range of 44° 04′ ~ 46° 41′ N, and the longitude 125° 42′ ~ 130° 10′ E, which endow the city with a unique location. Harbin is located in the center of Northeast Asia and is described as the pearl of the Eurasia Land Bridge. It is the transportation hub of the Eurasia Land Bridge and the Air Corridor. Five major railways including Hada (Harbin-Dalian), Binsui (Harbin-Suifenhe), Binzhou (Harbin-Manzhouli), Binbei (Harbin-Beian) and Labin (Lalin-Harbin) pass here. The waterway covers Songhua River, Heilongjiang River, Wusulijiang River and Nenjiang River, linking some harbors of Russian Far East. Through the river-sea shipping, ships can sail eastward from the Tartar Strait to Japan, Korea and Southeast Asia. Harbin Taiping International Airport is capable of handling 6 million passengers annually. Furthermore, it provides passenger-cargo shipping service for more than 110 countries. Harbin features a monsoon-influenced, humid continental climate. It is known for the "Ice City", as winters here are long and summers are short.

Harbin is the capital of Heilongjiang province, which serves as a key political, economic and cultural center. Harbin has direct jurisdiction over 8 districts, 3 county-level cities and 7 counties, covering an area of 53 800 square kilometers. Therefore it boasts the largest area among the capital cities of China. The city's urban area has 4.755 million inhabitants, while the total population of the city is up to 9.901 million. It has 48 ethnic groups, of which the population of minority nationalities is 660 000. It is also China's industrial production base and grain production base.

Now I'd like to tell you a bit of history about Harbin. It is a unique historic and cultural city. The humans set foot here about 40 000 years ago. The people living here in the early time were named the Sushen. After years of evolution, they were named the Nuzhen after Tang Dynasty (618-907).

In 1115, one of the Nuzhen tribal leaders, by the name of Akuta, defeated Liao (916-1125) and Northern Song (960-1127), then established the Jin Dynasty (1115-1234) in Huining (currently the Acheng District of Harbin) with the official title Great Jin. At that time, it was called Huining fu, Upper Capital of Jin. After 38 years of 4 emperors' reigns here, the capital of Jin Dynasty was moved to Yanjing (currently Beijing). Huiningfu, Upper Capital, was the biggest city of the Northeast Asia in the 12$^{th}$ century, which served as the political, economic and cultural center. It left massive wealth for the formulation of the northern culture, becoming the source and core of the Harbin's special culture.

After the Jin Dynasty, Yuan (1271-1368), Ming (1368-1644) and Qing (1644-1911) Dynasties all set up their central governments in Heilongjiang. In 1616, the last chieftain of the

Jianzhou Jurchens Nurhaci declared himself Khan (king) and founded the Later Jin Dynasty. In 1636, his son Hong Taiji renamed the dynasty Great Qing and united Manchu people. In 1644, the Qing Dynasty went into the central China. From then on, Harbin was governed by the vice-general of Alechuka (recently Acheng), regaining its ancient name "Halabin" (recently Harbin).

In the late 19th century, the Russian Tzar forced the Qing government to sign an unequal agreement that allowed Russians to build a railway in Northeast China. After the Chinese Eastern Railway being put in use, Harbin established some trading ports, attracting hundreds of thousands of people from more than 30 countries to start thousands of business enterprises and trading companies. Later, 19 countries set up the consulates here. In the early $20^{th}$ century, Harbin became the biggest financial and trading center in Northeast China. The first cinema, the first music school, and the first brewery in China were built in the city.

This city has been prettied up with various types of architecture around the era of Renaissance, so it looks like an architectural museum. The architecture in Harbin brings the city the name of "Oriental Moscow" and "Oriental Paris". You can appreciate not only China's classical buildings but also European architectural styles of Renaissance, Classicism, Romanticism, Eclecticism, Art Nouveau and Baroque. You can also enjoy the "Chinese-Baroque" buildings. Filled with the world's four major religions—Christianity, Islam, Buddhism, Judaism, and full of three main branches of Christianity—Catholicism, Eastern Orthodoxy, Protestantism, Harbin is renowned for the "Cathedral City". There are two synagogues in Harbin, which are extremely rare in China. As one of the only two Saint Sophia Cathedrals in the world, Saint Sophia Cathedral in Harbin, also named Harbin Museum of Architecture, is the biggest Orthodox Church in the Far East. You may be surprised that it is not in Russia but in Harbin. The newly-built Hallelujah Church is the biggest Christian Church in the northeast of China. Here you can enjoy numerous exotic buildings in various artistic styles and harmony that you can not see in other parts of China, which constitute the precious heritage of Harbin's culture and history as well as human civilization. Since the opening of Harbin, this modern city has sped up its international development, enriching the cultural composition in Harbin as many foreign migrants swarmed in.

In 1926, Russian administrative jurisdiction towards Harbin was replaced by the Harbin Special City. Later, Japan invaded Harbin outright after the Mukden Incident in 1931. On April $28^{th}$, 1946, the city was liberated from the puppet regime supported by Japan. It was the first liberated city as well as the home front both for the national liberation and the War to Aid Korea. It was also the candidate city for China's capital.

After the founding of new China in 1949, Harbin has become the key industrial base of China. Harbin has "Three Powers Plants" and "Ten Military Factories" as well as many enterprises, such as measuring plant, bearing plant, flax factory, electrical carbon factory, etc. For decades now, Harbin has established a comprehensive and wide-ranging industrial system with mechanical and electrical industries as its mainstay, and automobile manufacturing, medicine, food processing and chemical industry as its advantages. In the strategy of rejuvenating the old northeastern industrial base of China, Harbin has become the leading city of "Harbin-Daqing-Qiqihar Industrial Corridor". Harbin also has the comprehensive strength in science and technology, especially the aerospace, the intelligent robot's research and development, as well as the welding technology, and all of these have met or exceeded the advanced world standards.

The development of Harbin's street names witnesses the city's history. For example, the Zhongshan Road was called Horvat Street in the Tsarist Times, Tufeiyuan Road in the Japanese Puppet Regime period, and the recent name after the liberation. The city layout is planned depending on the rivers and railways. The downtown has more squares with radial streets. There is no north-south axis and even no city wall. There are 8 districts including Daoli, Daowai, Nangang, Xiangfang, Pingfang, Songbei, Hulan and Acheng. Daoli District lies in the west of the railway, whereas Daowai District in the east. Nangang District is located in the downland, south of the railway station. Xiangfang District is named for the joss-stick workshop a hundred years ago. Pingfang District is named for the bungalows of the Manchu village a hundred years ago. The newly constructed Songbei District lies on the northern bank of the Songhua River, hence comes the name. Hulan District gets its name for the Hulan River.

Harbin is known as "Ice City & Summer Capital" thanks to its distinct seasons of short summer and long winter. In spring, the city flower—lilac comes into bloom. The fragrance permeates everywhere. In summer, the trees and grass are luxuriant. It is a season for summer resort. In autumn, gold and red leaves on the outskirts of the city make you linger on. In winter, the exquisite and artistic ice lanterns are glorious at night. Of course, it is also the best time to ski, play and watch on the snow.

Harbin is the Historical and Cultural City of Heilongjiang province. You will find here everything from some of the most visited historical and cultural landmarks to the beautiful natural sceneries. The beautiful Songhua River crosses over the city like a jade belt with the Sun Island embedded like a bright pearl. Along the river bank, you can enjoy the wonderful landscapes. In summer, it presents the pastoral scenery surrounded by the greenwood; while in winter it presents the northern scenery wrapped in snow. After the reform and opening up, Harbin has become much more beautiful than before with more buildings and streets. The city features some of the exotic streets like the European-style Central Street, Russian-style Gogol Street, Indian-style Street, Jewish-style Street, and Buddhist Cultural Street in Jile Temple (Temple of Ultimate Bliss). Some of the major landmarks of the country are the Saint Sophia Cathedral—the biggest Orthodox Church in the Far East, Northern Forest Zoo—one of the largest in the country, Siberian Tiger Park—the largest natural park for wild Siberian tigers in the world, Dragon TV Tower (Heilongjiang TV Station)—the tallest steel structure in northeastern Asia, Harbin Polar Land—the most professional polar land in China with complete polar animals, etc. The traditional culture is an important part of Harbin's multi-culture. For example, Harbin Confucius Temple is the witness of enhancing the national spirit and fighting against the foreign invasions. There are also numerous cultural relics like Jin Shangjing Huining Fu Site, Five City Sites, Former Residence of Xiaohong, etc. Some national forest parks like Xianglushan, Hengtoushan, Songfengshan, Maoershan, Fenghuangshan, etc. are worth visiting. Harbin's ski resorts with the top-class facilities like Yabuli Ski Resort, Erlongshan Ski Resort, Jihuachangshoushan Ski Resort are famous scenic attractions that the ski enthusiasts won't miss.

Harbin's tourism is thriving with the activities all the year round, such as International Economic and Trade Fair in spring, Harbin Summer Music Festival in summer, Swan Art Festival in autumn (held every two or three years), Harbin International Snow and Ice Festivals and Ice Festival in winter. Whenever you come here, you will feel happy and satisfied.

Now I will tell you something about Harbin's food culture.

First of all, you can enjoy the best food here. Huamei Western Restaurant is the most popular Russian restaurant in Harbin. It is one of the Top Four Western Restaurants in China, along with Beijing Maxim's Restaurant, Shanghai's Red House Restaurant and Tianjin's Kiessling Restaurant. And Laoduyichu Restaurant is known for its dumplings, especially dumplings stuffed with three fresh delicacies. If you would like to try the local flavor "Shazhucai"—a stew dish with the ingredients of pork, Chinese vegetable and inners of a pig, you could go to the Laoliushazhucai or Da Feng Shou (Big Harvest). You can also enjoy the farm-flavored dishes in northeast restaurants like Nongjiadayuan and Nongjiaxiaoyuan. Of course you could buy some Dazhong Sausage of Harbin Meat-packing Joint Plant, Churin Leadfoods Sausage, Air-Dried Sausage and Songren Xiaodu (Pinenuts tripe) of Zhengyanglou, Da Lie Ba (large Russian bread) of Churin Company to give your relatives and friends.

Secondly, you can have a good drink here. Harbin Brewery, founded in 1900, is the oldest brewery in China. The consumption of Harbin beer ranks first in China and the third in the world after Munich and Paris. The annual Harbin Beer Festival has upgraded to the national level. Here you can enjoy the excellent beer from all over the world.

We are going to be pulling up to the hotel in a few minutes. Please get off with me and take all your belongings. You may have a rest at the lobby before the registration. We will meet in the hall at half past eleven and begin our Harbin tour.

Thank you very much!

## 哈尔滨市概况

尊敬的游客朋友们,大家好!"有朋自远方来,不亦乐乎。"我很高兴迎接来自海外的朋友们。热烈欢迎大家来哈观光旅游。我是中国国际旅行社的导游员,我叫白雪,大家叫我小雪就可以了,我们的司机师傅姓安。我们会努力为大家服务。诸位有什么要求,敬请随时随地向我们提出来。工作中如有不当之处,欢迎批评指正。

游客朋友们,从机场到酒店行车约需30分钟。借此机会向大家介绍一下哈尔滨的概况。

哈尔滨,坐落于中国东北部,美丽的松花江穿城而过,带来了无尽的秀美和丰饶;东经125°42′~130°10′,北纬44°04′~46°41′的方位赋予她得天独厚的黄金时空。哈尔滨地处东北亚中心位置,被誉为欧亚大陆桥的明珠,是欧亚大陆桥和空中走廊的重要枢纽。哈尔滨铁路主要有哈大、滨绥、滨州、滨北、拉滨5条铁路连通国内。哈尔滨水运航线遍及松花江、黑龙江、乌苏里江和嫩江,并与俄罗斯远东部分港口相通,经过水路江海联运线,东出鞑靼海峡,船舶可直达日本、朝鲜、韩国和东南亚等地区。太平国际机场年旅客吞吐量超过600万人次,可办理110多个国家的客货联运业务,哈尔滨的气候属中温带大陆性季风气候,冬长夏短,有"冰城"之称。

哈尔滨是中国黑龙江省省会,是黑龙江的政治、经济、文化中心。全市辖8区10县(市),总面积5.38万平方公里,总人口990.1万人,市区人口475.5万人,共有48个民族,其中少数民族人口66万人。哈尔滨是中国省会城市中面积最大的,也是我国主要的工业生产基地和粮食生产基地。

哈尔滨也是一座独具特色的历史文化名城。大约在4万年前,哈尔滨地区就有人类活动。早期生活在这一带的人被称为"肃慎人",以后经多次演变,至唐朝以后称为"女真人"。

公元1115年,完颜部女真人完颜阿骨打灭辽后,建立了区域性政权——金朝,国号大金,定都会宁(今哈尔滨阿城),时称金上京会宁府。金王朝在这块土地上历经四代皇帝,共38年之久,于1153年迁都燕京。上京会宁府是12世纪东北亚地区最大的都市和政治、经济、文化中心,为北方文化构成留下了厚重的财富,成为哈尔滨特色文化的源头与核心。

金朝以后,元、明、清三个王朝的中央政权均在黑龙江地区设置管辖。1616年,建州女真领袖努尔哈赤称汗,建立"后金"政权。1636年改国号为清,族名为满族,1644年入关。此后,哈尔滨地区属清王朝阿勒楚喀(阿城)副都统管辖,恢复了古地名,汉语俗称"哈拉滨",后称"哈尔滨"。

19世纪末,沙俄政府胁迫清政府签订了《中俄密约》,攫取了在中国东北修筑铁路的权力。随着东清铁路的修筑和全线通车,哈尔滨开埠通商,30多个国家的十几万侨民汇集到了哈尔滨,开办了数以千计的工商金融企业和贸易公司,有19个国家在此设立领事馆,哈尔滨成为20世纪初中国东北最大的国际商埠。哈尔滨有了中国第一家电影院、第一家音乐学校、第一家啤酒厂等全国之最。

这座城市也荟萃了文艺复兴前后的各类型建筑,犹如一座建筑艺术的博物馆,因此当年的俄国人称哈尔滨为"东方的莫斯科",法国人称这里为"东方的小巴黎"。在这里不仅可领略中华民族传统的古典建筑,更可饱览欧洲文艺复兴、古典主义、浪漫主义、折中主义、新艺术运动、巴洛克建筑艺术,还可看到中华巴洛克建筑群体。哈尔滨又有教堂城之称。世界上四大宗教基督教、伊斯兰教、佛教、犹太教,哈尔滨都有。基督教的三大派天主教、东正教、基督新教,也是一个不少。在我国极为少见的犹太教堂,哈尔滨有两处。索菲亚教堂(建筑艺术博物馆,世界目前仅存两处)是远东地区最大的东正教堂,但它不在俄罗斯,却在中国的哈尔滨。新建的哈里路亚教堂是东北地区最大的基督教堂。哈尔滨的异域风情建筑其数量之大,艺术风格之多,整体之和谐实属罕见。它是哈尔滨历史文化的沉积,也是人类文明的宝贵遗产。哈尔滨的开埠,加快了这座近代城市的国际化发展步伐,大量侨民的涌入也为哈尔滨的文化构成增加了浓重的色彩。

1926年,哈尔滨的行政管辖权被全部收回,设立哈尔滨特别市,1931年"九一八"以后哈尔滨沦为日本帝国主义统治。1946年4月28日哈尔滨解放,是全国解放最早的大城市,是全国解放的大后方,也是"抗美援朝"的大后方,曾是共和国首都的候选城市。

新中国成立后,哈尔滨市国家重点建设的工业基地。"三大动力""十大军工"等都曾落户哈尔滨,还有量具厂、轴承厂、亚麻厂、电碳厂等企业。经过几十年的发展,哈尔滨现已形成以机电工业为主体,以汽车制造、医药、食品加工、化工产业为优势,门类齐全的工业体系,在振兴东北老工业基地的战略中,成为"哈大齐工业走廊"的龙头。哈尔滨还拥有较强的科技综合实力,特别是哈工大的航空航天、智能机器人的研发和焊接技术,都达到或领先于世界先进水平。

哈尔滨的街区名称演变见证了城市的历史。如现在的中山路,沙俄时期叫霍尔瓦特大街,日伪时期叫土肥原路,新中国成立后改为中山路。哈尔滨的城市格局是以河流和铁路为依托进行规划的。市区广场多,街道呈放射网状,没有南北中心轴线,更没有城墙。以铁路为界,铁道西称道里区,铁道东称道外区。火车站南是岗地,称南岗区。香坊区因百年前曾有线香作坊得名。平房区,百年前是满族村屯,因平房而得名。新设的松北区因位于松花江北岸,呼兰区因河而得名。

哈尔滨四季分明,每到春天,哈尔滨的市花——丁香花相继开放,多种颜色争奇斗艳,满城飘香;夏天一到,树木葱茏,百花盛开,草地如毯,凉风习习,是消夏避暑的好时节;秋季城市周边的"五花山"会让游人在大自然中流连忘返;而冬天,到处是冰雕冰灯,千姿百态,五颜六色,夜夜辉煌,让人目不暇接,当然冬季更是玩雪、赏雪、滑雪的好时节,所以哈尔滨又被称为"冰城夏都"。

哈尔滨是国家级历史文化名城,美丽的松花江像玉带从市区穿过,幽雅的太阳岛像一颗明亮的珍珠镶嵌在松花江上。两岸风光秀丽、景色宜人。夏季这里绿林成荫,一片田园风光。冬季这里银装素裹,一派北国风光。改革开放后哈尔滨的房子长高了,街道拓宽了,城市变得漂亮了,相继开辟了欧陆风情的中央大街步行街、俄罗斯风情的果戈里大街、印度风情街、犹太风情街,还有极乐寺的佛教文化街。游览的景点还有远东地区最大的东正教堂——圣·索菲亚教堂,全国最大的北方森林动物园,世界上最大的东北虎野化基地——东北虎林园,亚洲最高的钢架结构的黑龙江广播电视塔——龙塔,全国最专业也是极地动物种类最齐全的极地馆等。哈尔滨的多元文化中浓重的一笔是传统文化。哈尔滨的文庙是弘扬民族正气,抗击外来侵略的历史见证;哈尔滨还有金代上京会宁府遗址、"五国头城"遗址、萧红故居等文化遗迹;哈尔滨的周边群山环绕,有香炉山、横头山、松峰山、帽儿山、凤凰山等国家级森林公园,都值得您去参观游览。对滑雪发烧友来说,亚布力滑雪场、二龙山滑雪场、吉华长寿山滑雪场等设施一流的滑雪胜地绝对不能错过。

哈尔滨旅游事业日益兴旺,春天有"国际经贸洽谈会",夏天有"哈尔滨之夏音乐会",秋天有"天鹅艺术节"(每两三年举办一次),冬天有滑雪节、"冰雪节"和"冰灯游园会"。一年四季,不论什么时候来哈尔滨观光旅游,都会令您快乐和满意。

下面我给朋友们介绍一下哈尔滨的饮食文化。

首先要吃得好:

俄式西餐首推华梅西餐厅,与北京马克西姆、上海红房子、天津起士林并称"中国四大西餐厅",另外老都一处三鲜水饺久负盛名;想吃地道的东北菜——杀猪菜可以到老六杀猪菜、大丰收。在农家大院、农家小院等东北菜馆都能吃到正宗的农家菜。当然也不能错过买点儿肉联厂产的大众牌红肠、秋林公司产的里道斯牌红肠和大列巴面包、正阳楼的风味干肠和松仁小肚等带给亲朋好友。

其次要喝得爽:

哈尔滨啤酒厂是中国最早的啤酒厂,诞生于 1900 年。哈尔滨市啤酒消费量居全国第一,世界第三,居慕尼黑、巴黎之后。每年一度的哈尔滨啤酒节已升格为国家级,在这里可以品尝世界各地的优质啤酒。

说话间,我们的车已到了我们下榻的酒店。请大家带好随身物品随我下车,先到大堂休息,等我安排好房间,稍事休息,简单洗漱后,11 时 30 分准时在大厅集合开始我们的哈尔滨之旅。

谢谢大家!

### 3. The City of Qiqihar

Qiqihar is the second largest city and the municipality in Heilongjiang province, which serves as the political, economic, technological, cultural and business center as well as the transportation hub of the western part in the province. It is designated to be one of the 13 large cities of China by the State Council. Qiqihar administers 7 districts, 1 city and 8 counties with a total population of 5.716 million, including the urban population of 1.439 million.

Qiqihar is located in Nenjiang Plain, northeast of Heilongjiang province, and it is 328 km west to Suihua, 282 km north to Baicheng of Jilin Province, 524 km east to Hulunbeir of Inner Mongolia, 483 km south to Heihe and 359 km to the capital of the province—Harbin. The geological structure belongs to the connection of the Neocathaysian No. 2 subsidence zone and No. 3 up-warping zone with the Nenjiang geofracture running through the whole plain. In general, the land is high in the north and descends to the south. The southern foot of Lesser Khingan Mountains lies in the north and east, and Nenjiang Alluvial Plain in the central and south.

Qiqihar is an ancient city with a history of more than 300 years. In 1674, Jilin Fleet was moved here by the Qing Dynasty. In 1683, the Naval Camp was set up. In 1684, a military depot with barracks and an arsenal was set up. In 1691, a stronghold was constructed in Qiqihar because of the Qing government's campaigns against the Mongols. The vice-general and the general of Heilongjiang moved from Morgan to Qiqihar in 1698 and 1699 respectively. In 1895, the Heishui Office was set up to administrate Qiqihar. In 1907, Qiqihar was designated to be the capital of Heilongjiang province. In 1936, Qiqihar implemented the municipal system. Qiqihar was established as the capital of Nenjiang Province, Heinei Province and Heilongjiang province after the foundation of People's Republic of China in 1949. However, since Songjiang Province was merged into Heilongjiang province, the provincial capital was transferred to Harbin in 1954. Then Qiqihar became the municipality.

Qiqihar is an emerging city with a huge potential. As one of the earliest old industrial bases, it has the solid industrial foundation with a focus on light industry, chemical industry, textile industry, building materials, electronics, medicine and food, particularly the heavy machinery and metallurgical industry. There are China First Heavy Industries praised as "National Treasure" and "Pearl in Palm" by Premier Zhou Enlai, Beiman Special Steel Co., Ltd., Qiqihar First and Second Machine Tool Group ranking at the top of the "Top Eighteen" in machine tool industry of China, the largest railway rolling stock manufacturer in China—Qiqihar Railway Rolling Stock Co., Ltd., two large chemical enterprises—Heilongjiang Chemical Plant and Qiqihar Chemical Plant, and three major military enterprises once made outstanding contributions to national defense—Heping Machinery, Huaan Factory and Jianhua Factory.

Qiqihar is a transportation and communication hub connecting Heilongjiang province, Jilin Province and Inner Mongolia. Railways are ramified all over the country. Qiqihar Airport operates daily flights to Beijing, Shanghai, Guangzhou, Wuhan, Shenyang, Dalian, Heihe, Hailar and other major cities in China. The waterway leads north to Heihe and east to Harbin, Jiamusi and other cities. The telephone communication has connected the international direct dialing.

Qiqihar is an ideal ecological tourist resort with unique features. Zhalong Nature Reserve, renowned at home and abroad, is the largest reserve of China for inhabitation and multiplication of waterfowls and birds, especially for the rare birds—red-crowned cranes. So Qiqihar is honored as the "Crane Hometown".

Of all the cities situated above the 47th degree of northern latitude, Qiqihar is the largest in China. The culture in the north of the Great Wall integrates with the nomadic culture on the grasslands, which brings the natural and unique human landscapes and historical and cultural sites. The nationallevel Zhalong Nature Reserve is the world-famous wetland and the reserve of waterfowls and birds. Of the 15 types of cranes in the world, China has 9 types, and you could see 6 types at Zhalong, including the rarest red-crowned cranes. The tourist spots are scattered all over the city. The Longsha Park with a history of hundred years is the largest urban comprehensive park in the Northeast China. The provincial-level scenic spot Bright Moon Island, whose former name is Sishui Island, is located at 7 km northwest of Qiqihar, with an area of 7.66 hectares. At the center of the island, there stands the Wanshan Temple built in 1925 and the rebuilt Heilongjiang Martial's Mansion, increasing some historic and cultural connotation. Built in 1943, the magnificent and grand Mahayana Temple is listed in China's Top Religious Sites and is the famous Buddhist sanctuary in the Northeast. The temple is a haven of peace and tranquility. The Pukui Mosque, which was first built in 1684, under the reign of Kangxi (1654-1722, emperor 1661-1722), is the largest Islamic church in Heilongjiang province. Besides these beautiful sceneries, there are other tourist attractions such as the fully enclosed Pine Pheasant Hunting approved by the State Forestry Department with an area of 4667 hectares, ancient site of the Neolithic culture at Ang'angxi, historical and cultural site protected at the national level—Puyulu Road of Jin Dynasty, Red Bank Park of Fularji, Snake-Cave Mountain in Nianzishan District Scenic and Erkeshan Park of Kedong, etc.

In recent years, the municipal Party committee and the municipal government have taken the opportunity of building an excellent tourism city by integrating the unique wetland culture, ice and snow culture, border area's culture, religious culture and other tourist resources to spread the city brand of "Large Wetland in the World" and "Crane Hometown of China" as well as to vigorously develop ecotourism, green agriculture, equipment industry and other characteristic tourism. Qiqihar has won the approval of national appraisal group to build the excellent tourism city of China; moreover, the dream of building the hometown of northern ecotourism is well on the way. In Qiqihar, you could enjoy the snow-covered landscapes and appreciate the ice lanterns as well as the artificial products in winter; you could view the lakes and marshes or watch the crane dancing, experiencing the natural charms in summer; you could visit the scenic spots and the ancient temples to listen to the morning bell and the evening drum in spring; you could walk on the isolated islands and go through the woods to experience the fruitful harvest in autumn.

## 齐齐哈尔市概况

齐齐哈尔市是黑龙江省第二大城市和省辖市,是黑龙江省西部地区的政治、经济、科技、文化教育、商贸中心和重要的交通枢纽,全市辖七个区、一个市、八个县,人口 561.1 万(市区 143.9 万)。齐齐哈尔是被国务院批准的全国 13 个较大城市之一。

齐齐哈尔市位于黑龙江省西北部的嫩江平原。东与本省绥化地区、南与吉林省白城地区、西与内蒙古自治区呼伦贝尔盟、北与本省黑河地区接壤。距省会哈尔滨市 359 公里,距绥化市 328 公里,距白城市 282 公里,距海拉尔市 524 公里,距黑河市 483 公里。地质构造属于新华夏系第二沉降带和第三隆起带的交接处,嫩江大断裂贯通平原全境。地势北高南低,北部和东部是小兴安岭南麓,中部和南部为嫩江冲积平原。

齐齐哈尔市是一座历史悠久的文化古城,有三百多年的历史。1674 年清政府移吉林水师驻齐齐哈尔。1683 年定齐齐哈尔为水师营制。1684 年于齐齐哈尔设火器营。1691 年齐齐哈尔建城。1698、1699 年黑龙江的副都统和将军先后由墨尔根移驻齐齐哈尔。1895 年在齐齐哈尔设黑水厅。1907 年齐齐哈尔为黑龙江省省会。1936 年齐齐哈尔实行市制。新中国成立后,齐齐哈尔先后为嫩江省、黑嫩省、黑龙江省的省会,1954 年黑龙江省与松江省合并,省会设在哈尔滨市,齐齐哈尔改为省辖市。

齐齐哈尔是一个开发潜力巨大的新兴城市。齐齐哈尔具有雄厚的工业基础,是国家最早兴建的老工业基地之一。以重型机械、冶金工业为主体,包括化工、轻工、纺织、建材、食品、电子、医药等门类齐全的工业体系。既有被周总理誉为"国宝"和"掌上明珠"的第一重型机械厂、北满特殊钢厂和被列为全国机床行业"十八罗汉"的第一、二机床厂,又有全国最大的铁路货车生产企业齐齐哈尔车辆厂和大型化工企业黑龙江化工厂、齐齐哈尔化工总厂,还有和平、建华、华安等为共和国作出卓越贡献的三大军工生产企业。

齐齐哈尔是跨黑龙江、吉林、内蒙古三省区的交通、通信枢纽,铁路四通八达,民航已开通北京、上海、广州、武汉、沈阳、大连、黑河、海拉尔等航线。水上运输北通黑河,东通哈尔滨、佳木斯等地。电话通信已进入国际直拨网。

齐齐哈尔旅游景观独特。境内的扎龙自然保护区是驰名中外全国最大的水禽、鸟类保护区。世界珍禽丹顶鹤就在这里休养生息,因此齐齐哈尔被誉为鹤乡之城。

齐齐哈尔作为北纬 47°以北的中国最大城市,塞北的黑土文化与草原的游牧文化汇聚交融,荟萃了风姿独特、古朴自然的人文景观和历史文化遗址。境内的扎龙国家级自然保护区是驰名中外的国际重要湿地、水禽、鸟类保护区。世界现有鹤类 15 种,中国有 9 种,扎龙自然保护区就有 6 种,其中尤以丹顶鹤最为珍贵。拥有百年历史的龙沙公园,是东北地区最大的市内综合性公园。省级风景名胜区明月岛,原名泗水岛,位于市区西北 7 公里处,面积 7.66 公顷。岛上有始建于 1925 年的万善寺建筑群,近年又将黑龙江将军府在岛内重建,给岛上增添了厚重的历史文化内涵。始建于 1943 年并列入《中国宗教名胜》的大乘寺,气势雄伟,规模宏大,静谧深幽,是东北著名的佛教圣地。始建于康熙(二十三年)1684 年的卜奎清真寺,是黑龙江规模最大的伊斯兰教堂。还有占地7万亩国家林业部批准建设的全封闭型青松山鸡狩猎场,昂昂溪新石器古文化遗址,国家级文物保护单位金代蒲峪路遗址,富拉尔基红岸公园,碾子山蛇洞山风景区,克东二克山公园等,都别有洞天,别具意趣。

近年来,市委、市政府以创建中国优秀旅游城市为契机,整合特有的湿地文化、冰雪文化、边疆民族文化、宗教文化等旅游资源,把"世界大湿地、中国鹤家乡"的城市品牌叫响,大力开发生态、绿色农业和装备工业等特色旅游,齐齐哈尔市已通过"创建中国优秀旅游城市"国家验收组的验收,建设北方生态旅游之乡的目标正在逐步成为现实。在齐齐哈尔,冬可赏雪景品冰雕,感受人造美;夏可游湖沼观鹤舞,体会自然神韵;春可览胜境行古刹,倾听晨钟暮鼓;秋可履孤岛踏林间,体味芳华物换。

## 4. The City of Mudanjiang

### Natural Landscape

With its beautiful natural scenery, the city of Mudanjiang is titled as China Excellent Tourist City authorized by the National Tourist Administration. As for its pleasant weather in summer and good quality of snow in winter, the city is crowned as the northern lush field, the Land of Snow, and so on. The Jingpo Lake in Mudanjiang, the largest volcano barrier lake in China and the second in the world, is National Key Scenery Attraction, approved as World Geopark in 2008. In Jingpo Lake Scenic Spot, the world famous Underground Forest is a crater primitive forest, and the national forest park. In the city of Mudanjiang, there are also some attractive spots, such as Mudan Peak, the nearest primitive forest to the city, which impresses visitors with its majestic and precipitous appeal; the picturesque Lotus Lake is the biggest artificial lake in northern area; the breathing-taking Tiger Park, the unique scenery in winter, and so on. The city has held 10 sessions of snow tourist festival, and the Summer Holiday of Jingpo Lake is also held from 2007, opening the ceremony of Big Ten Programmes in Tourism.

### History and Culture

The city of Mudanjiang is situated in the southeast of Heilongjiang province. Dating back to its long history, it is the homeland of ancient Manchu. In AD 698 of Tang Dynasty, the nation of Bohai was established here. Today, we still could see its historical remains, which were built more than 1 300 years ago. The city of Mudanjiang was set up in 1937, and achieved its liberation in August 1945. In the early 1960s, it was listed in the national historical and cultural heritage. The city remains ancient customs and people are simple and honest. Many heroes and revolutionists were born here, and the city witnessed some historical events, such as Eight Women Fighters and the War of Yakesa. Thus, there are many tourist attractions of revolution theme, including the Martyry of Majun, the Martyry of Yang Zirong, the Sculpture Group of Eight Women Fighters and Dongning Fortress.

Those architectures record the achievements of the past and remind us of the present happy life.

### The Custom

As for the local minorities, the city has its special custom and culture, and custom travel has developed rapidly in recent years. All kinds of Korean-style streets and Manchu nationality villages have been built in the downtown and some nearby regions. Those constructions not only promote the minority culture, but also attract numerous visitors and people domestic and overseas.

### Cross-country Travel

The southeast of Mudanjiang borders on Russia, stretching over 204.9 kilometers. Ports and border trades develop successfully here. The downtown is about 381 kilometers apart from Vladivostok, and 421 kilometers from Nakhodka which is the biggest ice-free port in the Far East. It serves as the communications hub connecting with Korean Peninsula and Tumen River. The cross-country travel of Mudanjiang develops vigorously and some popular routes have been open, for example, route on the natural scenery traveling from Changbai Shan to Jingpo Lake then to Vladivostok; route on international travel providing Seoul-Mudanjiang-Yanji or Harbin-Mudanjiang-Vladivostok. Mudanjiang is moving forward to the international tourism city and has received 948 400 inbound and outbound visitors in 2008, with 20% year-on-year growth.

### The sightseeing in the City

Mudanjiang has a style of its own. In the city, you could see tourist attractions such as the sculptures of the eight heroines who drowned themselves in the river and the cemetery of revolutionary matyrs in Beishan. Besides, you can enjoy natural and cultural landscape such as snowcastle on central island, People's Park, and Beishan Park. Dong Yi Street is a walking street that one can go shopping, dining and entertaining, and Culture Square is a place for recreation. Jinding International Hotel is the peak building in the city. Buildings are well-proportioned and rivers are scattered all over in the city.

### The Resources in Agriculture and Forestry

With rich natural resources, Mudanjiang is one of the major forest regions in Heilongjiang province. At present, 2.9 million hectares of forestry land occupies 75% of the total land area; 308 000 hectares of farmland are abundant in soybean, corn, wheat and the famous Xiangshui rice. Besides, it has 3.846 million mus (256 528 hectares) of uncultivated land, and 45.62 million mus (3 042 854 hectares) of forest land which covers 62.8% of the forest. As for the resources, there are 77 varieties of trees, and 210 million steres of living forest stock which becomes the home of Amur cork, Manchurian ash and walnuts. It is also the national seed forest of Pinus Koraiensis, rare medicinal herbs include ginseng, Astragalus mongholicus and wilsonii, rare animals like Manchurian tiger, sable and pterosaur live here. The wild industrial crops differentiate in 2 200 kinds, and half of them could be developed and used, including 15 kinds under national protection. More than 300 wild animals belong to 30 families, 14 of which are first class national protected animals. There are 96 different mineral products including metal and metalloid, among which coal, gold, marble and plumbago reserve most and are in good quality, with 1.2 billion reserves of plumbago ranking the first in the nation. Those resources provide great opportunities for development in economy of Mudanjiang.

## 牡丹江市概况

### 自然景观

牡丹江自然风光秀美旖旎，景色天成。夏季气候宜人，冬季雪质优良，享有"塞外江南""中国雪乡""中国雪城"等诸多美誉，被国家旅游局授予中国优秀旅游城市称号。中国最大、世界第二大的火山熔岩堰塞湖——镜泊湖，为国家重点风景名胜区，2008 年被评为世界地质公园。镜泊湖"地下森林"是世界著名的"火山口"原始森林，为国家级森林公园。国内离城市最近的原始森林牡丹峰雄伟壮观，中国北方地区最大的人工湖——莲花湖山清水秀，森林虎园惊心动魄，冰雪旅游独具特色，跨国旅游风情迥然……牡丹江已连续举办十届雪堡旅游节，自 2007 年开始举办"镜泊湖之夏"旅游文化节，全面启动建设"十大旅游精品工程"。

### 历史人文

牡丹江市位于黑龙江省东南部，历史悠久。牡丹江流域，古为肃慎地。帝舜禹始，一直是满族的祖先及其后裔生息之地。公元 698 年建立了唐朝地方政权——渤海国，上京龙泉府遗迹尚存。牡丹江市是历史的城市，唐代渤海国上京龙泉府遗址距今已有 1 300 多年的历史，1937 年设市，1945 年 8 月获得解放。早在 20 世纪 60 年代初就被列为国家级历史文化遗产。至今古风犹存，民风淳朴，历代多出民族英雄和革命志士，雅克萨之战、"平南洋"抗日、八女投江、杨子荣剿匪等可歌可泣的历史事件就发生在这里。牡丹江市是英雄的城市，作为红色旅游基地的马骏烈士纪念馆、杨子荣烈士陵园、"八女投江"群雕记录了革命先烈的丰功伟绩，作为日军侵华罪证的东宁要塞警醒着中华儿女牢记历史、勿忘国耻。

### 民俗风情

朝鲜族、满族等浓郁的少数民族气息，赋予了牡丹江市独特的民族风情文化。近年来，牡丹江市少数民族民俗风情旅游蓬勃发展，建成了市区朝鲜民族风情街、海林市新合朝鲜族民俗风味一条街、宁安市镜泊湖瀑布朝鲜族民俗村、依兰岗满族民俗村等一批少数民族风情游景点，弘扬了少数民族文化，吸引了众多的国内外游客和城市居民。

### 跨境旅游

牡丹江沿边邻境，区位优越。东南部与俄罗斯滨海边区接壤，边境线长达 204.9 公里，口岸众多，边贸畅通。市区距俄罗斯滨海边疆区首府海参崴市 381 公里，距远东最大不冻港纳霍德卡 421 公里，是南下图们江到朝鲜半岛的交通枢纽。牡丹江的中俄、中朝、中韩等跨境旅游发展迅速,现已开通了长白山—镜泊湖—海参崴"名山名湖出境游"、首尔—牡丹江—延吉"中韩国际热线游"和哈尔滨—牡丹江—海参崴等多条跨国旅游精品线路,牡丹江正向着国际旅游城市方向迈进。2008年全市共接待进出境旅游者94.84万人次,同比增长20%。

**市容市貌**

牡丹江市容别具风韵,有以八女投江雕塑、北山烈士陵园为标志的城市旅游景点,有以江心岛雪堡、人民公园、北山公园为核心的城市自然人文景观,有集购物、餐饮、文化、娱乐、休闲于一体的东一步行街和文化广场为重点的城市休闲场所,有以金鼎国际大酒店为最高建筑的城市建筑群,山、水、园、林错落有致,江、河、湖、海星罗棋布。

**农林资源**

牡丹江是黑龙江省重点林区之一,资源丰富,得天独厚。现有林业用地290万公顷,林地面积占土地总面积的75%以上,现有耕地30.8万公顷,盛产大豆、玉米、小麦,其中响水大米为千年贡品。有宜林宜农荒地384.6万亩,林地4 562万亩,森林覆盖率62.8%,主要树种77种,活立木蓄积量达2.1亿立方米,素有"林海"之称,是水曲柳、黄菠萝、胡桃楸"三大硬阔"之乡,也是国家红松母树林基地。人参、黄芪、刺五加等名贵药材及东北虎、紫貂、飞龙等珍禽异兽闻名遐迩。野生经济植物有2 200多种,可供开发利用的达1 100余种,其中国家重点保护的有15种,被称为"天然植物基因库"。野生动物有30科300多种,其中国家一级重点保护的东北虎、棕熊等14种。有金属、非金属矿产96种,煤、黄金、大理石、石墨储量大,品质好,其中石墨储量达12亿吨,居全国之首。如此丰富的资源是牡丹江市得天独厚的优势,为其经济的发展带来了可遇而不可求的契机。

## 5. The City of Jiamusi

Jiamusi lies in the hinderland of Sanjiang Plain. The plain is in the northeastern part of the country and is formed by the Heilongjiang River (Amur River), Songhua River and Wusuli River (Ussuri River). Located at latitude 45°56′–48°28′N and longitude 129°29′–135°5′E, Jiamusi is the first place where the sun rises and is called "East Pole in China". separated by the Wusuli River and the Heilongjiang River, the city lies across Russia's Khabarovsk and Birobidzhan. It administrates two county-level cities, four counties and four districts with an area of 32 700 km and a population of 2 450 000.

Jiamusi is the key city of the Eastern Heilongjiang province, which serves as the economic center for its unique location, the logistics center with a strong capacity of transportation and commodity distribution, as well as the business center with convenient traffic and excellent environment. Situated along the rivers, it is one of the livable cities with the pleasant environment, which attracts businessmen at home and abroad to set up offices. It borders Russia and links Northeast Asia. On the one hand, located in the center of the Northeast Asia economic circle, it links Mongolia, Russia,

Japan, South Korea, North Korea and Southeast Asian countries through the river-sea shipping, forming a grand economic cycle between 6 countries of the Northeast Asia and other Southeast Asian countries. On the other hand, the transportation towards Russia works well including railway, public, waterway and airport. Jimusi has 5 national first-class ports and a Jimusi-Khabarovsk international airline. In a word, Jimusi will provide an economic and trade platform to link Russia and extend the Northeast Asia.

Jimusi has a long history. According to archaeological records, human activities were found more than 7 000 years ago. With more than 670 historical and cultural relics, it was once the country of the Sushen ethnic group, the capital of Yilou (an alias of Sushen from the $3^{rd}$ century to the $6^{th}$ century), the birthplace of Five Cities (five tribes built by Jurchen) and the hometown of the present Manchu group. In the early Qing Dynasty, Jiamusi was the village of the Hezhe Minority named Giyamusi, originally meaning the inn in Manchu Language. Later Jiamusi was an ancient bridle path of the Songhua River, leading to the estuary of Heilongjiang River. In 1888, Jimusi became a small town of Huachuan county with the name Dongxingzhen. In 1937, the city of Jiamusi was established. It was set up as the administrative center for three places—the puppet Sanjiang Province, Huachuan County and the city of Jimusi. In 1945, it was the administrative center of the government of Former Hejiang Province. And now the border city Jiamusi serves as the hub of policy, economy, culture, technology, trade, tourism, communication, information and transportation in the Northeast Heilongjiang province.

Jiamusi has rich resources. It enjoys a great fame in the world for its vast lands, black soil plain—one of the only three in the world, including 14 300 km black soil wetland. The excellent green and environmental resources promote the leading enterprises of the grain intensive processing, the meat processing, the dairy processing, the green food processing and other agricultural industrialization. With the three major tributaries—Heilongjiang River, Songhua River and Wusuli River, this city is crisscrossed by the rivers and dotted with lakes, so all of these abundant water resources provide favorable conditions for developing industries especially for those energy-intensive and water-intensive industries. The main mineral reserves in Jiamusi are the gold, coal, oil, natural gas, facing stone, mineral water, etc. Recently, 43 kinds of mineral resources are found. Furthermore, Jiamusi has the geological condition for the hydrocarbon generation. It has been ascertained that the natural gas reserve is nearly 10 billion cubic meters and the gold 38 745.4 kg (metal quantity) in total. Meanwhile, Jiamusi has a huge potential to develop the wind power generation because of its abundant wind energy resources. As the riverside and border city in North China, Jiamusi has four distinctive seasons with the unique charm. Here are some splendid tourist activities such as the ecological tour, the snow and ice tour, the Hezhe folk-custom tour, the exotic tour, the revolution recalling tour, etc. You could enjoy some excellent scenic spots such as the unique cross-border river, the endless plain, the renowned wetland, the charming agriculture, the well ecological forest, the special snow and ice, as well as the fascinating island.

Jiamusi has a solid industrial foundation with sufficient factors of production. There is a rich land, where a few industrial development zones are programmed, offering some advantages for the companies to use the land. The energy supply is abundant, especially the coal resources with a high quality and low price. It supports the energy-intensive industries by reducing the electrovalence for those using large quantities of electricity. Besides the land and energy resources, the water resources are also rich including the industrial water, making Jiamusi the rare region with the abundant water compared with other cities of the same size. It has the complete industrial sectors and the strong capacity of carrying on the industrial transfer, gradually forming three pillar industries—green food, mechanical manufacturing and pharmaceutical chemicals. The technical force and the talent pool are abundant. Under the influence of the old industrial base, a lot of skilled workers are trained and talents are provided by the largest comprehensive provincial university with enrollment of more than 30 000 students on campus. With the agricultural modernization, the famers master the technology and move to the urban area. It is convenient to exchange with Russian technology and human resources, because there are massive technologies and talent reserves in the fields of heavy industry, military industry, and medical industry. Importantly the average educational level in Russia is high and the human resource cost is low, so it is convenient to bring in or communicate.

Jiamusi has a fine ecological environment full of ecological diversity, stable system and beautiful environment. There are 20 nature reserves with an area of 400 112 hectares, accounting for 12.23% of the total area in Jiamusi. Among them, Sanjiang wetland is the largest fresh water wetland in China and also one of the rarest primitive wetlands in the world. There are over 600 kinds of helad, over 120 kinds of waterfowls and migrant birds. It is an ideal paradise for inhabitation and multiplication of the national-level protected birds—white storks, also for the white whooper swans and elegant red-crowned cranes. Jiamusi is especially beautiful, surrounded by the dense primeval forests and myriad man-made forests. Daliangzihe Forest Park of Tangyuan County and the Jinkou Forest Park in Tongjiang Street are both the national-level forest parks, and you could relax on holidays in summer and go hunting or skiing in winter. With a hill and rivers nearby, Jiamusi looks like a bright pearl in Sanjiang Plain.

## 佳木斯市概况

佳木斯位于祖国东北边陲的松花江、黑龙江、乌苏里江汇流而成的三江平原腹地,南起北纬45°56′至48°28′,西起东经127°27′至135°5′。隔乌苏里江、黑龙江与俄罗斯哈巴罗夫斯克、比罗比詹相望,是祖国最早迎接太阳升起的地方,被誉为"中国东极"。全市幅员 3.27 万平方公里,现辖两个县级市、四县、四区,总人口 245 万。

佳木斯是黑龙江省东部地区的中心城市。优越的位置使佳木斯自然成为黑龙江省东部的经济中心。强大的运输、商品集散能力及交通枢纽打造了佳木斯的物流中心地位。便利的交通、优良的环境打造了佳木斯的商务中心地位。佳木斯是黑龙江省东部环境优美、适合人类居住的江城,吸引了各地客商在佳木斯建立办事机构。佳木斯是通往俄罗斯、连接东北亚的桥头堡。佳木斯处于东北亚经济圈的中心位置,通过江海联运,可连接蒙古、俄罗斯、日本、韩国、朝鲜和东南亚各国,形成东北亚经济圈六国与东南亚各国的经济大循环。佳木斯是通向俄罗斯、连接东北亚的大通道。目前佳木斯对俄贸易的铁、公、水、空通道运行良好、畅通无阻。佳木斯市拥有 5 个国家一类口岸,开辟了佳木斯至俄哈巴罗夫斯克国际空中航线。佳木斯将成为面向俄罗斯、延伸东北亚的经贸大平台。

佳木斯历史悠久。据考古资料证实,距今已有 7 000 多年的人类活动历史。这里曾是肃慎之国,挹娄古都,五国盛地,满族故乡,有各类历史文化遗存等 670 余处。据皇清职贡图、大清一统图、盛京吉林黑龙江等处标注战绩图,对佳木斯都有记载。清朝初年为赫哲族村屯,满语为"嘉木寺噶珊","噶珊"意为"屯"。佳木斯清朝年间是松花江通往黑龙江至庙街东海口古驿道站中的一站,汉语为"站官屯"或"驿丞村"。建镇于 1888 年,原是桦川县的一个小镇,史称东兴镇。1937 年改建为市,是原伪三江省会、桦川县和佳木斯市三署辖地。1945 年是原合江省政府所在地,现今是黑龙江省东北部地区政治、经济、文化、科技、外贸、旅游、通信、信息、水陆空交通重要边境城市。

佳木斯资源富集。这里土地广袤,是世界上仅有的三块黑土平原之一,包含世界上仅存的三大黑土湿地 2 145 万亩(1 亩≈667 平方米),在国际上享有极高的声誉。极好的绿色环境资源孕育着粮食深加工、肉制品加工、乳制品加工、绿色特色产品加工等农业产业化龙头企业。佳木斯区域内江河纵横,大小湖泊星罗棋布。境内有黑龙江、松花江、乌苏里江三大水系,充足的水资源为发展工业,特别是高耗能、高耗水产业提供了有利的条件。佳木斯市矿产储备以黄金、煤炭、石油、天然气、饰面石材、矿泉水为主。目前已发现矿产资源 43 种。佳木斯具备油气生成的地质条件,现已探明天然气储量近百亿立方米,全市黄金已累计探明储量 38 745.4 公斤(金属量)。同时,佳木斯还是我国风能资源的富集区,发展风力发电潜力巨大。佳木斯作为北国江城、边境城市,四季分明,独具魅力。原始生态游、冰雪特色游、赫哲民俗游、异国风情游、革命缅怀游等旅游项目异彩纷呈。大界江独具一格;大平原一望无际;大湿地闻名世界;大农业魅力无穷;大森林生态优良;大冰雪极具北国特色;大岛屿风光无限。

佳木斯产业基础雄厚。主要生产要素充足配套。土地资源极其丰富,规划了十几个产业发展园区,给予企业发展用地极大的优惠。能源供给十分充沛,煤炭资源丰富,质高价低;电力敞开供应,对耗电大户还给予电价优惠,支持高耗能产业发展。水资源极其丰富,工业用水完全有保证,是全国同等规模城市中极少的水利富集地区,工业门类齐全。逐步形成了绿色食

139

品、机械制造、医药化工三大支柱产业,承接产业转移的能力较强。技术力量和人才储备雄厚。佳木斯市作为老工业基地,多年来培养了大批的熟练技术工人,佳木斯拥有省属最大的综合性大学,在校生人数已达3万多人。现代化的农业培育了现代化的农民,现代化水平的提高,支持了技术农民向城市转移。与俄罗斯技术、人力资源交流便利。俄罗斯远东地区的重工业技术与人才、军事工业技术与人才、医疗技术与人才储备量巨大。俄罗斯平均教育水平较高,人力资源成本较低,引入和联系都十分便利。

佳水斯生态环境良好。生态多样,系统稳定,环境优美。佳木斯市建有20个自然保护区,总面积400 112公顷,占辖区面积的12.23%。其中,三江湿地是中国最大的淡水沼泽湿地,也是世界仅有的原始湿地之一。有各种沼泽植物600多种,水禽候鸟120多种。国家一级保护鸟类白鹤在这里繁衍生息,洁白的大天鹅、优雅的丹顶鹤在这里自由飞翔。茂密苍翠的原始森林、波涛万顷的人工林海把佳木斯装扮得分外妖娆。汤原大亮子河森林公园、同江街津口森林公园都是国家级森林公园,夏可休闲度假,冬可狩猎滑雪。良好的生态环境使依山傍水的佳木斯市犹如三江平原上的一颗璀璨的明珠。

### 6. Mohe County

Ladies and Gentlemen,

  Good morning/afternoon. I would like, on the behalf of all the staff of our travel agency, to extend a warm welcome to all of you. Welcome to the northernmost of the Heilongjiang province, the Arctic Polar of China—Mohe County.

  I'm ×××, your tour guide from Mohe Travel Agency, and this is our driver, Mr. ××. In this trip, you will visit Mohe's natural, geographic, and cultural landscapes. If you need help or have some suggestions, do not hesitate to let me know, and I will try my best to help. I hope our service will make you feel at home and this trip will be one of the special memories you'll take home with you.

  I wish you a pleasant stay in Mohe. Have a smooth journey!

  Ladies and gentlemen, we have arrived at the Chinese Arctic Polar—Mohe, and now we are driving straight to the hotel that we've arranged for you. During this period, I would like to introduce Mohe briefly.

  Mohe is located in the far northwest of Heilongjiang. It is located at latitude 52° 10′53° 33′ N and 121° 07′124° 20′ E with a total area of 18 233 square. Located at the north foot of Greater Hinggan Mountains, Mohe is in the northern most of the country with the reputation as "golden crest on the bright pearl".

  Mohe County is subdivided into four towns and one village, including Xilinji, Jingtao, Tuqiang, Xingan, and Arctic Village. Mohe's population has reached approximated 100 000, and this creates a population density of only 4.64 persons/km². The majority of the county's population is Han nationality, and there are other 13 Ethnic minorities living here.

Mohe, by virtue of its far northern location, is one of the few locations in China with a subarctic climate, long and severe winters, and short and warm summers. Due to the large temperature difference, it enjoys the reputation as the city with "four seasons in one day".

(In summer) Today's temperature is ×× ℃. Due to the large temperature difference, please add the clothes at any time in case of getting cold. Now we are on the No.2 Bridge over Dalin river, on your right-hand there is a hill which is called Xishan District by local residents.

We are driving on the Zhengxing Road, on both sides of which are banks, hotels, savings agencies, and it is a commercial street. The city has a feature of "Bustling but not noisy, quiet but not desolate".

Now we are driving on the Zhonghua Road, which is lined with several shops and attractions including Mohe Conference Center, Lianxin Square and post office. The clean and tidy street and the beautiful flowers along the streets are greatly enjoyed by locals and visitors alike.

(In winter) Today's temperature is ×××. Mohe in this season is covered with ice and snow, and even the air we breathe is cool. If this is the first time to visit Mohe, you might not adapt to the nippy weather, so please add the clothes to avoid getting the flu or cold injury.

It gets dark early in winter, so you cannot see the scene clearly outside.

There is still a light through the night to light every street. It is a prelude to welcome guests from afar. What you'll see tomorrow will be a more beautiful place.

Now I will introduce this hotel for you.

Located on the Zhonghua Road at Xilinji Town, Mohe Hotel was built in 1988, a two-star hotel regaling foreign guests. It covers an area of 5 000 square meters and its building area is 3 100 square meters. The Mohe Hotel features 36 guest rooms with 118 beds offering 24-hour room service and 12 restaurants in different size. You can taste the Northeastern Chinese cuisine and also other regional cuisines in here. It can provide whatever you would love to, and what you would never taste in other places.

Mohe Hotel will greet the guests with first-rate service.

Here we are at the hotel, please get off.

## 漠河县概况

女士们、先生们：

大家好！

首先,我代表漠河旅行社全体同仁,真诚地欢迎各位来到祖国的最北端——神州北极漠河！

我是漠河旅行社的导游×××,和我一起为大家服务的是我们的司机×师傅,我们将带领大家参观漠河的自然景观、地理景观、人文景观。如果您在旅行途中遇到什么困难或有什么建议,请您不客气地提出来,我将尽最大的努力帮助大家。希望我们的服务能使大家在漠河有宾至如归的感觉,希望漠河的美丽风光能留给各位最美好的回忆。

预祝各位漠河之游顺利、愉快!

女士们、先生们,我们现在已经踏上了祖国北极漠河的土地,我们的车正驶向今晚大家下榻的宾馆。利用这段时间,我先向各位介绍一下北极漠河基本的概况。

漠河县位于黑龙江省西北部,东经121°07′至124°20′,北纬52°10′至53°33′,地域总面积1.8万平方公里。地处大兴安岭山脉北麓,是中华人民共和国疆域的最北端,素有"金鸡之冠,天鹅之首"的美称。

漠河县辖西林吉、劲涛、图强、兴安四镇,一个乡,即祖国的最北端——北极乡(北极村),全县人口近十万,以汉族为主,有少数民族13个,人口密度为每平方公里4.7人,昼夜温差较大,有"一日四季"之说。春、秋二季不甚分明,冬季漫长而严寒,夏季短暂而温润。

(夏)漠河早晚温差较大,今天的气温是××℃,请大家注意随时添加衣服,防止感冒。漠河山美水美,空气清新,我们经过的是大林河二号桥,在我们车辆行驶方向的右侧是一座小山,县内的居民都称其为西山小区。

现在我们走的这条路叫振兴路,路两边有银行、饭店、储蓄所、商业一条街,虽繁华却不喧闹,虽安静却不冷清,这正是小城市的特点。

我们现在正在中华路上行驶,路两边有邮局、漠河会议中心、连心广场,这干净、整齐的街道,芳香四溢的鲜花,行人友善的面孔,都在欢迎着远方客人的到来!

(冬)现在漠河正值冰天雪地,天寒地冻之时,就连呼吸的空气都是清清凉凉的。今天的气温是××℃,因为各位团友是第一次到漠河来,所以一定不太适应这寒冷的天气,所以请大家做好御寒措施,以防冻伤、感冒。漠河的冬季天黑得早,现在车窗外已经看不清什么景色了,但仍有透过寒夜的灯光,为我们照亮漠河的每一条街道,这是欢迎远方客人的序曲,明天大家所看到的,必将是更加美丽的漠河!

现在,我向大家介绍一下这家宾馆。

漠河宾馆位于西林吉镇中华路西侧,1988年建成,是漠河县一家涉外的二星级宾馆。

漠河宾馆占地5 000平方米,建筑面积3 100平方米,共有客房36间,床位118张,无论您入住高档客房还是中、低档客房,都将享受到让您满意的客房服务。漠河宾馆内设大中小餐厅12个,南北特色,东北大菜,只做您想吃的,爱吃的,在别处吃不到的。

漠河宾馆将以一流的服务迎接远方的客人。

我们现在已到达今晚下榻的漠河宾馆,请各位准备下车。

## 7. Songhua River and Sun Island

Ladies and gentlemen, we are going to visit the Harbin Highway Bridge, a channel for traffic between South and North of the Songhua River. The bridge was built on May $10^{th}$, 1983, and completed on August 30, 1986 after three years and four months. It looks like a pair of scissors, cutting the river into two parts. With a length of 1 565 meters, it was the longest road bridge of China at that time. In the 1980s of China, lady was always regarded as a tailor at home, and it is said that the scissors-shape bridge comes from a female designer. The bridge indeed looks like gardener's scissors, trimming the river more fascinating.

Now, let's see through the window. The river under us is the Songhua River. The river rises in Nenjiang River in north, and has its southern headstream in Baitou Mountain of the Changbaishan Mountains. The streams flow from Tianchi, lakes on top of Changbaishan Mountains, which looks like river coming down from the clouds. Thus, the ancient nationality Nvzhen calls it Songgagda, meaning a river from heaven. Later according to the similar pronunciation, it was translated into the Songhua River. The Songhua River is 1 840 kilometers long, flowing through Heilongjiang province and Jilin Province, and empties into the Heilongjiang River in Tongjiang City of Heilongjiang province. The Songhua River is the largest branch of the Heilongjiang River, and covers a drainage length of 117 kilometers in Harbin downtown, navigable for 200 days a year. It is the third largest inland river for its navigation capacity, and ships of 2 000-ton displacement can run through safely. Harbin Port, located in Daowai District, is the largest port along the Songhua River. In summer, the river becomes an ideal swimming area. There are yachts and passenger ships shuttling in the river, corresponding with visitors and colorful tents on the riverside. The sands are soft in the riverbank, and visitors pitch camping tents which keep themselves away from city noises, making a separating paradise to enjoy the peaceful and quiet natural world.

Have you heard a story about the pine tree which fruits but never blossoms. Now let me tell you the reason in folk legend. It is said that in the area of Heilongjiang province, there is a white dragon always making troubles and bringing disasters to the people. One day, a black dragon with sense of justice decides to get rid of it for people's sake and he makes a life-and-death struggle with it under the support of the public. When the white spray appears, people throw stones into the river, because it means the white dragon is on the upper position. When the river turns to black, people will throw some food for the black dragon to keep strength. Finally, the white dragon is completely tired and runs away. From then on, people live in a favorable climate weathers and have good harvests. In order to commemorate the hero dragon, people names that river Heilongjiang, black dragon river in Chinese.

However, the white dragon doesn't mend his wrong way and still makes troubles in other places. So, the black dragon continues to pursue him along another river, beside which there are full of pine trees with white flowers. The white learns from his last failed experience and scouts in the sky, as when the black dragon arrives, the river turns black. Therefore, the white attacks on him when he is weak and escapes when he is energetic. As a result, the black dragon is totally exhausted and can't fight with the white. In order to help the black dragon, the white pine flowers beside the river fall on the river to cover his track. Thus, the white can't trace the black dragon, and confuses about what happened. At the moment, the black dragon strikes back and finally wins this battle. The white dragon escapes in Wudalianchi, and never comes out from then on. After that, everything goes well except for the pine trees, which can not blossom any more. As to commemorate the brave pine flowers, people called the river Songhua River, which means a river of pine flowers. Of course, it is just a happy story and contradicts with the Songgagda we have introduced before. This legend just wants to tell an old truth, the good one will finally prevail.

Next we will visit Sun Island. There is a famous Chinese song named On the Sun Island, just to describe it. Sun Island is situated on the north bank of Songhuajiang River, seeing downtown across the river, and occupies 380 000 square kilometers on the whole. Several years ago, bream is rich in this island, and bream in ancient Chinese language Nvzhen called Taiyian, similar with the pronunciation of sun in Chinese. As time goes by, it has its today's name—Sun Island. The island is embosomed in water, and it is a popular summer resort. The main place we visit in Sun Island is Sun Island Park, which has more than 300 000 trees of 100 varieties, such as pinus, sylvestris, larch, poplar, willow, elm, and so on. In the park, the total area is 114 hectares, including Shuigeyuntian, the house of teens, waterside pavilion, the theme park of Japan, etc. In Shuigeyuntian, you will see lots of architectures in European style and you can see the whole landscape in different positions. During the ice and snow festival of Harbin, the international and national snow sculpture matches are held here once a year.

Made of snow, snow sculpture is carved into various images. It is a work of art. A complete snow sculpture should go through two processes, carving and modeling. Its producing environment should be below zero degree, and snow and water are used to create lots of wonderful sculptures. In China, snow sculpture was developed in early 1960s, and the first snow sculpture match was held in the Sun Island in January 1988. After that, this match is held once a year and it attracts many people to visit here.

In summer, it is also a place with beautiful lakes and mountains, especially the sino-Japan friendship park. It is a garden within garden which is built to commemorate the tenth anniversary for Xinxi of Japan and Harbin to be sister cities. It is a typical Japanese style park, and opened in September 1989, attracting 150 000 visitors each year.

Now, we will see one of the most famous tourist attractions in Harbin, the Sun Island. When people talk about Sun Island, they always think of the island in early times. A few hundred years ago, Harbin was just a small fishing village, with abundant headwaters and rich aquatic products. After Songhua River flew year by year, there was a large sandbank on the north bank. In this primitive land, which combined hills, marshes, grasslands, reed ponds and bushes, it also had several crisscross continental rivers. In springs and summers, it is a natural paradise of plants and animals, green grass carpeting the ground, bushes everywhere, and flowers blooming accompanied by birds' clear singing. This is the primitive Sun Island, and at that time, there wasn't people living there for long. While in fishing seasons, some fishermen would put up small sheds to fish breams and lived there three or five days. It is said that there was an official fishery at ancient times, and in fishing seasons, there would be some small colorful flags on fishing boats. The river was covered with boats in the daytime, while in the night, fishermen got together on the island, with their boats on the bank.

The history of Sun Island could date back to 300 years ago. In 1683, the island had ever been used to be the navy's camp in Qing Dynasty. At that time, the island includes not only this small beach, but also the primitive land around. In Qing Dynasty, this area was in the jurisdiction of governor in Hulan of Heilongjiang province, and produced pearls and fishes especially for the emperor. According to the historical shipping materials of Heilongjiang, Emperor Kang Xi, a great emperor of Qing Dynasty, built a series of navy along its borders, and being a fortress of northeast that was always invaded by others. Heilongjiang owned a navy division, including four battalions such as Qiqihar, Bayan, Songhuajiang, and Hulan. The battalions paraded on Heilongjiang, Songhuajiang and Nenjiang river valley, and Hulan battalion's location was in the area of Sun Island. As for the military power, Hulan Navy with 180 soldiers was just a middle sized one, much smaller than Qiqihar. However, it was treasured by the government because of its well-trained soldiers, well equipped weapons, and brave spirit. The villages all around Sun Island were very poor except in Hulan, the county government's location, but it was very bustling because of ships' moving and soldiers' passing. In 1690, Hulan Navy went along the Songhua River to attack the strong Yakesas, who often invaded our border and grabbed villagers' possession. In this battle, Yakasa's provincial castle was captured, which made Hulan Navy well-known. This is the earliest prosperity of Sun Island.

In the late period of Qing Dynasty, the government was corrupt and incompetent. After being defeated in the Sino-Japanese War of 1894–1895, Qing Government was forced to sign an unfair treaty with tsarist Russia, which gave tsarist Russia the legal right to build railway in the east of China. In 1898, tsarist Russia's railway project started in the small fishing village along the Songhua River. With the building of railway, the village gradually changed into the city we are living now.

The construction of railway brought many Russians to Harbin. When they found it peaceful and secluded, the young Russians treated it as a place of love and romance. They dated here and bathed in the river. In historical records, the water police ever forbaded bathing in the river for its bad influence to the morals. However, the island was full of bushes and it had a wavy terrain, making a good environment to hide. Besides this, most Russians were good at swimming, so the forbiddance didn't effect, and vice versa. With more and more people coming here, it became a summer resort. People drank beer and sang Russian folk songs, enjoying themselves in the foreign land. Because of the beautiful scenery and improving infrastructure, there were more and more villas built by foreigners. We will see some European buildings later, which were built then.

With increasing tourists, Sun Island became a cherished paradise of water sports. In the 1920s, Russians organized some water races between Sun Island and the south bank, including sailing boat, Canadian single, and motorboat that just rose in Europe and America. You would always see the sailing boat racing and Russian girls surfing on the motorboats. Until 1930s, thousands of people spent their summer holidays on the bank and made renting boat a profitable occupation. In winter, the most convenient vehicle in Sun Island was sledge and sitting on sledge to spend holiday in Sun Island was not only the most fashionable way of life but also a symbol of status. It was a regional enjoyment when you sat on the sledge galloping across the frozen river and felt the cold wind passed by.

As the saying goes, he that lives with cripples learns to limp. Russians had lived in Harbin for more than 20 years and the remains they left contained a romantic sense of petty bourgeois, which retained until now. Though suffering from wars, natural disasters, and the Great Cultural Revolution, people never forgot to bring bread, sausages, and beer to enjoy the primitive beauty of the island at weekends. After years, the island has changed, but I still remember it now. Trees behind trees, and jungles after jungles, waved a boundless stretch of green, making you a part of nature. If you came here in May, you would experience the lilacs' sweet fulfilling the whole island and even wafting across the river. Sometimes, you would see an ancient Russian villa standing in lilacs, mysterious and beautiful, adding the finishing touch of a painting. Besides, the sand beach was clean and soft, with the golden and shining sand stretching over the whole island. The song of On the Sun Island just describes the original island and the real life in Harbin. People in Harbin live in a happy and harmony atmosphere with clear sky, blue water, green trees, fertile grassland, river fishes, small shrimps, wild hare and ducks, making up a distinctive character of loving life and nature.

However, in a period of time, tourists became disappointed to Sun Island. I guess it is because the primitive environment was destroyed. At that moment, there were too many visitors coming here with admiration, but we didn't have enough awareness of protecting the environment, plus the excessive manmade construction in later period, resulting in Sun Island an undeserved reputation. But this condition didn't last too long, the rebuilding program of Sun Island Scenic Spot started in the spring of 2003 and ended five years later. The government of Harbin invested much capital in the program, and determined to improve it by employing all means available. Therefore, the Sun Island in our sight now is the one after rebuilding. You won't believe the rumor that one will regret after visiting Sun Island after you visit her.

In the history, the name of Sun Island is originated from the ancient name of bream, which was abounded in the Songhua River near the Sun Island. Of course, there is also another story among people. It is said that the sun-god had ever lived in the island and the children could play with him everyday. Thus, it was called the Sun Island.

Now we have seen a big stone which is called the Sun Stone. Carved with name of the island, it is the first spot of Sun Island Scenic Spot. The stone is 7.5 meters long and 2.6 meters wide with a heavy weight of 150 tons, and it is the typical symbol of the island. The stone was not on the island at the beginning. It has an extraordinary historical background. It was found upstream of Ashi River in Acheng city. In ancient China, the army of Nvzhen nationality would have a military conference before fighting, and they always used branch to draw the marching route on sand, then erased it. The big stone was found in the place where the first emperor of Jin Dynasty drawing their marching route to the Huanghe River valley. In the period of the war with Japan, the place was the rest area of famous general Li Zhaolin and the lyric of the song of camping also was accomplished here. Moreover, the stone was used to observe the weather. People said that if the color of stone was bright, tomorrow would be a sunny day; if it was gloomy, the weather would be overcast; if there were some drops of water, it would rain; and if it was frosted, it would snow. Now, let's see the words on the stone. The three Chinese words were written by the famous calligrapher Zhao Puchu in 1984, vigorous and forceful, vivid and intangible, making the stone a more legendary existence. When you go through the Sun Stone, you will see the Gate of Sun, designed by Chinese and Russian designers. Its designing theme is the window of sun, meaning to see sunrise and sunset through the gate. With white-spray typed decoration stretching from both grounds, the gate is designed 74 meters long and 12.5 meters high. In front of it, you will see the imitated blocks drawn on the ground, having a moral of visitors going across home, Songhua River and beaches to step on the Sun Island. The whole design is coordinated with the metaphor of sun, shining place and rising from the east.

Entering the scenic spot, you will see a huge plant sculpture which is 6 meters high and occupies 60 square meters. Three dragons look up at the sky as if they will roar to fly, establishing the regional character and historical culture. Then, it's the Center of Flowers and Plants. Divided into 12 parts, it provides tourists with different gardens of constellation. You can walk clockwise and find your own garden of constellation according to your birthday. Now, the Art Exhibition Center of Ice and Snow is on our eyes. Founded in 2000, it is the world largest inner exhibition center of this area. You could image that the outside is hot to sweat, and inside is all covered with ice and snow sculptures, becoming a superior enjoyment in the north. Situated in the west of Sun Island Scenic Spot, this wide land is the Deer Garden. There are over 30 domesticated sika deer bred here freely, together with wooden ropeways, floating bridges, single-plank bridges, and playing wooden barrels. It is children's favorite place because they could also play slide, swing, and maze here. The Center of Deer Culture is also situated here. Next is the Garden of Lilacs. The garden was built in 1996 with various kinds of lilacs, and lilac is also the city flower of Harbin. There are also some Russian spots, such as the Russia Style town, the Russian Royal Golden Theatre, and the Russian Art Exhibition Center. Situated in the northeast, it is the largest private collection center in China. The Gallery of Yu Zhixue is the first individual gallery of Harbin, and Mr. Yu is the founder of ice and snow landscape painting. The Northern Folk Art Gallery is raised and built by Mr. Liu Hengfu, the youth photographer and national industrial artist. These works of art are about one thousand which are all made by him. In the following, we will see the Northern Culture Art Exhibition Hall, the Gallery of Sun Island, and the Sculpture Land of Yu Qingcheng. This mysterious place is the Squirrel Island, situated in the north and having more than 1 600 domesticated squirrels. This is the Swan Lake, also north of the garden, gathering many kinds of swimming birds, including black swan, whooper swan, cygnet, mandarin duck, mallard, swan goose, and graylag. In the map of China, Heilongjiang is just like a flying swan, and Harbin is the pearl on her neck, glittering with its attractive light.

## 松花江及太阳岛

各位朋友,下面我们要去哈尔滨市太阳岛参观浏览松花江公路大桥,公路大桥是赴太阳岛的陆路通道,松花江公路大桥建于1983年5月10日,建成于1986年8月30日竣工,历时三年零四个月,大桥呈剪子形状,给人以若大个松花江被一刀剪断之感,大桥全长1 565米,当时为全国公路桥之最。这座桥的设计者是一位女士,当时人们说女人总是喜欢剪剪裁裁,所以设计成剪刀形状,它的确好似园丁手中的剪刀一样,把松花江秀丽风景修剪得更加迷人。

大家往车窗两侧看,下面就是松花江,松花江有南北两源,北源嫩江,南源是第二松花江的源头,发源于长白山脉的白头山,因水流顺天池飞腾而下,似从天降,女真人称它为"松嘎里乌拉",意思为"天河",后来演变成"松花江"。松花江全长1 840公里,流经吉林、黑龙江两省,在我省的同江境内注入黑龙江。松花江是黑龙江流域最大的支流,流经哈尔滨市区117公里,年通航期可达200天,能通过2 000吨位的船舶,它是中国内河航运的第三大河流,位于道外区的哈尔滨港是松花江上最大的中心港。夏季的松花江是理想的天然浴场。江中游艇、客船穿梭行驶,岸边红篷绿顶、游人如织。细软的江畔沙滩上,一排排旅游账篷是旅游者躲避城市喧器,感受大自然恬然宁静的理想乐园。

  大家有没有听过松树不开花就结果的故事呢?现在我给大家讲松树不开花就结果的民间传说。相传在黑龙江地区有一条白龙总是兴风作浪,造灾于民,一只来自关内的一条富有正义感的黑龙决心为民除害,就在当地民众的大力支持下与白龙在江中展开了生死搏斗。当江水翻白色浪花时表明白龙在上,两岸的老百姓就扔石头砸,当江水变黑时,表明黑龙在上,老百姓就往江里扔馒头以便补充实力,结果筋疲力尽的白龙被打走了,然后风调雨顺,连年丰收,当地百姓为了纪念富有正义感的黑龙,就把那条江命名为黑龙江。

  可落荒而逃的白龙还是好比腊月的大葱——皮干叶枯心不死,它又在别处兴风作浪,连续作恶,于是黑龙又沿着另一条江开始追剿,这条江的两岸长满了松树,那时的松树是开花的,并且是雪白的花。"吃一堑,长一智"的白龙闻讯后就腾云驾雾到了高空侦察,不巧黑龙游到哪里,哪里的江水就变成黑色,所以就暴露了目标,于是白龙就采取了"避其锋芒,击其惰归"的战术,当黑龙疲惫不堪的时候连连出击打得黑龙防不胜防,只有招架之势,无还手之力。于是为了掩护黑龙的"军事"行为,这条江两岸盛开的白皑皑的松树花就纷纷落在江面上,罩得严严实实,黑龙有了松树花的掩盖,白龙就再也无法掌握黑龙的行踪,最后黑龙"出其不意,攻其不备",取得了决定性胜利,一败涂地的白龙一头扎进了五大连池再也不敢出来了。从那以后黑龙江地区就年年五谷丰登、国泰民安了。可是松树却从此再也不能开花了,为了纪念为正义之战作出巨大牺牲的松树花,人们把这条江命名为松花江。当然这是个美丽的传说,因为它和我们前面说的满语"松戈里乌拉"是相矛盾的,但这个寄予了古代劳动人民美好愿望的传说却告诉我们一个道理,正义终究会战胜邪恶。

  下面我们即将看到的就是太阳岛,大家一定听过郑绪岚的《太阳岛上》吧!太阳岛位于松花江北岸,与市区仅一江之隔,总面积达 38 万平方公里,很多年以前,这个岛屿盛产鳊花鱼,女真族鳊花鱼的发音是"太宜安",所以这个岛就被人称为太宜安,久传至今被称为太阳岛。太阳岛四面环水,是著名的避暑胜地,我们到了太阳岛上,主要参观太阳岛公园,在公园里树木茂密,全岛遍植各种树木 100 种 30 多万株,树种有江松、樟子松、落叶松、杨树、柳树、榆树,还有丁香等。整个公园面积是 114 公顷,园内建有水阁云天、青年之家、水榭、哈尔滨中日友谊园等游乐场所,一幢幢别墅式的建筑隐现在树丛中富有浓厚的欧式情调的"水阁云天"是园中之园,园内有长廊、方阁、荷花湖、太阳湖、太阳山和瀑布,平台遥望可以观赏到不同角度的岛上风景,冰雪节期间,还在此举行每年一次的国际及国内雪雕比赛。

  雪雕也叫雪像,它是以雪为材料雕出千姿百态,异彩纷呈的各种不同形状的艺术形象以供人们观赏和娱乐,他有两种表现形式,即雕和塑,雪雕则是选用雪和水进行塑造,在 0 ℃以下将雪和水搅和后,通过冻结黏合,可以塑造各种形态,创造出不同的艺术形象。我国的雪雕艺术活动是 20 世纪 60 年代初期发展起来的,1988 年 1 月在太阳岛公园组织了首届群众雪雕比赛,以后每年举办一届吸引日益众多的中外游客。

  夏天的时候这里湖光山色,其中中日友谊园是园中园,全名哈尔滨新潟友谊园,是哈尔滨和日本的新潟市建立友好城市十周年之际,在太阳岛公园内部投资修建的日式庭院风格的友谊园。在1989年9月正式对外开放,每年接待中外宾客达十五万左右。

　　我们接下来要参观的就是哈尔滨最负盛名的一个景点——太阳岛。

　　不过现在说起太阳岛,外地人也好,哈尔滨当地人也好,最最怀念的,还是早年的那个太阳岛。几百年以前,在哈尔滨还是一个小渔村时,这里就水源充沛,渔产丰厚。滚滚流经的松花江,在北岸围成一片不小的沙洲,由丘陵、沼泽、草原、苇塘、灌木组成的这片原始荒原,内有纵横交错的旱河,每当春夏季节,芳草茂盛,灌木丛生,山花野草,伴着清脆鸟鸣,一派自然风光。这就是沉睡了几千年而后被人们日渐关注的早年的太阳岛。那时,作为江中的一个小岛,并没有居民在岛上居住。因为太阳岛附近盛产鳊花鱼,渔民们自然会时常来这里打鱼,偶尔也会到岛上晒渔网。鱼汛期,顶多会有几户人家在这里搭个小马架,住上三天五夜。据传说,太阳岛江面曾是一个官渔场,每到捕鱼旺季,江面就出现了繁忙的捕鱼景象,渔船插有小旗,旗色各不相同。白天,大小渔船布满江面;夜间,岸边的渔船排列如织,渔民聚集到这里过夜,颇有渔家生活的味道。

　　太阳岛最早的史料记载要追溯到300多年前,早在公元1683年,太阳岛一带就曾经被清朝时的康熙帝国作为水师营地开发利用过。不过,那时的太阳岛并非只是这片小沙滩,它还包括与这片沙滩相邻的一片原始荒原。在清代,太阳岛是由黑龙江呼兰副都统管辖,当时,这里生产贡珠、贡鱼,曾被清廷封禁200余年。据黑龙江航运史料记载,为抵御外敌,康熙皇帝从南到北建立水师。黑龙江省地处东北要塞,外力的骚扰相当频繁,康熙皇帝决定在黑龙江建立水师,这个水师统辖齐齐哈尔、巴彦、松花江、呼兰四个水师营。这四个水师营分别活动在黑龙江、松花江和嫩江流域,其中,呼兰水师营的营地就在太阳岛一带,归呼兰府管属,指挥权直接归黑龙江水师。从军事力量方面说,呼兰水师营属中等规模的一个水师营,共有水师兵丁180多人,比齐齐哈尔水师营的人数少得多。但这个水师营训练有素,装备精良,作战十分勇敢,深得朝廷的赞赏,那时,除了呼兰是府县的所在地外,太阳岛四周都是十分贫穷的渔村。而太阳岛因为是水师营的营地,舰船来来往往,军人进进出出,显得十分热闹。康熙二十八年(1690年),为了平息外力的入侵,呼兰水师营奉命从太阳岛出发,开着舰船顺松花江而下,入黑龙江后溯流而上,攻打当时经常称霸一方、掠夺我边民财产、骚扰我国北方边境的雅克萨人。这一役大获全胜,一举攻克了雅克萨人的省府克萨城堡。呼兰水师营的营地也声名鹊起。这可以说是太阳岛最早的繁荣。

　　那么到了清朝后期,清政府变得腐朽而无能,尤其在中日甲午战争失败后,沙俄威逼利诱清政府与之签订了所谓的《中俄御敌互相援助条约》,这个条约的签订使沙俄取得了在中国东省境内修筑铁路的合法权利。1898年,沙俄的铁路工程局开进了松花江边的这个小渔村,开始修筑中东铁路,随着中东铁路的修建,这个小渔村变成了我们今天所在的城市——哈尔滨。

　　随着中东铁路的建设,大量的俄罗斯人涌入了哈尔滨,当时太阳岛上灌木丛生,十分幽静,一些俄罗斯青年男女发现了这一远离喧嚣的"世外桃源",纷纷在休闲时间来到这里,伴着江风与绿草、树荫谈情示爱。渐渐地,这里竟成了俄罗斯男女幽会的场所。据记载,当时的特区水上警察,还以有伤风化为由进行过取缔,但是岛上灌木丛生,地势起伏不平,处处可以藏身,加上俄罗斯侨民大都精通水性,水上警察也无可奈何。取缔不但未见成效,到太阳岛野浴的人反而越来越多,后来逐步发展成为盛夏季节游人游泳避暑的旅游胜地。俄侨男女争往这片小岛沐浴、戏水,并有卖饮料食品的凉棚。人们喝着啤酒,唱着俄罗斯民歌,如醉如痴地体验着异国的乡野情趣。正因为太阳岛景色宜人,再加上商业等服务设施相继建成,越来越多的各国侨民到太阳岛建别墅,等一下我们到了岛上之后所看到的欧式建筑便都是那时留下的。

随着游人增多,太阳岛成为人们进行丰富水上运动的场所。早在20世纪20年代,俄国人就开始在太阳岛和松花江南岸之间进行帆船比赛、单人划艇比赛等水上运动,尤其帆船比赛成为松花江上夏日一景。当时刚刚在欧美兴起的摩托艇滑水运动也迅速传入哈尔滨,在太阳岛畔,经常可以看见俄国姑娘乘摩托艇滑水冲浪的景观。到20世纪30年代,夏天每逢节假日,到太阳岛野浴的人已达万人之多。夏季出入太阳岛,没船不行,出租舢板般便是当时很好的谋生手段。而到了冬季,人拉的冰爬犁是当时出入太阳岛最便捷的交通工具,乘坐在冰爬犁上前往太阳岛度假不仅是当时最时尚的事,更是乘坐者身份的一种象征。那么坐着爬犁,听着耳边呼啸而过的寒风,驰骋在冰冻的江面上奔向太阳岛,仅过程来说便是一种别样的情趣。

那么俗话说得好:"近朱者赤,近墨者黑。"俄罗斯人在哈尔滨只不过停留了二十多年的光景,但他们在给哈尔滨人留下的事物中,却多了一种浪漫的"小资"情调。于是,在俄国势力从哈尔滨消退之后,尽管这里又经历了诸如战争、自然灾害、"文化大革命"等的浩劫,但是,这里的人们却从没有忘记在节假日的时候,带上面包、红肠、啤酒……带上亲朋好友,大家结伴来到岛上,共同享受那原始的、生态的美。尽管这种美只能留在我童年的记忆中,但我至今也不能忘记,那时上得岛来,大树连着大树,丛林接着丛林,摇摇曳曳,一望无际。站在其中,天、地、人浑然一体。如果五月到这里来,丁香的芬芳便笼罩着整个太阳岛,整整一个月,那股幽香悄悄地向江面飘散过去。偶尔会有一幢童话般古朴的俄罗斯小别墅从丁香丛里显露出来,画龙点睛似地神秘而又美丽……还有沙滩,绵延数里绕着小岛,那沙滩特别干净,而且是金黄金黄的,阳光一照,好像金子铺就的一般,你都舍不得伸脚去踏碎它。大家所熟悉的《太阳岛上》那首歌描绘的正是那种原生原态的太阳岛,也是我们哈尔滨人原生原态的生活写照,没有任何雕饰,没有任何浮夸。因为我们哈尔滨人就是这样和太阳岛的蓝天、碧水、树林、草地、江鱼、小虾、野兔、野鸭……一起快乐而和谐地相处着,形成了哈尔滨人热爱生活、热爱大自然的本色。

但是不知从什么时候起,大家对太阳岛流露出了越来越多的失望,我想是因为慕名而来的人太多,我们的保护措施又不当,便破坏了太阳岛的原始美,加上后期对太阳岛的开发人工的痕迹太重,所以使得太阳岛落下了"名不符实"的名声。不过,哈尔滨市政府已经决定要投入大资金、运用大手笔对太阳岛进行改造,而且,太阳岛风景区的改造工程已经在2003年的春天正式启动!所以,我们今天看到的太阳岛是经过初步改造后的太阳岛,整个改造工程持续到2008年,相信您接下来看到的太阳岛,肯定不会说像"到哈尔滨不到太阳岛很遗憾,到了太阳岛会更遗憾"之类的话。

关于太阳岛名称的起源有两种美丽的传说：一种是人们传说岛上曾有过太阳公公住过的房子，连岛上的孩子，天天都能同太阳公公一同玩耍，由此得名太阳岛；另一种流行的传说是，太阳岛附近水域盛产松花江"三花五罗"之一的鳊花鱼，当地的满族人称鳊花鱼为"太要恩"，其音与太阳发音十分相近，久沿成俗，人们在太阳后面加一个岛字，便泛指今天松花江北岸的这片岛屿了。

现在我们看到的这块上有"太阳岛"三个大字的石头便是岛上的第一景了，它叫作太阳石。这块石长 7.5 米，高 4.3 米，宽 2.6 米，重达 150 吨，是太阳岛上颇具灵性的标志物。不过它并不是岛上的石头，据说这块石头的来历不同寻常，它是阿城市阿什河上游发现的，而且发现它的地方，正是当年金太祖完颜阿骨打逐鹿中原时"画灰而议"（当时金人作战之前高级将领的军事会议，灰土当纸，以树枝做笔勾勒进军线路图，会后将灰一抹不留痕迹）的地方。抗日战争时期李兆麟将军也曾在发现这块石头的地方休息，著名的《露营之歌》"荒原水畔战马鸣""敌垒频惊骊不前"的歌词就是在这块石头上写成的。而且这块石头非常有灵性，在它没有被运到这里之前，当地的老百姓以其观天象，便可知阴晴冷暖，据说在傍晚时分，如果石头色泽光亮，第二天则晴；石头色泽晦暗，第二天则阴；如果石头挂水珠，第二天则雨；如果挂霜，第二天则雪。而太阳石上"太阳岛"三个字是由著名书法家赵朴初先生于 1984 年为哈尔滨日报太阳文学副刊题写"太阳岛"刊头时所书，字迹苍劲有力，空灵传神，也为这块巨石增添了凝重的色彩。而在太阳石后面，便是由中俄设计师联合设计的太阳岛大门"太阳之门"。太阳之门的创意主题为"太阳的窗口"，也就是说，透过大门能看到日出和日落。大门总长 74 米，主门高 12.5 米，门旁涌起的曲线形如白色浪花，大门前的地面设计有模拟街区图，象征着游人越过大地、松花江和沙滩，登上太阳岛。整个设计与太阳含有的"阳光明媚的地方"、"朝日在东方升起"的深意吻合。

进入到风景区，一座高 6 米，占地 60 平方米的大型立体花坛展现在游人眼前。三条巨龙翘首苍穹，啸吟欲飞，既展示着深厚的地域文化特色，也显示着文化渊源之所在。接下来是花卉馆。花卉馆按照黄道十二宫划分为 12 个花苑，游客可以根据自己的生日，由北至南，按顺时针方向行走，即可找到自己所属星座的花苑。现在我们看到的是冰雪艺术馆，冰雪艺术馆建于 2000 年，是目前世界上规模最大的室内冰雪艺术场馆。填补了哈尔滨三季看不到冰雪的空白。室外夏日炎炎、室内冰天雪地，堪称是超时代的享受，也是北国一大奇观。这篇开阔的花园就是鹿苑。鹿苑位于太阳岛风景区西部，岛内放养着人工驯养的梅花鹿 30 余只，木结构的索道、浮桥、独木桥和钻筒连成一体，滑梯、秋千、迷宫等会将孩子们带入童话般世界。鹿文化展馆也位于此地。下面是丁香园，丁香园建于 1996 年，及众多品种于一体，而丁香花同时也是哈尔滨市市花。俄罗斯艺术展览馆位于公园内东北部，是目前我国最大的私人（刘明秀）收藏展览馆。除此之外，我们还将看到极具俄式特色的俄罗斯风情小镇和俄罗斯皇家金色剧院。于志学美术馆是哈尔滨市第一座个人美术馆，于志学先生是冰雪山水画创始人。汇集了近千件艺术品的北方民艺精品馆是由我省年轻的摄影家、国家级工艺美术师刘恒甫自筹资金建立的,院内展品皆出自他一人之手。下面我们还将参观北方文化艺术馆、太阳岛美术馆,以及于庆成雕塑园。这片神秘的地方就是松鼠岛了,松鼠岛位于太阳岛风景区围堤内北部,散养着人工驯化的松鼠1 600余只。这就是天鹅湖了,天鹅湖位于太阳岛公园北部,散养着黑天鹅、大天鹅、小天鹅、鸳鸯、绿头鸭、鸿雁、灰雁等游禽。在中华人民共和国的版图上,黑龙江犹如一只展翅翱翔的天鹅,妩媚多姿,哈尔滨就是这天鹅项下一颗璀璨的明珠,闪闪发光。

## 8. Heilongjiang Northeast Tiger Park

Now, we will visit the Northeast Tiger Park which is the largest base for wild Siberian tigers' artificial feeding and propagation around the world.

With an area of 1 440 000 square meters, the park is located on the north bank of the Songhua River in the northwest of Harbin, neighboring the Sun Island Park. You can take the No. 85 bus to the park. There are over 300 pure bred Northeast tigers with different ages here. The park enjoys a favorable foundation for ecotourism and splendid scenery and it is an ideal place for holiday and leisure. In the park, you will enjoy the fresh air, and the aroma of earth and grass. Since its opening-up in 1996, the park has attracted more than 1 800 000 tourists from home and abroad.

The park is built to protect, study and raise the Northeast tiger. Through a variety of wild training, the Northeast tiger would restore their wild nature and independent viability of wildlife. Then these tigers will be sent back to the wild in order to increase their population in the wild.

The large park is divided into five areas, including the young tiger area, the raising tiger area, the mature tiger area, the African loin area and a walking area. The entire journey will take approximately one hour. 15 luxurious and comfortable tourist cars are available in the park. You can see the trace of tigers and enjoy their elegant demeanour in car.

There are 30 variegated Northeast tigers in the mature tiger area. Such large population of the Northeast tigers can not be seen in other places. Unlike common zoos, the Northeast Tiger Park exchanges the roles between visitors and animals. The tourists take the bus to visit the scenic spots while the tigers roam freely in the fields. In addition to viewing the tigers walking leisurely in the open-air, visitors can buy poultry or animals to feed them, including ducks, chickens, and even cows. The staff will help visitors bring the animals to the tiger group, and the visitors will see the unique scene that tigers hunt in packs.

Now I will introduce the characteristics of the Northeast tiger. The Northeast tiger, also known as Amur tiger, Ussuri tiger, and Changbai Mountain tiger, is a tiger subspecies inhabiting mainly the mountain region in the east of Heilongjiang province, Changbai Mountain area in Jilin Province and Northeast region in Russia. The Northeast tigers are huge and possess imposing body frame.

There is an old saying that the tigers live in the remote mountains and virgin forests. The wild Northeast tigers prefer to live a solitary life and have large territories; some of these areas cover from 30 to 100 square kilometers. They primarily eat large mammals, such as deer and wild boar. When they find their prey, they will attack them swiftly and violently. Due to their excellent springing capacity and strong explosive force, when the tigers prey on huge animals, they will spring at their prey with their fore paws and then kill them with bites. Generally, the Northeast tigers are inactive during the daytime. After eating, they will hide themselves in the depths of the forest or the high mountains to have a sleep; however, they still look around from time to time for fear of hunters or the other enemies' invasion. Moreover, the male Northeast tigers would delimit their own territory by leaving urine deposits to warn other tigers. But if the tigresses pass by, they will be friendly and send them out of their territory. Even the tigress cannot stay in their territory.

For raising the quality of the species and evoking the Northeast tigers' wild instinct, the park has offered a series of wild training. At first the cubs will improve their bounce ability by catching chicken and rabbit, and then learn to get food by themselves, and gradually they will prey on large animals independently. In addition to the predation training, the wild training also includes the training for hidden capacity, reproductive capacity, and adaptability against harsh natural environment. Currently, the wild training is still in a primary stage, for example, tigress need to give birth to babies in the prepared "delivery room", and before the two years old the cubs need to live in an enclosed 30-square-meter space. However, with their adaptability gradually increasing, they have to return to the park'though unwillingly. The cubs, born after the year of 1998, have got ferocious eye expression and shown the desire of attacking strangers.

The courtship of Northeast tigers involves a variety of behaviors. When they are in heat period, the male tigers would run in the mountains and forests and roar loudly in order to attract the female tigers. The female tigers will make an immediate response to the roar. If they fall in love at first sight, they will wag their tails and heads to express their satisfaction. Then they would run into the higher mountains, chase and play in the open space; sometimes they scratch lightly, bite pretentiously, and hug with each other. After playing for a certain period, they will mate with each other.

However, their "marriage" just ranges from December to March in the following year, mating is frequently in winter, and gestation lasts around three months. The female tiger will typically give birth to cubs in March or April, which can help the cubs pass the winter safely and increase their survival rate. The litter size usually consists of anywhere from 1 to 6 cubs, though 2 to 4 is usually the norm. In the wild, the cubs are often capable hunters by the time they are around 1~2 years old. Females reach sexual maturity at 3~4 years, whereas males reach sexual maturity at 4~5 years. After sexual maturity, the cubs will be driven away by their mother and then make a living by themselves. The female tigers reproduce every 3~5 years in the wild. The natural life-span is around 20~25. In the park, there is a great mother, called "the gorgeous beauty", because she has over 30 children.

In the young tiger area, besides the northeast tigers, lives the white tiger. The white tiger, also named lion-tiger, is a variant of the Bengal tiger. It is a hybrid of male lion and a tigress; therefore, it combines the characteristics of the tiger and lion. It has a lion-like short fur and tiger-like shape and striping pattern.

The gene for white coating is quite common among Bengal tigers, but the natural birth of a white tiger is still a very rare occasion in the wild. In addition, you can see a strange scene that tigers live with dogs. If the mother tiger has no experience of nursing, the keepers will find a dog acting as a wet nurse, which can ensure the healthy growth of the tiger cubs.

Well, we have arrived at the Northeast Tiger Forest Park. We will visit the park in a group, and please do not open the car window and the door during the visit. We will stay here for one hour, and then drive back to the city.

## 黑龙江东北虎林园

游客朋友们,我们现在即将前往游览的景点是东北虎林园。它是哈尔滨市独具特色的旅游景区,也是目前世界上最大的人工饲养、繁育东北虎(又称西伯利亚虎)的基地。

东北虎林园坐落在松花江北岸,与太阳岛毗邻,联运85路公交车直达景区。它占地面积144万平方米,拥有各种不同年龄的纯种东北虎300多只。东北虎林园自然特色十分浓郁,具有良好的生态旅游基础。这里的空气质量优良,到处散发着泥土和野草的芳香,使人充分地享受与自然的融合,是一处旅游、休闲、度假的理想之所。自1996年对外开放以来,东北虎林园以它浓厚的野趣和迷人的魅力吸引着海内外的游人慕名而来,7年来累计接待游客人数达到了180多万人次。

建园的宗旨是在保护、研究、饲养东北虎,再通过种种野生训练,恢复东北虎的野性、本性和野外独立生存能力,最后达到还虎灵性、放虎归山,补充东北虎野生种群的目的。收取门票,提供专用设备供游客观赏,也是以虎养虎的一种手段。

东北虎林园目前建有成虎园、育成虎园、幼虎园、非洲狮园和步行区5个景点,游人需要用1个小时的时间才能游完全程。其中成虎园、育成虎园、幼虎园、非洲狮园需乘车观赏。东北虎林园拥有15台豪华舒适的旅游观光车,人们可以坐在车内去寻觅虎踪,领略东北虎的风采。

园内自然放养着30只斑斓猛虎,数量之多状态之好,堪称世界一流,游人可乘坐专用旅游车辆,漫游于群虎之间,和一般动物园相比,人与虎交换了位置,别有一番情趣,使人油然产生许多遐想……特别值得一提的是,为了对东北虎进行野化训练,园林准备了从鸡到牛的一系列动物。游人可根据自己的喜好和经济情况,选购其中的几种或一种,由工作车投放到虎群之中,那种群虎捕食的场面,绝对是世界上绝无仅有的。当然,这些都要另行收费的。

现在介绍一下东北虎的情况:东北虎又叫满洲虎、西伯利亚虎、乌苏里虎、长白山虎和长毛虎。它们是虎种中形体最大、最健美、最凶猛的一族。主要分布在黑龙江省的东部山区、吉林省的长白山地区及俄罗斯的西伯利亚地区。俗话说:"深山密林有大虎。"野生的成年老虎,都有自己独立的栖息领地,从30公里到100公里不等以满足它的食物来源。东北虎的主食是大型的哺乳动物,如鹿、野猪等。野猪的繁殖速度很快,老虎也在不停地捕杀。老虎见到食物,会以迅雷不及掩耳之势猛冲猛攻,它的弹跳性好,爆发力强,在捕食大的动物时,它会先用利爪扑倒后再下口去撕咬。它白天是不活动的,人们常说"盘龙卧虎",当虎吃饱后,就选一山高林密之处,卧下休息酣睡,而且还不时抬头四望,以防猎人的接近和其他天敌的进犯。东北虎会用自己的尿液来划定自己的领地,以让别的老虎"闻而却步"。但母虎来临,它还是客气,会送它过境但也不许停留。

为了让东北虎重振森林之王的凛凛雄威,虎林园对虎进行了一系列野化训练,幼虎从捕活鸡、活兔开始学习弹跳,训练速度,设法自己填饱肚子,渐渐地再让它们捕食大型动物。虎的野化训练不仅仅是捕食,它们还必须具备隐蔽能力、繁殖能力、对恶劣自然环境的适应能力。目前对虎的野化训练还是初级的,比如说母虎还得到人们给它准备的"产房"生产,小虎2岁前还得到围起来的30平方米的小天地里活动等。但是,经过训练,虎的适应能力不断提高,现在,老虎已经渐渐不愿回窝了。时间最长的已经在野地里生活了8个多月,1998年以后出生的小虎,已经初具凶猛神态,面对生人,已表现出进攻的欲望。

东北虎的择偶性强。一旦发现自己喜欢的对象,会执着追求,每当它们的发情期一到,体质健壮的雄虎,除漫山遍野的奔跑外,还发出极其洪亮的吼声,其目的是呼唤正在发情的雌虎,雌虎会闻声而至,见面后,如"一见钟情、情投意合"时,它们便双双地摇尾巴、摆头表示满意,而后双双奔向山更高、林更密的山间空地上,双双嬉戏,追逐奔跑,又互相轻轻地扑抓、假咬、搂抱,然后进行交配。但是它们的婚姻生活只从12月到次年的3月份左右,在冬季交配,怀孕期是3个月左右,分娩期多在三四月,这样可以使它们的后代能平安过冬,提高了成活率。每胎2~4仔较多,在野外自然的环境里,东北幼虎长到1岁半至2岁时,就能跟母虎捕猎小型动物,4至5岁时,就性成熟了。当小虎性成熟后,母虎就会不时地狠狠地咬它们,赶它们,让它们自食其力地生活。在野外的环境里,东北虎雌虎,要每隔3到5年才能繁殖一次。东北虎的自然寿命是20~25年。虎林园里有位"大美人"是英雄母亲,因为她的子女已超过30只。

另外值得介绍的是在幼虎园里除了东北虎还有变异的白虎。白虎是孟加拉虎基因变异的产物——狮虎,就是雄性狮子和雌性老虎的爱情结晶,它兼有老虎与狮子的特点,体形似老虎,短毛似狮子,身上的花纹像老虎。这当然是人工饲养的结果,自然界中它们是无论如何也结合不到一起的。另外就是我们会看到小老虎和狗在一起的怪现象,这是因为这只狗不是别人而是小老虎的"奶妈"。因为初为"人母"的老虎,没有哺乳的经验,为了让虎宝宝更健康地成长,工作人员就给它们请来了"狗妈妈",这也只能是在人工饲养情况下才能出现的怪现象。也让人认识到狗的伟大。

好了,东北虎林园到了,请大家注意集体行动,参观时不能打开车窗和车门,我们预计在这里逗留1个小时,然后会乘车返回市区。

## 9. The Zhongyang Street

Ladies and gentlemen, we are going to arrive at the Zhongyang Street, and will visit there for an hour. Then we will gather in the parking lot of Songhua River Gloria Plaza Hotel. Our plate number is Hei A12345. Now, let's get off the coach, and take a walk on this hundred-year old street. Don't forget your valuables.

Zhongyang Street measures 1 450 meters from Jingwei Street in the south to the Flood Control Monument in the north. There are 71 European-style or simulated European-style buildings including 13 city-level protected buildings within the 3-li(1 500 meters) street. In 1986, it was granted the protected street by the People's Government of Harbin Municipality.

On June $1^{st}$ 1997, the pedestrian street was officially open to the public. Now the number of commercial stores has been over 700 here. We can find some specialty shops or counters of international brands such as Armani, Dunhill, Louis Vuitton, Rolex and Ports. There are also many international chain brands, KFC and Mcdonaldo's, mingling with some old buildings on this street. After some repaired protected buildings and more recreational space since 2002, the street has been in a beautiful environment. The European-style buildings, European classical streetlights, flowering leisure districts and diversified cultural life have made Zhongyang Street more magnificent. Zhongyang Street—with its special features—has become Harbin's splendid scenery.

In 1994, the city of Harbin gained its reputation as the Famous Historic and Cultural City on National Level. The Zhongyang Street is one of the most prominent streets in Harbin and an image and cultural brand of the whole city. In 2005, this street won the Model Prize of China Habitat Environment from the Ministry of Construction. In 2006, it got one of the Harbin the Ten Big city card from the Government of the Harbin Municipality. The street won the title for the Famous Street of First China's History and Culture in the first appraising, which was hosted by Chinese Culture Newspaper, Chinese National Culture Promotion Association and Chinese cultural relic newspaper at the approval of the Ministry of Culture and the State Administration of Cultural Heritage in 2010.

### The Origin of Zhongyang Street

Just like Harbin City, Zhongyang Street came into being with the construction of the Middle East Railway. Then on July $14^{th}$ 1903, from Manchuria to Suifenhe with Harbin as the center, the Binzhou line and Bin Sui line opened to traffic. Before long, the construction of the railway from Harbin to Dalian made Harbin become hub of Chinese Eastern Railway. From then on, Harbin officially began to develop as an international metropolis with a very strong colonial style. As a result, a mass of big powers, rich people and foreign residents came to Harbin for robbery, trade and shelter, while Zhongyang Street turned into a prosperous area for international commercial and trade and foreign settlers from a shipping cargoes passageway. At that time foreign settlers in Harbin were actually accounted for more than half of the urban population. Different cultures in different periods display on the street and impress us with the architectural culture.

In June 1898, thousands of railway workers from Shandong and Hebei province settled in vicinity of Central Street when the Chinese Eastern Railway started to be built in Harbin. They made mud into walls and turned grass into sheds. Therefore this street owned its original name—China Street. And in 1925, Chinese government renamed Zhongyang Street from China Street after with drawing the power of Harbin's municipal management. Then during the period of Culture Revolution in 1968, Zhongyang Street again renamed Fangxiu Street and regained the title of Zhongyang Street until 1976. The old weather-beaten street witnessed century of vicissitudes and the rise and fall of Harbin as a witness to history.

**The square stones road on Zhongyang Street**

In 1924, Zhongyang Street was floored with square stones according to a Russian engineer's design and supervision. It is interesting that the size of these granite stones in the road is all 18 cm long, 10 cm wide, exactly the same shape and size as Russian bread. When you first visit here, you've never imagined this used to be a huge project. For some reasons, the railway workers had to do much more than we've expected, for example, digging 3 meters down out of loosened sandy soil and putting them into thick roadbed paved by many large rocks. It is said that one square stone was worth one dollar (silver) which was much enough to buy one month's food for one adult. It is really a road paved with gold. Now everyone, when visit, I'm going to introduce the street's architectural features.

**Architectural style**

The special historical conditions created a unique style of the city. Zhongyang Street only took two or three decades to form an architectural style which cost the westerners for centuries. At that time, Zhongyang Street was a famous street in Far East.

The distinct street contains the most influencing four architecture genres, covers the most charming literature phylogeny of 300 years of Europe, including Renaissance style in $16^{th}$ century, Baroque style in $17^{th}$ century, Eclectic style in $18^{th}$ century and Art Nouveau style in $19^{th}$ century. And then Zhongyang Street became a real "Architecture Art Gallery" in China. For this reason, Central Street became cultural center of Far East, Europe and America and was compared with Regent Street in London, the Champs Elysees in Paris, the Unter den Linden in Berlin, Tokyo's Ginza

Street, Nanjing Road in Shanghai, and Tianjin, Victoria Street.

If you are walking on the Zhongyang Street, it seems you are entering into a foreign country. At the end of this street, we can see the Flood Control Monument built by Harbin people commemorating heroes who fought against the devastating floods in 1957. Just because of this, the Monument also became one of the landmarks in Harbin. In 1997, government of Harbin Municipal appointed the street as a pedestrian street.

**Typical Architecture**

The most remarkable building along Zhongyang Street is the Modern Hotel built in 1906. Once as a large luxury hotel, this hotel now lists first-class city-level Protected Building. It has a typical Baroque style of the Neo-artistic period. The name of Modern Hotel means fashion and modern. It is a commercially creative masterpiece and the most luxurious hotels in the most prosperous street in Harbin. Joseph Keith, a Russian Jew, came to Harbin. At first, he opened a Shop repairing clocks and watches. And soon he changed to deal in Silverwares and jewelries and benefited much. We can see how good the investment environment in Harbin is from the great achievement he made in just two years. So we really welcome everyone to invest in Harbin, and make a fortune.

Modern hotel has all the facilities of a modern hotel including well-equippedand well-decorated suites, medium and small-sized meeting rooms in European palatial styles. In the past few decades, this hotel has catered to many famous people, such as well-known Chinese writers Guo Moruo and Ding ling, and a renowned painter, Xu Beihong. Those who have stayed here also include distinguished American celebrities such as Anna Louise Strong and Edgar Snow. What's more, some movie studios have also shot movies, such as "Harbin in the Dark Night" "London Inspiration" "The Orient Express to Moscow". These movies have left people wonderful memories here.

Opposite the Modern Hotel, there is Huamei Western Food Restaurant. It was originally the Malse Western Restaurant set up by a Russian Jew. In 1957, the Restaurant moved here and changed its name as Huamei Western Food Restaurant. Together with Maxim in Beijing, Red House in Shanghai, Kissling in Tianjin listed as China's four western restaurants. Now Huamei Restaurant serves many specialties, such as Russian dishes, potted cattle tails, French eggs and fried prawns.

Now we are on the Red Brick Street, a newly opened Leisure Square. The sculptures of trumpeter and accordion girl also can be seen there. Another sculpture shows that a carter is driving his carriage telling the transportation condition at the time.

Further in the front, we can see the Education Bookstore constructed in 1909. It was originally Matsuura Matheson in a Baroque construction, now is Protected Building. It is magnificent with bold lines and strong contrast. Over the entrance, there are two statues. They are Titans in Greek fairy tales, the male is Atlas and the female is Galliached.

The building across Education Bookstore was originally the Churin Company in Daoli Branch created by the Russian merchant named Iraq Churin. It was built in 1919 and later changed its name as Churin Department Store in Daoli. The building in the Neo-artistic style is first-class Building in Harbin. The main three layers of the building are separated by waist lines. These top-down windows are gradually reduced showing a sense of stability. Now Youngor, a speciality Store settles here.

Now we come to Youyi Road in the north of Zhongyang Street. The tour of Zhongyang Street comes to an end. We can see the landmark building—The Flood Control Monument of Harbin. Now free activities for 30 minutes. You can review sceneries and cultures of this street and reshoot some buildings. So please get back at 10 a.m. in the parking lot of Songhua River Gloria Plaza Hotel. Then I will introduce the Flood Control Monument for you and take you to visit the country's largest riverside park and the beautiful Songhua River.

Thank you so much!

## 中央大街

尊敬的游客朋友们,我们要游览的中央大街马上要到了,我们在这儿将游览1小时,请大家于1小时后在松花江凯莱大酒店停车场集合,我们旅游车的号码是黑A12345。现在,请大家带好您的贵重物品和摄影、摄像器材随我下车,一同步行游览这条百年老街。

游客朋友们,从我们现在所处的位置经纬街到我们看到的北边的防洪纪念塔,中央大街全长1 450米。在这条不足3里(1里=500米)的街道上,有欧式和仿欧式建筑71处,其中保护建筑13栋。1986年,哈尔滨市人民政府将中央大街确定为保护街路。1997年6月1日步行街正式开通,是全国较早的步行街。目前中央大街历史街区的商业店铺已经超过了700家,国际著名品牌阿曼尼、登喜路、路易·威登、劳力士、宝姿等在中央大街都设有专卖店或柜台,肯德基、麦当劳等著名国际连锁机构的招牌与古老的建筑交相呼应。2002年以后,哈尔滨市对街区内的辅街进行了整治,对历史街区内的保护建筑全面修缮,增加了休闲空间。改建后的步行街环境优美。她以其独特的欧式建筑、欧式古典路灯、花团锦簇的休闲小区以及异彩纷呈的文化生活,成为哈尔滨市一道亮丽的风景线。

哈尔滨市1994年被确定为国家级历史文化名城。中央大街是哈尔滨市最突出的街路代表,是整个城市的名片和文化品牌。2005年中央大街被建设部评为"中国人居环境范例奖",2006年被市政府定为"哈尔滨十大城市名片"之一,2010年经文化部、国家文物局批准,由中国文化报社、中华民族文化促进会、中国文物报社主办的首届"中国历史文化名街评选"中,中央大街荣获首批中国历史文化名街的称号。

### "中央大街"街名的来历

中央大街和哈尔滨市一样,也是随中东铁路的建设而生。1903年7月14日,从满洲里至绥芬河,以哈尔滨为中心的滨州线和滨绥线正式通车。之后又修建了哈尔滨至大连的铁路,使哈尔滨成为中东铁路的枢纽。从此,哈尔滨正式开始了殖民色彩极浓的国际都市发展时期。大量的外国列强、富豪、侨民来这里掠夺、经商、避难,而中央大街也从当年经松花江运货物进市区的通道,变成了繁华的国际商贸区和外侨居住区。一时间在哈尔滨居住的外国侨民竟占城市人口的一半以上。各种不同时期产生的不同的文化也同时来到这里展现,留给我们最完整的要属建筑文化了。

1898年6月中东铁路在哈尔滨破土动工时从山东、河北来了数千名筑路劳工落脚在今天的中央大街一带。他们垒泥为墙,束草为棚。于是这条街就有了她最初的名字——中国大街。1925年,中国政府收回了哈尔滨的市政管理权,将中国大街改称中央大街。1968年的"文化大革命"岁月中,中央大街被改称"防修大街",1976年其名称又恢复为中央大街。这条历经风雨的老街,如同历史见证人,目睹着哈尔滨百年沧桑和荣辱兴衰。

### 中央大街的马路方石

1924年中国大街铺上了方块石。当年铺设方块石路的设计监工是俄籍工程师科姆特拉肖克,有趣的是,铺在路上的花岗岩方块石的尺寸都是长18厘米、宽10厘米,形状大小和俄式面包一模一样,初来参观的您不会想到这曾经是一项浩大的工程,最初这一带都是古松花江河床,地下水位高,沙土疏松,为了保证方块石路不会因为冬冻春融而翻浆变形,施工时不得不掘地3米,挖出疏松的沙土,放入许多大石块垫起厚厚的路基,再敷以碎石充填后夯实,最后才在上面整齐划一地铺上了从帽儿山和玉泉一带开采来的花岗石块。虽然它在地上露出的是我们现在所看的大小,实际立在地下的高度却长达20~30厘米不等。据说当时一块方石的价格就值1块大洋(银元)。1块大洋足以买来一个成年人一个多月的口粮,真可谓金子铺成的路。现在,大家随我边漫步游览,边听我介绍一下它的建筑风格。

### 建筑风格

特殊的历史条件造就了独有的城市风格,中央大街的建筑涵括了西方建筑史上最有影响的四大建筑流派。在西方建筑史上几百年才形成的建筑风格,在中央大街只用了二三十年的时间就形成了,当年中央大街成为远东著名的街道。

中央大街的建筑包括了西方建筑史上最有影响力的四大建筑流派和欧洲最具魅力的近300年的文化发展史。有16世纪文艺复兴式,17世纪的巴洛克建筑,18世纪折中主义建筑,19世纪的新艺术运动建筑。中央大街成为一条建筑的艺术长廊。正因如此,人们将中央大街同伦敦的摄政王大街、巴黎的香榭丽舍大街、柏林的菩提树大街、东京的银座大街、上海的南京路和天津的维多利亚大街相提并论,成为远东欧美文化中心。

走在中央大街上,就仿佛进入了异国他乡。长街尽头便是为纪念英雄的哈尔滨人民抵御1957年特大洪水而修建的防洪纪念塔,该塔也由此成为哈尔滨的标志性建筑之一。1997年,经市政府批准,中央大街被改造为步行街。

### 典型建筑

中央大街上最引人注目的建筑要数我们面前这座马迭尔宾馆。它建于1906年,属典型的新艺术运动建筑,是哈尔滨市一类保护建筑,原来为大型豪华旅馆。"马迭尔"这个名字便代表着"摩登"与"现代"。在哈尔滨最繁华的街道上建成最华美的建筑,开设最豪华的旅馆,成为商业创意上的杰作。俄籍犹太人约瑟·开斯来到哈尔滨,起初,他开一个修理钟表的小店,不久经营银器和珠宝,获利丰厚。短短两年就取得了这么大的成就,足以证明哈尔滨的投资环境是多么优良。欢迎大家来哈尔滨投资、发财!

作为哈尔滨当时最现代化的宾馆,不但室内设备齐全,装修华丽,还设有欧洲宫廷式中小型会议室,这里曾接待过众多中外知名人物,如宋庆龄、郭沫若、丁玲、徐悲鸿、斯特朗、斯诺等。影视界也以马迭尔宾馆为景多次拍片,《夜幕下的哈尔滨》《伦敦启示录》《开往莫斯科的东方列车》等电影都给观众留下了美好的回忆。

马迭尔宾馆对面的华梅西餐厅原是俄籍犹太人创办的"马尔斯西式茶食店",1957年迁到这里,改名为"华梅西餐厅"。与北京的马克西姆、上海的红房子、天津的起士林并列为中国四大西餐厅。"华梅西餐厅"的风味菜肴有俄式大菜、纸包小牛肉、软炸鸡脯、罐牛尾、法国蛋、炸板虾等。

现在我们位于红专街,是新开辟的休闲广场,我们看到小号手和演奏手风琴的少女的雕塑。对面广场的雕塑是车夫在驾驭一架马车,反映出当年的交通状况。

再往前走,我们就会看到教育书店。它建于1909年,原为松浦洋行,是哈尔滨市最大的巴洛克式建筑,是哈尔滨市一类保护建筑。它富丽堂皇,新奇变幻,线条自由,对比强烈。它的入口上方镶嵌着一男一女两尊人体雕像。它们是古希腊神话传说中的两个擎天神,男的叫亚特拉斯,女的叫加里亚切德。

与教育书店相对的建筑原来是俄国商人伊·雅·秋林经营的秋林商行道里分行,后改为道里秋林百货商店。建于1919年,属新艺术运动建筑,是哈尔滨市一类保护建筑。建筑物主体三层,各层间以腰线分割,自上而下窗口逐渐缩小,显现出稳定感。现为雅戈尔专卖店。

现在我们来到了友谊路。这里是中央大街的北端。中央大街的游览到现在告一段落,我们看见对面是哈尔滨市的标志性建筑——哈尔滨市人民防洪胜利纪念塔。现在自由活动30分钟,大家可以回顾一下这条街道的景色和文化,补拍一些刚才没有来得及拍照的建筑。10点整准时在对面的松花江凯莱大酒店停车场集合,我向大家介绍防洪纪念塔,并请大家游览全国最大的沿江公园和美丽的松花江。

谢谢大家!

## 10. Jile Temple(The Temple of Ultimate Bliss)

Ladies and gentlemen, we are going to arrive at Jile Temple. Before the visit, I have several suggestions to you. Firstly, photo taking and video recording are prohibited in the hall except the courtyard of the Temple. Secondly, please make sure you don't step on the threshold. It is said that the Ormazd God is lying there, so lift your legs high and stride over it. Now, please get off the coach with your valuables. We will gather here after two hours, and please remember our plate number "HA12345".

The Jile Temple is a Buddhist temple. Speaking of its founding, there is a special reason. Harbin is located on the verge of Songhua River. After the Opium War in 1840, China became a semi-colonial and semi-feudal society step by step. So churches of the Orthodox Eastern Church, of the Catholicism and the Christianity were built at Dazhi Street. At that time, a folk legend spread, to frighten western churches away, therefore, the local people appealed to build a Buddhist temple. That was the very reason of the founding of Jile Temple in Harbin.

In 1922, Master Tanxu, the 44$^{th}$ generation of disciple of the Tiantai Budhist clan, came to Harbin to set up this temple. With an area of 57 000 square meters, the construction of the Temple was completed in 1924. It was formally opened to the public in 1928. It has become a northern holy place of Buddhism and been listed as a unit of historical relics under national protection. Now it is also an important tourist attraction for domestic and international visitors to Harbin.

It is one of the four well-known Buddhist temples in Northeast China. The others are Banruo Temple in Changchun, Ci'en Temple in Shenyang, and Lengyan Temple in Yinkou.

The temple obtained its name because of two people, i. e. Tanxu and Chen Feiqing. Master Tanxu first preached AMiTabha Scriptures in the temple. Besides, as a lay Buddhist, Chen Feiqing initiated the name of the temple should indicate ultimate bliss and pure land because he believed in pure land Buddhism. The name Temple of Ultimate Bliss was proposed and adopted, hence Ji Le Si in Chinese. The three Chinese characters, each measuring one by one meter, were written by Zhang Jian. He was a Number One Scholar in the Imperial examination in the Qing Dynasty from Nantong, Jiangsu Province. It is said he devoted himself to commercial and industrial enterprises and became a famous entrepreneur in the modern history of China.

The architecture of the temple is in conformity with the traditional style of Chinese temples. The temple faces to the south at the eastern end of Dazhi Street. The Drum Tower and Bell Tower are in the entrance of the main gate of Jile Temple. The complex of the temple consists of the Heavenly King's Hall, the Grand Hall, the Three Bodhisattva Hall and the Buddhist Book Storage Hall.

What is often said "when hearing the bell, you will clear troubles, increase your wisdom and believe in Buddha". The Buddhists stress striking the bell in the morning and the drum evening, and they call this procedure assignment. They will strike 108 times respectively for bell and drum every morning and night. There are two reasons for this action. One connects to month, solar terms and Hou. The other is that there are 108 troubles in human beings, these strikings can help people relieve troubles. If we have any chance we can try. Now, of course, you can hear the sound from bells and drums only for the major Buddhist activities.

Now let's visit the first hall—Heavenly King's Hall, Inside, we can see a shrine of Maitreya Boddhisattva, images of Four Guardians and a shrine of Weituo Boddhisattva. Behind Maitreya, we can see Weituo Boddhisattva, who is famous for its braveness, and one of eight generals under the control of the Southern Guardian. He always cruised in eastern, western and southern continent to protect Buddhist doctrine.

The Laughing Buddha, you can see how nicely he smiles. As he always carries a bag with him, he is also known as the Bag Buddha with a bag. There are also images of Four Guardians. The Southern Guardian has a sword in his hand. The Edge of the sword is pronounced the same as "wind" in Chinese. So he is in charge of wind. The Eastern Guardian has a "Pipa", a string musical instrument. As the string can be tuned and adjusted, he has the function of making adjustment. The Northern Guardian holds an umbrella and is in charge of rain. The Western Guardian has a dragon around him. Since the dragon can stretch and shrink, he can make things run smoothly. It is said that the Four Guardians work together to ensure good weather and good harvests so that the country enjoys peace and the people enjoy a stable life. Behind the hall, we can see the tall and golden painted Weituo Boddhisattva with a steel stick (a weapon) in his hand. He is a fearless guardian and his weapon can keep devils away. One sentence circulated among the people like this: worship Maitreya Boddhisattva entering the gate, while Weituo Boddhisattva out of the gate.

Now we are at the front of the Grand Hall. The four Chinese characters were written by Mr. Zhao Puchu, late chairman of Buddhist Association of China.

Here we can find a Shrine of Sakyamuni Buddha, his disciples and other Boddhisattvas. About the Sakyamuni Buddha, is known in history for sure. Sakya was the name of the clanto which his family belonged, Munim was the meaning of the saints. He was a prince and was brought up in luxury, but he became discontented with the world when he was confronted with the sights of old age, sickness, and death. He was determined to save the world. Around the age of 30 he made his break from the material world, and plunged off in search of "enlightenment". After six years' cultivation, in his 30s he finally succeeded under the banyan in founding the Buddhism which delivered people from the bitterness. He became the founder of Buddhism. Standing on the left of Buddha was Sakya, on the right Ananda, they were Buddha's favorite disciples. After the death of Buddha, Sakya presided in the first Buddhist meeting. with his skill of great wisdom and good memory, Ananda, a cousin of Buddha, wrote all words Buddha had said onto the leaves and then these words became Buddhist sutras. Eighteen arhats are standing on both sides of the hall. Turn right and keep going, we can see Manjusri Buddisattva, symbols of wisdom and sharp, riding on the lion with sword in his hand. Turn left we can see Samantabhadra Buddha, whose responsibility is to make the good universal to all places, riding on an elephant with six teeth and his favorite stick in his hand. On the back wall of the hall, Avalo-kitesvara Boddhisattva stands there. He is also known as the God of Mercy and has a vase in his left hand and a twig of willow in his right hand. People say he is a drip Samantabhadra Buddha, since he shows mercy on all the people and solves all their problems.

Now let's visit the Three Bodhisattva Hall where Amitadha, Avalokitesvara and Mahasthamaprapta are worshiped. Amitabha, original name Dharmakara, vowed to build up a perfect Buddha world and to influence sentient beings with extraordinary skill. Later he became a Buddha and also the hierarch in the World of Ultimate Bliss. Avalokitesvara and Mahasthamaprapta are his disciples. Mahasthamaprapta, was a alias of Bodhisattva who owned the stronggest power to protect dharma and to influence sentient beings.

The two-storied Buddhist Book Storage Hall is where Buddhist sutras were placed and many statues were worshiped. The bell in the hall was built at the construction of the temple.

Backyardis Avalokitesvara yard where 32 elaborate-style paintings about Avalokitesvara Bodhisattva are hung. Furthermore you can also see the Deceased Bhikku Stupa and Seven-Storied Stupa, an eight-angle and seven-storied building which was built in 1924.

We can see the rare two-storied bell tower and drum tower both in the east and west. The windows are just open above the third floor and the others areniches for statue of the Buddha with over 30 active Arhats. From the first to the fourth floor, four Bodhisattvas are worshiped such as Ksitigarbha Bodhisattva, Avalokitesvara, samantabhadra and Manjushri, each at the height of 1.6 meters. From the fifth to the seventh floor, the three Bodhisattvas are worshiped such as Pharmacist, Sakyamuni and Amitabha, each at the height of 1.8 meters.

We can see the stairs within the tower and also the active pictures based on Buddhist stories on the wall of the both sides of the stairs. Relievoes, dragon, wind, lion and crane, are vivid and elegant. The styles of western buildings are introduced into the towers.

In the yard stands the statue of Amitabha. We can see Hall of Five Hundred Arhats, which was built in 1999, both in the east and west of the statue, and the Palace of Forty-Eight Wishe is also here.

Now the Temple is managed by monks here. On Buddhist holidays, thousands of believers come here to celebrate. The temple is over crowded with believers and visitors. If you come on these occasions, I am sure that you will be likely to enjoy more.

Now you have free time to enjoy your visit. Do not forget the gathering time. Thank you for your attention.

## 极乐寺

游客朋友们,我们将要游览的极乐寺马上就到了,在参观过程中,请注意:第一,殿堂内不允许拍照、摄像,院落可以;第二,进入殿堂内不要踩门槛。传说门下睡着善神,所以请大家脚下留情。请大家带好随身携带的贵重物品随我一起下车。我们将于两小时后在现在的停车场集合,记住我们的车号是黑A12345。

极乐寺是一座佛教寺院。说起极乐寺的建立,还有一段缘由。哈尔滨,濒临松花江畔。1840年鸦片战争后,中国一步步沦为半封建半殖民地社会,大直街上建起了东正、天主和基督教堂。当时民间传说,大直街上潜伏着一条巨龙,是哈尔滨的风脉所在。洋教堂正建在龙脊上,于是,人们呼吁建一座佛寺,以震慑洋气,这就是哈尔滨极乐寺兴建的"缘起"。

1922年北方名僧天台宗第44代亲传弟子倓(tán)虚法师来到这里开始创建寺庙,1924年落成,1928年开光典礼,占地面积5.7万平方米。它既是佛教徒参谒朝拜的北方佛教圣地,也是中外游人参观游览的名胜,已被列为黑龙江省级重点文物保护单位。

极乐寺是东北三省的四大著名寺院之一,与长春般若寺、沈阳慈恩寺、营口楞严寺并称为东北四大佛教丛林。

因为倓虚法师第一次开讲的是《阿弥陀经文》,又因发起人陈飞青居士信奉净土宗,与极乐净土相关联,"极乐寺"庙名由此而得。庙门正额上方浮刻"极乐寺"3个一米见方的大字,落款有"民国十三年七月南通张謇(jiǎn)"字样。张謇是清朝末年的状元,后来"下海"办实业,成为中国近代著名的民族实业家。

极乐寺的整体设计、形式布局和建筑结构,都保留了我国寺院建筑的风格和特点。寺院坐北面南,临街。进入山门,首先是钟楼和鼓楼。庙庭内,横向分左、中、右三个序列,众多的殿堂各向纵深依次排列。正中一列为四重殿:前殿为弥勒天王殿,正殿为大雄宝殿,后殿为三圣殿,最后是藏经楼。

常言道:"闻钟声,烦恼清,智慧长,菩提生。"佛家弟子讲晨钟暮鼓。从早上敲钟开始到晚上撞鼓结束一天佛事,也称功课。每早每晚要各撞108下,为什么呢?对此持有两种看法,第一种是说,一年有12个月、24个节气、72侯,古代五天为一侯,按360天计,一年分72侯,大家加一下,是不是正好是108?那么另一种说法是众生界有108个烦恼,撞一下就解一个烦恼,若大家有机会不妨亲身尝试一下。当然现在只有重大佛事活动才敲钟鼓。

现在请大家随我进入天王殿吧!天王殿里供奉有弥勒佛像、四大天王像和韦驮菩萨像。弥勒佛身后的站将为韦驮菩萨。他是南方天王部下的八将之一,以武勇著称。他常于东、西、南三洲巡游,守护佛法,故称"三洲感应"。

首先映入眼帘的就是这位笑口常开、大肚宽怀的佛像,他叫弥勒佛,根据佛教说法,弥勒佛是释迦牟尼的"法定"接班人,不过它要在56亿万年后才能降临人间,普度众生,所以弥勒佛就是人间崇拜的未来佛。还有一个说法是弥勒佛是五代时的布袋和尚,因传说为弥勒化身,后人塑像供奉。他常以杖荷一布袋,见人就行乞,能示人吉凶,预知风雨,圆寂前说过:"弥勒真弥勒,分身千百亿,时时示世人,世人自不识。"面前的相对而立,各个好似我国古代的将军,这就是四大天王,俗称四大金刚,他们手持的法器通过谐音和联想分别象征着"风""调""雨""顺":手持青锋宝剑的是守护南方的增长天王,"峰"和"风"同音;手持琵琶而没有弦,需要调音,表示"调"的是东方的持国天王;守护北方的多闻天王,手持雨伞显示"雨";而西方广目天王手绕缠龙,降魔降妖,保护众生,他是群龙之首,众龙都顺从他。四者合起来就誉为:风调雨顺,国泰民安。民间流传着这样一句话:进门拜弥勒,出门拜韦驮,大家请随我转到殿后,眼前这尊佛像,木制贴金,高大威武,手托金刚杵(chǔ),这就是位居四大天王手下的三十二位神将之首的韦驮菩萨。为何韦驮菩萨面向大雄宝殿呢?据说古印度佛寺内的大雄宝殿,为佛祖灵堂,宝殿前安放的释迦牟尼舍利塔,有个"捷疾鬼"偷走了佛祖的两颗佛牙,韦驮菩萨见状便行走如飞,抓住盗贼,夺回佛牙,之后他就担负起守卫佛祖舍利塔的任务,所以在寺庙中他总面向内。

现在我们来到的是大雄宝殿。"大雄宝殿"这四个字是我国已故佛教协会会长赵朴初老先生所书。

大雄宝殿里供奉有释迦牟尼佛和他的弟子阿难尊者、迦叶尊者的雕塑以及大行普贤菩萨像、大至文殊菩萨像、滴水观音菩萨像和十八罗汉像。关于释迦牟尼,历史上确有其人,释迦是一个种族的名字,牟尼是圣人的意思,相传他是古印度北部迦毗罗卫国,现为尼泊尔境内,净饭王的儿子,原名为乔达摩·悉达多,他从小善于思考,虽然自己过着舒适的生活,但有感于现实人生中的生、老、病、死等种种现象,认为要拯救人类,只有通过出家修行,才能找到解脱苦难的道路,他29岁那年,进入森林,去寻找解脱苦难的真理,经过六年含辛茹苦修行,到了35岁终于在菩提树下修炼成功,创立了能使众生脱离苦海的佛教,成为佛教的创始人。佛祖左边站着的长者叫迦叶,右边站立的青年叫阿难,他们是佛祖的得力弟子,佛祖逝世后,迦叶主持了佛教信徒第一次聚会,阿难是佛祖的堂弟,聪明智慧,擅长记忆,跟随佛祖25年,把佛祖生前的话写在贝叶树的叶子上成为佛经。大殿的两旁塑有罗汉像,东南两边加起来共有18位。这些罗汉都是释迦牟尼佛祖的亲传弟子。佛祖圆寂时特意嘱托,让他们不入涅槃,永驻人间,弘扬佛法,普度众生。大家请随我右行前走,这位身骑狮子,手持宝剑的就是文殊菩萨,他象征着智慧和锐利,左边这位手持如意棒,身骑六牙大象的是普贤菩萨。普贤菩萨的职责是把"善"普及到一切地方。在大殿的后壁,就是大家熟悉的观音塑像,左手持净瓶,右手持杨柳枝,因其大慈大悲,救苦救难,人称滴水观音菩萨。

大家请随我前往后殿西方三圣殿参观。三圣殿里供奉有被称为西方三圣的南无阿弥陀佛、观音菩萨和大势至菩萨像。传说中,阿弥陀佛,原为法藏比丘,发愿成就一个尽善尽美的佛园,以最善巧的方法来度化众生;后来成佛,他是西方极乐世界的教主。观音菩萨和大势至菩萨是他的徒弟。大势至,是菩萨的别号,指菩萨势力最大之极,以此护持佛法,度化众生。

藏经楼是双层结构的收藏佛经的地方,里面供奉两尊释迦牟尼佛白玉石雕像,内东侧供奉寒山、拾得、丰干禅师和济公罗汉,殿内的钟为建寺时所铸。

后院为观音院,内悬挂32幅观念菩萨说法的工笔画。极乐寺所属寺院内设有七级浮屠塔和圆寂比丘塔。七级浮屠塔建于1924年,是一座八角七层楼阁式砖建筑。

大家看,塔与殿前,东西各设两层塔式钟鼓楼,布局为国内罕见。塔三层以上开窗,其余都设有佛龛,塑有生动的罗汉浮雕30多尊,殿和塔相通,从一层到四层,供奉着地藏王、观世音、普贤、文殊四大菩萨像,各高1.6米;从五层到七层,供奉着药师、释迦牟尼和阿弥陀佛三尊佛像,各高1.8米。

塔内有木梯,楼梯两侧的墙壁上绘有以佛教故事为题材的生动画面,殿和塔檐下的龙、凤、狮、鹤等浮雕,造型生动、典雅。塔的局部构件和装饰吸收了西方建筑的风格。

在院中的这尊为阿弥陀佛站像,塔身东西各建罗汉堂一座,1999年建成,内供奉500尊金漆木雕罗汉。塔后24孝长廊,将两罗汉堂连接一起。卧佛殿的对面为千手千眼观音殿,南面是延寿功德堂(地藏王殿),圆寂比丘塔供存放已故僧人骨灰。阿弥陀佛殿,供奉48尊同一造型阿弥陀佛站像,代表阿弥陀佛的48愿(48个理想)。舍利殿,供奉开山祖师倓虚法师的舍利。

现在寺庙完全由僧人自己管理。极乐寺每年农历四月初八、十八、二十八日的浴佛节,都要举行盛大的庙会,熙熙攘攘,热闹非凡。

好了,极乐寺就介绍到这儿,下面请大家自由活动。请别忘了集合时间。

## 11. Stalin Park & Flood Control Monument

Dear friends,

Welcome to Stalin Park. It is a belt-shaped open park rebuilt from the Riverside Park in 1953. It is located on the southern bank of Songhua River, extending 1 750 meters from Songhua River Railway Bridge to the east and Jiuzhan Park to the west, with a total area of 105 000 square meters. Across the river, you can see the renowned Sun Island. It is characterized by coleus blumei flowerbeds and 16 groups of art sculptures distributed among green fields.

Flood Control Monument is the centerpiece of Stalin Park, which is a symbol of Harbin with a classical European style. It was erected in 1958 in memory of the Harbin people's heroic fight against the flood in 1957. It is designed and constructed by engineers of Harbin Architectural Designing Institute like Bages of Soviet Union and the Chinese Li Guangyao. The monument is 22.5 meters in height. Its foundation was made of rock, implying the river dike is as strong as rock. At the foot of the monument, there are two fountains. The fountains imply that the people of Harbin have tamed the flood to benefit the people. In 1990, a music fountain was added here. There are two-layer pools under the pedestal. One represents the highest water level of 119.72 meters in 1932, when the flood inundated parts of Daoli and Daowai districts; the other represents the water level of 120. 30 meters reached by the devastating flood in 1957. The copper tubes above the ponds mark the highest water level record of 120.89 meters in 1988. The Monument Square is also a place for holding political, cultural and sports activities. This Square was the eastern end of Asian torch relay in 1990 Beijing Asian Games. Furthermore, it was also the starting point of Harbin torch relay in 2008 Beijing Olympic Games.

As we walk along the bank, we can see an attractive building—the Riverside Restaurant. It is the classical Russian style with a wooden structure. The roof ridges scatter randomly with clear edges, and you will find the restaurant looks like building blocks. The veranda is open to the river. The roofs and veranda embodies an elegant European style.

Now we can see the magnificent "taming the dragon" sculpture, which was built in 1958. It means that man is the master of his own fate and the working people can overcome formidable enemies. During the Cultural Revolution, the sculpture was destroyed and then rebuilt as the original design in 1982. The fountains were also rebuilt in 1988.

Now we come to the Railway Workers' Club. This club covers an area of 5 000 square meters. It was first constructed in 1912 with the name "Yacht Club". It is popular for the unique location along the Songhua River, the classical European style and exquisite pavilions. The boat-shape main building is located on the dyke close to the water, which looks like a colossal ship about to set off on its maiden voyage. The club has many facilities for leisure activities.

Tourists can refresh and relax while walking along the avenue in Stalin Park with the flowing Songhua river by side.

## 斯大林公园和防洪纪念塔

游客朋友们,大家好! 欢迎各位来到斯大林公园观光游览。斯大林公园是1953年在原"江畔公园"的基础上改建而成的沿江开放式公园。公园位于市区松花江南岸,东起松花江铁路大桥、西至小九站,全长1 750米,是顺堤傍水建成的带状开放式公园,与驰名中外的"太阳岛"风景区隔江相望,占地面积10.5万平方米,它因园内遍布五颜六色的"五色草花坛"及分布在绿地之间的16组艺术雕塑而名扬海内外。

斯大林公园景区的核心是防洪纪念塔,防洪纪念塔为欧洲古典风格建筑,是哈尔滨城市的象征,是为纪念哈尔滨市人民战胜1957年特大洪水而于1958年修筑的。哈尔滨建筑设计院的工程师巴吉斯、李光耀等人参加了该塔的设计和施工。纪念塔塔身高22.5米,塔基用块石砌成,意味着堤防牢固,坚不可摧。塔基前的喷泉,象征着勇敢、智慧的哈尔滨人民,正把惊涛骇浪的江水,驯服成细水长流,造福人民的幸福之水,1990年改建成彩色音乐声控喷泉。塔座下部的两段水池,下阶表示海拔标高119.72米,含义是日伪时期的1932年,松花江水淹没哈尔滨道里、道外的部分市区时的最高水位;上阶表示海拔标高120.30米,标志1957年全市人民战胜特大洪水时的最高水位;现在大家看到的位于两层水池上方的金色铜管,是1998年哈尔滨市人民战胜百年不遇特大洪水的最高水位120.89米。防洪纪念塔广场还是哈尔滨市举行大型政治、文化和体育活动的场所之一。1990年,第11届亚运会在首都北京举行,这座广场成为亚运火炬传递的东端起点,这座广场还是2008年北京奥运会哈尔滨段火炬传递的起点。

现在展现在我们面前的江畔餐厅,是仿造俄罗斯的古典木结构建筑。屋脊高低错落,棱角分明,外观呈现积木形状,迎江通透式的外廊,体现了古朴典雅的欧式建筑风格。

现在大家看到的就是著名的"伏龙"雕塑。该雕塑建于1958年,气势磅礴,它向人类宣告:人定胜天,劳动人民能"伏龙降虎"。"文化大革命"时期,伏龙雕塑遭到严重的破坏,后于1982年按原设计造型修复,1988年,改建了池内的喷泉。

我们现在来到了铁路江上俱乐部,它建于1912年,占地面积5 000多平方米,原名"游艇俱乐部"。该建筑依江傍水的独特地理位置、古朴典雅的欧式建筑风格、精巧别致的楼台亭阁深受世人瞩目,特别是船形的主建筑,半卧江堤,半伸江面,就像一艘整装待发的巨轮靠于岸边,这是一处集多功能服务为一体的休闲俱乐部。

游人漫步在斯大林公园的林荫道上,身旁就是静静流淌的松花江水,阵阵江风吹拂,令人神清气爽,心旷神怡。

## 12. Yabuli Ski Resort

Ladies and gentlemen,

Good morning! Today we are going to Yabuli Ski Resort—the largest ski resort in Asia. Friends, do you know three admitted tourism resources in the world? Yes, they are ocean, forest and snow, and two of them are rich in Heilongjiang province. In particular, Yabuli has the best snow. Skiing, golfing, equestrianism and billiards are four sports for the noble. Today let's enjoy skiing like a nobleman.

The resort is 197 km away from Harbin. It will take us 4 hours by coach there. We will stay one day in the ski resort. Tonight we will live in the hotel here, while tomorrow morning we will go skiing and return to the city in the afternoon.

While on the bus, I will introduce the Yabuli resort to you. Located in the southeast of Shangzhi City in Heilongjiang province, Yabuli was under the jurisdiction of Jilin province in history. During the Jin Dynasty, it was a farm for Chinese medicinal herbs. In the Qing Dynasty, it was a forbidden area as the hunting ground for feudal lords. In 1861, the forbidden area was open, and the pine trees and wild fruits were scattered all over there. In autumn, fruit was abundant. In 1897, when Chinese Eastern Railway was constructed in this area, Chinese laborers lived in the northern makeshift sheds, so this place was called northern shed at that time. Russian engineers saw an apple orchard full of crab apples in the mountain and called it Yabuli(Yabuli in Russian means apple orchard). It is the origin of its name, and the name is still in use today.

Yabuli ski resort is 20 kilometers (12 miles) southeast of Yabuli town, 197 kilometers (122 miles) west of Harbin city and 90 kilometers (56 miles) east of Mudanjiang City. The 301 National Road leads straight to the resort. The whole area consists of three peaks of Zhangguangcai Mountain in the Changbai Mountain Range (First Guokui Peak at 1 374 meters above sea level, Second Guokui Peak at 1 100 meters above sea level, and Third Guokui Peak at 1 000 meters above sea level). Most of the area is covered with pristine forest. There are some rare fujithions in the highest hill. The rock-block field is distributed over the hill, which is formed during the crustal movement 100 million years ago. The Anti-Japanese Amalgamated Army of the Northeast and the movie Tracks in the Snowy Forest left many stories here. Its gross area is 68 square kilometers (26 square miles), protection area is 87 square kilometers (34 square miles) and the mountainous terrain is 22 square kilometers (8 square miles). The ski resort is located in the higher latitude area and features a monsoon-influenced, humid continental climate. The annual average temperature varies from 2 to 10 degrees centigrade. The highest temperature reaches 34 degrees centigrade while the lowest drops to minus 43 degrees centigrade. The snow period here is 170 days with skiing period of 120 days annually. The snow can be as deep as 100 centimeters at the foot of the hill and 1.5 meters on top. And the snow is neither too hard nor too powdery. The rarely excellent ski resort ranks the Top Ten Ski Resorts in the world, which is suitable for training and competition, as well as for ski vacations. It enjoys equal popularity with the Lake Placid Ski Resort that has hosted many Olympic Winter Games.

The ski arena was built in the 1970s. Now it is the largest ski resort in Asia. It has good facilities for hosting large-scale international competitions such as National Winter Games. In February 1996, the resort was chosen to host the 3$^{rd}$ Asian Winter Games, where all the events on snow were competed here. In February 2009, the 24$^{th}$ Winter Universiade was also held here successfully. Yabuli Ski Resort is the biggest competitive section and the leisure skiing section. It is also the training venue for the Antarctic expedition. It has been approved as a "4A-Level National tourism resort"

The period frommid November to late April of the next year is the best time to ski at Yabuli Ski Resort. The ski resort includes two distinctive areas—the alpine competitive section and the leisure skiing section with international standard.

Yabuli Ski Resort has perfect reception and recreation facilities. There are eleven enterprises and institutions such as Sun Mountain Yabuli Resort, Avaunce (Yabuli) International Convention & Exhibition Center, Tiwei Ski Resort and Yabuli Village. It also has seven competitive ski resorts. The ski run is 50 kilometers long with 16 rope tows, hanging box ropeways and chairlift ropeways.

Besides, there is also a 2 680-meter-long summer toboggan run.

International skiing racing includes 10 sports and 62 events, and Yabuli has 9 sports and 59 events winning the approval of International Ski Federation with a certificate. It ranks among the Top Ten Ski Resorts in the world and receives over 500 000 visitors per year.

The ski resort provides integrated services and is willing to accommodate and entertain you as few other resorts can. For example, the five-star hotels and other star-rated hotels have the capacity of 3 000 tourists.

Sun Mountain Yabuli Resort is originally called the Yabuli Windmill Resort. Yabuli Windmill Resort was the largest skiing and four-season resort with well-equipped facilities, maximum ski runs and the best snow quality. In July 2007, the Yabuli Windmill Resort was purchased by Melco China Resorts ("MCR"), an associate of Melco International Development Limited ("Melco"). Sun Mountain Yabuli Resort is the flagship of MCR's five premier destination resort properties. It is China's first resort that offers more than a venue for the wintertime skiing but a range of year-round activities. So far, it has been named a 5S-level ski resort in China.

Tianyin Lake is the oldest natural lake in Yabuli. It is said that when the Buddha visited the Gangkui Peak, he left the trace of his footprint on the peak, so the lake appeared. There are all kinds of recreational facilities here. In summer, you can go swimming, go fishing, go boating and driving a motorboat. While in winter, you can participate in a host of activities like skating, iceboating and dog sledding.

The resort boasts 17 ski runs for beginner, intermediate, advanced skiers respectively. It has invested more funds in high-speed 8-passenger heated gondolas, 6-passenger heated bubble chairlifts from POMA of America and 5 magic carpets(conveyor belt machines for carrying beginners), which save the time from the foot to the peak of the mountain, bringing the visitors a comfortable experience. There is also an all-weather summer toboggan run, which is built in Germany and boasts the longest run of its kind in the world. The 2 680-meter-long run snakes through the forests and drops 570 meters from the peak to the foot of the mountain, with 48 turns. It features in the list of the Guinness World Records because these indexes rank first in the world.

"Tiwei Ski Resort" is used for professional competition, literally meaning a ski resort owned and managed by Heilongjiang provincial Sports Administration. It is one of the competitive places that host ski events of the 24$^{th}$ Winter Universiade. It is not only the biggest and well-equipped competitive skiing resort, but also the training venue for Chinese Antarctic exploration. In winter, a large number of researchers come here to go camping and receive adaptive trainings such as glacier escape, snow rescue and so on. There are the shooting range with 14 targets, 125-meter and 90-meter alpine ski jumping, U-shaped skiing pool for freestyle aerial skiing, alpine skiing runs (3 060 meters, 1 200 meters and 800 meters), alpine slide downhill runs (3 500 meters and 2 500 meters) as well as slalom and giant slalom(GS) run (1 500 meters). All these are accepted by International Ski Federation.

The five-star hotel Avaunce (Yabuli) International Convention & Exhibition Center is invested by Hong Kong Avaunce Group with 0.32 billion RMB. It is a comprehensive service site which combines conferences, lodging, eatery, skiing, tourism, recreation projects of all seasons together. Furthermore, it succeeded in accomplishing the 2009 Winter Universiade reception work. Convention center has various view suites. The multi-functional hall is well-equipped with multi-language simultaneous interpretation, computer projection, and world-class stereo equipment. Apart from this, the basic amenities provided here comprise Chinese and Western restaurants, large Karaoke Room, KTV rooms, food regimen, massage, gymnasium, badminton hall, playroom, tennis court and table tennis room.

As the most important supporting facility of the Convention and Exhibition, Avaunce ski resort has two alpine ski runs and a ski yard for beginners. Compared to Yabuli's numerous competitive alpine skiing runs, the Avaunce is undoubtedly the best accessible skiing and tourism paradise.

At the foot of the Second Guokui Peak, there are Lingzhi lake and Haohan lake reservoirs. It is said that when the young people fall in love with each other, they always drink water from Lingzhi spring to pray for their pure, honest and eternal love like the couples of Haohan and Lingzhi. They will also take a photo under the Wuzhi Tree and Love Tree and pray for the Buddha to let them be happy all the life. You can also visit the alpine garden and enjoy the pristine forest. Yabuli ski resort charms and entices in every season where you can ski in winter, go sightseeing in spring, escape the heat in summer and go vacationing in autumn.

For our safe and happy skiing, the following precautions should be taken. The most important thing is to prevent frostbite. Frostbite is the damage that is caused when the skin is exposed to cold temperature. The areas most likely to be affected by frostbite are hands, feet and ears. So please keep them warm. Furthermore, you should pay attention to the following points. Firstly, have enough outfits for cold weather. Secondly, do not go skiing alone for fear that nobody can know and save you. Thirdly, do not slip off the boundary of the ski resort. Fourthly, do not go skiing after drinking alcohol so as to avoid the frostbite while lying down. Lastly, wear bright clothes so as to be found immediately. I hope everyone can pay attention to the above suggestions and do not drop your guard.

We are going to pulling up to the ski resort. Please get off with me and take all your belongings.

# 亚布力滑雪旅游度假区

尊敬的游客朋友们：

早上好！今天我们将前往亚洲最大的滑雪场——亚布力滑雪旅游度假区参观游览。朋友们，你们知道世界上公认的三大旅游资源是什么吗？对了，是海洋、森林和冰雪。黑龙江就占有其中的两项。雪资源以亚布力为最佳。人们常把滑雪、高尔夫、马术和台球并称为四大贵族运动。今天也让我们体验一下做贵族的感受和滑雪的乐趣吧！

亚布力滑雪旅游度假区距哈尔滨市 197 公里。从我们住地到雪场约 4 个小时的行程。我们将在雪场停留一天，今晚住在雪场的宾馆，明天上午滑雪，下午返回市内。

下面利用车上的时间，我把亚布力的概况简单向大家做个介绍。亚布力位于黑龙江省尚志市东南部，在历史上属于吉林省。金朝时期是王公贵族们培育中药材的地方，清朝时代，这里一直作为皇室狩猎围场，禁止百姓入林垦荒涉猎。1861 年，封禁大开，那时这里松树满山岭，野果遍沟壑。1897 年，中东铁路修建时，在这里筑路，在此筑路的华工住在北面临时搭建的大棚里，所以那时此地还被称为北大棚。在此筑路的沙俄工头经常发现成片成片的果树，秋天结出累累的果实，以为是野生苹果，于是将此地用俄语命名为"亚不洛尼"，即"苹果园"的意思，音译为亚布力，这个名称沿用至今。

亚布力滑雪旅游度假区，位于亚布力镇东南 20 公里处，西距省城哈尔滨市 197 公里，东距牡丹江市 90 公里，有 301 国道直通度假区，整个区域由长白山山脉张广才岭的三座山峰组成，它们是海拔 1 374 米的主峰大锅盔山、1 100 米的二锅盔山和 1 000 米的三锅盔山。亚布力滑雪场大部分处于原始森林之中，大锅盔山顶长有全国稀有的伏地松，分布着 1 亿年前地壳运动形成的高山石海。当年东北抗日联军及后来的《林海雪原》曾在这里留下了许多故事和传说。全区规划面积 68 平方公里，保护面积 87 平方公里，启动面积 22 平方公里，度假区纬度较高，气候特点属于中温带大陆性季风气候，年平均气温 2～10 摄氏度，最低气温零下 43 摄氏度，最高气温 34 摄氏度。冬季山上积雪厚度可达 100 厘米，雪质优良，硬度适中。年积雪为 170 天，滑雪期为 120 天，山顶积雪可达 1.5 米，是世界上少见的优良滑雪场地，也是世界十大滑雪场之一，可与多次举办冬奥会的美国普莱西德滑雪场相媲美，很适于开展竞技和旅游滑雪的各项运动。

滑雪旅游度假区始建于 20 世纪 70 年代，经历 20 余个寒冬酷暑，已经成为当今亚洲最大的滑雪旅游度假区，完全具备承办大型国际比赛的条件，曾多次举办过全国冬运会，1996 年 2 月举办了第三届亚洲冬季运动会全部雪上项目比赛。特别是于 2009 年 2 月成功举办了第 24 届世界大学生冬季运动会，是我国目前规模最大的国际滑雪比赛和旅游滑雪场地及南极训练基地，是 4A 级旅游度假区。

每年 11 月中旬至次年 4 月中旬是这里的最佳滑雪期。雪场由具有国际标准的高山竞技滑雪区和旅游滑雪区两大部分组成。

亚布力滑雪旅游度假区接待、娱乐设施完备，度假区现有新濠亚布力阳光度假村、雅旺斯

(亚布力)国际会展中心、黑龙江省体育局滑雪场、亚布力山庄等11家企事业单位,7处体育竞技滑雪场。滑雪道总长度50公里,有16条吊箱、吊椅和拖牵式索道,还有一条全长2 680米的旱地雪橇滑道。世界竞技滑雪的10个大项、62个小项之中,亚布力已有9个大项,59个小项得到国际雪联的认可,并被授予了相应的证书,跻身世界十大滑雪场之一,度假区年接待游客超过50万人次。

滑雪场地提供综合服务,有中国接待能力第一的服务设施,以五星级酒店为代表的数家星级酒店可同时容纳3 000余名游客。

新濠亚布力阳光度假村(原亚布力风车山庄)是加拿大上市公司——新濠中国度假村控股有限公司旗下5个中国滑雪度假村中的旗舰,是国内首家以冬季滑雪为主体并提供全年休闲度假体验的目的地型度假村。原名是亚布力风车山庄企业集团,它曾是我国规模最大、设施最全、雪道最多、雪质最好的滑雪旅游和四季度假旅游胜地。2007年8月由香港新濠国际集团旗下中国度假村控股有限公司并购,是目前国内最高等级5S级滑雪场。

天印湖是亚布力地区最古老的天然湖泊,相传是如来佛祖降临锅盔山时留下的足印。天印湖上游乐项目齐全,夏季可以游泳、垂钓、划船、驾驶摩托艇,冬季可以滑冰、冰帆、乘狗拉雪橇。

阳光度假村西侧的山麓,有17条初、中、高滑雪道。亚布力阳光度假村重资新购了POMA 8人电加热坐椅箱式缆车、POMA 6人电加热坐椅吊椅缆车、魔毯5条,大幅度缩短从山脚到山顶所需的时间,大大提升了身处冰天雪地的舒适度和温暖度,大幅提升了滑雪体验的舒适度。另有一条由德国引进的世界最长的四季全天候旱地雪橇道,全长2 680米,落差为570米,有48个弯道,这几个指标均居世界第一,已载入《吉尼斯世界纪录》。

黑龙江省体育局滑雪场,是亚布力滑雪旅游度假区中的专业竞技滑雪场,也是第24届世界大学生冬季运动会雪上比赛的主要场地之一。这里不仅是我国规模最大、条件最好、设施最完备的竞技滑雪场,而且是中国南极考察队的雪上训练基地。每到冬季,就有大批科研工作者来这里进行露营野炊,以及冰川脱险、雪地救生等适应性训练。它拥有14个靶位的射击场、125米及90米级高山跳台、自由式空中技巧U形池滑雪场地、高山滑雪道(3 060米、1 200米、800米)、高山速降雪道(3 500米、2 500米)及大小回转雪道(1 500米)都已通过了国际雪联的验收。

雅旺斯(亚布力)国际会展中心是由香港雅旺斯集团投资3.2亿元人民币兴建的五星级酒店,是集会议、住宿、餐饮、滑雪、旅游、四季室外娱乐项目为一体的综合性服务场所,是2009年第24届世界大学生冬季运动会主要接待场馆。拥有不同规格的观景客房,多功能厅配置有多种语言的同声传译、电脑投影及一流音响设备,会展中心配有中、西餐厅,大型卡拉OK厅,KTV包房,食疗养生馆,按摩室,健身房,羽毛球馆,游戏室,网球场,乒乓球馆等休闲娱乐设施。

作为会展中心最为重要的配套项目的雅旺斯滑雪场,拥有两条高山雪道、一座初级滑雪场。在高山竞技雪道林立的亚布力，这里无疑是具有亲和力的旅游滑雪天堂。

在二锅盔山的脚下，有两座水库，名叫灵芝湖和好汉泊。据说山里的年轻人热恋时，总要到好汉岭前，喝几口灵芝泉的水，以祈求自己的爱情像"好汉"和"灵芝女"的感情一样纯洁、忠贞、永恒！还要到五指树、情侣树下留下一张难忘的照片，愿佛祖保佑，一世幸福，百年好合，事业腾达。此外可游览高山植物园，享受原始森林的乐趣。亚布力滑雪场已经成为冬季滑雪、春季观光、夏季避暑、秋季度假的四季旅游胜地。

为了我们能安全、快乐地享受滑雪的乐趣，我想提醒大家注意以下事项：首先是防冻伤。冻伤是指人长时间处于低温环境中产生的伤害事故。人体产生冻伤主要发生在手部、脚部、耳朵等部位，所以对上述部位应格外注意保暖。另外，还应注意以下几点：①备足御寒衣物。②不要单独一人外出滑雪，以免出事后既无人知晓，又无人救援。③不要擅自滑出滑雪场界线。④饮酒后不要外出滑雪，一旦醉卧在外，非常容易发生冻伤。⑤要穿鲜艳服装，以便能及时被发现。希望大家在滑雪活动中注意以上建议，切不可麻痹大意。

好了，雪场到了，请大家带好自己的物品随我下车。

## 13. The Zhaolin Park and Harbin Ice Lantern Show

Ladies and gentlemen, welcome to Zhaolin Park. The Zhaolin Park of Harbin covers an area of 6.5 hectares and is the oldest park in Harbin. It was constructed in 1906 as the park of Red Cross Board of Directors. In early 1930s, it changed its name to the Park in the Daoli District. Since General Li Zhaolin, who was a leader in the war against the Japanese invasion, died on March 9, 1946 and later buried in this park, the park was renamed Zhaolin Park by the provincial government on August 15, 1946.

Owing to the unique climate in Harbin, Zhaolin Park is popular in both summer and winter. In summer, green trees and grass are matched with colorful flowers, and small boats ripple through birds' twitter and fragrance of flowers. In winter, it is the world of ice. The Harbin Ice Lantern Show is held here.

The Harbin Ice Lantern Show was founded in 1963, and had another name as Art Exhibition of Ice Lantern during 1999-2001. The amount of ice used for ice lantern each year is over 20 000 cubic meters. Over 1 500 pieces of art work make it the biggest outdoor ice Lantern show in the world.

Some of the lanterns have been recorded in the Guinness Book of World Record, such as St. Sophia Church of 26.25 meters high as the highest ice building, and the ice and snow Great Wall of 958 meters long as the longest ice structure. As you can see, the Harbin Ice Lantern Show is world wonder on snow and ice.

As one of the elite tourism projects in China, the Harbin Ice Lantern Show is listed as one of the 35 fascinating attractions in China. It has become a window to show the city's economic development and folk's spirit, and a bond between people in the city and the world.

Ice lanterns are a traditional form of art in the northern part of China and they are first made in Heilongjiang province. It is said that long long ago, farmers and fishermen in groups of three and four came to Songnen Plain of Heilongjiang every night in winter. They came here to feed horses or fish leisurely. At that time, their lanterns are made of ice, which became the earliest ice lantern. The original way of making ice lantern was very simple. People used a pail of water, and let it freeze for a certain time. Then they pulled this block of ice out of the pail. They drilled a hole in the middle; poured out the unfrozen water, and put oil light inside. The outside ice protected the light from blowing out. Thus, there was a light that never went out, which helped people a lot. Afterwards, people decorated it for viewing and made it into a unique art form of expression, which exhibited to the public in Spring Festivals and Lantern Festivals. In the History of Heilongjiang, which was written in Qing Dynasty, it was said that in Lantern Festival, various lanterns were exhibited for five days and attracted lots of people especially the ladies, making the street busy all nights. The lantern carved the god of longevity was 2 meters high and had two lights inside, looking like the crystal figure. Actually, ice Lantern appeared not only in the northern area but also in the southern part. During the reigns of Emperor Qianlong (1736–1796) and Emperor Jiaqing (1796–1821) of the Qing Dynasty, a poet named Zhang Wentao of Sichuan province ever wrote the poem called Ice Lantern, which said ice lantern lighted the dark and relived the heat, being a miracle that astonished the public.

Today the ice Lantern in our eyes is not as simple as before. It is a unique art of ice carving, combining the culture of gardens, architectures, lanterns, paintings, beauties, literature and music. With modern technologies including shaping, color, sound, light, and electricity, people create an exquisite and colorful world of ice. The ice lantern embodies the history of ancient China and the values of foreign architecture and custom, being a special and splendid wonder in the world.

Well, ladies and gentlemen, I guess you must be curious about how the ice Lantern is made. Actually in winter, the temperature is 20 degrees centigrade below zero. The ice block cut from the Songhua River has a good plasticity and compression strength similar with the construction material. According to the designing paper, the blocks are cut into different shapes, and then processed into ice bricks and components by using special tools like carpenters' saws, chisels, planes, and so on. At last, with the help of water and light, lofty buildings, majestic sculptures and miniscapes present in our eyes.

The Harbin Ice Lantern Show has become world famous. Every year, an international ice Lantern contest during 1$^{st}$ January ~ 15$^{th}$ January is held in Zhaolin Park. Artists from Japan, Russia, Singapore, the United States, Canada and many other countries and regions come and demonstrate their works of art. These works are in different themes and different styles, contributing a multicultural collection of ice lanterns.

There is a saying that getting married on the ice and promising in the snow. The wedding on the ice is a unique and pioneering activity promoted by the youth of Harbin. Nowadays, not only the youth, but the seniors and foreign friends come here to hold their romantic and memorable wedding.

The ice lantern creates a beautiful life and builds a wonderful world. Artists of Harbin have ever been to Russia, Japan, Singapore, France, the United States, Korea, Canada and many countries and regions. It becomes a bridge for communicating with the world. It is a pity that the ice lantern can only last for about 2 months, but it is a fairy tale that never repeats for people who love it.

Now, let's go to the fairyland of ice and snow, and enjoy the miraculous journey!

## 兆麟公园与冰灯游园会

游客朋友们,欢迎您到兆麟公园参观游览。哈尔滨市兆麟公园占地6.5公顷,始建于1906年,曾是红十字董事会花园,是哈尔滨市内历史最久的公园。20世纪30年代初改名"道里公园",后因李兆麟将军被害葬于园内,为纪念这位抗日民族英雄,公园于1946年8月15日被命名为兆麟公园。

由于哈尔滨市独特的气候条件,使得兆麟公园形成了冬夏完全不同的两种自然景象。夏季,绿树成荫,百花盛开,轻舟荡漾,鸟语花香;冬季这里又成了冰的世界,灯的海洋,驰名中外的哈尔滨冰灯游园会,就在这里举行。

冰灯游园会创办于1963年,1999~2001年一度更名为"冰灯艺术博览会"。2002年以后恢复原名。每届冰灯游园会的总用冰量都在两万立方米以上,冰景作品达1 500余件,可以说它是目前世界上形成时间最早、规模最大并已成为传统项目的大型室外露天冰灯艺术展。

这里曾有载入吉尼斯纪录的世界上最高的冰建筑——圣·索菲亚教堂,高达26.25米;有世界上最长的冰建筑——冰雪长城,长达958米,成为冰雪造园艺术史上的奇迹。

冰灯游园会作为中国冰雪旅游的一张王牌,已经跻身于国家旅游局评出的"绝奇美胜"35个旅游景点之列,成为哈尔滨向国内外游客展示社会经济发展水平和人民精神风貌的重要窗口,成为哈尔滨人民同各国朋友友好往来的纽带。

冰灯是流行于中国北方的一种古老的民间艺术。黑龙江是制作冰灯最早的地方,据说在很早以前,每到冬季的夜晚,在松嫩平原上人们总会看到三五成群的农夫和渔民,在悠然自得地喂马和捕鱼。他们所使用的照明工具就是用冰做成的灯笼,这便是最早的冰灯。当时制作冰灯的工艺很简单,把水放进木桶里冻成冰罩,放个油灯在里面,用以照明,冰罩挡住了凛冽的寒风,黑夜里便有了不灭的灯盏,冰灯成了当时人们生活中不可缺少的帮手。后来,每逢新春佳节和元宵节,人们又把它加以装饰,成为供人观赏的独特的艺术表现形式。清代《黑龙江外纪》里对此有过详细的记载:"上元,城中张灯五夜,村落妇女来观剧者,车声彻夜不绝。有镂五六尺冰为寿星灯者,中燃双炬,望之如水晶人。"其时,冰灯在我国南方一些地方也相继出现过。乾隆、嘉庆年间,四川诗人张问陶曾写过一首专门描写冰灯的诗,题名就叫《冰灯》,诗云:黑夜有炎凉,冰灯吐焰长。照来消热念,凿处漏寒光。影湿星沉水,神清月里霜。三冬足文史,底用探萤囊。

古时,冰灯的制作技术比较简单,现在我们所看到的冰灯要远远比这复杂得多,它是以冰为载体,集园林、建筑、雕塑、绘画、舞美、文学乃至音乐等多学科为一体的独特的冰雪造园艺术,同时应用形、色、声、光、电等现代科技,创造出玲珑剔透、五彩缤纷的艺术世界。它融合了华夏民族悠久的历史、中外建筑和民俗风情等广阔领域里的文化,是世界民间艺术宝库中一朵绚丽的奇葩。

游客朋友们,您一定想问冰灯是怎么制成的? 冬季,在零下20摄氏度以下的严寒中,先从松花江里凿出可塑性强,抗压强度与一般建筑材料相差无几的坚冰,根据设计图纸的要求用电锯切割成不同规格的冰料,再用木工使用的刨子、扁铲等工具加工成冰砖或冰配件,以水为黏接剂,制造出巍峨的冰建筑、雄伟的冰雕塑和小巧的冰盆景等。晶莹的冰体雕成后,再用灯光赋予它美丽的灵魂,一道绚丽的风景便这样走进了你的视野。

每年的1月1日~15日,兆麟公园都要举行大规模的群众性冰雕比赛和国际冰雕邀请赛,来自美国、日本、新加坡、加拿大、俄罗斯等十多个国家和地区的冰雕艺术家与我国各城市及地区的冰雕艺术爱好者云集于此,挥刀弄铲,同园竞技。他们制作的不同主题、不同风格的冰雕作品争奇斗艳,巧夺天工,为冰灯艺术博览会锦上添花。

"冰上成婚配,雪中结连理。"冰上婚礼是哈尔滨市青年开展群众性冰雪文化活动的一项创举,独具北国特色和时代风采。不仅是青年人,还有许多老年朋友,甚至还有外国朋友也不远万里慕名而来,在这里喜结良缘。

冰灯创造了美的生活,创造了美的世界。作为传播友谊和文化的友好使者,哈尔滨冰灯走出了国门,走向了世界。哈尔滨冰雕艺术家曾出访俄罗斯、日本、新加坡、法国、美国、韩国、加拿大等数十个国家和地区,虽然冰灯是一门遗憾的艺术,它的生命只有短短的两个月,但是对于热爱她的人们来说,冰灯,却是一个永不重复的童话。

现在,请大家跟我一同走进这冰雕雪塑的童话世界,去领略冰雪艺术的神奇和美丽吧!

## 14. The Jingpo Lake Scenic Area

Ladies and gentlemen,

Now, we're leaving the downtown and we will visit Jingpo Lake one and half an hour later. Then we will have a boat ride on Jingpo Lake. Now I'm going to introduce Jingpo Lake to you.

Jingpo Lake is the largest volcano barrier lake in China and the second in the world. It is 110 kilometers away from the southwest part of Mudanjiang. It is a historical and mysterious place. In ancient times, it was called Meituo River, and in Ming Dynasty, it was named Jingpo Lake. In the

Qing Dynasty, it was called Birteng Lake in the Manchurian language, meaning smooth like a mirror. Now we call it Jingpo Lake, which can be translated into Mirror Lake.

But how did the lake come form? The answer is the diastrophism. The expert told us that more than 10 000 years ago, there was a rift zone because of diastrophism. Afterwards, volcanoes erupted many times, and a great amount of lava blocked the Mudan River, raising the water level to form the present lake in the mountain. With a total area of 90.3 square kilometers, the lake has its average altitude of 350 meters and average depth of 40 meters, reaching maximum depth of 70 meters when it gets deeper. It is flowing from northeast to southwest, with 45 kilometers long and 9 ~ 45 meters wide. The shape of the lake is like letter "S", and it is divided into North Lake, Center Lake, South Lake and Vpper Lake.

Crowned as "West Lake in the North", it can be compared with Lake Geneva at an altitude of 375 meters. Big and small islands are scattered all over the lake, namely Baishilazi (White Stone Hill), Dagushan (Big Isolated Hill), Xiaogushan (Small Isolated Hill), Chengqianglazi (Rock Wall), Zhenzhumen (Pearls Gate), Daoshishan (Taoist Hill), and Laogualazi (Crow Hill). These seven islands together with the following Diaoshuilou Falls are the famous Eight Spots of Jingpo Lake Scenic Area. The eight spots all have their own features and make the whole area more beautiful.. The most famous one is the falls, although it has a weird name. The local people prefer to call the waterfall as Diaoshuilou in dialect, and name it Diaoshuilou Falls for its huge size. According to the appearance, the waterfall looks like the well-known Niagara Falls. It is also the biggest basalt falls in the world, and we will see it soon.

Jingpo Lake is one of first national key scenic spots approved by the State Council in 1982. It is surrounded by high cliffs and forests. The calm water reflects the mountains. It looks like the mountains rise from the water, and the water comes from the mountains; mountains and the water stay close to each other like lovers. Inspired by the beautiful scenery of the lake, the well-known General Ye Jianying once composed a poem about the scenery of the lakeJingpo. "One can see mountain above the lake, and water uphill, the scenery in the north beats the one in the south." Jingpo Lake is not only spectacular for its scenery but also is rich in natural resources. The forest areas in the lake region covers 600 000 hectares, and can be felled over 100 years. Jingpo Lake serves as a reservoir, which harnesses an area of 120 000 square kilometers. Now two hydropower stations have been built which contribute to the production of agriculture and industry and the people's livelihood. With its vast water resources, Jingpo Lake is good for fish farming. There are over 40 kinds of fish, including crucial carp, carp, red-tail carp, Chinese bass, and great whitefish. During holidays, anglers come here and fish in the woods or around jagged rocks. They can catch Chinese bass which weighs 2 kilograms with a small fish as bait. You can come and try your luck if you are interested. In the lake area, there are grapes, mountain plums, mountain peaches, pine nuts and mountain dates. The annual-output of these exceeds 20 tons. There are also a great variety of mushrooms, including Hericium mushroom fungus. The lake area can be regarded as a zoo with a natural environment. There are over 200 species of birds and animals including Sika deer and sable.

As tourism develops, hotels of various sizes and styles have been built, including Jingpo Lake Hotel, Villa Hotel and Crescent Hotel. These hotels are located at the lakeside with modern facilities and excellent services, being the ideal places for upscale tourists and convalescents.

Please look at the stone in my hand, and maybe you could see its difference. It is black and full of little holes. Why are there holes in the stone? I'll tell you the reason. The stone is called basalt which is formed after lava cooling. When the volcanoes erupt, lava flow meets air and turns into hard crust. However, there is also some gas remaining to vent after lava's cooling and these holes form. During low water period, we could find karst caves of various styles in the lava beds. These caves were made of lava blocks that experienced perennial abrasion of running water, as glossy as artificial works.

Well, ladies and gentlemen, we are going to visit the Jingpo Lake and I believe that the beautiful scenery will impress you deeply. By the way, as we are arriving, remember to take your belongings especially the camera, watch your step and follow me to begin the wonderful journey.

## 镜泊湖风景区

各位游客：

接下来我们要乘坐一个半小时的车程离开市区,到达大家期盼已久的旅游胜地镜泊湖。进行今天游览的重头戏——乘船游览镜泊湖。下面我就利用这段时间向您介绍一下镜泊湖的概况。

镜泊湖是我国最大、世界第二大的火山熔岩堰塞湖。它位于牡丹江市西南110公里处。镜泊湖是历史悠久、充满神奇传说的地方。镜泊湖,古称湄沱河。明代开始称镜泊湖,清代又称毕尔腾湖,满语中的"毕尔腾"也是平如镜面的意思。因此,我们至今仍称它为镜泊湖。

那么镜泊湖是怎样产生的呢？据专家考证:距今一万多年前,由于地壳变迁,这里形成了牡丹江断裂带。此后,这里又发生了多次火山群爆发,大量熔岩阻塞了牡丹江古河道,抬高了水位,在高山上就形成了现在的镜泊湖。全湖面积约90.3平方公里。平均海拔350米,水位高时,平均水深40米,最深处达70米。湖身呈东北至西南走向,纵长45公里,最宽处9公里,最窄处约400米。湖面呈S形,全湖分为北湖、中湖、南湖和上湖四个湖区。

镜泊湖被誉为"北国的西湖",可与世界上海拔375米的著名的瑞士日内瓦湖相媲美。湖中大小岛屿星罗棋布,分布着白石砬子、大孤山、小孤山、城墙砬子、珍珠门、道士山、老鸹砬子。它们与我们一会将要参观的吊水楼瀑布并称"镜泊八景"。这些景观各有特色,有的风光优美,有的历史悠久,仿佛八颗璀璨的明珠点缀在镜泊湖中。镜泊湖八景中最为著名的是吊水楼瀑布。乍一听,这个瀑布的名字好怪啊。原来,当地人习惯把瀑布称为"吊水",而这里的瀑布又高又大,于是人们就叫它吊水楼瀑布了。吊水楼瀑布酷似闻名世界的尼亚加拉大瀑布,是世界上最大的玄武岩瀑布。一会我就会带领大家去亲眼目睹它的壮观景象。

镜泊湖是1982年国务院公布的第一批国家级重点风景名胜区之一。湖岸群崖陡立;湖周峰峦叠翠;湖中水平如镜真是山在水中起,水在山中生,山山水水,相依相恋。叶剑英赋诗镜泊湖:"山上平湖水上山,北国风光胜江南。"可谓画龙点睛,概括了镜泊湖的旖旎风光。

镜泊湖不仅风景秀丽,各种资源也十分富饶。湖区森林面积达60万公顷,可采伐100年以上。镜泊湖本身也是一个大水库,控制流域面积达12万平方公里,已经建立的两座采用压力隧道引水的发电站,被称"地下明珠",为牡丹江地区的工农业生产和人民生活作出了巨大贡献。镜泊湖湖面辽阔,水质肥沃,是鱼类繁殖的良好场所。湖中除了驰名中外的湖鲫以外,还盛产鲤鱼、红尾、鳌花、大白鱼等40多种鱼类。每逢假日,垂钓爱好者来到这里,在怪石中或树丛中,用小小的活鱼作饵,即可钓上三四斤重的大鳌花。大家有兴趣的话,也可以在那里一试身手。湖区还产葡萄、刺梅果、山桃、松子、大枣等,年产量达20多万吨。湖区出产的圆蘑、冬蘑、青蘑、榛蘑及珍贵的猴头蘑、木耳等山产品畅销国内外。湖区还是一座天然的动物王国,野生动物及各种鸟类有200多种,梅花鹿、紫貂等都是举世闻名的珍贵动物。

随着旅游业的发展,镜泊湖周围建立了许多精巧别致、风格各异的休闲、疗养、避暑别墅和游乐场所。其中的镜泊湖宾馆、山庄宾馆、抱月湾宾馆、杏花村宾馆,依山傍水,设备先进,服务优良,是旅游者理想的休息和疗养的好地方。

大家看我手中拿一块石头,细心的游客可能会发现这石头与普通的石头不一样,它颜色乌黑而且还有许多小孔,大家能不能告诉我这是为什么呢?好,下面我就揭开这个谜底。这块石头叫作玄武岩。首先它是岩浆冷却后形成的,所以它的颜色乌黑。上面的这些小孔是因为镜泊湖的火山群的爆发时,喷出的熔岩在流动过程中,接触空气的部分首先冷却为硬壳,而硬壳内流动的熔岩中尚有一部分气体未来得及逸散,及至熔岩全部冷却后,这些气体才从硬壳中排出,形成了许多气孔和空洞。也就是我们看到的这些石头为什么会有小孔了。如果在枯水期,在熔岩床上我们还可以发现许多常年被流水冲击磨蚀的熔岩块形成的大小深浅不等的溶洞,这些溶洞犹如人工凿成的一般,光滑圆润,十分别致。

好了各位朋友,一会我就带大家一起去游览镜泊湖,我相信湖中的美景一定会给大家留下深刻印象的。镜泊湖马上就要到了,带好您的随身物品,请您注意脚下安全跟我一起下车吧。在这里我还要提醒您一句千万别忘记带相机哟……

## 15. Wudalianchi World Geopark

With a total area of 1 060 square kilometers, Wudalianchi World Geopark is located in the north Heilongjiang province, China, at the intersection between Lesser Hinggan Mountains and

Songnen Plain. Miraculously, it remains the layers in the period of Hercynian, Yanshan, and Cretaceous. With the eruption ages ranging from 2.1 million years prehistory to 230 years before now, 42 eruption centers are known up to now, from which this landscape received its dominant morphological shaping, including over 225 volcanoes, basalt lava platform with an area of over 800 square kilometers, 10 barrier lakes, 3 rivers, 127 natural cold springs and a great deal of rivulets. Moreover, here is home to 1 044 plants and 397 wild animals. The five connected lakes, like a string of beads, are formed by the latest volcanic magma filling the ancient sag basin lake Wudalinchi Lake, thus named Wudalianchi (five connected lakes). From the perspective of aesthetics and science, Wudalianchi represents the remarkable monogenetic volcano of the world.

Wudalianchi boasts the micro-topographic landscapes in various forms, such as crater, felsenmeer, fumarolic cone and disc, lava ice cave, lava sea, barrier lake and Longmen Stone village, named "Natural Museum of Volcano" and "An Open Textbook on Volcano" by the geologist. It is also reputed as "A Space-time Theatre of Biological Evolution" and "The Natural Kingdom of Ecological Harmony" by the botanists, also "The Tiptop tourism resources of the world" by the international tourism experts.

The rich geographical resources bestowed by nature create six natural environments rarely seen in the world for Wudalianchi: the world's purest natural Oxygen bar; the world's top quality magnetized and mineralized ionized water with medical care function; mineral water treatment and mud-bath treatment that have the functions of health care, facial care and medical care; natural volcanic lava mesa—solar thermal therapy field; multi-functional and large scale volcanic magnetic environment; non-polluted green mineral water food series. Thus Wudalianchi is now a natural therapy base with the best comprehensive conditions in the world.

The human beings in Wudalianchi has a long history. According to the Archaeology research and the document records, there are humans living here as early as 4 000 years ago. It belongs to Sushen, the ancient of Manchu, in Zhang and Zhou Dynasties, to Wuhuan or Hansui in Qin and Han Dynasties, to Beifuyu in the Three Kingdoms Period, to Tungusic Mohe tribes, the ancient of Manchu, in the Sui and Tang Dynasties, to Nurkal (Nuergan). There are many ethnic groups living in Wudalianchi, including Daur, Ewenki, Manchu, Mongol, Oroqen. The ancesters of these ethnic groups created various folk cultures, such as the culture of Shamanism, Buddhism, Taoism, Christianism. In addition, the culture of refugees, anti-Japanese, defending the frontiers and opening up wasteland as well as literate youngster also widely spread in here. Wudalianchi is the origin of the dragon culture in northern part of China, and the cradle of the culture of volcano and mineral spring. Thus, it is reputed as the earliest tourist attraction in the northern part of China.

Wudalianchi is rich in seasonal tourist products. Currently, it has developed six geological sightseeing areas, three original ecological adventure areas and three recreation areas, a total of twelve different sightseeing tourist areas, including Heilong Mountain, Bailong Lake, Longmen Stone village, Medical Spring Mountain, Crystal Palace, Bailong Cave, Medical Spring, Warm Lake, Wuhu Mountain, Heaven Lake, Grey Crane Wetland, Medical Spring Town as well as Longmen Mountain. Moreover, you can also visit the most dazzling tourist town, the Pearl Mineral Spring City and the most fashionable Healthy Therapy SPA City.

Up until now, Wudalianchi has won three world level awards and 13 state honors, such as World Geopark, World Biosphere Reserve, China National Geopark, 5A-Class Scenic Spot, China Biosphere Reserve, Home of Mineral Water, etc. Wudalianchi has a great significance in the development of the earth and ecological science, and has unique values in geo-aesthetics, spa environmental medicine, biology, hydrology and etc. Generally, visitors are impressed and shocked by the brilliant and spiritual landscapes. You might have travelled to a lot of historic sites, famous springs and tourist resorts in China, but you will find what Wudalianchi offers is the best. It is a trip for scientific exploration and longevity. I'm sure you will fall in love with it.

## 五大连池世界地质公园

五大连池世界地质公园位于东北亚大陆裂谷的轴部,小兴安岭西部隆起和松辽断陷盆地交界上,总面积1 060平方公里。这里奇迹般地保留着海西期、燕山期、白垩系古地层,从史前210万年到近代230年间,相继由42个火山口喷发形成了井字形排列的新老期层状、盾形、爆裂式火山25座,渣锥寄生火山200多座,玄武岩台地800多平方公里;形成了由低等到高等种类繁多的寒温带植物1 044种,野生动物397种;形成了10个如串珠状火山堰塞湖泊、3条河流、127眼天然冷矿泉和星罗棋布的溪流水泊。五大连池也因新期火山岩浆填塞凹陷盆地湖"乌德林池"而得名。大自然把地球亿万年的演化过程完整地压缩到五大连池,系统地展示给我们。从审美和科学的角度上看,五大连池是地球上单成因火山的卓越代表,奇异的自然地理结构造就了具有突出普遍价值的天然名胜。

"旷古绝作铸火山,罕世上善造神泉。熔岩腾飞化石海,万古酿就圣水传。"这里有保存最完整、分布最集中、品类最齐全、状貌最典型的微地貌遗迹:雄峻陡峭的山巅火口、波澜壮阔的翻花石海、造型奇绝的喷气锥碟、霜花似玉的熔岩冰洞、碧水一泓的天池胜景、云雾蒸腾的石龙温泊、鬼斧神工的龙门石寨、景色如画的堰塞湖泊;这里有中国北方最复杂的植被类型,是世界上研究生态演化的天然实验室;这里有神奇季相变幻下,复杂多样的生态系统所组成的山水画卷。这里山奇、石怪、泉神、洞异、湖秀、林幽,被地质学家称为"打开的火山教科书""天然的地质博物馆",被植物学家称为"生物演变的时空剧场""生态和谐的自然王国",被国际旅游专家称为"世界顶级旅游资源"。

得天独厚的环境因素和地质资源,造就了具有医疗保健价值举世罕见的六大天然理疗环境:高负氧离子含量的纯净空气、磁化矿化带有电荷的离子水,集康体、美容于一身的矿泉、矿泥洗疗区,太阳热能熔岩台地理疗场,规模宏大的火山全磁环境和矿泉系列生态食品。这些都是人类最理想的康体养生天堂。

五大连池的人类历史源远流长,通过考古和文献记载,景区内早在4000年前就有人类活动,商周时期这里属肃慎族居地,秦汉时属乌桓地或汉岁地,三国时属北夫余地;隋唐时属黑水靺鞨部居住地,明代归奴尔干都司所属,在古湖东岸建乌登河卫管辖,民国初年在三池湖畔建制湖山镇。这里的达斡尔、鄂温克、满、蒙、鄂伦春等各族先民创造了丰富的民俗文化,不仅有萨满、佛教、道教、基督教文化,而且还有浓郁关东风情的流民文化、抗联文化、屯垦、知青文化。神鹿示水、黑龙白龙的传说流传大江南北,这里是北方龙文化的起源地,是火山文化、矿泉文化的摇篮。游溶岩王国、品天下名泉、享民俗盛宴、观绝世奇景,五大连池是中国北方历史上最早的旅游胜地。

五大连池四季旅游产品丰富,目前已开发了6个地质观光区、3个原生态探险区、3个休闲游憩区,总计十二个不同类型的旅游区:有黑龙山、白龙湖、龙门石寨、药泉山、水晶宫白龙洞、药泉、温泊、卧虎山,还有天池、灰鹤湿地、药泉古镇、龙门山,涉及景观五百多个。还有黑龙江最耀眼的旅游名镇,工业观光游的明珠矿泉城,国际上最时尚的康疗SPA城等,是集生态观光、休闲度假、康体养生、科考探险为一体的多功能、综合型国际旅游区。

从开发建设至今三十年内已荣获了世界地质公园、世界生物圈保护区、世界自然遗产题名地三项世界级桂冠和国家重点风景名胜区、国家自然保护区、国家森林公园、国家5A级旅游区、中国矿泉城等十三项国家级荣誉。五大连池在地球发展史、生态科学方面对人类有重大意义,在地质美学、矿泉环境医学、生物学、水文学等方面更有独特价值。这里的景观会给人以生命灵动的震撼,踏山寻水之旅,更是意想不到的科学探讨之旅、健康长寿之旅。相信通过这次难忘的旅程,您一定会爱上这块珍奇的世界瑰宝。

### 16. Sino-Russian Border Lake—Lake Xingkai

  Dear tourists, imagine a place where the water flows clearly, the fish grows big and Mother Nature surrounds you with its entire glorious splendor. Welcome to Lake Xingkai, reputed as the emerald of north China. I believe the trip will be well worthwhile.

  Lake Xingkai is located on the border of China and the Russia. The lake is called Lake Xingkai in China and Khanka Lake in Russia. It is situated in the Jixi city, in the southeast of Heilongjiang province, 35 kilometers from Mishan City. It is a remarkable site for its beautiful natural landscape, eco-tourism as well as rich cultural heritage. Dating back to 6 000-year ago, Sushen, the ancient of Manchu, lived in the Lake Xingkai area and created the unique culture of hunting and fishing in the history of Chinese Civilization. Khanka Lake was once an inland lake in China. After the signing of Sino-Russia Convention of Peking in 1860, the lake became Sino-Russian Boundary Lake. Historically recorded, Khanka Lake was called Meituo Lake in the Tang Dynasty and was called Beiqin Sea in the Jin Dynasty. In the Qing Dynasty, it was renamed again as Khanka Lake. In Manchu language, Khanka means the water flowing down from a higher to a lower place.

Jiang Zemin, the President of the People's Republic of China, and Boris Yeltsin, the President of Russian Federation signed the agreement, then Lake Xingkai became National Nature Reserve. In the same year, it was appraised as Provincial Scenic Resort. Currently, it has become a tourist area with a considerable scale and unique features through the tireless efforts of Lake Xingkai people. The visitors can appreciate the natural landscape with special beauty and the wetland habitat. If lucky enough, you may encounter with millions of birds gathering on the Songacha River. Moreover, it is a land of heroes and you can visit the site of former Northeast Aviation School, the Memorial Hall for Great Northern Wilderness Development, the Tomb of Wang Xia, who was a general, all of which show us the history of heroes. All in all, the landscape of Lake Xingkai can be summarized in the following words: miraculous beauty, picturesque landscape, unsophisticated culture, and majestic appeal. A poet once praised Lake Xingkai that, "blue sky, blue lake; white beach, white wave; green grass, green hill; gold history, gold resource."

The formation of Lake Xingkai is a result of volcanic eruption and the continental collision between the Eurasian Plate and the Pacific Plate. Lake is composed of two lakes, one large and one small, which are divided by a 98 km-long sandy hill. The Lesser Lake Xingkai is an inland lake belongs to China. And the Greater Lake Xingkai totals an area of 4 380 kilometers, of which 1 080 kilometers within the boundaries of China. The widest place of the lake from east to west reaches to 60 kilometers, the longest distance from south to north is 130 kilometers, the deepest place is 10 meters and the depth on average is 3 meters.

There are 26 rivers in the area of Lake Xingkai emptying into the Lesser Lake Xingkai and the Greater Lake Xingkai respectively, 9 of which are within the boundaries of China. There is only one river flowing out of the Lake Xingkai and into the Wusuli River, which is the Songacha River.

The water area of Lake Xingkai is vast and the fish resource is rich. According to the relevant statistics, there are 6 fish orders, composed of 12 families and 48 species, such as the Culter alburnus, colloquially named big white fish, is one of the four major freshwater fishes in China; and the delicious "Sanhua", including Jihua, Aohua, and Bianhua. In addition, the white shrimp is the local delicacies in Lake Xingkai. Currently, the big white fish and the white shrimp have become the unique specialties of the Lake Xingkai. Dear friends, while enjoying the beautiful scene of Lake Xingkai, welcome to taste the delicacies—the big white fish and the white shrimp. I believe that you will never forget their delicious tastes.

Lake Xingkai is not only a National Natural Reserve and a National Geopark, but also an important wetland habitat and a natural habitat of migratory birds. You can find beauty in each season. In spring, it is vigorous. We can hear the sound of the ice surface splitting. With the calling of the spring the Lake Xingkai returns to life, and in the spring breeze, those unmelted ice rafts are rushed towards the shore by lake water, which represents its boundless vitality and its explosive force. Sometimes, the height of ice raft can be splendidly up to dozens of meters in the lakeshore, which embodies the mighty power of nature. In addition, the wild apricot and cherry come to flower competitively in the mound of the lake, putting on a beautiful garland for the Lake Xingkai. In summer, it is cool. It impresses visitors that the surface is smooth as a mirror, the water and the sky merge in one color, and the air is cool and refreshing as well as the scene is enchanting. The lakeshore is a vast sand beach stretching hundreds of miles, which has attracted lots of tourists. Definitely, this is the best choice for summer resort. In autumn, it is splendid. The visitors can feast their eyes with the beautiful scene, which is composed of the bird migration, green water, blue sky, and white reed catkins. In winter, it is a world of ice and snow. Lake Xingkai is covered by thick ice and looks like a silver kingdom. If you come here, you will see a special landscape: the unfrozen Songacha River, whose surface is covered in mist. The fog on the trees along the riverbank is transparent, crystal and exquisite which forms a fabulous world for you. The city leads the way in border-lake, wetland, eco-tourism and the ice and snow, so it is one of the best eco-tourist resorts, and is praised as "Oriental Hawaii" by the tourists.

## 中俄边界湖——兴凯湖

各位游客朋友,当你耳边响起辣妹子宋祖英那圆润甜美的歌声,伴着《月亮妹妹兴凯湖》那优美旋律,美丽神奇的兴凯湖是否会引起你无限的遐想?今天我就带领大家一起去游览素有"北国绿宝石"之称的兴凯湖。相信大家一定会不虚此行。

兴凯湖是中国与俄罗斯的界湖,位于黑龙江东南部鸡西境内,距密山市35公里处,它有着美丽神奇、生态完好的自然风光,还有着深厚的文化积淀。早在6 000年前,满族的祖先肃慎人就在兴凯湖畔生活,创造了中华文明史上独具特色的渔猎文化,据文字记载,从西周王朝开始,兴凯湖就是属于中国版图的内陆湖,唐代称兴凯湖为"湄沱湖",金代称为"北琴海",清代才改称为"兴凯湖","兴凯"为满语,是水往低处流之意。1860年通过不平等的《北京条约》,沙俄把中国的内陆湖改变为中俄界湖。1996年经中俄两国元首江泽民与叶利钦于4月25日在北京签署协议后,兴凯湖被列为国家级自然保护区,同年,它也被黑龙江省评为省级风景名胜区。经过兴凯湖人不懈的努力开发建设,兴凯湖现已成为颇具规模、颇具特色的旅游区。这里有独具风韵的自然景观、童话般的大沼泽湿地、万鸟云集的松阿察河盛况。这里还是一片英雄的土地,东北老航校旧址、北大荒开发纪念馆、王震将军墓,为我们展现了一部部英雄的历史。兴凯湖景观可用十六个字概括:美丽神奇,风景秀丽,文明古朴,气势磅礴。有一位诗人曾经这样赞美兴凯湖:蓝色的湖水蓝色的天,白色的浪花白色的滩,绿色的草地绿色的山,金色的历史金色的资源。

兴凯湖是由火山喷发、欧亚大陆板块与太平洋板块相撞,造成地壳陷落而形成的。一条98公里长的沙岗将兴凯湖分为大小两湖,小兴凯湖是中国内陆湖。大兴凯湖总面积4 380平方公里,中国境内面积为1 080平方公里,东西最宽处60公里,南北最长纵距130公里,湖水最深处10米,平均水深3米。兴凯湖共有26条河流分别注入大小兴凯湖,其中在我国境内9条,颇有海纳百川的气魄。从它流出的河流只有一条,这就是由东北溢出的松阿察河,随后注入乌苏里江。

兴凯湖水域辽阔,鱼类资源丰富,据有关资料统计,共有鱼类6目12科48种之多,其中翘嘴红鲌(俗称大白鱼)是我国四大淡水鱼之一,以及味道鲜美的"三花"(吉花、鳌花、鳊花)等鱼种。白丽虾,也是兴凯湖鱼宴上一道佳肴。现在,大白鱼和白丽虾都已成为兴凯湖的独有特产。游客朋友们,在观赏兴凯湖美景之际,请你品尝大白鱼和白丽虾佳肴,定会给你留下"不吃不知道,一吃忘不掉"的美好印象。

兴凯湖不仅是国家级自然保护区和国家地质公园,而且还是国际重要湿地及候鸟栖息地。这里一年四季景色各异:春天是活力世界,我们首先听到的是隆隆的开湖之声,沉寂了一冬的兴凯湖,在春姑娘的召唤下焕发出勃勃生机,融化的湖水在春风的吹动下,不断地将未融化的冰块冲向岸边,展现它无穷的生命力和永不停息的爆发力,有时在岸边能形成蔚为壮观的高达几十米的冰排,使我们不得不感慨大自然力量的伟大。此时节,百里湖岗野生的杏花和樱花竞相开放,如同给兴凯湖戴上了美丽的花环。夏季是清凉世界,兴凯湖波平如镜,水天一色,清爽宜人,风光旖旎。大湖环形的百里沙滩充满生机,游人如织,这里绝对是你避暑旅游的最佳选择。秋天是美妙世界,百里湖岗层林尽染,秋色斑斓。经过一春一秋的繁衍生息,候鸟开始集群南徙,湖水与蓝天相接,清白的芦花与秋鸟共舞,渲染出"落霞与孤鹜齐飞,秋水共长天一色"的美景。冬季是冰雪世界,兴凯湖到处是白雪茫茫、银装素裹。若您置身其中就会发现,还有一道独特的景观,那就是不冻的松阿察河,河上面雾气蒙蒙,两岸树上挂满了雾凇,冰清玉洁、千姿百态,犹如仙境一般,令人赞叹。界湖、湿地、生态、冰雪构成了兴凯湖独领风骚的旅游优势,是人们回归自然的最佳生态旅游胜地之一,被游人誉为"东方夏威夷"。

## 17. Qiqiher Zhalong Nature Reserve

Distinguished ladies and gentlemen,

  Welcome to Zhalong Nature Reserve!

  I am your guide ××× from Zhalong Reserve Administration. I am so glad to be with you. If you have any requirement or comment, please do not hesitate to ask, as long as conditions permit, I will definitely try to help you, I am willing to better serve you and also hope you will cooperate with me and give valuable advice on my work.

Maybe you've already heard about Zhalong Nature Reserve, but it is the first time for most of you to come here, so I want to ask a question first:

Do you come here for the red-crowned crane? Or just want to see the endless reed marshes?

All my dear friends, your answers are right, but far from comprehensive. While visiting here, you will have a very different tour from other places of interest and cultural landscape—Zhalong wetland eco-tourism. There are many definitions of eco-tourism. For example, what our country and other countries accept and quote is the definition determined in 1994 by Australia, which refers to enjoying education about natural environment while traveling in nature as well as sustainable ecological management. The tourism is to promote a viewpoint, to propose a culture that one can enjoy, love and protect nature.

Firstly, I will introduce the overview of Zhalong Nature Reserve to you. In our country Zhalong Nature Reserve is the biggest nature reserve of rare birds and wetland ecosystems which is mainly to protect cranes and other waterfowls. It is located on the lower reaches of the Wuyuer River and covers a wetland of 210 000 hectares and the average altitude is 142.5 meters with temperate continental monsoon climate.

Wuyuer River is an inland river. Originated from Lesser Khingan Mountain, it flows to the Zhalong, and makes an astonished wetland landscape, among which 80% is reed swamp. Many dotted lakes and meandering streams and rivers flow here and make aquatic, wet and plants widely distributed; furthermore, fish, frogs, aquatic insects and molluses bloomed and waterfowl's food sources are abundant as well. Because of this area's special high latitude, the sunlight lasts for more than 14 hours per day from April to June, which is favorable for waterfowls' mating, breeding and nestlings' growth. Vast water area, contiguous lakes, luxuriant reed and soft mud here all make this area a natural protection place and shelter of the waterfowl since ancient time, for in spring, summer and autumn, it is difficult for people to go inside to hunt or fish; it is also difficult for wolves, foxes and other predators enter this region with harassment.

Unique natural conditions and great location make birds resources abundant in this region. There are 296 kinds of birds among which mostly are waterfowls, especially large quantity of cranes. It is said that among 15 species of cranes in the world, 9 species live in China, and in Zhalong, you can find 6 ones. The red-crested crane, white-napped crane, demoiselle crane and gray crane belong to breeding birds; white crane and white-headed crane are migratory birds. Other rare birds, swans and great egrets also stay here. As Zhalong has so many kinds of cranes and birds, it is also known as the Paradise of Birds and Cranes.

The worldwide attention is attracted by the four features of Zhalong Nature Reserve, vast land, original wetland landscape, abundant bird resources and short distance from the urban area.

Dear friends, when you go inside this reserve you will first see the mission center opposite the park. VIP lounge, visitors service center and video hall which can accommodate 80 people at the same time are available in the mission center. The video film, *The International Important Wetland and Home of Red-Crowned Crane* is played all day long to introduce the wetland landscape and various waterfowls and birds in Zhalong, which will bring you into a world of birds and a kingdom of cranes. Here you can see hundreds of thousands of gulls, egrets and other birds flying in the sky and hordes of waterfowls frolicking in the lakes. Also you can enjoy the unique courtship of love from red-crowned cranes. The male crane expresses his dedicated pursue with his high-pitched voice. When you hear a duet from male and female in the wilderness, that must be the joy of a successful puppy love they are claiming. It is most exciting when a couple of red-crowned crane holds a wedding ball, the beautiful pas de deux of the crane can beat the first-class dancer in the world. Having seen the video film I believe you guys have already got a preliminary understanding about Zhalong Nature Reserve. We are now at the second stop of this one-day tour in the crane's home, "the Platform for Watching Cranes". First you can see a pair of white marble statue of red-crowned cranes standing on the Taihu Lake Stone in the middle of the platform. They have a pretty posture and a good look which can arouse one's expectation and aspiration for all the beautiful things. Take a photo with them! I believe staying with these lucky living creatures, you and your family will live a long and happy life and your love will have a perfect end.

Wandering along the classical long corridor, we can see the new tourist attraction "Fishing Garden" in the west. Along the green and luxuriant reed pond, mushrooms look especially attractive within the green reeds. Walking in the tranquil environment, taking a shower with fresh air, which may make you relaxed, happy and refreshed.

Opposite the platform we can see the Immortal Crane Lake on which you will enjoy a wonderful world with lotus just like shy girls around you.

The Wetland Monument in the reeds is to remember the event in 1992 China government joined the Convention on Wetlands, at the same time Zhalong Nature Reserve was ranked into the list of international important wetland.

The full name of the treaty is International Important Convention on Wetlands of the Habitant of Waterfowls which was signed in Ramsar city, Iran on February 2nd 1971 also called Ramsar Convention. The aim of the treaty is to admit the mutual relationship between human and environment and makes sure the wetland of many waterfowls can be protected well by the coordinated international actions. 18 countries started the treaty and 105 countries have joined it by the end of 1997. In 1992, Chinese government joined the treaty and pointed six wetlands into the international important wetland list, namely, Zhalong Natural Reserve in Heilongjiang province, Xianghai in Jilin province,

Poyang Lake in Jiangxi province, Dongting Lake in Hunan province, Bird Island of Qinghai in Qinghai province and Dongzhaigang in Hainan. With the return of Hongkong in 1997, Mipu became the seventh international important wetland in China.

There are at least over 50 different definitions about the wetland, mainly can be divided into broad and narrow sense. The definition of Convention on Wetlands is from the broad one which means wetland is, no matter how natural or man-made, permanent or temporary swamp, wet prairie, peat land or water land, static or flow, fresh water or semi-salt water including water under the six meters when meet low tide. Even though there is a doubt about the Scientific nature of this definition, till now there is no more definition like this accepted by human.

Usually the narrow definition of wetlands deems the wetland as aneco-zone which means that is a transition zone between lands and the one between land and waters or the marshes, peat land.

The Convention on Wetlands divided wetland into three categories, namely, the marine and coastal wetlands, inland waters wetlands and artificial wetlands.

Zhalong Protected Area is an inland swamp wetland.

The wetland is a versatile unique ecosystem on earth; the ecological landscapeis rich in biodiversity in nature and the most important living environment of human being with high biological productivity, usually close to or even more than productivity of intensive agricultural system. The drinking water of human being all comes from wetlands, 80% of the towns are built on or around wetlands and 60% of human being absorbs wetlands property. The wetlands have unique features of stored water and adjusting flood, regulating climate, controlling soil erosion and reducing environment pollutants, so it is known as "Kidney of Nature" and "the Cradle of Life". Wetlands are also an important species gene pool and breeding grounds of endangered birds, of migratory birds and other wildlife habitat.

Here is the Memorial Monument of Zhalong Natural Reserve. The year of 1979 witnessed the foundation of Zhalong Natural Reserve which was promoted to the National Nature Reserve after the approval of the state in 1987. In our country the Natural Reserve is divided into four levels, namely national level, provincial level, city level and county level.

Approved by the state council, the natioanl natural reserve has a high scientific, cultural and economic value in our country or the world.

National Nature Reserve of natural ecosystems must meet the following conditions:

(1) Its ecosystem should be in a high degree of representativeness and typicality in the world or in its respective domestic bio-climatic zones.

(2) Its ecosystem should be rare in the world, only biome or habitat type in the country.

(3) Its ecosystem should be considered with high abundant biodiversity in its respective domes-

tic bio-climatic zones.

(4) Its ecosystem should not be damaged or at least should be damaged softly with a good nature.

(5) Its ecosystem should be all or basically completed and there are enough space for keeping this integrity including core area and buffer area over 1 000 hectares.

In front of us are egret shed, bird cage and crane's feeding farm with different architecture and style. Libai, a great poet in Tang Dynasty, once composed a poem about the big egret here. We can find a lot of rare birds such like white spoonbill, heron, purple heron, big swan, swan goose and peacock, and the most attractive red-crowned crane. There are totally 15 species of cranes, but you can find 13 species wild or tamed in Zhalong, especially the rarest red-crowned crane ranked national-level. At present it is world-renowned to watch cranes in the home of cranes.

The red-crowned crane is also known as "Immortal Crane" and symbolizes longevity and luck and left only no less than 2 000 in the world. Through the efforts of researchers in our administration, we have been successfully established China's first red-crowned crane to dissipate and tame breeding populations, which make migratory birds become resident birds just to go outdoor throughout the year, and never move south any more. The red-crowned cranes can take off, fly and land down in a group according to the command of the breeders. You can also see light and beautiful crane dance, just like fairy arriving the earth. A famous writer, Liu Baiyu, once created one beautiful poem to praise it. If you are lucky enough you can take photos of this moment. Accompanied by the cranes, hearing their songs and blessing you will feel the unprecedented charm of life given by the nature.

Surrounding the breeding center, you can see the scattered area of rare waterfowls where you are always reluctant to go away from the bridge. On the water of the both sides of the bridge, you can see many kinds of waterfowls play just like flowers competing for beauty of looks, big swans hold up their long necks seemingly to make salute to people. If you feed them you will get the worship from birds. I'm sure the friendly communication can recall your responsibility for protecting nature and treasuring birds.

Getting out of breeding farm along the path in the forest, you can see "Watching Building for Crane" built in 1984. It was a comprehensive facility with science, research and mission, inside you can see s specimen display hall, rest room and telescope.

In the specimen hall, you can see the biggest within province and vivid model of wetlands eco-landscape, tiny eco-sand plate of wetlands represent the whole scene. Here you can find six kinds of animals and over 130 bird specimen from 15 sections, 29 divisions. In the first floor rest room, you can see the photos when our country's leader such as Deng Xiaoping, Li Peng and Tian Jiyun inspected here. The picture exhibition of insect specimen, wetlands mission and science and research achievement can be seen from the second floor to the fourth floor.

Entering the main building of Watching Building for Crane, you will feel standing on the cloud and suddenly become extensive before your eyes with your whole body melt into the hug of the nature. The endless reed swamp spreads over the distant horizon and numerous riverway embellish the reed swamp bright. From your deep heart you will highly praise the miracle of nature. You can experience a more interesting life with telescope searching for the trace of cranes and hearing hundreds of birds sing.

There is a sea of flowers in front of the building. Rows of lilac trees, trimmed hedges, three-dimensional flower bed with a flying crane surrounded by yellow Cestrum, purplish red cockscomb and intoxicating canna.

Opposite the building locates a new special flavor restaurant which can hold 120 people one time with fresh environment, complete equipment and first-rate service. With birds' twitter and fragrance of flowers and rural interest, you want to linger on. In order to adapt the development of tourism, the restaurants of the protection zone are open to the outside with double room, big and small meeting rooms, activity room, western buffet and multifunctional karaoke. Every room is equipped with air condition and hot water. The protection zone can receive all kinds of meeting, group tour and family outing for holiday. You can enjoy reservation and all-round service including eating, staying, visiting and shopping accompanied by guide.

Since the foundation of the protection zone, we have already received many international organizations such as International Crane Fund, the World Natural Association, the International Union for Conservation of Nature and Natural Resources and World Wildlife Fund, etc. We also welcome 1 500 000 ornithologists, ecologists, nature lovers and many visitors from 42 countries such as US, Japan, Russia, UK, France, etc., to come here for investigation and research, practice teaching and a sightseeing tour.

In 1995, as The world-famous Wetland Waterfowls Nature Reserve and The Home of Red-crowned Crane, Zhalong Protection Zone was chosen the most honorary award of China by state council. In 1998, Zhalong Protection Zone was honored with National Children's Hand in Hand Global Village and National Environmental Education Base. In 2000, it won National Youth Science and Education Base.

Zhalong Nature Reserve is to be built as the Center of publicity and education on birds' protection in china, as well as the cranes' breeding research center, but also as "Waterfowl Park" and "Important International Wetland with unique Chinese characeristics". The world-famous Zhalong Nature Reserve with its unique charm has become a bright pearl in the northern part of the country.

Our trip will come to an end. I believe everyone has already known the outlook of this nature reserve. You must be deeply impressed by the endless reed swamp, fresh air with the flavor of flower, original wetland landscape, enthusiastic staff from Zhalong, and especially the beautiful red-crowned crane.

You will leave Zhalong Nature Reserve and start a new journey, I wish everyone healthy and happy and welcome to Zhalong again!

Thanks!

## 齐齐哈尔扎龙自然保护区

尊敬的各位女士、各位先生、朋友们：

你们好！

欢迎您到扎龙自然保护区参观游览。

我是扎龙保护区管理局的导游员，我叫×××。我很高兴陪同诸位在扎龙保护区游览观光。您如有什么要求和意见，请随时提出来，只要条件允许，我一定尽力去办，我愿意为您服务，也希望您能同我合作，对我的工作提出宝贵意见。

诸位可能很早就听说过扎龙自然保护区，但大部分人都是第一次来扎龙保护区，我先提一个问题：

你到这里是看丹顶鹤吗？

还是看一看一望无际的芦苇荡？

来宾朋友你们都说对了，但不全面，您会感受到与其他名胜古迹、人文景观所不同的旅游——扎龙湿地生态旅游，生态旅游的定义有多种解释，我国和大多数国家所认可和引用的是1994年澳大利亚为发展生态旅游下的定义：到大自然中去的、将自然环境教育和解释寓于其中的、受到生态上可持续管理的旅游。主要内容是宣传一种观点，倡导一种文化即享受自然、热爱自然、保护自然。

我首先为来宾朋友介绍一下扎龙自然保护区概况。扎龙自然保护区是我国最大的以保护鹤类等水禽为主体的珍稀鸟类和湿地生态类型自然保护区。位于黑龙江省西部松嫩平原乌裕尔河下游，区址在齐齐哈尔市区东南26.7公里处，是齐齐哈尔市所辖铁锋区、昂昂溪区、富裕县、泰来县和大庆市所辖林甸县、杜尔伯特蒙古族自治县交界地域。绝对地理坐标介于东经123°35′~124°46′，北纬47°34′~46°35′之间。面积2 100平方公里，平均海拔高度142.5米，气候属中温带大陆性季风气候。

小兴安岭发源的乌裕尔河是一条外流区中的内陆河，流至该区处于无尾状态，河水囤积漫溢形成80%以芦苇沼泽为主的湿地景观。湖泊泡沼星罗棋布，溪流河道蜿蜒迂回，水生、湿生和中生植物广泛分布，鱼、蛙、水栖昆虫、软体动物大量繁殖，水禽的食物来源十分丰富。该区纬度较高，4~6月鸟类繁殖期日照长达14小时以上，鸟类繁殖期光照时间长既刺激亲鸟性激素分泌增多,有利于配对繁殖,又因采食时间长,有利于雏鸟生长发育。该区水面广阔,湖泊连片,苇草繁茂,淤泥绵软,春、夏、秋三季以水禽为主的候鸟居留期间,不便渔、猎和其他生产活动的开展,狼、狐狸等天敌也难进入区内骚扰,自古以来就是水禽的天然保护地和隐蔽所。从世界动物地理来看,该区位于东北亚内陆,居西太平洋、日本海与东北亚大陆之间,是很多沿海越冬,内陆繁殖鸟类的繁殖地与迁徙过渡带,也是澳洲、东南亚越冬,北部近极地区繁殖鸟类的迁徙过渡带和繁殖地;根据中国动物地理区划,该区位于东北区的大兴安岭亚区、长白山亚区和蒙新区的东部草原区之间的过渡地带。

得天独厚的自然条件和优越的地理位置,使该区鸟类资源十分丰富,据调查,该区分布以水禽为主体的鸟类269种,尤其以鹤的种类多、数量大为举世瞩目。世界现存鹤类15种,中国有9种,该区即分布有6种,其中丹顶鹤、白枕鹤、蓑羽鹤、灰鹤为繁殖鸟,白鹤、白头鹤为迁徙停息鸟。其他珍稀鸟类还有白鹳、黑鹳、天鹅、白琵鹭、大白鹭、小杓鹬及沼泽猛禽多种,和数量众多的鸥类、雁鸭类、鹭类等,成为驰名中外的"鸟的乐园、鹤的故乡"。

该区辽阔的地域,原始的湿地景观,丰富的鸟类资源,距离城市较近的特征已为世人瞩目。

来宾朋友,您进入保护区后,首先迎接您的是位于停车场对面的宣教中心。宣教中心内设贵宾休息室、游客服务中心和可容纳80人同时观看的录像厅。全天滚动播放介绍扎龙自然保护区湿地景观和各种水禽鸟类的录像片《国际重要湿地、丹顶鹤的故乡》,它将把您带入鸟的世界、鹤的王国中。在这里您可以看到成千上万只的鸥、鹭等鸟类在天空翱翔,成群结队的水禽在湖中嬉游。清澈的溪流泛起团团银光,摇曳的芦缨、茂密的苇塘在微风中奏响大自然的瑰丽诗章。在这里您还可以领略到对爱情专一的丹顶鹤独特的求爱方式,那"一鸣九皋,声闻于天"的男高音,表达了对心上人的执着追求,当原野上回响起互诉柔肠百转的"男女声二重唱"时那是它们为初恋而发自内心的喜悦。等到一对喜结良缘的丹顶鹤在大自然的礼堂中举行婚礼"舞会"时,那是最令人兴奋的场面,轻快协调而优美的"双人舞"让人间最优秀的舞蹈家也为之逊色。

看完录像片我们已对扎龙自然保护区有了初步的认识,现在我们来到鹤乡一日游的第二站"观鹤台"。首先映入您眼帘的是台中央太湖石上耸立的一对洁白无瑕的丹顶鹤汉白玉塑像。它们体态秀丽,亲密和谐,相亲相爱。它们的神情能唤起世人对一切美好事物的向往与追求。留下一张照片吧!只要这吉祥的生灵永远陪伴我们,我们每一个人和家庭就一定会幸福安康、爱情美满、白头偕老。

环绕古典长廊,西侧是新建的旅游景区"垂钓园"。青翠茂密的苇塘怀抱着一泓碧波,朵朵蘑菇在绿色的苇丛中显得格外醒目。幽雅恬静的环境,沐浴在草木野花清香的空气中,让人心旷神怡、倍感清爽。

观鹤台的对面是萍飘苇秀的仙鹤湖。荡起一叶小舟,轻摇双桨,您将观赏到清澈的湖水托出的一个斑斓的水上世界。随着您双桨的起浮,片片浮萍撩起点点玉珠,在阳光下放射出迷人的光彩。亭亭玉立的莲花像含羞的少女一样簇拥在您的船边。

位于芦苇丛中的是湿地纪念碑,用于纪念中国政府1992年加入《湿地公约》,扎龙自然保护区被列入国际重要湿地名录。

该公约全称是《关于特别是作为水禽栖息地的国际重要湿地公约》。1971年2月2日签订于伊朗的拉姆萨尔城,又称拉姆萨尔公约。其宗旨是承认人类同其环境相互依存关系,并通过协调一致的国际行动确保众多水禽栖息地的湿地得到良好的保护而不至于丧失。公约由18个国家发起,至1997年底已有105个国家加入,是世界上影响较大的政府间合作的环境保护公约。中国政府1992年加入《湿地公约》并同时指定黑龙江扎龙、吉林向海、江西鄱阳湖、湖南东洞庭湖、青海鸟岛、海南东寨港6个湿地保护区列入国际重要湿地名录。1997年随着香港的回归,香港米埔保护区成为中国第7块国际重要湿地。

湿地的概念世界上至少有50多种不同的解释,大体可分为广义和狭义的湿地概念。《湿地公约》的定义是广义的。湿地是指,不问其为天然或人工,长久或暂时的沼泽地、湿草原、泥炭地或水域地带,带有或静止或流动,或为淡水、半咸水体者,包括低潮时不超过6米的水域。目前,尽管对这个定义的科学性还有些争议,但迄今为止还没有比它更好的定义,而且是国际公认的定义。

通常狭义的定义把湿地视为生态交错带,是陆地与陆地和水域之间的过渡区域,或者是指沼泽地、泥炭地。

湿地公约把湿地分为三大类,即海洋和海岸湿地、内陆水域湿地、人造湿地。

扎龙保护区属于内陆沼泽性湿地。

湿地是地球上具有多功能的独特生态系统,是自然界最富集生物多样性的生态景观和人类最重要的生存环境,具有很高的生物生产力,通常接近甚至超过集约农业系统的生产力,人类的饮用水100%来源于湿地,80%的城镇建立在湿地及湿地周围,60%的人类以湿地的物产为摄取物,湿地具有蓄水调洪、调节气候、控制土壤侵蚀、促淤造陆、降解环境污染物等独特功能,被誉为"自然之肾""生命的摇篮",是濒危鸟类、迁徙候鸟及其他野生动物的栖息繁殖地和重要的物种基因库。

这里是扎龙自然保护区纪念区碑,扎龙自然保护区建于1979年,1987年经国家批准晋升为国家级自然保护区。我国自然保护区分为国家级、省(自治区、直辖市)级、市(自治州)级和县(自治县、旗、县级市)级四级。

国家级自然保护区,是指在我国或全球具有极高的科学、文化和经济价值,并经国务院批准的自然保护区。

国家级自然生态系统类自然保护区必须具备下列条件:

(1)其生态系统在全球或在国内所属生物气候带中具有高度的代表性和典型性。

(2)其生态系统中具有在全球稀有、在国内仅有的生物群落或生境类型。

(3)其生态系统被认为在国内所属生物气候带中具有高度丰富的生物多样性。

(4)其生态系统尚未遭到人为破坏或破坏很轻,保持着良好的自然性。

(5)其生态系统完整或基本完整,保护区拥有足以维持这种完整性所需的面积,包括具备1 000公顷以上面积的核心区和相应面积的缓冲区。

眼前是建筑风格各异、造型别致的鹭舍、鸟笼和鹤类饲养场。这里有李白笔下"一行白鹭上青天"中的大白鹭,有嘴似琵琶的白琵鹭,以及俗称"缩脖老等"的苍鹭、草鹭、大天鹅、鸿雁、孔雀等珍禽鸟类,更有您到鹤乡最想看到的丹顶鹤。全世界共有15种鹤而扎龙保护区野生及人工驯养的鹤类就达到13种之多,其中尤以国家一级保护珍禽丹顶鹤最为珍贵,"鹤乡观鹤"早已闻名世界。

丹顶鹤又称"仙鹤",是吉祥和长寿的象征,现世界仅存不到2 000只。它体态秀丽,能歌善舞,站则亭亭玉立,动则缓步轻移,飞则直冲云天,鸣则声震九霄。经区科研人员的努力,现已成功建立了我国第一个丹顶鹤散放驯养繁殖种群,使候鸟变成留鸟,一年四季均在野外活动,不再南迁。丹顶鹤能根据饲养员的口令"整体起飞,群体飞翔,定点降落"。还能为您表演世人罕见的"鹤舞",看它舞姿轻盈,袖舞霓裳,洁白的体羽上,轻笼着黑纱巾,随风飘过,似仙女临凡,美不胜收。著名作家刘白羽曾以"翔鹤飘然落,美在自然中"的诗句来赞美它。如果运气好,您一定能拍下这难得的瞬间。在仙鹤的陪伴下,聆听云雀的歌唱、百鸟的祝福,您会感受到大自然的绿色赋予我们的生命的魅力。

环绕鹤类繁育中心,是珍稀水禽散养区,一座座木桥依恋地挽留着您的脚步。木桥两侧的水面上多种水禽像一片花朵一样争奇斗艳,尽情嬉戏。鸬鹚捕鱼,鸳鸯戏水,大天鹅竖起长长的可自转360°的脖颈,在行独有的注目礼。您若大方地撒上一把食物,就会享受到群鸟的朝拜。这友好的感情交流肯定会唤起您保护自然爱惜鸟类的责任感。

离开饲养场,沿林间小径来到"望鹤楼"。望鹤楼建于1984年,是集科研、宣教一体的综合设施,内设标本展厅、商服网点、休息室、高倍观鹤望远镜等。

标本展厅内有省内最大的形态逼真的湿地生态景观模型,有反映保护区全貌的微缩湿地生态沙盘。在这里你可以观赏到形态各异栩栩如生的大到黄羊,小到刺猬等6种兽类和15目29科130多种鸟类标本。在一楼休息室,悬挂着党和国家领导人邓小平、李鹏、万里、田纪云等同志来区视察的照片,二至四楼设有昆虫标本展及湿地宣传教育和保护区科研成果图片展。

登上望鹤楼主楼,您会产生腾云驾雾之感,眼前豁然开朗,仿佛整个身心都溶化在大自然的怀抱里了。凭栏远眺,一望无际的芦苇荡一直铺展到遥远的地平线,随风荡漾的绿色波涛雄浑坦荡极有气势地向天际涌去,又向您涌来。纵横交错数不清的港汊河道把万顷芦苇荡点缀得生机盎然。您会由衷地赞叹大自然的鬼斧神工。手持高倍望远镜寻觅仙鹤飞踪,耳听百鸟争鸣婉转优雅,更是别有一番情趣在心头。

观鹤楼前是一片花的海洋。成排的丁香树,修剪整齐的绿篱,立体花坛中央有一只仙鹤在振翅高飞,四周簇拥着黄色的夜来香、紫红的鸡冠花和红的醉人的美人蕉。

望鹤楼的对面是装修一新的风味餐厅,内部环境典雅清新、设施齐全、服务一流,可容纳120人同时就餐。在这里掬一注清水烹茶煮鱼,斟一杯家乡北大仓。此时此刻,伴着窗外鸟语花香,眼前涌动着苇木葱茏,这乡野情趣会令您流连忘返。

为适应旅游业发展,保护区的宾馆对外开放,设有双人客房、大小会议室、活动室、西式冷餐厅、多功能卡拉OK等配套旅游商服网点,房里都装有空调,备有热水,可接待各种会议、团体旅游、家庭节假日野游。并可预约、预定,还有导游陪同等吃、住、游、购物一体化全方位服务。

建区以来,共接待了国际鹤类基金会、世界自然协会、世界自然与自然资源保护联盟、世界野生生物基金会等国际性组织和美国、日本、俄罗斯、英国、法国等42个国家,中国港、澳、台地区及内地150余万人次的鸟类学者、生态学者和大自然的爱好者及游客考察研究、教学实习、参观游览。

1995年扎龙保护区作为"闻名中外的湿地水禽自然保护区"和"丹顶鹤的故乡"同时入选国务院颁发的中华之最荣誉大典,1998年被授予"全国少年儿童手拉手地球村""全国环境教育基地",2000年被授予"全国青少年科普教育基地"。

扎龙保护区不仅要建设成为中国的鸟类宣传教育保护中心和鹤类繁殖研究中心,还要建设成为中国独具特色的"水禽乐园"和"国际重要湿地"。物宝天华、人杰地灵、举世闻名的扎龙自然保护区正以其独具特色的魅力成为祖国北疆的一颗璀璨的明珠。

鹤乡的游览活动就要结束了,我想大家对扎龙保护区已有了大致的了解。那一望无际的芦苇荡,清沁飘着花香的空气,原始的湿地景观,热情好客的扎龙自然保护区工作人员,特别是美丽的丹顶鹤,一定会给大家留下令人难忘的美好记忆。

各位女士、各位先生即将离开扎龙保护区,踏上新的旅程,预祝大家精神愉快、身体健康!欢迎再次来扎龙保护区观光游览。谢谢!

## 18. Mudanjiang Snow Village—Snow World in China

Located on the Jiangxin Island of Jiangbin Park, Mudanjiang City, the Mudanjiang Snow Village covers an area of 46 000 square meters. Every winter sublime and majestic Snow village will be constructed on the Jiangxin Island, bearing much resemblance to the Harbin Ice and Snow World in structure. The biggest differences between these two works of art lie in the fact that the latter displays the beauty of the ice, and the crystalline world of the ice with ice being the raw materials while the former embodies the elegance of the snow and the pure white paradise of the snow with snow being the theme. The Snow Village in Mudanjiang City boasts its present status of No. 1 in the world in terms of area coverage, snow used and active involvement, which can rival those in Kemi, Finland, and in Sapporo, Japan.

Each year, the Snow Village will be planned and constructed with different themes, which has become a focus of attraction in the winter tours of Heilongjiang province and as such tourists from various places come with admiration for its reputation to enjoy the charm of these art treasures.

### 牡丹江雪堡——中国雪城

中国雪城牡丹江雪堡,位于牡丹江市江滨公园江心岛内,占地4.6万平方米。2001年开始,每年冬季牡丹江的江心岛上都要建造气势恢弘的雪堡,雪堡的建设与哈尔滨冰雪大世界有许多相同之处,但最大的不同在于哈尔滨是以冰为原材料,是冰的展现、冰的天地,牡丹江是以雪为题材,是雪的艺术、雪的世界。目前,牡丹江的雪堡在占地、用雪量及规模上成为世界之最,可与芬兰开米、日本札幌的雪堡相媲美。

雪堡每年都围绕不同的主题进行规划建设,现已成为黑龙江省冬季旅游一大亮点,各地游客慕名而来,感受这份艺术精品的魅力。

## 19. Wanyan Aguda Mausoleum

At the distance of 300 meters east of thesite of Huiningfu, the upper capital of the Jin Dynasty the first Emperor of Jin Dynasty, Wanyan Aguda's original burial site is located in southern suburb, Acheng City, Heilongjiang province. The Mausoleum, locally referred to as execution site for army officers, is a huge mound of 10-meter high, assuming the shape of a turtle, covering an area of approximately 1 000 square meters, the base circumference of the mound being as long as more than 100 meters.

The first Emperor of Jin Dynasty (1068–1123) was the second son of Jielibo, his autonym Wanyan Aguda and Chinese first name Wen. Aguda proclaimed himself emperor of Jin Dynasty in 1115, naming the first year of his reign Shouguo. He was an outstanding hero of the Jurchen Nationality, for completing two great causes in his lifetime, one founding a new dynasty, the other defeating Liao Kingdom. In the second year of his reign (1116), he was respectfully called "Emperor Mahatma", and called "Emperor Wuyuan" posthumously in the third year of Tianhui (1125), his shrine name "Founder".

### 金太祖完颜阿骨打陵址

金太祖完颜阿骨打的初葬陵址位于黑龙江省阿城市南郊,东距金上京会宁府遗址约300米,当地俗称"斩将台"。陵址是一个呈龟形、高约10米的大土阜,封土堆底周长百余米,占地近千平方米。

金太祖为世祖劫里钵第二子,本名完颜阿骨打,汉名雯,生于1068年,卒于1123年。阿骨打于1115年称帝建金,建元收国,他一生完成了建国、破辽两件大事,是女真族杰出的英雄。收国二年(1116年)他被尊为"大圣皇帝",天会三年(1125年),被溢为武元皇帝,庙号太祖。

## 20. History Museum of the Upper Capital of the Jin Dynasty in Acheng

History Museum of the Upper Capital of the Jin Dynasty is located 2.5 kilometers from the southern suburb of Acheng City, Heilongjiang province, to the east is the Site of Huiningfu, one of the sites to be protected at the national level; the south, the original graveyard of the first emperor Wanyan Aguda—Jintaizu Mausoleum Park; and the north, the ancient temple of Jin Dynasty, Baosheng Temple, to be rebuilt. All of these sites form the unique resort of Jin culture.

The politics, economy, culture, military affairs and history of Jin Dynasty are shown by pictures, documents, and valuable historical artifacts respectively in 9 exhibition halls. The museum stores over 1 500 pieces of cultural relics, including 21 pieces of national first class, such as crouching copper dragon fixed on the emperor's sedan chair, copper mirror with carp veins and "Cheng'an Baohuo" sycee, precious treasure in the world currency history. It is also worth mentioning that in the nationally famous exhibition hall of copper mirrors, there shows 246 copper mirrors that are made with exquisite craftwork and characterized by their diversified and colorful designs. They reflect the perfect arts and crafts of mirror making in Jin Dynasty, and also provide us valuable materials for historical research.

## 阿城金上京历史博物馆

金上京历史博物馆位于黑龙江省阿城市南郊2.5公里处,东临国家级文物保护单位——金上京会宁府(皇城)遗址,南傍金代开国皇帝完颜阿骨打的初葬地——金太祖陵址公园,再加上北侧即将复建的金代古寺宝圣寺,共同构成了别具风格的金源文化旅游区。

博物馆设9个展厅,以翔实的图片、文字资料和弥足珍贵的历史文物展示了金代的政治、经济、文化、军事及发展历程。博物馆馆藏文物1 500余件,其中国家一级文物就有21件。如皇帝御辇上的饰物铜座龙、双鲤纹铜镜、世界货币史上的珍宝"承安宝货"银锭等。尤其值得一提的是名冠全国的铜镜专题展厅,共展出246面铜镜,其制作工艺精湛,图案丰富多彩,反映了金代极高的制镜工艺水平,也为今人研究金代历史提供了宝贵的资料。

## 21. Site of Huiningfu, the Upper Capital of the Jin Dynasty in Acheng

Site of Huiningfu, the Upper Capital of the Jin Dynasty, commonly called Baicheng (the white city), is located four miles south of Acheng City, Heilongjiang province. It was once the capital of Jin Dynasty in its early stage, which was established by the ancient Jurchen nationality—the ancestors of the Manchu nationality.

From the date the Jin Dynasty was founded by Emperor Wanyan Aguda to the year of 1153 in which Wanyan Liang, King of Hailing moved the capital to Yanjing (later called Central Capital, now Beijing), Huiningfu is under the rule of four emperors of Jin Dynasty for 38 years.

Since the capital was moved here, Huiningfu was once destroyed. But as the birth place of Jurchen nationality and the location of the Shangjinglu and Huiningfu prefectures, it was still the political, military, economic and cultural center in northeast of Jin Dynasty. During the reign of Jin Dynasty, Huiningfu held a very important strategic position. The Dynasty divided the North China into nineteen parts that were equal to today's administrative division—province. These divisions were administrated by five capitals and fourteen prefectures. The site of Huiningfu was named by the State Council one of the major historical and cultural sites under state protection.

## 阿城金上京会宁府遗址

金上京会宁府遗址,俗名白城,位于黑龙江省阿城市城南四里,是中国满族的先世女真族所建金朝(1115—1234年)的早期都城。

自金太祖完颜阿骨打建国称帝,至1153年海陵王完颜亮迁都到燕京(后改称中都,即今北京)止,金政权在这里历四帝,统治达38年之久。

迁都后,这里虽然一度受到破坏,但作为女真族的发祥地和上京路、会宁府的治所,仍是金朝在东北北部的政治、军事、经济和文化的中心。在整个金代,上京会宁府所处的战略地位十分重要。金朝将其统治的北部中国划分为十九路(路是相当于现在"省"的大行政区域名称),分别由五京和十四总管府管辖。金上京会宁府遗址于1982年被国务院公布为全国重点文物保护单位。

### 22. Yagou Moya Stone Carving Statues of the Jin Dynasty

There are two stone statues carved on two neighboring pieces of granite, situated on the south halfway up Stone-man (Shiren) Mountain in Yagou. Of the two stone carving statues, one is male, the other female, and in terms of size, they are like real man.

The two statues are sitting side by side and looking forward. The male one wears a headpiece, boots with tine head and a short stick in hand. It is 185cm in height, 105cm in width. The length of its head is 33cm and the width of its face is 22cm. It sits up crossing his left leg. The female is blurred, but from the rubbings, we can know it wears a hat, a straight collar, and the two hands joined under sleeves, the body leaned to the right with two legs crossed.

According to the modern visual habits, the male one is at the left and the female one is at the right, the size of the male a little bigger. The two statues were both carved on the face of the granite with the natural radian. As for the carving technique, linear carving is the main method used. But the skills of using the knife inengraving are diversified, combining straight carving, side carving and circle carving when depicting various lines of the human body. With the distinctive main and minor parts, the whole carving shows the craftsmen's superb skills.

## 金代亚沟摩崖石刻像

亚沟石刻像为两幅,分别刻凿在石人山南旅半山腰的两块相邻的花岗岩上。石刻像由男、女两幅像组成,就人体比例而言,与真人略同。

两像并坐前视,男像头戴头盔(帽),足着尖头靴,手执短杖,通高185厘米、宽105厘米、头部高33厘米、脸宽22厘米,左腿盘回端坐。女像已很模糊,但通过拓片尚可辨识,女像头戴帽,衣直领,左枉,双手合袖,双腿盘坐,身体略向右倾斜。

按现代人视觉习惯男像在右,女像在左,男像画面较大。两幅像均刻在自然弧度的岩面上,从刻凿技法上看,是以线刻手法为主进行创作的,但采用刀法都不尽相同,有直刀、侧刀和圆口刀等深浅转折手法,描绘了多变的人体线条,主次分明,体现出匠人高超娴熟的技艺。

### 23. Ice and Snow Sculpture World of Harbin

Ice and Snow Sculpure World is located on the sand beach of the river center, Song Hua River, the length of 1 030 meters, the widest point of 25 meters, the area of about 200 000 squre meters, the ice gross of 60 000 steres, the snow gross of 130 000 steres. The park, building with the center of Century Gate, Merry Gate and Cartoon Gate, falls into three sections—the east, the west and the certer, including such fivescenic spots as Sound of Century, Cartoon World, Adventure Eden, Romance on Ice, and Snow Field Carol.

Sound of Century, based on the theme of millennium celebration, is comprised of four squares—Gargoyles, Century Clochard, Sound of Regres and Century Arena, where there areMillennium Dragon, Century Gate, Double Paddling Dragons、Century Bell, Ornamental Columns, Happiness Portico, Hong Kong Convention and Exhibition Centre, Ruins of St. Paul, Taiwan Chi Xiang and the exhibiting veranda of the 50-year refulgent achievements of Harbin.

Cartoon World is characterized by the children's entertainment, which consists of the following-the Clusters scenic spots: Rabbits Welcoming the Spring, North Country Scene, Chasing Deer on Snow, Lunar new year pictures with a pine and crane, Submarine World, Little Snow-white, Santa Claus and Russian Trip, as well as some scattered scenes—Colorful Pagoda, Horizontal Buddha on Jokul, Affections in an Ancient Castle, Snow Child and Snow House and so forth. Besides, there are many amusing facilities for the children to enjoy themselves, such as the Great Wall, Sliding Boards with Animal Figure and Merry Labyrinth.

Adventure Eden is the theme of enjoying a few interesting activities, where we can participate scuh adventruous and irritative amusement as taking jokul ropeway, climbing ice cliff, seeking the track in Arctic Pole.

Romance on Ice, the theme of activity on ice, is composed of ice-skating field, ice scripture show, playing peg-top, mystery canyon and the timetunnel.

Snow Field Carol, the activity on snow, includsski resort, snow pitch, snowmotor, together with some scenes—Snow Pagodam, Windmill in north of the Great Wall etc.

For the sake of the impressive souvenir after the ice and snow melting, Harbin made a decision to build a Centry Bell hanging in the . It is located in Sound of Century, the weight of 5.3 tons, the height of 2.58 meters, marking the rapid development of Harbin in 2000, the diameter of 2000 millimeters (the symbol of the year 2000) and 12 crouching dragons cast on the surface, which is copied the bronze one of Jing Dynasty excavated in A'Cheng District of Harbin, marking that legend of the dragon celebrating the millennium with rapture. The round striking point represents the rising sun, water waves below Song Hua River. In addition, there is inscription on the bell carved in Lishu by the calligraphers in Harbian, the total of 188 characters.

## 哈尔滨冰雪大世界

哈尔滨松花江冰雪大世界位于松花江段江心沙滩,全长1 030米,最宽处25米,总占地面积近20万平方米,总用冰量6万立方米,总用雪量13万立方米。整个园区建设以"世纪门""欢乐门""卡通门"三座大门为中心,形成东、西、中三大部分,包括"世纪之声""卡通世界""冒险乐园""冰上风情""雪场欢歌"五大景区:一是以千年庆典活动为主题的"世纪之声"景区,由神龙、世纪钟楼、回归之声和世纪舞台四个广场组成,主要包括千禧龙、世纪门、二龙戏水、世纪钟、华表、欢乐柱廊、香港会展中心、澳门大三巴牌坊、台湾赤嵌楼、哈尔滨50年辉煌成就展廊等景观;二是以少年儿童娱乐活动为主题的"卡通世界"景区,设有玉兔迎春、北国风光、雪地逐鹿、松鹤延年、海底世界、白雪公主、圣诞老人、俄罗斯之旅八个组团式景区和七彩宝塔、雪山卧佛、古堡情思、雪孩子、雪屋子等多处景点,以及长城、动物造型的滑梯和欢乐迷宫等适合少年儿童年龄特点的冰雪娱乐设施;三是以趣味性参与活动为主题的"冒险乐园"景区,设有雪山索道、攀冰岩、北极寻踪等惊险刺激的娱乐项目;四是以冰上活动为主题的"冰上风情"景区,设有滑冰场、冰雕区、抽冰尜区、神秘峡谷、时光隧道等冰上娱乐项目,以及供游人取暖、休息的暖房、蒙古包风情园;五是以雪上活动为主题的"雪场欢歌"景区,设有滑雪场、雪地足球场、雪地摩托项目,以及雪塔、塞外风车等景点。

为了使冰雪融化后的冰雪大世界留下一件纪念品,哈尔滨决定建一口"世纪钟"悬挂在园区内。该钟位于"世纪之声"景区,重5.3吨,钟高2.58米,象征着2000年哈尔滨要加快发展,直径2000毫米(象征2000年),钟的外表铸有12条座龙,取材于哈市阿城出土的金代千年铜座龙,象征着12亿龙的传人欢天喜地贺千年。圆形撞击点,象征升起的太阳。下部水纹象征着松花江。钟上刻有哈市书法家用简体隶书书写的铭文,共188字。

### 24. Daqing Grassland Racetrack in Daqing

Daqing Dumeng Grassland Racetrack is located in the western suburbs of Taikang Town in Dorbed Mongolian Autonomous County. It covers 150 000 square meters with convenient transport facilities.

The racetrack was built in 1993, and was used as the race venue for the Nadamu Assembly. Afterbeing reconstructed and added other functions, it was renamed Daqing Grassland Racetrack in 1997 and became a tourist attraction for horse-racing events.

The race has adopted the international starting rules. In the mean time, the racetrack has professional riders and all the racing horses are well trained. In addition, on the basis of the original national race activities, a set of standard and integral management rules for the racing game is developed, which make the race more competitive, exciting and entertaining and attracts more public participation.

The modern Daqing Grassland Racetrack, together with the Lianhuan Lake and Shoushan Leisure Resorts, has become the Golden Triangle of tourist hot spots in Daqing.

## 大庆草原赛马场

大庆市杜蒙草原赛马场坐落在杜尔伯特蒙古族自治县泰康镇西郊,交通便利,占地面积15万平方米。

赛马场始建于1993年,是那达幕大会赛马的场所。1997年通过重新维修改造,增加其功能,成为有奖赛马的旅游景点,改名为大庆草原赛马场。

赛马采用国际通用的胡特马闸起跑规则,同时配备骑术高超的专业骑士,所有赛马均经过悉心调教,并在原有民族赛马活动的基础上,开发制定了规范和完整细致的现代有奖赛马管理规则,使赛马更具有竞争性、可观性、大众参与性及民族娱乐性。

现代的大庆草原赛马场连同连环湖、寿山休闲度假村已经形成了大庆的金三角旅游热线。

### 25. Uhomill Scenic Spot in Daqing

Uhomill is a natural scenic spot with an area of 0.6 square kilometers. It is located in the junction between Xindian Forest Farm and Aolin Town, Dorbed Mongolian Autonomous County in the City of Daqing, Heilongjiang province. Uhomill is a Mongolian name, which means Dunes of Death or Death Valley. Later, the local people gave it the present name—the Five-Horse Dunes. The dunes are composed of a dozen of other dunes, reaching an altitude of 170 meters.

Wild apricots are abundant on dunes, which cover the dunes from the top to the slope of the valley. There are also 15 other kinds of trees such as mulberry and ancient Elm, etc. Besides those trees, there are more than 30 species of wild animals, such as wild wolves, Mongolian gazelles, mountain rabbits, foxes, pheasants, quails and so on. Every year in May, when spring brings warmth to the northern China, the wild apricots on the sunny slope blossom lavishly, while on the other slope they are still in buds.

## 大庆乌呼穆勒风景区

乌呼穆勒占地0.6平方公里,是一处自然风光景区。风景区地处大庆市杜尔伯特蒙古族自治县新店林场和敖林乡交接处。乌呼穆勒为蒙古语,意为死亡沙丘或死亡沙谷。随着历史的发展,当地人将它化成今名——五马沙坨。沙坨由高高低低十余座沙丘汇集而成,海拔高度170米。

沙坨内野杏繁茂,从沙丘顶端迤逦而下,直至坡谷,都有杏树生长,其他的还有桑葚、古榆树等树木达15种之多。沙丘内有野狼、黄羊、山兔、狐狸、山鸡、鹌鹑等30余种野生动物。每逢5月,北国春暖,杏花怒放,阳坡花开茂盛,阴坡蓓蕾初绽。

## 26. Harbin Huatian Wujimi Ski Resort

Huatian Wujimi Ski Resort is located 9 kilometres west of Shangzhi City, 115 kilometers away from Harbin, and is close to National Road No. 301.

It opens up a ski field of 230 000 square meters, with ski runs of 120 meters in width for beginners, and also very challenging ski runs of 1 400 meters in length for advanced skiers. To improve the quality of the snow and extend skiing period in a scientific way, Huatian Company has introduced a very scientific and advanced water supply snow-making system, providing water directly to the top of the hills through the underground seamless steel pipes. Meanwhile, the company has also introduced other equipments like six sets of snow-making systems from France and snow compacters from Germany.

The 10 000-squremeter Viewteam Club, combining skiing services, catering, accommodations, entertainment and meeting service, provides high quality and convenient services for skiers. In particular, the ground villas catering to different tastes of people are also available for guests to enjoy the snow scenery.

## 哈尔滨华天乌吉密滑雪场

哈尔滨华天乌吉密滑雪旅游度假区,位于尚志城西9公里处,距离哈市115公里,紧邻301国道。

乌吉密滑雪场一期开放雪道面积23万平方米,既有宽达120米的初级雪道,又有极富挑战长达1 400米的高级雪道。为提高雪道雪质并科学延长滑雪期,华天公司引进科学先进的造雪供水系统,利用无缝钢管地下供水直达山顶,同时引进法国约克6套造雪系统及德国凯斯鲍尔压雪车等设备。

万米的 Viewteam 会所,集滑雪服务、餐饮、客房、娱乐、会议接待为一体,为滑雪者提供优质便捷的服务,更有风情迥异的山涧别墅供您欣赏雪地风光。

### 27. Harbin Moon Bay Ski Resort

Harbin Moon Bay Ski Resort is located in the City of Harbin and neighbors the beautiful Sun Island. It covers an area of 200 000 square meters with a comprehensive building of 2 000 square meters, and it is an integrated leisure and holiday resort that provides catering, accommodation and entertainment.

Within the skiresort, the skiing ground for intermediate skiers is 25 meters high, 40 meters wide, 450 meters long and has a slope of 36 degrees. The ski run for beginners is 16 meters high, 25 meters wide and 240 meters long. Its total skiing area is nearly 65 000 square meters. A ski area for children is also available. The resort provides exclusive night skiing and some other entertainments like horse-riding and dog-driving sleds, which would create a new field for tourists to enjoy themselves in the snow.

### 哈尔滨月亮湾滑雪场

哈尔滨月亮湾滑雪场坐落在哈尔滨市区内,与美丽的太阳岛为邻,总占地面积20万平方米,设有2 000平方米的综合楼,是集餐饮、住宿、娱乐为一体的综合休闲和度假的场所。

雪场内中级滑雪场高度为25米,宽度40米,坡度36°,长450米,初级雪道高度为16米、宽25米、长240米,总滑雪面积达65 000平方米,滑雪场内还备有儿童滑雪场。月亮湾滑雪场在哈尔滨独家推出灯光滑雪,另备有雪地骑马、狗拉爬犁等娱乐项目,给游人创造一个冰雪娱乐的新天地。

### 28. Jihua Longevity Mountain Ski Resort

Longevity Mountain belongs to Zhangguangcai Range in Changbai Mountain. The entire region is surrounded by winding mountains on four sides with a basin in the center. The Longevity Mountain Ski Resort lies in the middle and becomes a haven for tourists.

Longevity Mountain Ski Resort is located in the National Forest Park in Bin County. The park possesses a unique natural landscape with well-preserved natural forests. Now there are eleven ski runs, which are divided into beginner, intermediate and advanced levels in accordance with international practices, satisfying the demands of different skiers. In addition, there's a special ski area for children. The longest ski run is 1 600 meters and the maximum width of the ski run for beginners is

100 meters. There are three hanging-chair trams with the length of more than one thousand meters.

The skiresort is equipped with more than 8 000 sets of high quality ski equipment and has set up a professional ski training school. It can accommodate thousands of tourists, with an office building of 13 000 square meters, the Forest Training Center of 4 000 square meters, a hotel of 2 800 square meters, an independent villa and farmhouses with Chinese kang (heated brick bed).

Besides the regular ski items, theski resort also offers more than twenty related recreation items like curling and hunting.

## 吉华长寿山滑雪场

长寿山属长白山张广才岭余脉,整个区域四面环山,中心为盆地,群山逶迤,把长寿山滑雪场围在了中间,形成了避风港湾。

长寿山滑雪场坐落在宾县长寿国家森林公园内,园内自然景观独特,自然林保存完好。现共有11条雪道,按照国际惯例分为高、中、初级,满足不同滑雪者的需求,并设有儿童专用滑雪区。最长雪道1 600米,最宽初级道100米。有千米吊椅式缆车3条。

滑雪场备有8 000余套高档雪具,并创建了专业滑雪学校。另外有13 000平方米的滑雪大楼,4 000平方米的大森林培训中心,2 800平方米的滑雪宾馆,独立的滑雪别墅以及农家火炕可接待千余名游客住宿。

除正规的滑雪项目外,还推出了雪地冰壶球、自然狩猎等20余个与滑雪相关的游乐项目。

### 29. Langxiang Rock Monkey Mountain Ski Resort

Langxiang Rock Monkey Mountain Ski Resort is located within the boundary of the Forestry Bureau of Langxiang County in Yichun City, Heilongjiang province. It covers an area of about 40 hectares, with an altitude of 400 meters. The slope length can be thousands of meters and the average angle of the slopes is 15 degrees.

This scenic resort consists of the Rock Monkey Mountain and the Ski Field. On the main peak, there is a large and grotesque rock, with a monkey-shaped black rock on the top, so the mountain was named Rock Monkey Mountain by the local people. Rock Monkey Mountain is rugged with bizarre rocks standing out quite predominantly. Some look like the eagle with extended wings, others are like fish playing in the water or like a sitting frog observing the sun. The scenery is quiet and elegant and could be very pleasant to enjoy. The ski course is more than 1 000 meters long equipped with the push-and-pull cableway and entire sets of ski equipment. It is suitable for primary ski lovers to learn skiing.

### 朗乡石猴山滑雪场

朗乡石猴山滑雪场位于黑龙江省伊春市朗乡林业局内,占地约40公顷,海拔400米,坡长千余米,平均坡度15°。

由石猴山和滑雪场两大旅游景点组成。主峰上一座高大怪异的岩石,顶有一块形状如猴的青石,当地人称此山为石猴山。石猴山山体嶙峋,怪石耸立,有似雄鹰展翅,有似游鱼戏水,有似青蛙观日,幽静清雅,景色十分怡人。滑雪场雪道长千余米,有托牵式索道,雪具健全,适宜初级滑雪爱好者学习滑雪。

## 30. The Longzhu Ski Resort in Double-Dragon Mountain

The Longzhu Ski Resort is located in Double-Dragon Mountain scenic area, 60 kilometers from the eastern outskirts of Harbin, covering an area of 780 000 square meters.

The snow period here is 170 days with skiing period of 120 days annually. There are 8 ski runs for beginner, intermediate and advanced skiers respectively where the ski runs are broad and the snow slopes are gentle, with German equipment and first-class consummate facilities. Equipped with tourist cable cars and telescopic traction cableways, covering an area of 12 000 square kilometers, the two huge ski yards for beginners have the capacity for thousands of skiers. The total length of the ski runs is 2 000 meters and all the skiing equipment is of the latest products from Austria. First-aid staff from the Red-cross Society is available as well as night ski yards, ski training schools, fast food restaurants.

Intercity Transportation: Trains or airplanes to Harbin. Then transfer to the tourist coach to the Double-Dragon Mountain Ski Resort. The ride takes approximately 40 minutes.

### 二龙山龙珠滑雪场

龙珠滑雪场,位于二龙山风景区,距哈尔滨东郊60公里,占地面积78万平方米。

滑雪场年积雪期170天,滑雪期达120天,雪道坡度适宜,雪道开阔。滑道引进德国设备,配套设施完善。拥有初、中、高级雪道8条,两座大型初级滑雪场,面积1.2万平方公里,可同时容纳数千名滑雪者,雪道总长度2 000米,还设有空中旅游缆车和伸缩拉杆式拖牵索道。雪具均为奥地利最新产品,并设有夜间滑雪场、滑雪学校及快餐店、咖啡店和红十字救护店员。

交通:游客可乘火车或飞机先到哈尔滨,从哈尔滨再转乘至二龙山滑雪场的旅游专线车,约40分钟的车程。

## 31. The Riyuexia Ski Resort in Tieli

The Riyuexia Ski Resort ofis located in Mayongshun Forest Farm of Tieli Forestry Bureau, Yichun City, Heilongjiang province, 37 kilometres from Tieli City.

With an area of approximately 2.6 millionsquare meters, and 85% of forest coverage, the ski yards enjoy SSS-standard. There are 3 ski runs for beginner, intermediate and advanced skiers respectively and a U-shaped ski run for single skiing, totaling more than 5 000 meters in length. Snow yards for sliding on buoys, snowmobiling and snow cycling are available as well. Equipped with a ski lift of 1 400 meters long, and two 400-meter and two 200-meter tramways, the resort has a skiing capacity of 2 000 people.

## 铁力日月峡滑雪场

铁力日月峡滑雪场位于黑龙江省伊春市铁力林业局马永顺林场,距铁力市37公里。

雪场占地面积约为260万平方米,森林覆盖率达到85%。滑雪区按照SSS级标准建设,拥有三条高、中、初级和一条单板U型滑道,总长度5 000多米,还有滑雪圈、雪地摩托及雪地自行车场地;一条1 400米长的吊椅索道,两条400米和两条200米的拖牵;雪场可同时接待2 000人滑雪。

### 32. The Wofuo Mountain Ski Resort

Located in Dalai town on the outskirts of Jiamusi City, Heilongjiang province, the Wofuo Mountain Ski Resort sits on the site of ancient caldera which dates back 67 million years.

There are 4 ski runs for beginner, intermediate and advanced skiers respectively, the total length being 4 000 meters, equipped with double-chaired ski lifts, and a telescopic cableway. Currently, colorful activities have been launched namely touring skiing, snowmobiling, snow bobbing, kite flying etc. With a capacity of 300 skiers, it is the tourist attraction ensuring both leisure and vacation all year round.

Transportation: 19 kilometers from Jiamusi City, 30 minutes ride via scheduled bus service.

## 卧佛山滑雪场

卧佛山滑雪场位于黑龙江省佳木斯市郊区大来镇,坐落在距今6 700万年前古火山口遗址群地带。

卧佛山滑雪场,4条初、中、高级雪道总长度4 000余米,安装了双人吊椅缆车和伸缩拉杆式牵引索道。目前,雪场已开展了旅游滑雪、雪地摩托、雪上飞碟、雪地爬犁、雪地风筝等项目,可同时容纳300人进场滑雪,是集休闲度假为一体的四季旅游胜地。

交通:距佳木斯市区19公里,乘班车至雪场需30分钟。

### 33. The Amota Tourist Resort in Daqing

The Amota Tourist Resort is located on the Amota Peninsula, 30 kilometers west of Hujitomo Town, Dorbed Mongolian Autonomous Country. It is the largest field recreation ground in that county.

Amota means in Mongolian "delicacy", whose name was inspired by the lush grass and crystal-clear water, rich natural resources, deep lake and its abundant population of fish. Surrounded by water on three sides, the Amota Peninsula occupies approximately 6 800 acres and is eight kilometers from north to south. The primitive features in the Amota Peninsula have been preserved intact, thus, attracting a large number of rare birds such as wild geese, mallards and black-headed gulls to dwell on it. In the late spring and early autumn each year, we will occasionally have red-crowned cranes as our visitors.

There are 11 traditional yurts (traditional dome-shaped tents), one Aobao (Mongolian house), one Japanese-style wooden house of 600 square meters, and a lake-viewing platform in the Amota Tourist Resort.

Since the opening of the Amota Tourist Resort, professional Mongolian singers, musicians, and Matouqin (a type of traditional Mongolian musical instrument) players from Inner Mongolia Autonomous Region have been invited to entertain the guests. Typical Mongolian foods such as roast sheep, roast lamb legs, and milk tea are provided for the tourists to enjoy.

## 大庆市阿木塔旅游区

阿木塔旅游区位于杜尔伯特蒙古族自治县胡吉吐莫镇北30公里处的阿木塔半岛,是杜尔伯特最大的一家野外娱乐场所。

阿木塔蒙古语意为"美味",是因为阿木塔半岛水肥草美、物产丰富、湖深水清、鱼肥而得名。阿木塔半岛三面环水,全岛南北长8公里、占地面积6 800亩左右。阿木塔半岛原始风貌保存完整如初,岛上栖息着大雁、野鸭、红嘴鸥等几十种珍禽。每当春末秋初,丹顶鹤也时有出现。

阿木塔旅游度假村有传统式蒙古包11座、敖包一处,有600平方米日式木屋和望湖台一处。

阿木塔半岛旅游区域营业以来,从内蒙古自治区请来了专职蒙古族歌手、马头琴手,还备有烤全羊、烤羊腿、蒙古族奶茶等民族食品。

### 34. The Shoushan Tourist Resort in Daqing

Vast in territory, long in history, the Shoushan Tourist Resort is located on the Linzhao Highway (No. 201 Provincial Highway), 71 kilometres from the city of Daqing. As early as the end of the 11$^{th}$ century, the primitive Mongolians in Dorbed began their hunting and fishing in this area. Much of their unique local custom is still found to prevail to this day. The Mongolians name the Village "elosibbo" which means "the sand tribes". The Shoushan Tourist Resort is a multifunctional resort with traditional Mongolian custom, typical Mongolian food, comfortable accommodation, and colorful entertainments.

## 大庆市寿山民俗休闲度假村

大庆寿山休闲度假村位于林肇公路(201省道)71公里处。寿山休闲度假村地域辽阔,历史悠久。早在公元11世纪末叶土著杜尔伯特蒙古族人就在这里进行牧猎活动,至今还完好地保持着奇特的地域性民族文化。蒙古族人称寿山休闲度假村谓"额勒斯锡博",即"沙地部落"。寿山休闲度假村蒙古族风情浓郁,具有吃、住、娱乐等多种功能的蒙古度假村(草原部落)。

### 35. The Oroqen Folklore Tour

Xinsheng Township of Aihui District in Heihe City is located on the beautiful riverside of Kuerbin where the the Oroquen people reside. Each year an increasing number of tourists are attracted to Xinsheng Township by its unique ethnic customs. Admired at the blooming Dazixiang flowers scarlet as blazing flame in spring; intoxicated in the enormous expanse of forest boundlessly stretching to the horizon in summer; excited by the maple leaves red like flaring fires mantling the mountains in autumn and in winter lost in the immense expanse of the pure snow white as polished jade.

Here tourists can feast their eyes on the typical ethnic costumes. The overcoat, called "su'en", is the leather gown worn in winter, meticulously sewn from roe-deer leather, with the smooth side being outside and the rough side inside, and is incredibly warm. The Boots, called "Qikemi", are made from the hides of 16 roe-deer legs. Soles are made from wild boar or bear hide, which are suitable for wearing in the snow for they are light and warm. "Mietaha" is the leather hat made from the roe-deer scalp. Among the folk crafts are the containers made from white birch barks, such as birch bark baskets and boxes, which are of excellent workmanship with beautiful patterns embroidered in colorful silk threads.

The dishes here have unique flavors. Thosemainly include "Kumingla" (jerked meat), roe-deer meat fried with "Kunbihaowa" (Artemisia integrifolia), wild boar cooked with "Kangulanuwa" (wild celery), roe-deer meat fried with "gilaosao" (day lily). Here you can also taste "Mogo" (fungus), "Dounenate" (Birch mushroom), enjoy many kinds of cold water fishes, such as Amur grayling, Golden-line barbell, etc. and sip "jiete'alahei" (persimmon wine).

## 鄂伦春民族风俗游

黑河市瑷珲区新生乡坐落在美丽的库尔滨河畔,这里是鄂伦春族聚居地。特有的民族习俗吸引着越来越多的游人到新生乡去旅游。春季观赏达子香花红胜烈火,夏季观赏绿色林海浩瀚无边,秋望漫山遍野的红叶,冬赏白雪皑皑。

游人在这里可以看到典型的民族服饰。大衣叫"苏恩",是冬天穿的皮袍,用狍皮精心缝制,狍皮为面、毛为里,穿起来非常暖和。皮靴叫"其克密",是用16只狍腿的皮拼制成的短靴,以野猪皮或熊皮做底。在雪地上穿着适用,轻便保暖。"灭塔哈"是用狍头做的皮帽。民族工艺有用白桦树皮制作的器皿,有桦皮篓、桦皮盒,做工精巧,上面用彩色丝线刺上美丽的图案。

治理的菜肴风味独特。主要有"库明拉"(晒肉干)、狍肉炒"昆比好哇"(柳蒿芽)、野猪肉炖"抗骨拉奴哇"(山芹)、狍肉炒"给老搔"(黄花菜),还能吃到"莫锅"(木耳)、"豆嫩阿特"(桦树蘑),吃红鳞、金线、柳根池等冷水鱼,喝"吉厄特啊拉嘿"(都柿酒)。

## 36. The Jiejinkou Hezhen Village

Hezhen ethnic group is the ethnic minority with the smallest population in China, with Jiejinkou being its settlement covering a total area of 160 square kilometers, of which the village takes up a floor space of 3 500 square meters. The basic layout of the village is in the shape of a square, and the buildings are largely tile-roofed houses of the Han style.

Hezhen people always take the three rivers as their home (Heilongjiang, Songhua and the Wusuli Rivers), and live mainly by hunting and fishing. This forms a truly unique style of life and custom. In the village, there's an ethnic museum that keeps rich collections of Hezhen relics unearthed, artifacts and production tools of all ages.

The Jiejinkou Hezhen Village is located in the northeast of Tongjiang City with mountains and rivers around it. Russia can be seen from here on the other side of Heilongjiang. The village borders on the Jiejinkou National Forest Park and both land and water transportation provide easy access. It was officially founded in 1936 and its population consists of Han, Manchu, Korean and Hezhen nationalities. At present there are 70 households and 3 000 people in the Village. Historically, the people of the Hezhen ethnic group are the descendants of the Jurchen in northern China.

## 街津口赫哲族民族村

赫哲族是我国人口最少的民族,街津口是赫哲族集居地,总面积160平方公里,其中村寨建筑面积3 500平方米。村寨布局基本为正方形,建筑多为汉族式瓦房。

赫哲族素以三江(黑龙江、松花江、乌苏里江)为家,渔猎为主,形成了独特的生活方式和风俗习惯。村里有民族博物馆，收藏赫哲族历代出土文物、手工制品和生产工具等。

津口赫哲族民族村位于同江市东北部，隔黑龙江与俄罗斯相望，依山傍水。水陆交通便利，与街津山国家森林公园为邻。1936 年建制，居民由汉、满、朝鲜、赫哲族构成，现有 70 户，3 000 人。赫哲族历史上是我国北方民族女真族的后裔。

### 37. Meilisi Daur Hala Village in Qiqihar

On the west bank of Nenjiang River in Meilisi Daur Nationality District, Qiqihar, situate 13 Daur villages, among which Hala Village has already had a history of 300 years. The Daur Nationality accounts for over 70% of the village's gross population. Some of the ancient houses have been preserved in the village, through which the original appearance of Daur Nationality villages is faintly visible. Thatched cottages, most of which have a history of over 50 years, are warm in winter and cool in summer by nature, and the peculiar westward windows ensure an abundance of daylight, so it is not necessary to make a fire indoors in winter. The "Leleche" was used as Daur people's living appliance for transportation and production. And now, it can only be found in the exhibition hall of Hala Village.

The Daur people are famous for their naturaltalent of singing and dancing. Today, the Daur people still get together often to sing sweet and melodious "Zhaendale" (a representative type of Daur folk songs) and dance lively "Hakenmai" (a kind of group dance usually performed by young Daur women).

## 齐齐哈尔梅里斯达斡尔哈拉新村

在嫩江西岸的齐齐哈尔市梅里斯达斡尔族区，有 13 个达斡尔族村，其中，哈拉村已有 300 多年的历史，全村人口达斡尔族占 70% 以上，村里仍然保留着一些古老的民居，依稀可见达斡尔族村寨的原貌。草房冬暖夏凉，大部分有 50 多年的历史，冬天屋里根本不用生火，独特的西窗户，能保证采光充足。"勒勒车"，是他们过去用来运输和生产的生活用具，如今，在哈拉新村的展览馆中仍可见到。

达斡尔族是能歌善舞的民族。如今，达斡尔人仍然经常聚集在一起，吟唱婉转悠扬的"扎恩达勒"，跳起欢快的"哈肯麦"。

### 38. Site of Longquanfu, the Upper Capital of the Bohai State

In the world-famous Jingpo Lake Attraction, there is a spectacular historical site—Site of Longquanfu, the Upper Capital of the Bohai State. Situated in Bohai town, Ning'an County, Heilongjiang province, less than 20 km from Jingbo Lake, this once renowned medieval metropolis is now listed among the major sites to be protected at national level.

Thesites visible today include Longquanfu, Gujing, Jinyuan, Jietan, and the sites of temples, ancient tombs, archaic bridges, and Xinglong Temple. The major artifacts are Stone Light Blocks, grand stone Buddha, a schelly box, huge Stone Turtle, and tiles with Chinese characters etc. No other sites here have been preserved more intact than Xinglong Temple, whose quintet palaces are of all wooden structure of corbel brackets. With glazed tiles on the eaves, they look resplendent and magnificent in the sun.

Longquanfu is the capital city of the Bohai State. It is 16 km in circumference outside, with ten gates on four sides, and the ramparts, averaging roughly two meters high, are of earth and stones while the inner circumference is approximately 4.5 km with stone ramparts. The palace stands on the axis of the imperial city and is around 2.5 km in circumference with stone ramparts of over 3 meters high on the average. Presently there only remain quintet palace foundations. Wu Men, in the south of the city, stands on a base of nearly six meters high, with side gates in the east and west originally. In the east of the second palace hall, there is a glazed well providing drinking water for the royal families. In the east of the city locates the Jinyuan Site, to the south of which, there is a 20 000-square-meter pond. On the eastern and western sides of the pond, are sites of rockeries and buildings and halls made of mainly stones and bricks. The Site of Longquanfu has gained an important position in the Chinese history of ancient architecture. In 755AD, the third king of the Bohai State decided to move the capital from Zhongjing to Shangjing (the Upper Capital), which had been kept as the capital for 160 years ever since. The Upper Capital exhibits the splendid civilization—"The Power of the East Sea" created by people of the Bohai State. It used to be the second largest metropolis in East Asia, only second to Chang'an, the Capital in Tang Dynasty.

## 渤海国上京龙泉府遗址

在驰名中外的镜泊湖风景名胜区中,有一个瞩目的史迹区——渤海国上京龙泉府遗址。这个中世纪赫赫有名的大都市,当年就坐落在距镜泊湖不足20公里的黑龙江省宁安渤海镇的位置上,被列为全国重点保护文物。

现今可见的遗址有:上京龙泉府遗址、古井址、禁苑址、街坛址、寺庙址、古墓、古桥址、兴隆寺。主要遗物有石灯幢、大石佛、舍利函、大石龟、文字瓦等。现今保存最完整的遗址是兴隆寺,五重庙宇均为木制斗拱结构,再加上屋檐上的琉璃瓦,在阳光照耀下金碧辉煌。

上京龙泉府是渤海国首府,外城周长16公里,四面十门,城垣土石建筑,城高平均约2米左右。内城周长约4.5公里,城垣石筑,宫城周长约2.5公里,城垣石筑,残垣平均高3米以上。宫殿在宫城中轴线上,今存五重殿基。宫城正南的午门,台基高近6米,其东西两边原为侧门。第二殿东侧有供皇族饮水用的八宝琉璃井。宫城东侧有禁苑遗址,其南有一面积近20 000平方米的池塘。池塘东西两侧有人工堆砌的假山和一些楼台殿阁建筑的遗址,建筑材料多用石料和砖瓦。上京龙泉府在中国古代建筑史上有一定的地位。公元755年渤海国三世自中京迁至上京为国都达160多年。它代表着渤海人创造的"海东盛国"的灿烂文明,为当年仅次于唐长安京城的东亚第二大都会。

### 39. The Dalizi Site

The Dalizi Site is located on theriverside of the Tangwang River, northern suburb of Jinshan Village, Yichun City, Heilongjiang province. It is called so by the local people because there is a cliff standing at a height of 30 m. Many a time, stone and pottery artifacts of the late Neolithic Age have been excavated at this site. The stone artifacts include residual stones, lower stone saddle-querns, broken chopping blocks, carved stones and small stone tools. The pottery artifacts are grey pottery, russet pottery, scarlet pottery and black pottery. The pottery is diverse in thickness, most of which were handmade with a small proportion of sand. Pots and bowls are commonly seen utensils bearing prick designs, scratching designs, finger-impressed designs, convex designs, rhombic designs and raised designs added, etc. The scientific research from the experts has proved that the stone and pottery artifacts unearthed here are typically utensils of the late Neolithic Age, dating back to more than 3 000 years. The plane surface of the lower stone saddle-querns is concave, and the broken chopping blocks remains solid after being unearthed, which is rare among stone and pottery utensils of the same type unearthed in China.

## 大砬子遗址

大砬子遗址位于黑龙江省伊春市金山屯区北郊的汤旺河畔,有一处30米高的悬崖,当地人称"大砬子"。这里多次挖掘出新石器晚期的石器和陶器,石器有残石、盘底、殊陶俎、石核、石片等。陶器有灰陶、红褐陶、红衣陶、黑陶等。陶壁薄厚不等,多属夹沙手制,器型多为罐和钵,有刺纹、划纹、指捺纹、凸弦纹、菱格纹、附加堆纹等。经专家考证,这里的石陶器是新石器晚期典型的石陶器具,距今约3 000多年,石磨盘的使用面呈凹形,残陶俎出土后依然坚挺,在我国出土的同类石陶器具中十分少见。

### 40. Heilongjiang Provincial Museum

Located at 50 Hongjun Street, Harbin, Heilongjiang provincial Museum is a Russian-style structure, formerly the Moscow Emporium built by Russians in 1904. In 1922, Russians sponsored the establishment of the Research Association of Cultural Relics in Dong Province and decided on the Emporium as a museum. The Museum was operated by Russians and Japanese successively before 1951 when the Chinese government took it over and renamed it Science Museum of Songjiang Province. Heilongjiang provincial Museum, the present name, began to be in use in 1954 when

Songjiang Province and Heilongjiang province were integrated.

Three sides of the building have been artistically adorned ensuring that its visitors can enjoy an excellent view of it from any directions (two sides of it adjacent to the main streets and the other a square). The whole contour of the museum consists of 3 rectangular-based flat domes and 2 square-based flat domes bearing styling classic French features which together greatly enriches its architectural style.

Not large architecturally, the museum is a 2-storey building with a basement whose individual parts on the facades are impressed by protruding pillars, the tops of which stretch out of the eaves forming part of the parapets, which is typically a new artistic fashion of constructing parapets in Harbin. The application has produced a striking rhythm. Each part is a feast to the eye, bringing the visitors into the intoxication of a melodious symphony with its domes as the most spectacular essence as the climax of the symphony. The color of the building—muted yellow walls decorated with white brickwork and dark red domes, looks bright and harmoniously elegant against the luxurious green foliage of the trees.

## 黑龙江省博物馆

黑龙江省博物馆,位于哈尔滨市红军街50号。博物馆为俄式建筑,是1904年俄罗斯人所建的莫斯科商场。该博物馆1922年由俄国人发起建立东省文物研究会,并于该处筹备成立了博物馆。该馆曾先后由俄国人、日本人经办管理,1951年由中国人民政府接管,更名为松江省科学博物馆,1954年松江省同黑龙江省合并,该馆开始用现名。

由于建筑两面临街,一面临广场,因而三个立面都做重点处理,使观者在每个角度都能看到良好的景观。首先在建筑整体轮廓线创造上,采用了三个长方形底扁形穹顶和两个方形底扁形穹顶,极大地丰富了建筑造型,这种穹顶造型带有法国古典主义的特征。

建筑整体尺度不大,地上为二层,地下一层。立面的每个独立单元通过突出的壁柱加以强调,壁柱末端伸出屋檐成为女儿墙的一部分,这种做法是哈尔滨"新艺术"建筑女儿墙的典型做法。这种手法创造出很强的节奏感,观赏建筑的每个部分犹如欣赏一段乐曲,而两个方底穹顶则是乐曲的高潮所在,建筑的色彩十分优雅——土黄色的墙面间以白色的线脚装饰及暗红色的穹顶,在葱郁的树木映衬下既鲜明又和谐。

## 41. The Site of Ancient Cemetery in Hengshan

The Site of Ancient Cemetery in Hengshan is located in Hengshan Business Agency, Jinshantun District, Yichun City, Heilongjiang province. The site is a horseshoe-shaped valley on a south-facing slope, covering an area of approximately 3 hectares where 56 ancient tombs lay scattered.

According to the *Chronicles of Jinshantun*, in Liao Dynasty, Hengshan was the territory of Jurchen nationality, which belonged to one of the five states—the Pennuli State. In Jin Dynasty, it was within the region of Tunhemengan, and the Jin army and troops stationed here and established the Headquarter of Commander-in-chief. In 1956, the Ancient Cemetery was discovered; thereafter, such cultural relics were unearthed as octagonal stone pillars with relief pattern of dancing and music instrument playing, a copper mirror, gallipots, sabots of Jin Dynasty, stone tables and stools, spades, copper coins and jade ornaments, etc. In addition, a copper seal and a gold tally of the Headquarter of Commander-in-chief were unearthed. Gold foil-coated and engraved with Jurchen characters, the tally is the first one ever unearthed in the archaeological studies of our country.

In 1998, theSite of Ancient Cemetery in Hengshan was authorized by Heilongjiang provincial Government to enter the list of major sites to be protected at provincial level.

## 横山古墓群遗址

横山古墓群遗址位于中国黑龙江省伊春金山屯区横山经营所,面积约3公顷,是一处向阳坡马蹄形谷地,分布有56座古代墓葬。

据《金山屯区地方志》载:横山在辽代,为女真人领地,属五国部之盆努里国。金代属屯河猛安,金人在此屯军,设都统所。1956年,古墓群被发现后,出土了八面乐舞浮雕石幢、铜墙铁壁镜、轮制陶罐、金代木鞋、石桌、石凳、铁锹、铜钱、玉石岛等文物。另外,还出土了都统所铜印一枚和金质符牌一块。金质符牌外包金箔,上面阴刻有女真文字,是我国考古界出土的第一块金牌。

1988年,横山古墓群遗址被黑龙江省人民政府批准为省级文物保护单位。

### 42. Ruins of Puyulu Ancient City (Jin Dynasty)

Oval in form, 3 000 meters in circumference, Ruins of Puyulu Ancient City (Jin Dynasty) is located in Gucheng Village (Jincheng Township, Kedong County, Qiqihar, Heilongjiang province), bordering the southern bank of the Wuyur River. Built with rammed earth, the city walls have a base of 23 meters broad, and 1.5 meters at the top. Currently, the remains range from 1.7 to 3.28 meters in height. There are North Gate and South Gate with enceintes, and a city moat 10 meters off the city. In the northwestern corner of the city moat stands earthen piers of oval-shape, the perimeter of which is 420 meters, which is considered as a wharf.

In 1975, an archaeological excavation of South Gate was conducted by the Archaeological Department of Heilongjiang provincial Museum, which revealed that the Gate was designed to be single access with lintel. Right in the middle of the gate opening there were stone doorstoppers and the roads inside were paved with pebbles and sand. The gate tower had already collapsed years before with caved eave tiles, arched tiles and plate tiles from the caved-in roof scattering over.

Further excavations in the northeastern corner of the inner city in 1979 uncovered a larger architecture site—the site of the government offices which consisted of a front courtroom and a back hall taking up floor space of 300 meters. As the essence of the building, the back hall had 3 rows of untreated plinths, spaced approximately 4 meters apart. The walls of the back hall were built with grey bricks except the north wall which was made of clay. In the east side of it were Huokang (traditional Chinese hot brick bed), and a kitchen range was in the northwest side, which was most likely the officials' residential area.

The excavation of these ruins providedthe geographical coordinates for China's northern boundaries in the $12^{th}$ and the $13^{th}$ centuries. More than 200 cultural relics were unearthed, including pottery, porcelain, bronze ware, ironware, bone objects, copper coins, etc., which provide valuable materials for future studies.

## 金代蒲峪路故城遗址

金代蒲峪路故城遗址位于黑龙江省齐齐哈尔市克东县金城乡古城村。古城濒临乌裕尔河南岸。故城址平面呈椭圆形，周长3 000米，城墙是夯土筑成，基宽23米，顶宽1.5米，残高1.7~3.28米，设有南、北二门，门外有瓮城。墙外10米处有护城河，城外西北角护城河处有椭圆形土埠，周长420米，被认为是水运码头。

1975年黑龙江省博物馆考古部对故城南门进行了发掘，了解到城门是过梁式单洞结构的。门洞正中立有档门石，门洞内的路面系河卵石的沙子铺成，城楼早已坍塌，漏顶上的瓦当、筒瓦、板瓦散布遍地。

1979年对故城内东北角的一处建筑址进行了发掘，这次发掘到一处较大的建筑址——官司衙址。它由前堂和后殿组成，一座背朝南，建筑面积300平方米。后殿是建筑的主体部分，室门有没经过任何加工的柱础三排，每排柱础的间距4米左右。后殿的东、西、南三面墙均砌青砖，北面墙是土墙。后殿内东侧有火炕，西北附有灶址，这应为当时官衙的起居场所。

蒲峪路故城的确定，为中国12~13世纪北部疆界找到了重要地理坐标。发掘出土文物有陶、瓷、铜、铁、骨器和铜钱等200余件，为今后的研究提供了宝贵的资料。

### 43. Yanzhigou Gold Mine in Mohe County

Yanzhigou Gold Mine is 43 km to the north of Xilinji Town, Mohe County, Heilongjiang province, and 32 km to the south of "North Pole Village". It was mined in 1889 and was known as Mohe Gold Refinery and Mohe Gold Mine Bureau successively. The name was later changed to Laogou Gold Mine. In Qing Dynasty, gold mined here was bartered for rouge for the Empress Dowager Cixi, thus another name Yanzhigou was born (yanzhi means rouge). The mine so far enjoys a history of more than 100 years.

In addition to the land for production in the mining area, there are groups of prostitute graves, Yanzhi Palivion, the Cultural Exhibition Center of Gold Mining as well as Site of Ancestral Hall of Li Jinyong (1853-1890), the founder of the gold mine and court official in Qing Dynasty, etc..

## 漠河胭脂沟金矿

漠河胭脂沟金矿位于黑龙江省漠河县西林吉镇北 43 公里,北极村南 32 公里处,始建于 1889 年,史称漠河金厂、漠河金矿局,现称老沟金矿。清朝时,这里的金子为慈禧太后换过胭脂,又称胭脂沟。至今已有一百多年的开采历史。

整个矿区除了生产用地之外,还有清朝廷官员金矿创办人李金镛(1835—1890 年)祠堂遗址、采金文化陈列馆、胭脂亭等。

### 44. Site of Ancient Human Beings of Daziyang Mountain in Songling District

Site of Ancient Human Beings of Daziyang Mountain is located in the southern part of Songling District, Daxinganling City, Heilongjiang province, and 120 km from Jiagedaqi City. In 1975, two bronze swords of the Warring States Period were found by the Forest Police on top of the precipice. In 1989, 112 pieces of Paleolithic artifacts were unearthed, most of which are chipped stone implements with some pressed tools from both the Paleolithic Age and Neolithic Age.

## 松岭大子杨山古人类遗址

松岭大子杨山古人类遗址位于黑龙江省大兴安岭市松岭区南部,距加格达奇 120 公里。1975 年,森警部队在峭崖顶发现两支青铜长剑(战国时期)。1989 年出土旧石器标本 112 件,主要为打制石器,有部分压制(含新石器时代)。

### 45. Site of Shibazhan Ancient Human Beings in Tahe County

Being the site of late Paleolithic Age, Site of Shibazhan Ancient Human Beings in Tahe County can be dated at over 20 000 years. Located in Shibazhan Town, Tahe County, Daxinganling City, Heilongjiang province, the site has been one of the major sites to be protected at the provincial level. As the site of late Paleolithic Age, Shibazhan is the first of its kind found in the farthest northern region of China, which is also unique in Heilongjiang province. On this site, within an area of 14 km east and west to Nenjiang-Mohe Highway, 1 070 pieces of chipped stone implements have been unearthed, most of which are in the shape of ships. Medium and small sized stone implements of 5-10 cm constitute the majority buried to a depth of the earth between 0.3 to 3 m.

The Shibazhan Site is located at the eastern foot of Greater Khingan Mountains and on a second-class platform on the right bank of Humahe River—a branch of Heilongjiang River, where there are winding mountains and flourishing forests. The discovery of the site is of great scientific importance for studying the origin and development of the primitive culture.

## 塔河十八站古人类遗址

塔河十八站旧石器晚期遗址,距今约 2 万多年。位于黑龙江省大兴安岭市塔河县十八站乡境内,现已列为黑龙江重点文物保护单位之一。十八站遗址是在中国最北部地区首次发现的旧石器朝代遗址,也是黑龙江省唯一的一处。此遗址在嫩-漠公路东西 14 公里范围内,采掘出土了 1 070 件以船形石为代表的打制石器,以 5~10 厘米的中小型石器为多,埋藏深度 0.3~3 米之间。

十八站旧石器晚期遗址位于大兴安岭山脉东麓,黑龙江支流呼玛河右岸二级台地,山势和缓起伏,森林茂密,它的发现对研究原始文化的起源和发展有着重要的科学价值。

### 46. The Former Residence of Xiao Hong

The Former Residence of Xiao Hong, 28 kilometers from Harbin, is situated at Wenhuazhan Road, Hulan District, and covers an area of 7 125 square meters. It was listed as one of the major sites to be protected at the provincial level.

The residence was built in $34^{th}$ year of the reign of Emperor Guangxu (1908). Born in May 1911, Xiao Hong, a famous female writer in China in the 1930s, spent her childhood here. In 1929, she left home, and became a famous Left Wing writer in China. On Jan 22, 1942, she died in Hong Kong, and left behind many literary works as a precious legacy to us, such as novels, short stories and essays that number more than 1 million words.

The Former Residence of Xiao Hong, a typical traditional Manchu residence with 30 rooms, is made of adobe and wood with black-tiled roof. Many artifacts are exhibited in the courtyard, such as some items used by Xiao Hong and her grandmother in their daily life, photographs of Xiao Hong, souvenirs, epigraphs, poems and letters from Chinese and foreign celebrities. In addition, a two-meter high statue of Xiao Hong can also be seen here.

Route: Take a bus to Hulan District from the bus station opposite the Harbin Railway Station.

## 萧红故居

萧红故居位于呼兰县城文化站路 29 号,距哈尔滨市 28 公里,占地面积 7 125 平方米,哈尔滨市省级文物保护单位。

故居始建于清光绪三十四年(1908 年)。1911 年 5 月,中国 20 世纪 30 年代著名女作家萧红出生在这里,并度过了她的童年和少年时代。1929 年离家出走,成为中国著名左翼女作家。

1942年1月22日病逝于香港。她一生中写出长篇小说、短篇小说、散文等文学作品共计100多万字。

故居为传统的八旗式住宅,青砖青瓦,土木建造,共有房舍30间。院内展有萧红及祖母用过的部分物品,萧红生前的照片,中外名人留影、题词、诗作、信函等,另有一座2米高的萧红塑像。

交通:可从哈尔滨火车站对面的车站乘开往呼兰县的长途汽车。

### 47. "Northern First Rafting"—Rafting On Balan River

Balan River is located in the hinterland of the natural scenic area of Danqing River in Yilan County. It measures more than 20 km in length and is surrounded by mountains and the water is clear.

Balan River originates from the south of Lesser Khingan Mountains, and is fed by many streams as it winds along its path. The water is so clear that you can see the bottom. Even in midsummer, the temperature never passes 14 ℃. This is how Balan River has earned its name (In Manchu, Balan means "Cool Water River"). Balan River, dozens of miles long, snakes through elevations and winding roads; the mountains seem to twine with the water; and the scenery is constantly changing which enhances its appeal. Along Balan River, the simple and serene natural scenery has been extremely well preserved.

## "北方第一漂"——巴兰河漂流

巴兰河地处依兰县丹清河省级自然风景名胜区腹地,流域全长20余公里,四周群山环绕,河水澄碧清澈。

巴兰河发源于小兴安岭南麓,沿途汇聚溪涧清流,千回百转,河水澄清碧绿,清澈见底,即使在酷暑难当的盛夏,水温也绝对不会超过14 ℃,巴兰河正是因此而得名(巴兰河系满语,意为"凉水河")。数十里水路,峰回路转,水绕着山走,山随着水转,山边是水,水边有山,移步换景,情趣各异。巴兰河沿途古朴清幽的自然风貌保存十分完好。

### 48. Rafting On Fenglin River

Rafting on Fenglin River, which has a length of 11 kilometers, starts at a tributary of Tangwang River in Yichun city, Heilongjiang province. The speed of flow and the width of the river are constantly changing. The average depth of the river is 1.2 meters. The Southern bank of Fenglin River is Fenglin National Nature Reserve, which has been listed as a member of International Man and Biosphere Reserve Network, while a dense and flourishing secondary forest lies on the northern bank. Drifting down the stream by rubber rafts, you can see the pines on both sides and enjoy the picturesque scenery of the brilliant nature.

When rafting along the river in a double rubber boat, the jolting and rotating of the raft over the rapids makes for an exciting adventure with endless rejoice. Rafting on Fenglin River is the earliest developed tourism project and has been hailed as "the best rafting in Lesser Khingan Mountains".

## 丰林河漂流

丰林河漂流起始于伊春汤旺河支流,全程11公里。河道时宽时窄,平均水深1.2米。河南侧是被列入世界人与生物圈网络成员的丰林国家级自然保护区,河北侧是茁壮的次生林。乘坐皮筏顺流而下,两岸松林交错、美景如画。

丰林河漂流水流湍急,乘上双人橡皮船顺流而下,颠簸旋转,乐趣无穷。丰林河漂流是伊春最早开发漂流旅游项目的地区,有"小兴安岭第一漂"之称。

### 49. Rafting On Jinsha River in Meixi District

Jinsha or Golden Sand Riverin Meixi District, with a length of 65 kilometers, is located in Songling Forest Farm in Yichun City, Heilongjiang province. It has a maximum width of 50-meters, and a minimum width of 20 meters, an average elevation of 400 meters and an average flow speed of 7.14 cubic meters per second. There are 4 dangerous shoals in the river and Woniu Rocks crisscross the river and sometimes the wave can reach 1 meter high.

## 美溪金沙河漂流河段

金沙河漂流位于黑龙江省伊春市松岭林场,河段全长65公里,水面最大宽度50米,最小宽度20米,平均海拔400米,平均流量7.14立方米/秒,险滩数4处。河中卧牛石纵横交错,弯多,最大浪高1米以上。

### 50. Rafting On Xiangshui River

Xiangshui River is located in Fangzheng County with convenient transportation available. The rafting journey travels through 10 km of rapids with a full gap of 23.4 meters, starting at Dragon Pearl Lake and ending at Magical Mussels Pool. The starting point in the north is "Lesser Mount Huang" which can be compared to Mount Huang in its beauty. In the west, one can start from the source of Xiangshui River and the forest Oxygen-bar. In the east, the starting point is a Mongolian style Birch Forest Park.

On both sides of Xiangshui River, we can see such beautiful scenery as the legendary Fairy Fox Hole, Bergamot Peak, Tiger Roar Crag, Magical Mussels Pool, Hump Peak, and Rhino Stone, etc.

Xiangshui River has many twists and turns, and the water intermittently changes from white water rapids to leisurely and calm drifting.

## 响水河漂流

响水河在方正县境内,交通便利。漂流河段10公里,全程落差23.4米,从龙珠湖起漂,到仙蚌潭收浆。漂流始发点北有与黄山媲美的"小黄山";西有湍急的响水河源头和森林氧吧;东有白桦林蒙古风情园。

响水河两岸美景绮丽,具有传奇、神秘色彩的狐仙洞、佛手峰、虎啸岩、仙蚌潭、骆驼峰、犀牛石等令人遐思。响水河九曲十八弯,河水时而起伏湍急,时而舒缓平静。

### 51. Rafting on Zhan River in Xunke County

Rafting on Zhan River starts from Zhanbei Forest Farm located upstream of Zhan River, Heilongjiang province and the destination will be Xin'e Township, totaling 80 kilometers. The maximum width of its water surface is 100 meters and the minimum width is 40 meters, whereas the deepest point measures 3 meters. The maximum current velocity is 3 meters per second, while the maximum flow capacity is 1 750 cubic meters per second, and the average flow capacity is 67 cubic meters per second with 1.14% declivity. The riverbed is covered with granite bedrocks and pebbles. Clear as crystal is the pollution-free water. The waterway itself is winding and the rafting course is zigzaging, along which exists a stretch of exposed rocks called "starriness" (for the rocks resemble stars in the sky), and 17 rapids and shoals.

## 逊克沾河漂流

逊克沾河漂流起点位于黑龙江省逊克沾河上游的沾北林场,终点新鄂乡,全长80公里。河面最大宽度100米,最小宽度40米,水深最深3米,最大流速3米/秒,最大流量1 750立方米/秒,平均流量67立方米/秒,河道比降1.14%,河床由花岗岩基岩与河卵石组成。河水清澈,无污染。河道弯曲,有一处河段岩石裸露,人称满天星,险滩17处。

### 52. Rafting on Yongcui River

Originated at the south foot of Cuiling, Huanshan Forest Farm, north of Dailing District, Yichun city, Heilongjiang province, Yongcui River runs in Tangwang River system, Heilongjiang River Basin, with 667 square kilometer catchment area and total length of 70 kilometers. Yongcui River falls in the category of mountain-stream rivers and as such its runoff is heavily affected by floods and rainstorms. It is a unique environment for cold-water fish, namely Capelins, Crucian Carps, Gambusia and Pikes, etc. Endowed with a view of rare birds and animals along the riversides, rafting on Yongcui River through green hills and waters is sure to be a great joy.

## 永翠河漂流

永翠河漂流发源于黑龙江省伊春带岭区北部环山林场翠岭南麓,属黑龙江流域,汤旺河水系,集水面积677平方公里,总长70余公里。永翠河属山溪性河流,径流受洪水和暴雨影响明显,特有冷水性鱼类,如细鳞、鲫鱼、柳根、狗鱼等。在此漂流,在穿流于青山绿树中的同时,还可一睹两岸的飞禽异兽,其乐无穷。

### 53. Baliwan National Forest Park

Officially approved by the State Forestry Administration, Baliwan Forest Park enjoys the status of a national forest park under the jurisdiction of Weihe Forestry Bureau in Heilongjiang province. Just eight kilometers off the Forestry Bureau, it borders National Road 301 and the Harbin-Suifenhe Railway with convenient traffic facilities and advanced communication system.

The tourist accessibility of the Forest Park totals 41 000 hectares, divided into six tourist attractions—Baliwan Scenic Area, Double-Peak Mountain Scenic Area, Virgin Forests on Cockscomb Mountain, Scenic Spot of Cliff where tigers stand ready to jump down, Area of Chinese yew forests, and Guokui Mountain scenic Area. In the Forest Park, there are hotels and restaurants with perfect facilities and excellent service available, providing high-quality accommodation and catering for the tourists.

## 八里湾国家森林公园

黑龙江省八里湾国家森林公园是经国家林业局正式批准的国家级森林公园,隶属于黑龙江省苇河林业局。距林业局八公里,毗邻301国道和哈尔滨至绥芬河铁路,交通便利,通信发达。

森林公园经营区总面积为41 000公顷,分为八里湾景区、双峰山景区、鸡冠山原始森林、虎跳崖景区、红豆杉景区、锅盔山景区六部分。森林公园内建有配备完善的宾馆和餐厅等高档服务设施,可为游客提供高质量的住宿和餐饮服务。

### 54. Longevity Mountain National Forest Park

Located within the boundaries of Bin County, southeast of Harbin city, covering an area of 773 hectares, Longevity Mountain National Forest Park is a natural forest park nearest to Harbin. It boasts breathtaking views of precipitous peaks, jagged rocks of grotesque shapes and substantial fauna and flora. Its major attractions include Longevity Stone, Prime-Minister Peak, Baboon's Stone,

Mainstay Peak, Camel Peak, Zigzag Cave, Bat Cave and Lesser Mount Hua, etc., all of which make Longevity Mountain National Forest Park a booming holiday and leisure destination. The two large skiing fields in the Park have a capacity of 1 000 skiers. In addition, a training base for field survival has been established here. Hotels and holiday villages are available and the geographical locations of these scenic spots are convenient. One-day, two-day and three-day package tours are offered.

Transportion: Via coach from the Highway Passenger Station near the East Harbin Railway Station to Binxi County.

## 长寿山国家森林公园

位于哈尔滨市东南宾县境内,占地面积773公顷,是距哈尔滨市最近的一处天然森林公园。园内奇峰险峻,怪石嶙峋,动植物资源非常丰富。主要景点有长寿石、丞相峰、狒狒石、擎天峰、骆驼峰、九曲洞、蝙蝠洞、小华山等,是新兴的休闲度假胜地。园内建有两座大型滑雪场,可容纳1 000人滑雪,开发了野外生存训练基地,并建有宾馆、度假村等接待设施。各景点分布合理,可安排1~3日游。

交通:可从哈尔滨东站公路客运站坐车至宾西镇。

### 55. Xinlin Virgin Forest Park of "Beauty Pines" on Greater Khingan Mountains

Stretching over an area of some 50 000 square meters, Xinlin Virgin Forest Park of "Beauty Pine" is of mainly Mongolian pines with Larch in a small amount. From the exuberance and towering, graceful trunks, derives the charming name known as "beauty pines". The average diameter of a trunk measures 0.4 meters; the height of the pines averages around 18 meters, whereas the largest one can grow as tall as 29 meters. The age of stand is estimated to be some 170 years.

Lying to the north of Xinlin Town, Xinlin District, Greater Khingan Mountains, Heilongjiang province, Xinlin virgin forests of "Beauty Pines" have remained intact ever since the establishment of the Xinlin District.

## 大兴安岭新林美人松原始森林公园

大兴安岭新林美人松原始森林公园,面积约5万平方米,以樟子松为主,夹生少量落叶松,园中树林茂密,枝干挺拔秀美,故称美人松。树干平均直径0.4米。林龄约170年,最大树木高度29米,平均树木高度18米。

大兴安岭新林美人松位于黑龙江省大兴安岭新林区新林镇镇北,是建区以来保留下来的原始森林。

## 56. Liangshui Nature Reserve in Dailing District

Lying 25 kilometers north of Dailing District, Yichun City, with a length of 11 kilometers from south to north, a width of 6.25 kilometers from east to west and a total area of 63.94 square kilometers, Liangshui Nature Reserve is one of the virgin forest bases of Korean pines extant in China, and with a status of national nature reserve it is the institutional forests for teaching and research in northeastern region.

The forest coverage in the reserve is up to 95%, and the stand volume totals 140 000 square meters. Of the rich varieties of species, natural Korean pines constitute the majority. And this vast virgin forest nurtures a wealth of wild fauna and flora and valuable Chinese medicinal herbs, thus, being generally referred to as "the small hometown of Korean Pines". It is a great pleasure to be intoxicated among the towering, gigantic, and luxuriant primeval pines of 30 to 40 meters high with stand age between 200 to 400 years.

## 带岭凉水自然保护区

凉水自然保护区距伊春市带岭区北25公里处,南北长11公里,东西宽6.25公里,总面积63.94平方公里,是我国现存红松原始林基地之一,为国家级自然保护区,也是东北地区林业教学、科研的实验区。

保护区森林覆被率达95%以上,总蓄积量为14万平方米。区内林木类型繁多,尤以天然红松树种比重居多。原始林中生长着各种野生动植物和珍贵药材,素有"小红松故乡"之称。走进原始林,干躯笔直的古松,傲然屹立,郁郁葱葱。红松树龄大多为200~400年,树高达30~40米。

## 57. The Virgin Forests Park in Fangzheng County

Traveling 164 km from Harbin along the Tongjiang Highway, will bring you to Fangzheng County. Another 28 kilometers south lies the Virgin Forests Park on the hilly land of the northern foot of the Laoye Mountain Range, west slope of Zhangguangcai Mountain of the Changbai Mountain. It lies between 200 and 800 meters above sea level, with the scenic area covering more than 600 hectares, and the forest coverage ratio at more than 90%.

The major scenic sites include Tiger Cave, Alum Pool, Expanses of Pines, and eleven other places of interest. The vegetation here is of typical flora in the Changbai Mountain, and mixed forests of broad-leaved Korean pine forest forms the major vegetation, mainly covering the gradual slopes and high slopes of the mountains. Spruce and larch account for the majority of the mixed trees. On the slopes many trees such as Linden, Betula costata and other kinds are growing, forming both a Betula costata and Pinus koraiensis forest, and Tiliaceae and Pinus koraiensis forest, with typical sub-trees namely Corylus mandshurica Maxim, Radix Acanthopanacis Senticosi and Philadelphus kansuensis and so on. There also grow some liana and Ampelopsis breipedunculata, wuweizi and Actinidia kolomikta in the mixed forest of broad-leaved Korean pine forest.

## 方正原始森林公园

从哈尔滨出发沿哈尔滨同江公路前行164公里，就到了方正县城。再向南行进28公里，就是方正原始森林公园。方正原始森林公园位于长白山张广才岭西坡老爷岭北麓的丘陵地带，海拔在200～800米之间，景区占地面积600多公顷，森林覆盖率90％以上。

景区内主要有老虎洞、明石塘、绿海松涛等14个景点。该旅游区内植被属于长白山植物区系，红松针阔混交林是旅游区内代表性植被，分布于山地的缓坡或斜坡上。混生树种一般以云杉和落叶松为主。在缓坡和斜坡混生树种为紫椴、枫桦等，组成枫桦红松林和椴树红松林。林中典型的下木有毛榛、刺五加、山梅花等，红松针阔混交林还混生一些藤本植物和山葡萄、五味子、狗枣猕猴桃等。

### 58. Fenglin Nature Reserve in Wuying District

Stretching on the Southern slope of Lesser Khingan Mountain, Wuying District, Yingchun City, Heilongjiang province, covering an area of 18 400 hectares, established in 1958 and listed as national natural reserve in 1988, Fenglin National Nature Reserve was brought into UNESCO (United Nations Educational Scientific and Cultural Organization) "Human and Biosphere" protection network in 1997 and it mainly protects the most typical forests of Northeastern Region—the needle and broad-leaved mixed forest with Korean pine as its main type.

This reserveis made up of many needle and broad-leaved mixed forests and it is the largest and perfectly-reserved virgin Korean pine forest, and it has enjoyed a history of over 300 years. The greatest of these trees have a maximum trunk diameter of 140 centimeters and can reach 37 meters in height. There stands a 40-meter-high watchtower where a bird's-eye view of the magnificent immense expanse of the Korean pines is available. Paved paths surrounding the mountains allow hikers to trek to the summit either by foot or by vehicle.

## 五营区丰林自然保护区

丰林国家自然保护区位于中国黑龙江省伊春市五营区，小兴安岭南坡，面积为18 400公顷。该保护区创建于1958年，1988年被列为国家级自然保护区，1997年被纳入联合国教科文组织"人与生物圈"网络。主要保护东北地区最有代表性的森林类型——以红松为主的针阔叶混交林。

保护区由针阔混交林组成,是中国保存最完整、面积最大的原始红松林,并已有300多年的历史。林中树木胸径最大可达140厘米、最高达37米。保护区内耸立着一座40米高的瞭望塔,登塔可鸟瞰壮丽浩瀚的红松林海。保护区内建有环山甬道,游客可步行或乘车登上山顶。

### 59. The Fenghuang (Phoenix) Mountain Forests Park

Over 150 kilometers off the urban area of Wuchang City in the vicinity of Harbin, stands a mountain named Phoenix. With its southern and northern ridges, it is the second highest mountain in Heilongjiang province, only next to the Mount Grand Baldhead. There used to be one narrow-tracked railway functioning as the only communication channel with the outside world. In the year of 2000 a highway was completed, which opened the door of this "grand natural park" long being called so by the local residents for its charming and beautiful scenery.

The Phoenix Mountain boasts its unique and special attractions such as high mountain wetland, 100-meter-drop waterfalls, two brooks, one being white water, the other being black, the great canyon as deep as 5 kilometers, azaleas all over the mountains and plains in spring and the attractive Wuhua Mountain in autumn as well.

Mountain Garden: Covering an area of 100 000 square meters, the Garden in the Air is located on the Laoye Moutain which enjoys the reputation of the highest mountain in Heilongjiang province.

High mountain wetland: The top of the mountain is a broad stretch of open wetland of oxalic carbon with high moisture. The mountains all over are mantled with flowers, grasses and bushes of more than 1 meter tall. Rising to 1 633 meters above sea level, this stretch of land totals an area of 500~600 hectares.

High mountain falsenmeer: There is also a broad stretch of high mountain falsenmeer which resulted from the gradual accumulation of huge rocks, covering an area of thousands of kilometers.

The Great Canyon: The Great Canyon lies just between the Northern and Southern Phoenix Mountain, the former rising to 1 668.9 meters high, while the latter being 1 633 meters high. It is 5 000 meters long and the narrowest place is less than 20 meters wide, with dazzling green hills on both banks and gurgling spring water running, a feast to both the eye and the ear.

The Grand Waterfall: The source of the Great Canyon in Phoenix Mountain is referred to as "the river to the sky" by the local forest workers for dozens of small and large waterfalls with vertical drops ranging from 10 to 15 meters form a terraced drop of over 1 000 meters, which might well be said to be No.1 waterfall in Heilongjiang province.

## 凤凰山森林公园

哈尔滨附近的五常县境内有座山叫凤凰山,距五常市区一百五十余公里,分南北两峰,是黑龙江省内仅次于大秃顶子山的第二高山。以前仅有一条窄轨铁路与外界联系,2000 年修通公路与外界相通,这里风景秀美,一直被当地人称为天然大花园。

凤凰山有独具特色的高山湿地景观,有落差百米的瀑布,有一白一黑的两条溪水,有纵深长度为 5 公里的峡谷,还有春日里满山遍野的杜鹃和秋日下令人陶醉的五花山。

高山花园:空中花园坐落在海拔 1 690 米,被誉为龙江第一大山的老爷岭上,占地 10 万平方米。

高山湿地:山顶是一大片开阔湿地,土壤属草碳性,含水量很大,遍布一米多高的花草和灌木。这片湿地海拔 1 633 米,总面积 500~600 公顷。

高山石海:山上还有一片由巨石堆积而成、面积数千平方米的石海。

大峡谷:北凤凰山高 1 668.9 米,南凤凰山高 1 633 米,峡谷纵深长度为 5 公里,最窄处不足 20 米,两岸青山耀目,泉水汩汩悦耳。

大瀑布:凤凰山大峡谷源头被当地林业工人又称之为"通天河",有 10~50 米落差的大小瀑布十数级,落差超过千尺,可谓龙江第一瀑。

## 60. Harbin Northern Forest Zoo

Harbin Northern Forest Zoo is located in Gezidong District of Acheng, only 43 kilometers away from Harbin urban area. It is the largest forest zoo in China at present, covering an area of 848 hectares. There are 240 species and 5 800 animals, such as white tigers, cheetahs, African elephants, polar bears, penguins, giant pandas, rhinoceros, hippos, alpacas and so on. Twelve functional zones with 39 scenic spots are set up in the reserve, such as animal performing zone and scientific breeding zone. In addition, three mountain stone stairs and many sight seeing platforms are built for tourists to enjoy the "forest walk".

## 哈尔滨北方森林动物园

位于阿城市鸽子洞的哈尔滨北方森林动物园,距哈尔滨市区仅 43 公里,占地面积 848 公顷,是目前中国占地面积最大的森林动物园。园内有白虎、猎豹、非洲象、北极熊、企鹅、大熊猫、犀牛、河马、驼羊等各类动物 240 种 5 800 只(头),设置了动物表演、科研繁育等 12 个功能区,共 39 个景点,此外还修建了 3 条山石阶和多处观光平台,供游客享受"森林浴"。

## 61. The Heilongjiang Forest Botanical Garden

The Heilongjiang Forest Botanical Garden was founded in 1958 and was later opened to the public in 1988. In 1992, it was approved by National Forestry Ministry as Harbin National Forest Garden.

Located in Xiangfang District of Harbin, covering an area of 136 hectares, the Garden is the most prominent cold-temperate zone botanical garden in Northeast China, and it is also the only one situated in a provincial capital. Thirteen specified plant gardens with different themes have been arranged in this botanical garden, such as tree specimen garden, medicinal botanical garden, tulip garden, rare and endangered plants garden, autumn leaves and winter scenery garden, flowers garden, fruits garden, rosaries garden and willow garden, etc. About 1 200 plant species from Northeast China, North China, Northwest China and abroad are available here.

Furthermore, in the Botanical Garden, there are also other sceneries such as the 12 000 square kilometers lake, the 48 meters Sky Tower, the Wanshou Mountain surrounded by trees and the 10 000 square meters ecological leisure square.

## 黑龙江省森林植物园

黑龙江省森林植物园始建于1958年。1988年正式对外开放,1992年被国家林业部批准为哈尔滨国家森林公园。

植物园位于哈尔滨市香坊区,占地面积136公顷,是中国最具代表性的东北寒温带植物园,也是唯一一处处在省会城市中的森林公园。园内建有风格各异的树木标本园、药用植物园、郁金香园、珍稀濒危植物园、秋叶冬景园、百花园、观果园、蔷薇园、杨柳园等13处植物专类园。栽植有东北、华北、西北及部分国外植物1 200余种。

园内还建有12 000平方米水面的园中湖、48米高的青云塔、绿荫环抱的万寿山、10 000平方米的生态休闲广场。

### 62. Huzhong National Nature Reserve

Huzhong National Nature Reserve is located in the middle of Greater Khingan Mountain with a climate of an obvious continental feature, and it is the southern edge of Eurasia frozen earth. The vegetation is the cold temperature zone conifer. The forest is the only well-reserved original cold temperate zone larches in China. The main species are Khingan larches and Mongolian scotch pines. National key protected animals living there include moose, musk deer, otters, mandarin ducks and so on. In addition, there are also some special cold-water fishes. Huzhong Nature Reserve is the research base of high-latitude frozen earth and various wetland vegetation colonies.

Huzhong Nature Reserve has been sealed off for a long time. Native vegetation, mainly Khingan larches, is well reserved and is the only representative of natural forest ecology in Greater Khingan Mountain area. Forest vegetation within the area falls to original north pole plant area, Eurasian forest plant subregion, Greater Khingan Mountain plant region, and is the cold temperate zone conifer, and is also the bright conifer forest vegetation in east Siberia mountainous region. The vegetations could be classified into 58 sections, 156 categories and 223 species. Because of geographical and historical glacier variance and local climate influence, special forest views are formed in this area, mainly by original cold temperate zone conifer forest, such as "drunkards" "lotus on dry land" "dwarves" and "a peacock shows its tail" sights.

## 呼中国家级自然保护区

呼中国家自然保护区地处大兴安岭中部,气候具明显的大陆性特点,为欧亚大陆多年冻土的南缘。植被为寒温带针叶林,是中国唯一保存较完整的寒温带原始落叶松林,主要树种为兴安落叶松和獐子松。国家重点保护动物有驼鹿、原麝、水獭、鸳鸯等,还生存着特有的冷水鱼类。呼中自然保护区可作为研究高纬度带多年冻土和各种沼泽地植被群落的基地。

呼中自然保护区长期处于封闭状态,以兴安落叶松为主的原生植被保存完整,是唯一的大兴安岭自然森林生态的代表,区内森林植被属原北极植物区、欧亚森林植物亚区、大兴安岭植物区系,系寒温性针叶林,是东西伯利亚山地明亮针叶林森林植被。植物种类分布58科156属223种。区内由于受地史变迁冰川和局部气候影响形成了独特的森林景观,主要有寒温带针叶原始森林景观、"醉林"景观、"旱地莲花"景观、"侏儒林"景观、"孔雀开屏"景观等。

## 63. Langxiang Garden in the Forest

Langxiang Garden in the Forest is situated in Langxiang District of Yichun in Heilongjiang province, 28 kms from Langxiang Forestry Bureau. The garden is established in the deep vigin forest, covering an area of 2 824 hectares. The main tree species are Korean pine, Faber fir, Chinese Spruce, Ribbed Birch, Elm and so on. The average age of the trees is about 170 years, and the oldest is 500 years. Most of them date from late Ming Dynasty and early Qing Dynasty.

The forests retained theoriginal look. A small-scale forest train of 4.5 km has been built to take tourists around in the garden.

## 朗乡林中园风景区

林中园风景区,位于黑龙江省伊春市朗乡区境内,距朗乡林业局所在地28公里处。林中园风景区,占地2 824公顷,是一处建在原始林中的森林公园。风景区中的主要树种有红松、云杉、冷杉、枫桦和黄榆等,平均树龄170年左右,最大树龄达500年,多系明末清初的古树。

景区内保持着林区开发初期的原貌,设有森林小火车,铁路周长4.5公里,游客可乘坐小火车穿梭于林海之中。

## 64. Meihuashan National Forest Park

Meihuashan Natianal Forest Park is 28 km to the east of Yichun District of Yichun, Heilongjiang province, covering an area of 78 square kilometers. The scenic spot includes the virgin forest of Korean Pine, Tiger Buttocks Mountains Adventure Area, Meihuashan Adventure Area and Meihua Lake Amusement Zone etc.

The main scenic spots and attractions are Path to the Heaven, Air Climbing Rock, Eastern Heaven Gate, Stone Buddha Watching the Sea, Longevity Platform, Laojun Mountain, Tiger Head Peak, Bear Head Peak, Wooden Club Mountain, Pap Mountain, Cloud Cave, Fairy Spring and Plum Blossom Lake.

The Meihua Lake is a cold-water lake formed by the Meihua River, which covers an area of 4.5 square kilometers. There are more than ten kinds of famous cold-water fishes such as Capelin and Hill Catfish.

## 梅花山国家森林公园

梅花山庄风景旅游区位于黑龙江省伊春市伊春区东郊28公里处,占地78平方公里,分红松原始林景区、虎臀山探险观光区、梅花山探险观光区、梅花湖娱乐区四个景区。

主要景点景观:通天路、登天石、东天门、石佛观海、万寿台、老君山、虎头峰、熊头峰、棒槌山、奶头山、穿云洞、仙女泉、梅花湖。

其中,梅花湖是利用梅花河水形成的冷水湖,湖面4.5平方公里,湖中有细鳞、山鲶鱼等名贵冷水鱼十余种。

## 65. The Mudanfeng (Peony Peak) National Forest Park

The Peony Peak is the main peak of Laoye Ridges. It is also named as Heaven Ridge or Large Hangers Mountain. It is situated in the southeast of suburb Mudanjiang and its peak is 30 kilometers away from the urban area, bordered with Muling and Ning'an. The Peony Peak is the watershed of Mudanjiang River and Muling River with an altitude of 1 115 meters, stretching from the south to the north. It covers an area of 400 square kilometers; the top of the Peony Peak is a round rectangular platform, which is surrounded by spruce and fir. The terrain of Peony Peak declines in the northwest like radiation, and the high-low gap is about 800 m.

Twenty-five million years ago, there were very active volcanic movements. After the eruption, the ridges are covered by basalt and become the rare lava hill. Crisscross gullies are around the park and the biodiversity is obvious, therefore, there are many scenic spots including Heaven Spring, Basalt River, Dragon Head Spring, Apricot Flower Mountain, Buddha Hands Mountain, Eagle Summit, Mopan Mountain, Birch Mountain, Thin Strip of Sky, Gin Ridges, Ancient City and Secret

Camps etc.

## 牡丹峰国家级森林公园

牡丹峰为老爷岭北上之主峰,又名天岭或大架子山,位于牡丹江市郊东南境,峰顶距市区仅30公里,与穆棱、宁安接壤,是牡丹江与穆棱河的分水岭,海拔为1 115米,南北走向。总面积约400平方公里,峰顶为一圆形的长方平台,四周为云杉、冷杉林所包围,地势向西北倾斜面呈放射状而下降,高低差近800米。

在2 500万年之前,曾有相当活跃的火山喷发,因此山岭为玄武岩所覆盖,成为少有的熔岩山。境内沟壑纵横,生物繁多,因而有天泉、玄武河、龙头泉、杏花山、佛手山、鹰峰顶、磨盘山、白桦川、一线天、杜松岭、古城、密营等众多的风景名胜。

### 66. Sandaoguan National Forest Park

Sandaoguan National Forest Park is situated in the northwest of Mudanjiang of Heilongjiang province and at the end of Anfang Mountain, Zhangguangcai Ridge, covering an area of 8 000 hectares.

The natural landscape of Sandaoguan National Forest Park is unique, and the main landscapes include forest, stream, grotesque stone and fantastic peak etc. The exuberant and productive forest also has precipitous and magnificent stone, such as Daiwang Stone and Cockscomb Stone to form many exotic sights like Camel Peak, Flying Stone and Thin Strip of Sky, which are naturally caved by prodigious craftsmanship.

The park has five major tourist attractions: Daiwang Stone Tourist Attraction, Cockscomb Stone Tourist Attraction, Little Mount Huang Tourist Attraction, Southern Frog Pond Tourist Attraction and Couple Stone Tourist Attraction.

## 三道关国家森林公园

牡丹江三道关国家森林公园位于黑龙江省牡丹江市的西北部、张广才岭安纺山脉之末,公园总面积8 000公顷。

三道关国家森林公园自然景观独特,森林、河溪、奇石、怪峰为公园主体景观。有枝叶茂盛的大森林,有陡峭壮观的石砬子:岱王砬子,鸡冠砬子等,有"鬼斧神工雕自然"的骆驼峰、飞来石、一线天等景观。

三道关国家森林公园有五大旅游景区:岱王砬子旅游景区、鸡冠砬子旅游景区、小黄山旅游景区、南蛤蟆塘旅游景区、夫妻石旅游景区。

## 67. Linhaiqishi National Forest Park

The Stone Forest Scenic Area in the Lesser Khingan Mountain in Tangwanghe District—the Linhaiqishi National Forest Park is situated in Yichun City of Heilongjiang province, 8 kilometers away from Tangwanghe District. It covers an area of 190 square kilometers, which is a new ecotourism scenic area and national geological relics park composed of natural and human sceneries.

The famous scenic spots in the south are: "A Tiny Sky View" "Arhat Turtoise" "Grand Mountain" "The Mountain General" and so on. The western area is formed of peculiar landscapes such as "Mountains cut by sword" "Angel-dog-shaped Rock", and "Cloud Boots Peak" etc., which are full of mythical legends. The northern area includes such scenic spots as "Zhongkui Cliff"—holding the pole by hands to make demons surrender and fastening the whip in waist to exorcise ghosts, "Deep and Secluded Valley" in green and "Flat Peach Ridge", and these scenic spots are famous for the folk legends related to them. The central spot is composed of pictographic rocks, including "Dragon Head Rocks" "The Auspicious Dragon and Phoenix" "The Goddess of Mercy" "The Crouching Ox" "Khingan Ganoderma Lucidum" "Sky Mending Rocks" and "Long-lived Turtles" etc. Besides, there are many geological phenomena, geo-structures and rock spectacle with great value of scientific research and popularization of science.

## 林海奇石国家森林公园

汤旺河小兴安岭石林风景区——林海奇石国家森林公园,位于黑龙江省伊春距汤旺河区址8公里处,占地面积190平方公里,是由人文景观和自然景观构成的生态旅游新区和国家地质遗迹公园。

南区著名的景点有"一线天""罗汉龟""雄峰""护山大将军"等。西区由"剑劈山""天犬岩""云靴顶"等充满神话故事的特异景观组成。北区是以手持降魔杆,腰系驱鬼鞭的"钟馗崖"及绿色深幽的"幽谷"和"蟠桃岭"为主要内容的民俗传说景观。中区景观以象形奇石为主,主要有"龙头岩""龙凤呈祥""林海观音""卧天牛""兴安灵芝""补天石""增寿龟"等。这里还有具有极高科研和科普价值的地质现象、地理构造和岩石奇观。

## 68. Taoshan National Forest Park

Taoshan National Forest Park, originally named Taoshan Primitive Forest Scenic Spot and officially approved in 1997, is situated 55 kilometers to the east of Taoshan Forestry Bureau of Yichun City, covering an area of more than 20 million square kilometers. The park is mainly covered with Korean Pines, with a small quantity of Elm, Tiliaceae and Manchurian ash etc. The average age of the trees is about 350 years; the diameter of the trees can reach 40 centimeters, and the height 25 meters. In the primitive forest, there are 999 steps leading to the mountain peak, with two viewing pavilions along the way.

Near the scenic spot, there are camping sites for hunters, which are of continental loft style and are equipped with guest rooms, bars, fireplaces and so on.

## 桃山国家森林公园

桃山国家森林公园位于伊春市桃山林业局东 55 公里处,面积 2 000 多万平方米,主要树种为红松,间杂有榆、椴、水曲柳等。平均树龄为 350 年左右,树径一般达 40 厘米,高 25 米。走进原始森林,绕山而上有 999 级台级,路经两处观景亭可到达山顶。

景区附近还设有猎人宿营地,为欧式层楼阁款式建筑,设有客房、酒吧、烧烤壁炉等。1997 年,桃山原始林景区被批准为国家级森林公园。

### 69. Taoshan Hunting Ground

Taoshan Hunting Ground lies 30 kilometers away from Taoshan Forestry Bureau of Yichun in Heilongjiang province, and 238 kilometers away from the northeast of Harbin. It stands 14 kilometers from the southeast of Taoshan Forestry Bureau, within the mountain area of the Lesser Khingan Mountain. Approved by the State Council in 1985, it is the first breeding and hunting ground of wild animals which opens up to the public. In the lush forest of the hunting ground, there are numerous wild animals, such as black bears, wild boars, red deer, roe deer, pheasants, hazel grouses, snow hares and so on. Except the rare species, all the other wild animals can be hunted. The hunting period is from early September to the end of the next February each year.

The hunting ground has two camps, providing special vehicles, hunting guides, shotguns and ammunition. It is well-known in Heilongjiang province and attracts thousands of visitors abroad to tour and hunt here every year.

## 桃山狩猎场

桃山狩猎场位于黑龙江省伊春市桃山林业局 30 多公里处,距哈尔滨东北 238 公里,位于桃山林业局东南 14 公里处,山地为小兴安岭山脉的一处山区。1985 年,经国务院批准,是中国第一个对外开放的野生动物饲养狩猎场。在狩猎场茂密的森林内,有黑熊、野猪、马鹿、狍子、山鸡、飞龙、雪兔等多种野生动物。这些野生动物除国家规定珍稀品种外都可猎取。每年 9 月初至翌年 2 月底为狩猎期。

猎场建有两处营地,备有狩猎专用车、导猎员和猎枪弹药等,每年吸引大批海外旅游者到此狩猎旅游,在黑龙江省久负盛名。

### 70. Weihushan National Forest Park

Weihushan National Forest Park is the largest national forest park in China. Situated in Chaihe Town of Hailin City, it covers an area of 41.4 hectares. There are Stone Murals dating from Western Zhou Dynasty, Korean Ancient Well in Bohai State, Ancient Tombs of Jin Dynasty in Bohai Bay, Beacon Towers in Qing Dynasty, Ancient Villages of Jin Dynasty in Guokui Bay, "Weihu Cave" in which Yang Zirong, a hero during the Chinese Liberation War, won a brilliant victory in suppressing the bandits, River God Temple and Taoist Temple. The Lotus Lake has formed three gorges, five bays and six islands, and has been enjoying the reputation of "Little Three Gorges of One Hundred Li in the city of Mudanjiang".

## 威虎山国家森林公园

威虎山国家森林公园是目前中国面积最大的国家森林公园,总面积为41.4公顷,位于海林市柴河镇。这里有西周时期摩崖壁画、渤海国高丽古井、渤海湾金代古墓群、清代烽火台、锅盔湾金代古村落,还有中国解放战争英雄杨子荣剿匪的"威虎厅"(山洞)及河神庙、老道庙等。莲花湖在这里形成三峡五湾六大岛屿,具有百里丹江小三峡美称。

### 71. Chinese Woodcarving Park in the City of Woods

Chinese Woodcarving Park was built in the year of 2002. It lies on the west of the Huayuan Road, Yichun, Heilongjiang province, covering an area of 8 800 square meters and neighboring the Stone Garden. All the carvings in the garden are made of woods and show good taste and natural style. The garden is divided into four parts: the Archway Zone, the Porch of Wood Carvings, the Central Viewing Zone, and the Leisure and Recreation Zone. All the sculptures combine concrete images and abstract concepts, some are carved in high relief while some in low relief. It embodies traditional Chinese culture and new concepts of modern design, conveying the theme of eternal life.

## 中国林都木雕园

中国林都木雕园建于2002年,位于黑龙江省伊春区花园路西畔,占地8 800平方米,与石苑相邻,是一个取材于林区,彰显自然,高文化品位的园林景观。木雕园分为牌坊景观区、木雕排廊区、中心观赏区、休闲娱乐区四个景区。整个雕塑采取了形象与抽象结合、浅浮雕与高浮雕相对比的手法,浓缩了中化民族传统文化与现代造型的新理念,传达永恒的生命主题。

### 72. The Lianhua (Lotus) Lake Scenic Area in Fangzheng County

Situated at 45°50′N and 128°45′E, 5 kilometers to the west of Fangzheng County (about 175 kilometers away from the city of Harbin), the Lotus Lake, once called the Lotus Pond, covers an area of 35 hectares, of which 17 hectares are dotted with over 5.1 million lotuses. The lake gets its name for its unique geographic location and naturally grown lotuses. It is the largest natural lotus lake with the most flowers at the same latitudes. The Lotus Lake is a natural lake, which enjoys a vast expanse of clear water from rainfalls and seven springs. Each year on July 28th, the Lotus Festival is celebrated in Fangzheng County.

## 方正莲花湖风景区

莲花湖,原名莲花泡,北纬45°50′,东经128°45′。位于哈尔滨市方正县西5公里处,距哈尔滨约175公里,水域面积35公顷,有莲花面积17公顷,池内莲花510万多株,因地理环境独特天然生长莲花而得名。是同纬度面积最大、有莲花最多的一处天然莲花池。

该池为自然湖泊,水面辽阔,水质清澈透明,池水来自池内7个泉眼和自然降水。每年的7月28日是方正的"莲花节"。

### 73. The Great White Mountain in Huzhong

Situated in the southernmost part of Huzhong Nature Reserve of the Greater Khingan Mountain, Heilongjiang province, the Great White Mountain is the highest peak in northern range of the Greater Khingan Mountain. With its summit at 1 528.7 meters above sea level, the mountain is gradual in the north and steep in the south. The high elevation enables it to be a typical vertical forest-vegetation-belt collection with its ridges orderly composed of various forest belts from the foot to the top, with orderly distribution of mountainous frigid-temperate zone coniferous forest belt, frigid-temperate zone sub-alpine Coniferous (broadleaved) forest belt and sub-alpine elfin forest belt.

It is usual to see the coexistence of beautiful snow at the top and lively green trees on the foot concurrently on the Great White Mountain. Moreover, it also provides seas of rocks on the top, rocky outcrops on the lower part, and rocks forming stacks, seas, and rivers on the flat ground.

## 呼中大白山

位于黑龙江省大兴安岭呼中自然保护区最南端,是大兴安岭北段最高峰。山势南陡北缓,海拔较高,峰顶为1 528.7米。整个山体由于海拔高,具有典型的森林植被垂直带谱景观特色,从山麓脚至山顶,有序地分布着山地寒温带针叶林带、山地寒温带亚高山型针(阔)叶林带、亚高山矮曲林带。

在大白山区往往可以见到山巅白雪皑皑,山下万木葱绿的景色。山顶夷平面多石海,山坡下部多岩屑裙,一些平坦地方形成石堆、石海、石河等。

### 74. Baleng River Scenic Resort in Jidong County

Situated 30 kilometers to the southwest of Jidong County in Heilongjiang province, the newly built Baleng River Scenic Resort was opened to tourists in June 1997. The Baleng River is a man-made multifunctional lake, bordering Russia and equipped with convenient transportation. It is used mainly for irrigation, and also for flood protection, tourism, as well as livestock-raising.

The charm of the Baleng River lies in both its unique artistic conception and intact natural ecosystem. It enjoys a vast expanse of water as well as precipitous mountains. Inside the resort many famous places are available for guests, such as the Hall of the Immortal Fox, the Slope of Apricot Blossoms, Natural Stones, Stone Forest, etc. Adding to this there are also numerous entertainments, such as swimming, exciting and adventurous rafting, water-playing in a 10-meter long water slide, etc. In addition, the Baleng River Scenic Resort is famous for its local products such as matsutake, wild mushrooms, Siberian frog, which greatly meet the needs of tourists.

## 鸡东县八楞河风景区

八楞河风景区位于黑龙江省鸡东县西南方向30公里处,是一处新建风景区。1997年6月开园接待游客,它是一座以灌溉为主,兼顾防洪、旅游、养殖多业发展的人工湖。与俄罗斯接壤,交通十分便利。

八楞河水面浩瀚,山峰险峻,著名的景点有仙狐堂、杏花坡、天然石观、石林等景观,其独特的意境和完好的自然生态体系成为景区魅力所在。八楞河的游乐项目丰富,漂流惊险刺激,标准游泳池、10米高水滑梯是嬉水者的理想之地。此外,八楞河景区盛产山珍——松茸、山菇、林蛙等山产品,可以满足游人的购物需求。

### 75. Unicorn Mountain Scenic Resort in Jixi City

Unicorn Mountain Scenic Resort in Jixi City, a rare scenic attraction, lies in Xingnong Township, Jidong County, Heilongjiang province. Against the resort stands the well-known Unicorn Mountain with its head ridge (the north peak) facing north and tail ridge south (the south peak), and the waist looks like the body of a unicorn. The mountain resembles a unicorn, hence the name, "Unicorn Mountain".

Along the southern slopes of the mountain the most distinguishing structures are 10 Japanese-style villas where you can experience the exotic appeal of Japan similar to that at Mount Fiji. The service center incorporates catering service and entertainment activities, while Building B provides lodging rooms together with an indoor swimming pool. Furthermore, the newly built Student Building adds cultural atmosphere to the resort.

Tickets: RMB 25.00 Yuan

## 鸡西市麒麟山风景区

麒麟山风景区位于黑龙江省鸡东县兴农镇,是一处不可多得的旅游胜地。麒麟山庄对面的山峰就是著名的麒麟峰。这座山峰头朝北、尾朝南,北峰似麒麟的头角,南峰似麒麟的尾,细看山脉,犹如麒麟的腰身,故叫麒麟山。

整个山庄最具特色的建筑是顺峰南坡修建的 10 栋日式风格别墅。到这里来可领略日本富士山下的异国情调。服务中心大楼集餐饮、娱乐于一体。B 楼是住宿房间和室内游泳池。新建成的学子楼给山庄带来了文化氛围。

门票:25 元

### 76. Tianci Lake (The Heaven-sent Lake)

Tianci Lake in Yichun City, made up of mountain springs, covers 5 sq km expanse of crystal clear and palatably sweet water. In summer, brimmed with bluish green water, the 5-meter deep lake reflects the mountains like a mirror and the two forms a harmonious picture. This draws the visitors into a world of picturesque waters and hills. Running across a dyke, the lake ingeniously weaves a water screen with the crystal white water in all directions, presenting a spectacular view.

### 天赐湖

伊春的天赐湖水是由清澈的山泉汇集而成,湖水清澈透明,甘甜可口。湖面 5 平方公里,湖水深 5 米,夏季湖水含碧,山水相连,倒映清山,使人如同进入一幅山水画中。湖水从坝上而过,形成水帘,翻花洒珠,别具情调。

### 77. Toulong Mountain Scenic Spot in Tieli City

Toulong Mountain Scenic Spot is located in Tieli city, Heilongjiang province. It is 240 kilometers from Harbin, only 2~3 hours' drive by train or car.

This scenic spot enjoys a good reputation both in and out of Heilongjiang province. Mainly composed of lucid and lively wooden structures, it echoes the characteristics of forest regions, providing satisfying catering, entertainment and accommodation services. There are mysterious thousand-year-old ancient caves, sweet and graceful spring and stream waters and precious primitive wetlands. There are also plunging mountain waterfalls along the winding path to halfway up the mountain. The right side is a cave, within which there are steep stone walls. What amazes many people is that there is a second small cave at the other end of the cave and the two caves are opposite each other. The area between these two caves is known as the famous "Toulong Mountain". Toulong Mountain consists of 9 mountains and 18 scenic sites, among which are the famous Mandarin Duck Trees, Crouching Tiger Mountain, Back-to-back Mountain, Celestial Bone, A Seam of Sky, Welcoming Pine and Azalea Mountain.

## 铁力透龙山风景区

铁力透龙山风景区位于黑龙江省铁力市。距哈市240公里,乘火车、汽车只需2~3小时。透龙山风景区以木质结构建筑为主,风格简洁明快,很有林区特色,可在此就餐、娱乐、住宿,是闻名黑龙江省内外的旅游度假区。这里有神秘的千年古洞,甘甜的清泉溪水,宝贵的原始湿地。沿景区蜿蜒的小径至半山腰处,有直泻而下的山间瀑布,右侧的有一个山洞,洞内石壁陡峭。令人称奇的是山洞的另一头还有一个小洞,两个洞口遥相对应,"透龙山"因此得名。透龙山有九峰十八景,景景称奇,著名的有鸳鸯树、卧虎峰、背靠峰、仙人骨、一线天、迎客松、杜鹃峰等。

### 78. Wogui Mountain (Crouching Turtle Mountain)

Wogui Mountain, being similar to a turtle in shape, is located in the northeast of Jinshan village in Heilongjiang province. It enjoys an elevation of approximately 400 meters. One side of the mountain is a 30-meter-high cliff, its two front foothills draws near to Tangwang River and the center part of the rear extends quite a distance. The shape is similar to an incumbent turtle leaning on the mountain. Seen from a distance, the turtle's head, back, shell, foot and tail are quite vividly connected with the mountain. The outline of the mountain is seen to be vague at dawn, just like a crouching turtle roaming in a sea of clouds. The area is a marvelous rocky scenic spot.

## 卧龟山

卧龟山位于黑龙江省金山屯区东北面,海拔高400米左右,是一座相形山,山的一侧是高三十多米的峭壁,前端的两个山脚临近汤旺河水面,后端中部向远处延伸,形似一只依山横卧的乌龟。远看卧龟的头、背、甲、足、尾都与相应的山体相连,形式十分逼真。晨曦微露时,山势时隐时现,如同卧龟在云海中遨游,是一处别具一格的相形奇石风景区。

### 79. Wusuli River

Wusuli River is a big branch on the right bank of Heilongjiang River, also an important boundary river on the Sino-Russia border in the Northeast. Wusuli River is one of the few unpolluted rivers in China with beautiful and natural scenery. Overlooking her west bank, we can see the flourishing forest on Nadanhada Ridge and the rich and luxurious Sanjiang Plain; another elegant and captivating scene is the continuous mountains and their shadows on the surface of the water at the east bank.

Her flat beach is covered with cobblestones of various colors; the silvery white water is very calm and glimmers in the sunlight, and occasionally, fish boat, yachts and cargo ships steering on the river may be seen, which adds liveliness to this serene environment. In addition, Wusuli River is rich in world-renowned salmon, carp, crucian carp, mandarin fish, bream, bighead fish and brown trout are also well known.

## 乌苏里江

乌苏里江是黑龙江右岸的一大支流,也是中国东北部中俄边境上的一条重要界河。乌苏里江的秀丽和自然风貌,是中国仅有的几条未被污染的江河之一。在这里可以看到江西岸连绵起伏的那丹哈达岭茂密的森林和丰饶富庶的三江平原。江东岸更是山岳连绵,山水相映,别是一派奇秀风光。平缓的江边铺满了五颜六色的鹅卵石,银白色的乌苏里江水,在阳光普照下,天光水色,静影沉壁,不时看到江水中行驶的渔船、游船、货船,给乌苏里江增添了几分热闹;另外,乌苏里江盛产的大马哈鱼(鲑)驰名中外,鲤、鲫、鳜、鳊、鱅、巨鳟等均是佳品。

## 80. Cuibei Wetland Nature Reserve

Cuibei Wetland Nature Reserve lies in the source of the Ximalu River and Kulebin River in Heilongjiang province. In the reserve, rivers crisscross and lakes scatter like stars in the sky. It is a typical wetland at higher latitude in North China.

Korean pine broad-leaved mixed forest and bright coniferous trees both exist in the reserve. Forest swamps, herbaceous swamps, peat bryophyte swamps, water plants and wet meadow pattern like islands. There are 164 kinds of birds in the reserve, including 9 types of Class-A and 29 types of Class-B protected species. There are 37 kinds of animals, including 1 type of Class-A and 36 types of Class-B protected species. And there are 1 120 varieties of plants, including 37 types of protected species at the national level, and about 100 kinds of medical herbs, which have potential to be further explored.

## 翠北湿地自然保护区

翠北湿地自然保护区位于黑龙江西玛鲁河和库乐滨河的源头。保护区内河流纵横交错、湖泊星罗棋布,是中国北方较高纬度地区具有代表性的湿地类型。

保护区为红松阔叶混交林、明亮针叶林交错地带,包括森林沼泽、草本沼泽、泥炭藓沼泽、水生植被和沼泽化草甸,成小片的岛状分布。湿地内有鸟类164种,其中国家一级保护鸟类9种,国家二级保护鸟类29种;兽类37种,其中国家级一类保护兽类1种,二类保护兽类36种;植物1 120种,其中国家级保护植物13种,具有可开发价值的中草药100余种。

## 81. Sanjiang Wetland Nature Reserve

Sanjiang Wetland Nature Reserve is located in Fuyuan County, Jiamusi City, 400 kilometers from Harbin. It is in the northeast of China and a lower alluvial delta wetland formed by Heilongjiang River and Wusuli River. The wetlands cover an area of 200 000 hectares. It is one of the best-protected wetlands in the world. The late summer is the best season for tourists to enjoy the beauty of the wild water lilies rare in north China and the sunrise in Wusu Town.

In Sanjiang Wetland Nature Reserve, anatidaes and mandarin ducks can be seen paddling about in the water. Red-crowned cranes and golden eagles can also be observed flying in the sky. Red deer and roe deer run in the grassland searching for food, and the large area of grass sways gently in the breeze, which makes the wetlands more lively and vigorous.

Route: Buses run every half hour from Harbin Bus Station to Jiamusi City, RMB 86 yuan per person. Then take buses or sleeping coaches to Fuyuan Sanjiang Nature Reserve (10 hours), RMB 90 per person.

## 三江自然湿地保护区

三江自然湿地保护区位于佳木斯抚远县,距离哈尔滨约400公里,地处中国东北角,是黑龙江与乌苏里江汇流的三角地带。整个湿地面积达20万公顷,是世界保护最好的湿地之一。来这里最好的季节是暮夏,那时可看到北国稀有的野荷花,也可到乌苏镇观日出。

在三江湿地保护区,雁鸭、鸳鸯成群结队在水中嬉戏;丹顶鹤、金雕等搏击长空;马鹿、狍子在草地上奔走觅食;湿地中的大片小叶樟草在风中沙沙作响,为湿地增添了生机与活力。

交通:哈尔滨客车站至佳木斯,每半小时就有一班,票价86元。到达佳木斯,有开往抚远三江自然保护区的班车,卧铺客车,票价90元,约10小时的车程。

## 82. Songfeng Mountain in Acheng District

Songfeng Mountain is located in Shanhe Township, Acheng District, 45 kilometers from the South of Harbin. It is a Forest Ecosystem Nature Reserve with an area of approximately 146 square kilometers and was considered a Taoism Holy Land in both Jin dynasty and Qing dynasty. It has earned its name due to the mountain being covered with many old pines. It once was the summer resort and hunting ground for royalty members of Jin Dynasty. Until now there are still many remains, such as the Cao Taoist Inscriptions, the Bowing Platform, the Carved Stone Chess Board, and the TaiXu Ancient Cave in Jin Dynasty and so on. Since Qing Dynasty it has been called the first marvelous sight among the eight famous mountains in the northeast.

The elevation of Songfeng Mountain is 627 meters, which is made up of the prominent peak, called Chimney Peak and the dissimilar peaks such as the Breast Peak, the Roaring Lion Peak, the

Chess Board Peak, the Rocky Peak and so on. The prominent peak is extremely steep, popularly called the Chimney Cliff Peak while the branch peaks have been named as Jinyuan Breast Peaks since old times for they look like two breasts.

The five peaks are side by side in the north mountain, while the rocks in various shapes stand in great numbers. On the mountain there are many trees and grasslands. Many ring peaks are on the top.

Under the beautiful Rocky Peak, there are still two remains: the two Taoist ancient temples during the reign of Emperor Jiaqing in Qing Dynasty, which are Haiyun Temple and Cangjing Temple. In addition, there are also many historic sites such as Bowing Platform, Spring Well, Precious Stone, Senior Taoist Temple and Chess Board on which the Taoists once played chess and so on. In the mountainside there is a natural cave, in which there are carved characters of "Taixu Cave in Songfeng Mountain", and some steles.

## 阿城松峰山

位于哈尔滨市南 45 公里处的阿城市山河镇,面积约 146 平方公里,是森林生态型自然保护区。区内松峰山是金清两代道教圣地,因其山多古松而称之为松峰山。松峰山是金代皇室避暑、狩猎的园林,至今仍有曹道士碑刻、拜斗台、石刻围棋盘、金源太虚古洞等遗存。清代以来被称为东北八大名山第一奇观。

松峰山海拔 627 米,由主峰烟筒峰和形态各异的乳头峰、狮张嘴峰、棋盘峰、石景峰等群峰组成。主峰俗称烟筒砬子,陡峭险峻,支峰状似双乳,自古有金源乳峰之称。

北山五峰并峙,怪石林立,相映成趣。山上林茂草丰,山顶有许多突起的环峰。

在风景秀丽的石景峰下,尚存两座清代道教建于嘉庆年间的古庙遗址,这就是海云观和藏经楼。此外还有拜头台、山泉井、石宝、老道观及当年道士对弈的围棋盘等古迹。山腰有天然石洞,洞内有"松峰山太虚洞"刻字,并有若干石碑。

## 83. Guogeli Street

Fendou Road, an old street with a history of one hundred years, has recently been restored and reconstructed into one of the Russian-style streets in Harbin-a famous city in Northern China. Its name was also changed to Guogeli Street by the Harbin Municipal Government. On this street, tourists from both home and abroad can enjoy the leisure and comfort the "Modian" (trolley car) brings and the melodious bells from Aleksev church, just like in the past.

Fendou Road was built in 1907, also called Commercial Street and later Guogeli Street, measuring 2 642 meters in length. This street was eventually named after Gogol, a Russian writer, due in part to the many Russians living in the area at that time, and the multitude of European-style constructions erected along the street.

The transformation of Fendou Road centers around three buildings: Number 167, Fendou Road residential building, Aleksev church and the Provincial Foreign Affairs Office. The buildings, together with the Russian River Garden, the Church Square, the "Modian", the constructions of "bar corridor" show the natural, simple and elegant style of Russian constructions.

## 果戈里大街

一条有着百年历史的老街"奋斗路"近日在中国北方名城哈尔滨被重新修复和改造成为俄罗斯风情街区,哈尔滨市政府也将其更名为"果戈里大街"。中外游客在这条老街上得以重温"摩电"(有轨电车)的闲适和阿列克谢耶夫教堂悠扬的钟声。

建于1907年的奋斗路,原名商务街、果戈里街,道路全长2 642米,由于当时在此居住的俄罗斯人较多,沿街欧式建筑林立,该街便以俄罗斯作家果戈里的名字命名。

奋斗路改造主要以奋斗路167号民宅、阿列克谢耶夫教堂、省外事办三处建筑为主,配以俄罗斯河园、教堂广场、"摩电"、酒吧长廊建筑小品等,再现了俄罗斯自然、古朴、典雅的建筑风格。

## 84. Dragon Tower—the Highest Steel Tower in Asia

Dragon Tower, officially called Heilongjiang province Broadcasting Tower, is a comprehensive and multifunctional tower, combining broadcasting, sightseeing, catering and entertainment, advertising and wireless communications into one. 336 meters high, it is the second highest steel tower in the world, and the highest in Asia.

The Science and Technology Paradise in Dragon Tower is reputed as "the best paradise in Heilongjiang" and one of the national bases for spreading scientific knowledge to the youth. The Terracotta Warriors and Horses during the reign of Emperor Qin Shihuang has recently been exhibited on the second floor, which is magnificent and imposing. In the Waxworks Museum of Dragon's Descendents, there are more than forty emperors' wax statues, such as Emperor Qin Shihuang, Genghis Khan, Wu Zetian and so on. The sightseeing floor, at an elevation of 181 meters, is the first exhibition hall in China to display celebrities' hand-imprints, in which more than 300 celebrities' hand imprints are collected, comparable to Hollywood's Star Boulevard. The Adventurous Ring Strolling in the Clouds, 60 meters in length, provides excitement without danger. The saucer-shaped revolving restaurant, built with a total floor area of 1,256 square meters and 186 meters from the ground, provides a comfortable and elegant environment for tourists to enjoy cuisines of both Western and Chinese style.

## 龙塔——亚洲第一钢塔

黑龙江省广播电视塔——龙塔是一座集广播电视发射、旅游观光、餐饮娱乐、广告传播、无线通信于一体的综合性多功能塔,塔高336米,为目前亚洲第一、世界第二高钢塔。

龙塔科技乐园被誉为"龙江第一乐园",是全国青少年科普教育实践基地之一;二楼新增"秦兵马俑军阵展",气势恢弘。"龙的传人蜡像馆",内有秦始皇、成吉思汗、武则天等帝王蜡像40余尊。181米高度的观光层有中国首家名人手型馆,收藏各界功成名就人士手型300余枚,可与"好莱坞"星光大道媲美;周长60多米的"云中漫步惊险环"有惊无险;186米空中飞碟旋转餐厅,面积1 256平方米,环境舒适典雅,中西佳肴款款精致。

## 85. Hengdaohezi Amur Tiger Garden

Hengdaohezi Amur Tiger Park lies 211 kilometers from the 301 State Highway, near the city of Hailin, which is in the eastern part of Heilongjiang province. It is the largest Amur Tiger breeding center in the world. It covers a total area of 250 000 square meters, including Tiger Garden, Training Zone, Entertainment Zone and Rare Animal Zone. Surrounded by mountains and forests, the Tiger Garden alone covers an area of 70 000 square meters. With the dense and flourishing forests surrounding the area, this provides the optimum environment for the Amur Tiger.

With the primary purpose of releasing the tigers back to the wild and reviving its primal instincts, the Amur Tiger Garden was furthermore constructed as a multifunctional rare animal garden combining sight-seeing, entertainment, scientific education, a summer resort and other functions. The garden includes Tiger Zone, Deer Zone, Bear Zone and Science Education Center. From the viewing platform or the tourist coach, the tourists can witness the fear-inspiring natural prowess of "the King of the beasts" and other rare animals.

## 横道河子东北虎林园

横道河子东北虎林园位于黑龙江东部海林市301国道211公里处,是世界最大的东北虎繁育中心。虎园占地25万平方米,包括猛虎园、教育区、高娱服务区、珍奇动物观赏区,其中猛虎园占地7万平方米,虎园四周群山环绕,林木葱郁,是东北虎生存的极佳环境。

东北虎林园本着放虎归山、还虎灵性的宗旨,建设了集观赏、游乐、科普教育、避暑度假等多功能于一体的珍稀动物观赏园。园内设有虎园、鹿园、熊园、科普中心等观赏、游乐区。游人可在看台上、缆车中一睹"兽中之王"的凛凛虎威和其他珍稀动物的风采。

## 86. Jingpo Lake Lava Tunnel Scenery

13 kilometers to the southeast of the underground forest lies a scenery rarely seen lava tunnel,

adding even more mystery as it mystically accents the Jingpo Lake. Scientists have speculated that the lava tunnel was formed from a volcanic eruption 4 000 ~ 8 000 years ago. Its appearance bears great resemblance to the karst water-eroded cave in the limestone areas of Guilin, Guangxi province, while each bares its own essential difference. When the volcano erupted, scorching lava turbulently plunged down along the lowlands of the valley. While its surface solidified into a stiff shell upon cooling, its insides still remained mobile at high temperatures forming an underground river of lava. As the lava source exhausted, a giant subterranean cave was formed within the lava stream, creating the lave tunnel.

The lava tunnels discovered up to date usually measure around 5 meters wide and 3 meters high with its length ranging from tens of meters to over 500 meters. All of the tunnels also have an arched ceiling, and the inside surface is naturally dark purple in color. The innate wonders are magically formed with various shapes and beautiful patterns, just like being designed and carved by human beings. Vertical stone pillars, and natural stone beds and steps can be seen in the tunnels.

## 镜泊湖熔岩隧道风景

在地下森林东南方约13千米的地方,有几处国内外罕见的"熔岩隧道",给镜泊湖又添上一层神秘的色彩。据科学家推测,"熔岩隧道"是距今4 000~8 000年前一次火山喷发时形成的,其面貌很像广西桂林石灰岩地区的喀斯特"溶洞",但与其有本质区别。当火山爆发时,汹涌炽热的熔岩流沿河谷低地奔腾而下,其表层先冷却凝成硬壳,而内部仍处于高温流动状态,形成地下熔岩河,当岩浆源枯竭时,便在熔岩流内部留下巨大的地下空洞,即"熔岩隧道"。

已发现的熔岩隧道短的几十米,长的在500米以上,一般宽5米余,高3米。隧道顶呈拱形,内表面全都是黑紫色。各种奇幻形成,犹如人工雕琢,图案精美。隧道中还可见到直立的石柱以及天然的石床、石阶等。

### 87. Shuangfeng Snow Town

Functioning as an eco-tourism scenic resort, Shuangfeng Snow Town lies within the boundary of Dahailin Forestry Bureau on the southern slope of Zhangguangcai Ridge in Heilongjiang province. With the winter season lasting up to 7 months, every year the intense snow surges into the mountains, leaving an accumulation of snow up to 2 meters in depth; thus the area is known to be an area to host the greatest snowfall in the country.

Taking the shape of whatever it falls upon, the snow creates many natural figures with thousands of shapes, including the typical northeastern houses, bringing out the best of both worlds. Shuangfeng Snow Town is also renowned as a world of fairy tales serving as the best place for tourists and "shutterbugs" alike to appreciate the winter scenery.

## 双峰雪乡

双峰雪乡地处张广才岭南坡黑龙江大海林林业局境内,属生态旅游风景区。每年秋冬开始,风雪涌山,积雪深达2米,雪期也长达7个月,号称全国降雪量最大的地区。

雪乡的皑皑白雪随物具形,堆积成一个个千姿百态蘑菇状的雪堆和典型的东北民居,相得益彰。雪乡还别称童话世界,是旅行者及摄影爱好者东北冬季观雪景之佳处。

## 88. Erke Mountain

Erke Mountain lies in the Kedong county, Qiqihar city and on the northern bank of Wuyuer River, a branch of Nenjiang River.

Erke Mountain can be categorized into extinct volcano. In recent years, when archaeologists inspected it, they discovered the relics of Neolithic Age in a saddle-shaped valley and collected a lot of stonewares. Then they found a nearly completed cooking tripod with hollow legs made of pottery clay near the hall side of the crater. According to the archaeologists, this tripod is a kind of bronze ware and has a history of at least three or four thousand years. So it can be assumed that Mountain Erke was formed by an eruption ten thousand years ago in the late Fourth Age.

If you view the mountain from a distance, you can see the two peaks stand erect. And during rain seasons, the two peaks appear in the fog occasionally as if you are in a fairyland. The bigger mountain and the smaller one depend on each other and there is another small mountain standing one mile from the western and northern side of the big mountain. The two peaks and a mound shape like the parents leading a child, full of appealing.

Erke Mountain has always been a famous place of interest from ancient times. In the year of 1919, a Taoist priest called Zhou Minghe came here and thought that this mountain was an auspicious place, then hold a campaign of donation in person. Then a Buddhist temple, an ancestral hall, a tower for storing a horizontal inscribed board, a bell tower and two caves called Chang Xian and Hu Xian respectively were built in the north entrance of the south mountain. The temples in commemoration of the Three Saints—Confucius, Guan Yu and Yue Fei (in China, they symbolize knowledge, integrity and patriotism respectively and are highly respected by ordinary people) and another one for the memory of a goddess were built in the south side of the north mountain. Then a pavilion and a temple were built on the top of the south mountain. When it came to the temple fair, pilgrims, men and women crowded here to light the candles and incenses and bent their knees in worship. And there are also the plays performed on a stage bustling with activity.

In recent years, a Buddhist from Wutai Mountain called Jue Hai built a temple named Lengyan with twelve rooms in the entrance of the south mountain. Another two-floor building called Jushi is under construction. A great number of Buddhists gather together to chant scriptures and sit in meditation, and the bell rings in the morning and at night, which together reproduces the prosperous scene in the past. On the southern slope of the mountain built 538 steps going through the top of the mountain, where a wayside pavilion was built for the tourists to rest and enjoy the sceneries. On the top of the mountain, a bird's-eye view of the landscapes in Kedong can be thoroughly obtained while in the north the waters of surrounding lakes ripple in the mist as if you are in the fairyland of Penglai.

## 二克山

二克山位于齐齐哈尔市克东县境内,在嫩江支流乌裕尔河的南岸。

二克山系熄火山,近年,考古工作者在对二克山进行考察时,在山马鞍形谷地上发现了一年新石器时代遗址,并采集了许多石器。在火山口厅侧的断崖地层发现了一件几乎完整的陶鬲,据考,此陶鬲系青铜器,距今至少三四千年,故推断二克山可能是在距今1万年前第四纪晚期爆发的。

遥望二克山,双峰屹立,每逢雨季,二峰时隐时现于云雾中,宛若仙境一般。大小二山相依,距大山西北1公里处有一小山独卧,双峰一丘,宛如双亲携子、情趣盎然。

二克山自古以来就是远近闻名的游览胜地,民国八年(1919年)游方道士邹明和云游至此,认为此山是吉祥之地,亲自主持求布募捐,在南山北口建禅房、神祠,筑匾楼、钟阁,凿长仙、狐仙二洞;在北山南麓建造孔、关、岳三圣庙,娘娘庙;在南山顶修筑凉亭一处,庙宇一座,每逢庙会,善男信女竞相前来,秉烛焚香,顶礼膜拜,唱台戏,热闹非常。

近年,五台山僧人觉海在南山瓮中建造了一处12间的佛教寺院——楞严寺,二层的"居士楼"正在建造中,寺院里聚集了众多的弟子诵经打坐,朝钟暮鼓,昔日的繁华景象再度出现。在山南坡修筑了538级台阶直通山顶,山顶处建一凉亭,供游人休息和观光。站在山顶,克东风光尽收眼底,回头北望,云雾缭绕处,五大边池的群水若隐若现,如蓬莱仙境。

### 89. Shedong Mountain Scenic Spot in Qiqihar

Shedong Mountain, one of the "AA" state level scenic spots, is located in the west of Nianzi Mountain, Qiqihar City, Heilongjiang province, covering an area of 300 hectare, with its highest peak 406 meters over sea level.

Within the resort, there are undulating ridges and peaks and rugged odd stones. In particular, the natural giant Buddha with a head of 4 meters high and 3 meters wide is the very image of Rulai Buddha, which has been authenticated as "rare statue across the country" by Buddhism Association. There are also various poem stele inscriptions, ancient plain and elegant pavilions, platforms and buildings with remote and rich cultural flavor. Shedong Mountain is also a discovering place of Paleolithic culture, where stone sword, stone axe, stone artifact and mammoth ivory have been excavated, thus the site of Shedong Mountain is of great value in historical research. In 1987, the spot was listed as a "key historical and cultural site under the protection of municipality" by Qiqihar Municipal Government.

An ancient legend about Shedong Mountain cannot be ignored. A famous writer in the Qing Dynasty wrote in *Longcheng Outdated Story*, "The Russian were building Dongqing Railway, when a snake appeared. The Russian attacked it with distant cannons, but in vain. The snake burst with anger and killed a number of Russians by beating stones. Local people regarded the snake as god, thus prayed often. So, it was also known as a cave of heavenly being". Shedong Mountain was thus named.

## 齐齐哈尔蛇洞山风景区

蛇洞山位于黑龙江省齐齐哈尔市碾子山区西部,占地面积 300 公顷,最高峰龙峰海拔 406 米,是国家 AA 级旅游风景区。

蛇洞山景区内峰峦起伏,怪石嶙峋。尤其是天然大佛,头像高 4 米、宽 3 米,其形酷似如来佛祖,已被佛教协会考证为"全国罕见"。景区内诗词碑刻繁多,亭、台、楼、阁古朴典雅,文化底蕴悠久而丰富。蛇洞山又是旧石器文化发现地,曾挖掘出石刀、石斧、石器和猛犸象牙等,因此蛇洞山遗址在历史研究上很有价值。1987 年被齐齐哈尔市人民政府确定为"市级重点文物保护单位"。

蛇洞山有着古老的传说。清朝著名文人魏毓兰《龙城旧闻》"俄人筑东清铁路时,蛇出,被俄人所见,以炮遥击之,不中,蛇怒鼓石,毙俄数人。当地土人以为神,多往祈祷者,亦曰仙人洞。"蛇洞山由此得名。

### 90. Jiayin Dinosaur National Geological Park

Covering an area of 38.44 square kilometers, Jiayin Dinosaur National Geological Park lies on the right bank of Heilongjiang River, Jiayin County, Yichun City, Heilongjiang province. Previously the site of Longgu Mountain in Jiayin County, it was established as Dinosaur National Geological Park by virtue of approval granted by the Review Committee of National Geopark in 2001.

It is the very place where dinosaur fossils were first discovered and unearthed in China. In 1902, a Russian paleontologist found the dinosaur fossils here, and assembled those unearthed fossils into an integrated dinosaur skeleton of 4.5 meters high and 8 meters long. It was named Mandschurosaurus amurensis, and displayed in Former Soviet Union Geological Museum in St. Petersburg. It was the first Chinese dinosaur skeleton stranded in the foreign country, and it is called First Dinosaur of the Divine Land.

Since 1977, Chinese geologists have found a large number of dinosaurfossils and other animal fossils such as fish, birds, turtles, lizards, alligators and so many angiosperm fossils as up to hundreds of genres. Archaeological studies proved that the dinosaur fossils unearthed here come under the sub-family of flathead Hadrosauridae, a new species in the dinosaur family. It is one of the last dinosaurs living on earth 65 000 000 years ago and it is the typical grand hadrosauridae of the late Cretaceous Period in the world as well.

### 嘉荫恐龙国家地质公园

嘉荫恐龙国家地质公园位于中国黑龙江省伊春市嘉荫县，黑龙江右岸。面积38.44平方公里，原为嘉荫县龙骨山旧址，2001年经国家地质公园评审委员会审定后批准建立。

这里是中国最早发现并出土恐龙化石的地方，1902年俄罗斯古生物学家在这里发现了恐龙骸骨化石，并把挖掘出的化石组装成一具高4.5米，长8米的完整恐龙化石骨架，定名为黑龙江满洲龙，陈列在圣彼得堡的苏联地质博物馆内。这是中国流落到外国的第一具恐龙化石骨架，被称为"神州第一龙"。

1977年以后，中国地质工作者在这里又发现了大量的恐龙化石和鱼、鸟、龟、鲟、鳄等动物化石及丰富的被子植物化石，多达上百个属种。经研究，这里出土的恐龙化石属平头鸭嘴龙亚科，是恐龙家庭中的一个新属种，是6 500万年前最后一批在地球上生存的恐龙之一，也是世界上晚白垩纪大型鸭嘴龙的典型代表。

### 91. Maolangou National Forest Park

Running 67 kilometers off Jiayin County, Heilongjiang province, over 400 meters above sea level, stretching over an area of 60 square kilometers, Maolangou Natural Scenic Zone is of a deep valley resulted from fold faulting caused by crustal movement, with its highest peak of 200 meters and its valley as deep as over 100 meters. The zone hosts vast expanse of virgin forests and secondary natural forests, in which extraordinary diversities of exotic flowers and rare herbs grow.

The unique geographical property of conglomerate texture in the natural zone and its peculiar topographic features have created such fascinating wonders as grotesque peaks and rocks, cascading waterfalls and streaming springs, precipitous peaks and cliffs, deep ponds shrouded in a milky-white mist. Hence, Maolangou Natural Scenic Zone enjoys the good reputation of "The Northern Jiuzhai Gullies" for its beautiful mountains, clear water, peculiar rocks and tranquil forests.

Maolangou boasts more than 30 tourist attractions including Maolangou Waterfall, Prince Peak, Three-Stepped Pool, Wild Pigeon Peak, Fairy Pool, Granny-shaped Stone, Red Phoenix Spring, General Cave, Maolan River, scene of Stone Bear listening to the waterfall, and scene of General Volunteering for Battle, etc.. The site of the Oroqen hunters has so far been seen in Maolangou Natural Scenic Zone—a place full of mystery and miracles.

## 茅兰沟国家森林公园

茅兰沟自然风景区位于黑龙江省嘉荫县境内。嘉荫茅兰沟国家森林公园距嘉荫县城 67 公里,面积 60 平方公里,海拔 400 多米,最高峰 200 米,沟深 100 多米,是地壳变迁的褶皱断裂而形成的深谷。这里不仅分布了大面积的原始森林和天然次生林,而且林下分布了种类繁多的奇花异草。

茅兰沟自然风景区属砾岩质地,独特的地质地貌造就了茅兰沟奇峰怪石、飞瀑流泉、险崖峭壁、深潭迷雾的奇妙景观。山美、水秀、石奇、林幽,茅兰沟自然风景区被誉为北方的"九寨沟"。

茅兰沟自然风景区有茅兰沟瀑布、太子峰、三阶潭、野鸽峰、仙女池、石老妪、三阶潭、丹凤泉、茅兰河、将军洞、石熊聆瀑、将军请缨等 30 多处旅游景点。弥漫着神秘与神奇色彩的茅兰沟自然风景区,至今还有鄂伦春猎户的遗址。

## 92. Stone Forest Scenic Area

Seven kilometers off Yichun city, Heilongjiang province, locates the Stone Forest Scenic Area, which is a level ground in the dense forests. From the gigantic and magnificent peaks of huge and column-shaped granite stones, derives its name—Stone Forest. The Stone Forest consists of six stone peaks, four of which in the north take on the form of a terraced row, each being remarkably vivid in shape. The distances between two or three Stone Peaks are as short as some one foot and their gaps are as narrow as a Jackknife, because of which they are referred to as "One Gleam of Sky".

## 石林风景区

石林风景区位于黑龙江省伊春市市区 7 公里处。在密林中,有一片平地,以一块块花岗岩巨石砌成的石峰,高大雄伟,其形似柱,称谓石林。石林由六座石峰组成。北面四座一字梯形排列。各峰成形惟妙惟肖,二三座石峰间相距极狭,仅尺许,缝如刀切,称"一线天"。

## 93. The Dinosaur Museum of Lesser Khingan Mountains

Located west of the Water Park in Yichun District, Yichun City, Heilongjiang province, with a total area of 4 500 square meters, the Dinosaur Museum of Lesser Khingan Mountains is a comprehensive museum largely housing exhibits of dinosaur fossils, incorporated by biological landscape, historic exhibitions and cultural exhibitions in addition to the Hi-tech Dinosaur Hall, the Hall of Dinosaur Skeletons, the Gallery of Historical Relics and the Hall of Forest Culture.

The seven dinosaur skeletons exhibited are the remains of dinosaurs living from the Cretaceous Period to the late Jurassic Period, two of which are flathead Hadrosaurs skeletons unearthed on

Longgu Mountain in Jiayin County (Chaoyang Town), Yichun City. Mamenchisaurus skeleton, the largest one, was unearthed in Chuan County, Sichuan Province. It is 22 meters long and 9 meters tall with cervical vertebrae as many as 19 joints and a tail as long as four meters.

Most of these dinosaur skeletons were excavated from Longgu Mountain in Jiayin County, which is located on the right bank, the middle reach of Heilongjiang River. There buried many ancient dinosaur fossils of 70 million years ago, from which the mountain derives its name and which captured great attention of experts and scholars from different countries. Experts, scholars, and tourists, domestic and overseas, come in streams for research, for sightseeing and for admiration.

## 小兴安岭恐龙博物馆

小兴安岭恐龙博物馆位于黑龙江省伊春市伊春区水上公园西侧,总面积4 500平方米,设有现代科技恐龙展厅、恐龙化石骨架展厅、历史文物和林区文化展厅,是一处以展示恐龙化石为主,集生物景观和历史文化展出于一体的综合性博物馆。

馆内展出的恐龙化石骨架7架,多是生活在白垩纪到侏罗纪晚期恐龙留存的化石骨架,其中有出土于伊春市嘉荫县(朝阳镇)龙骨山的两具平头鸭嘴龙化石骨架。最大的一具恐龙化石骨架是出土于四川省川县的马门溪龙骨架,长22米,高9米,仅颈椎骨就有19块,尾长有4米多。

这些恐龙骨架大部分取自嘉荫县龙骨山。嘉荫县龙骨山位于黑龙江中游右岸,因埋藏着大量的7 000万年前古生物恐龙化石而得名,由此引起了各国专家学者的极大关注,慕名考察观光的中外学者、专家和游客络绎不绝。

## 94. Wuying National Forest Park in Yichun City

Lying 8 kilometers north of Forest Administration, Wuying District, mid-hinterland on the southern slope of Lesser Khingan Mountains, the northernmost region in Heilongjiang province, covering an area of 114 square kilometers, Wuying National Forest Park is the national forest park, the national reserve of natural Korean Pines and it also serves as a place of interest in the far extent of Lesser Khingan Mountains.

The major tourist attractions in the park include Songxiang Bridge, Tianci Lake, Cuckoo Garden, Ecological Nursery Garden, Open Camping Zone, Live Shell Shooting Range, Mini steam train, Songtao Tower, Resort of Exotic Architectures, Man-made Lake, etc. Here tourists can have a bird's-eye view of the immense expanse of the forests, enjoy the forest air full of Negative Oxygen Ion, touch the evergreen Korean Pines 400 to 500 years of age—the symbol of Northern Territory, speeding through the boundless forest on the mini-train named "Shaoqi".

The park accessible to tourists achieves approximately 200 days in summer and autumn.

## 伊春五营国家森林公园

　　伊春五营区国家森林公园位于黑龙江省最北部,小兴安岭南坡中腹地带五营区离林经营所北8公里,占地面积141平方公里。五营国家级森林公园,是国家级红松天然林自然保护区、小兴安岭深处的旅游娱乐场所。

　　公园内有松乡桥、天赐湖、杜鹃园、苗圃生态园、野外露营区、实弹射击场、森林蒸汽小火车、松涛塔、异国建筑风景区、人工湖等。在此可鸟瞰莽莽林海,呼吸含负氧离子的森林空气,亲手触摸树龄在400~500年之间、四季常青的北疆象征树——红松,还可以乘坐"少奇号"小火车在林海中飞驰穿梭。

　　公园主要在夏、秋两季开放,约200天。

## 95. Pukui Mosque

　　Pukui Mosque, a fairly intact construction among other remaining buildings from a 300 year-old ancient city, with an area of over 4 000 square meters, is situated at No. 1 Limao Hutong in Jianhua District of Qiqihar City in Heilongjiang province. The Mosque is named after the city, which formerly named Pukui. It is comprised of three parts—the Eastern Mosque, the Western Mosque and the Female Mosque—as recognized by the hanging shingles. The three units were finally merged in 1958. It has been named Pukui Mosque since 1981.

　　The Eastern Mosque was established in 1684 (the 23$^{rd}$ year of Kangxi Period, Qing Dynasty), with a capacity of providing religious service for 400 people at the same time. Initiated in 1852 (the 3$^{rd}$ year of Xianfeng Period), the Western Mosque was made up of the back hall, the central main hall and the entrance hall. Initially built in 1990 and later joined to the Eastern Mosque, the Female Mosque was installed with a women's shower room. For religious services, the hall would be separated by a curtain. At present, rare handwritten copies of the Koran and ancient-styled private school textbooks—The Variorum of the Four Books—published in 1858 (the 8$^{th}$ year of Xianfeng Period), etc. are treasured up in the mosque.

　　Pukui Mosque, one of the largest, fully intact mosques in Heilongjiang province, is one of the sites to be protected at provincial level, which holds significant value in the study and research of religious history as well as architectural art.

## 卜奎清真寺

　　卜奎清真寺位于黑龙江省齐齐哈尔市建华区礼貌胡同1号(卜奎为齐齐哈尔旧称),是300余年前的旧城内保存较为完整的建筑,总占地面积4 000多平方米。该寺包括东寺、西寺、女寺三部分。过去分别挂牌为东寺、西寺、女寺,1958年合为一寺,1981年定为现在的寺名。

东寺始建于清康熙二十三年(1684年),西寺始建于1852年(咸丰三年),两寺相邻。西寺礼拜大典由后窑殿、中大殿、门厅组成。东寺礼拜大殿可容纳400人同时礼拜。女寺于1990年初建,后归于东寺院内,有女沐浴室,在大典内用围账隔开礼拜。寺内现珍藏有稀世手抄本《古兰经》和1858年(咸丰八年)出版的私塾教材《四书集注》等。

卜奎清真寺是黑龙江省清真寺中规模最大保存较完整的寺院之一,对研究宗教历史和建筑艺术有重要价值,为省级重点文物保护单位。

### 96. Jinshantun Orthodox Church

The Orthodox Church, a Russian woodcarving, prism-shaped building with an area of 82.8 m$^2$, is located in Jinfeng Agricultural Production Brigade of Jinshantun District, on the east side of the road to the south of Jinshantun. In the early 1930s, White Russians built this church and named it the Orthodox Church for short.

The Orthodox Church points southward with a broad west end and a narrow east end. The building edge is herringbone in shape and completely covered with wooden boards, and the eaves are of an inverted, three step shape. It is architecture in a typical European style. According to those who lived here in the late 1940s, it was a prosperous place where White Russians from both near and far prayed and discussed official business. In 1982, having been surveyed and authenticated by the Provincial Department of Historical Relics Management, the Orthodox Church was listed as a major historical relic to be protected at provincial level.

## 金山屯东正教堂

东正教堂位于金山屯区金峰村,金山屯南公路东侧,面积82.8平方米,为俄式木刻棱建筑。是20世纪30年代初,白俄罗斯人修建的东正教圣母升天教堂,简称东正教堂。

教堂坐北朝南,西宽东窄,房脊呈人字形,木板铺盖,房檐为三层倒台阶形,是典型的欧式建筑。据20世纪40年代未在这里居住的老人讲,当时这里是远近居住的白俄罗斯人祈祷议事的场所,十分繁荣。1982年经省文物管理部门考察鉴定,这座东正教堂被列为重点文物保护单位。

### 97. Mahayana Temple in Qiqihar

Mahayana Temple, originally named the Grand Buddhist Temple, stands in No.1 Dacheng Road, some 2.5 kilometers off the railway station in Qiqihar. Constructed in 1939, and completed in 1943, it covers an area of 40 000 square meters. The temple faces south with the Gate, theside halls, the main hall, the front hall and the rear hall. Its walls are constructed in accordance with Eight Trigrams (a combination of solid and broken lines joined in pairs to form 64 hexagrams formerly used in divination) and it is a typical corbel bracket building with glazed roofs. Centered around the Hall of Mahavira, two side halls stand symmetrically, each being 88 meters away from the Hall with their facades facing it. With yellow glazed roof, the gate tower and the Hall contrast pleasantly with the three green glazed characters on the tablet of the Mahayana Temple; the three add radiance and beauty to each other, rich in religious flavor.

Works of the modern times as it is, the temple has developed its unique style for its adopting the traditional aesthetics of ancient architecture construction. The towering primeval trees stand both inside and outside the walls, creating an elegant and quiet environment. Being one of the largest glaze-tiled structures extant in Heilongjiang province, the temple is a priority site under provincial protection.

## 齐齐哈尔市大乘寺

大乘寺(Mahayana Temple)原名大佛寺,位于齐齐哈尔市大乘路1号,火车站南约2.5公里。始建于1939年,1943年竣工,占地4万平方米。寺院坐北朝南,由山门、配殿、正殿、前殿、后殿组成。院墙按八卦建造,庙宇采用斗拱式建筑,玻璃瓦覆盖,以大雄宝殿为中心,各边有一座配殿,每座配殿距离大殿恰好88米,而且均面向大殿。大殿及门楼皆为黄釉琉璃瓦覆盖,与绿色琉璃瓦组成的"大乘寺"三个大字交相辉映,具有浓郁的宗教色彩。

寺院虽为近代所建,但因采用传统的古建筑形式而独具一格。墙内外古树参天,环境幽雅,是黑龙江省现存规模最大的琉璃瓦建筑之一,为省内重点文物保护单位。

### 98. The Huamei Western-style Restaurant

Harbin Huamei Western-style Restaurant was initially built in 1925, originally situated in the Western Eighth Street in Daoli District. Its founder was a Russian Jew called "Chaojiarman". The Huamei Western-style Restaurant was originally called "Malse", which only occupied more than 70 square meters for business and mainly dealt in Russian food, tea and snacks. Its owners were changed several times from 1925 to 1956, among whom were Russian, German, Polish, Czech or Chinese people. In 1957, its ownership turned to the state-private partnerships and the Restaurant was moved to No. 112 Central Street. Later it has become a state-owned enterprise with business operating area enlarged to about 280 square meters and renamed as the Huamei Western-style Restaurant.

The Huamei Western-style Restaurant mainly serves Russian dishes, and other dishes such as French and Italian as well. After several renovations, reconstruction and expansions, the newly increased business area was up to 850 square meters. The first floor is well-known for its modern European garden-style bars. The second floor is designed like the ancient Kremlin style in Moscow, Ex-

Soviet Union with several separate rooms. The third floor embodies the modern Russian style, which is divided into north and south halls. The south hall is luxurious and grand, and the north is valued for its quiet and elegance. The layout of the Huamei Western-style Restaurant is reasonable, elegant and luxurious. The famous Russian-style dishes are hot pot loin, butter chicken breast, roast milk mandarin fish, fried plated shrimp, iron braised chicken and Russian soup. The color, smell, taste and style of all dishes are better completed. The Russian staple food is bread, which dopts the Russian technology, using hops for fermenting and oak charcoal for baking. The flavors drawn from these two processes are what make this bread so famous.

## 著名的华梅西餐厅

哈尔滨华梅西餐厅始建于1925年,原址在道里西八道街,创始人是俄国犹太人,名叫"楚几尔曼"。华梅西餐厅原名"马尔斯",当时只有七十多平方米的营业面积,主要经营俄式西餐茶食小吃。1925年至1956年间几易经纪人。他们当中有俄国人、德国人、波兰人、捷克人和中国人。1957年公私合营,迁址到中央大街112号。营业面积二百八十平方米,成为国营企业,改名为华梅西餐厅。

华梅西餐厅以经营俄式大菜为主,兼营法、意式菜系。经几次装修、改造、扩建,新增营业面积850平方米。一楼突出现代派欧洲园林式酒吧风格;二楼突出古老的前苏联莫斯科"克里姆林宫"风格,并设有高级单间;三楼体现俄罗斯现代风格,分南北两厅,南厅豪华气派,北厅突出优雅安静。华梅西餐厅布局合理,典雅豪华,著名俄式大菜有火锅里脊、奶油鸡脯、烤奶汁鳜鱼、炸板虾、铁扒鸡、苏波汤等,色味香形俱佳。俄式主食槽子面包,采用俄式工艺酒花发酵,柞木炭烘烤,入口清香浓郁,素有盛名。

## 99. The Modern Hotel in Harbin

In the Zhongyang Street, Harbin, stands a magnificent building full of legends—the Modern Hotel of great eminence.

Early at the beginning of the last century, Harbin had embraced tens of thousands of Jewish refugees for reasons of war or others. They came mainly from Russia, Germany, Denmark, Poland and Austria, etc., the majority of whom were civilians who were forced to uproot. They had constructed various types of buildings, department stores, churches and private residences after their native culture and their aesthetic concept in this beautiful city. It was in this situation that the Modern Hotel made its appearance as the times required.

By the time when the Japanese-Russian War came to an end in 1901, China Avenue (the original name for this street) in Harbin had assumed its embryonic layout. Then, there arrived a retired Russian cavalry called Joseph Gasp. With the intention of doing business, this shrewd Jew first opened a small shop for watch repair and then jewelry shops, whose business grew so thriving and flourishing that with his savings he bought a row of shacks in China Avenue in which the Chinese laborers lived for he had foreseen the vigorous growth of business opportunities in this avenue. Thus, the idea to build a hotel for nobilities only took shape in his mind.

Joseph Gasp had a good friend named Yudinov, an architect who had majored in architecture in France years before. He was in favour of Joseph's plan so much that he made efforts to convince Joseph to display the spirit of the new times and to construct the hotel after the "architectural styles of the Art Nouveau Movement" which was then in vogue throughout Europe.

Joseph Gasp accepted Yudinov's views. In 1905, he invited Wisaen, the renowned grand master of architecture in Europe at the time, to make the architectural design and chose the finest building materials from the United States and European countries. And before long, a luxurious French building of King Louis XIV style in China Avenue had been erected. The hotel is a three-storey building whose architectural style is of European Art Nouveau that was very popular throughout Europe towards the end of the 19th century. Tastefully decorated with arcs or curves in form and large cycloidal windows with artistic touch installed, the building is unique in technique, natural and novel in style, adding exotic appeal to this modern city. Joseph Gasp named the hotel "модерн" (Russian from which the Chinese translation derives), which means "modern and trendy" in French.

Completed in 1906 and opened for business the same year, the Modern Hotel was one of the most luxurious and multi-functional hotels in Harbin at the time, though it was constructed later than the Qiulin Firm in Nangang District. According to the advertisement in Russian edition of the Harbin Guide published in 1931, "модерн" enjoys the most deluxe dance halls and restaurants, the modernized and the most comfortable guest rooms." In addition, the Modern Hotel had run a film theatre with shows of films and dramas domestic and overseas every day. The Modern Hotel of that time might well be said to "ring with intoxicating music and songs day after day and witness scenes of feasting and pleasure-seeking night after night."

Marvelous is the elevation of the building for the distinctive features of "Art Nouveau" are embodied primarily by such basic elements as windows, balconies, parapet walls and domes. The windows are designed in great diversity, the shapes of which vary from floor to floor. The varieties include radius top windows, elliptical windows, segment-top windows, and geometric windows, etc., with classification of single windows, double windows and triple windows. The varied decorations of skintled brickwork above the windows, combined with the division of exquisite walls produce a poetic warmth and tenderness.

On entering the building, you will be greeted with walls either ornamented with elegant murals or faced with mirrors, the carvings superb beyond compare, the railings of the brass staircases like young girls showing off their fine and charming figures, the large chandeliers in the lobby dazzling and glittering, the decorative marble facade adorned with delicate lines, manifesting its luxury and elegance. The guest rooms designed are graceful and comfortable, furnished with delicately carved cupboards, characterized by varied skintled brickwork on the walls, bright and refreshing tones, the beautifully draped mirrors and well-preserved lamps.

The Modern Hotel has once played host to both military and political VIPs of China and foreign countries and celebrities from all walks of life, namely Song Chingling, wife of Dr. Sun Yat-Sen, the Chinese revolutionary forerunner; Pu Yi, last emperor in China; Guo Moruo, Chinese historian and writer; Xu Beihong, grand master of painting, and so on. In March, 1936 when Chaliapin, Russian bass singer who enjoyed a good reputation of "best singer in the world" came to Harbin to perform live, he also made his stay in the Modern Hotel. His three concert shows in Harbin had been an important event in the Harbin history of culture.

Completed in 1906, Modern Hotel has so far enjoyed a history of nearly one hundred years, during which period, time brought drastic changes to the world and the Modern Hotel has been renamed six times. In recent years, the Modern Hotel has again become famed in Harbin and enjoyed high prestige domestically and universally with the honor of national four-star hotel conferred by the state and the international standardization of its business management.

## 马迭尔宾馆

在哈尔滨中央大街上,有一座辉煌而又充满传奇色彩的建筑,它就是名声显赫的马迭尔宾馆。

上个世纪初,由于战争等原因,哈尔滨接纳了流亡到这里的数以万计的各国犹太人。他们分别来自俄罗斯、德国、丹麦、波兰、奥地利等国,其中的大多数是背井离乡的普通侨民。他们在这座城市里,依照自己家乡的文化特色和审美理念,建设了各种各样的楼房、商店、教堂、民宅。正是在这样的背景下,马迭尔旅馆应运而生。

1901年,日俄战争结束,哈尔滨的中国大街已具雏形。这时候,有一位叫作约瑟·加斯普的俄国退伍骑兵来到这里。这位精明的犹太人打算在这里经商,他先开了一家修钟表的小店,之后经营珠宝,生意越做越火。于是他把手中积攒下的钱,在中国大街买下一排中国劳工住的简陋民房。他看好大街正在勃勃兴起的商机,盘算着在这里建筑一座专供富人下榻的宾馆。

约瑟·加斯普有一位做建筑师的好朋友叫尤金诺夫,早年曾在法国学习建筑。他十分赞成加斯普的计划,极力说服加斯普体现新时代精神,把宾馆设计成正风靡欧洲的"新艺术运动"建筑风格。

约瑟·加斯普听取了他的意见,1905年,加斯普聘请了当时欧洲著名建筑大师维萨恩做旅馆的建筑设计，并选购欧美各国上等的建筑材料，不久，一座法国路易十四风格的豪华建筑在中央大街拔地而起。

宾馆为三层楼房，属于欧洲新艺术派建筑风格，流行于19世纪末的欧洲各国。在造型上采用弧线或曲线装饰，摆线型大玻璃窗，其建筑手法独特，格调自然，大方新颖，给哈尔滨这座近代城市平添了异国情调。约瑟·加斯普为他的旅馆命名为马迭尔，法语为摩登、新潮之意。

马迭尔宾馆建造的年代晚于建于南岗区的秋林商行，于1913年建成开业，它是当时哈尔滨旅馆建筑中最豪华的多功能旅馆之一。1931年《哈尔滨指南》俄文版广告中有这样的记载："马迭尔宾馆拥有最豪华的舞厅及餐厅，最现代、最舒适的客房。"当时马迭尔开设电影戏园，每日放映外国电影，演出中外戏剧。那时的马迭尔真可谓是日日弦管闻客醉，夜夜酒色人灯红。

马迭尔宾馆建筑的立面处理十分精彩，鲜明的"新艺术"特征手法主要是通过窗、阳台、女儿墙及穹顶等元素体现出来。建筑物窗户的造型极富变化，每一层窗户的形式都有区别。有半圆额窗、圆弧额窗、圆额方角矩形窗以及圆窗等不同形式，又有单窗、双窗及三连窗之分。窗上装饰线脚非常丰富，与精致的墙面划分相结合，给人一种温暖、柔和的诗意。

步入建筑内部，你会看到室内的墙壁或饰以优雅的壁画，或装以镜子贴面；雕刻精美绝伦，黄铜的楼梯栏杆舒展柔媚的线条；大吊灯在厅内耀眼生辉；大理石饰面装点着精致饰线，透出豪华典雅的气质。客房的设计优雅舒适，精美的雕刻橱柜、丰富的墙面线脚、清新的色调以及优美的镜饰和灯饰都保存完好。

马迭尔宾馆曾接待了中国和外国的军政要人、各界名流，像中国革命先行者孙中山先生的夫人宋庆龄，中国最后的皇帝溥仪，中国历史学家、作家郭沫若，大画家徐悲鸿等，都曾在马迭尔下榻。1936年3月，有"世界歌王"美誉的俄罗斯男低音歌唱家夏利亚宾来哈尔滨演出，也是住在马迭尔。夏利亚宾在哈尔滨期间，演出三场，成为哈尔滨文化史上的一件大事。

马迭尔宾馆从1913年创建至今，几近一个世纪。这其中，风雨沧桑，社会变迁，马迭尔也曾先后六次易名。近年来，随着马迭尔宾馆通过国家四星级评审和经营管理的国际标准化，马迭尔宾馆已经誉满哈埠，蜚声中外。

# Appendix

## I. Folk Arts

### 1. Northeast Drums

The Northeast Drums has five big schools as a result of the differences in region, geographical environment, language and accent. "School of Lower Reach of the Songhua River" is one branch, which originates from the broad areas centered round Harbin in the lower reach of the Songhua River and features in diversified tunes and powerful expressions, suitable for long, medium and short programs, traditional and modern content.

### 东北大鼓

东北大鼓由于地域、地理环境及语言、语音的不同,形成艺术风格的差别,产生了五大流派。黑龙江省"下江派"东北大鼓就是其中的一派。"下江"指沿松花江下游以哈尔滨为中心的广大区域。"下江派"东北大鼓曲调丰富,表现力强,既适合演唱中、长篇书目,又适于演唱小段;既适于表现传统曲目,又能够演唱现代作品。

### 2. Northeast Song and Dance Duet

The traditional "North School" song and dance duet of Heilongjiang is a branch with unique regional features with about 100 years of history. It especially features in the loudness of the vocal sound and the clearness of the enunciation, rich emotion, graceful figure of the dancers and pungent charm. In particular, "Double Fan Dance" draws much attention. This art form appeals to the farmers in Heilongjiang because it shows deep emotion and love for the ordinary people, for the land and for the simple and unadorned character of the farmers in Heilongjiang.

### 东北二人转

黑龙江"北派"传统二人转,它有 100 年左右的历史,是东北二人转在本地区一个极具地域性特色的分支流派。演出尤其讲究唱腔的嘹亮豪放,吐字清晰,声情并茂,舞蹈身段优美,泼辣风趣,尤以"双扇舞"引人注目,特别是以它一身爱土地、爱农民的"土腥味儿",时刻保持与平民百姓息息相关、血肉相连的那一份深厚情感,紧紧地拴住了黑龙江广大农民们的心!

### 3. "Mosukun" of Oroqen Nationality

"Mosukun" means singing the story in Oroqen language and it is an ethnic art with unique features created through long hunting life of the nomadic Oroqen people. "Mosukun" features in talking and singing consecutively and telling stories of heroes and singers' own misery life experience, and it is mainly performed by one person in folk tunes, fixed or not fixed. "Mosukun" is passed on from mouth to ear until now and suffers a serious loss and variation, however, it still remains a popular performance with ethnic features and deeply loved by the Oroqen people.

### 鄂伦春族"摩苏昆"

"摩苏昆"是鄂伦春语,意为讲唱故事,是鄂伦春族人民在漫长的游猎生活中创造出来的独具特色的民族艺术。"摩苏昆"是说一段,唱一段,说唱结合的表演艺术形式,多讲唱"莫日根"英雄故事和自己苦难的身世,以一人表演为主。以民族曲调为主,有固定和不固定两种。"摩苏昆"凭口耳相传流传至今,已有严重的遗失和变异,但仍不失民族特色,深为鄂伦春族人民喜爱。

### 4. Hailun Paper-Cuts

As an important part of the traditional art of Heilongjiang paper-cuts, Hailun paper-cuts embrace the different styles of the northern and southern schools, vigorous but still exquisite, rough but still graceful. Its works, originally characterized by its folk style, are now developing more thematic and systematic. The representative works "Marriage Customs of Manchu Nationality" "Facial Make-up Series of Peking Opera" and many others sell well in more than 50 countries and areas, such as the United States, Japan, and France.

### 海伦剪纸

海伦剪纸是黑龙江剪纸重要的一支。它兼容南北各派风格,豪放中不失细腻,粗犷中蕴含优雅,其作品由民间化向标题化、系列化发展。代表作《满族婚俗图》《京剧脸谱系列》等,行销美、日、法等50多个国家和地区。

### 5. The Crafts of Birch-Bark Making

The people of Hezhen Ethnic Group and Oroqen Ethnic Group living along the Heilongjiang River Valley are accustomed to making their houses, canoes with birch skin and are good at turning birch skin into such varieties of household items as chests, boxes, pails and bowls, etc. They have followed, created, and developed the traditional art of birch bark making which involves four processes—first, peeling off the birch bark; next, softening the bark either by soaking it in water or by simmering it in pot; then cutting it into patterns needed and sewing them together or making them elaborately interlocked, and finally decorating with designs symbolizing auspiciousness and fortune, jubilation and festivity, wish for peace and plentiful harvests on the crafts by clipping and pasting as well as by hammering and pressing. However, this traditional crafts of birch bark making is on the verge of distinction with the successive death of those senior citizens of Oroqen Ethnic Group who are familiar and good at it. Presently, the profound academic worth and significant practical value of birch-bark crafts demand prompt succession and protection.

## 桦树皮制作技艺

古代黑龙江流域的赫哲族和鄂伦春族,习惯用桦树皮盖房、造舟,缝制各种箱、盒、桶、碗等生活器皿。他们承袭、创造并发展了桦树皮的传统工艺,工艺有四个步骤:一剥取树皮;二将皮子浸软或煮软;三剪裁缝合,或是精巧地咬合;四装饰图案,有砸压、剪贴,将象征吉祥、喜庆,企盼平安、丰收的图形装饰在桦树皮制品上。如今,熟悉传统工艺的民族老人相继离世,传统的桦树皮工艺濒临消亡。桦树皮工艺深远的学术价值和实用价值,亟待保护传承。

### 6. Leather-Silhouette Show Association of Xiangbai Township

Leather-silhouette Show Association of Xiangbai Township, Wangkui County, Heilongjiang province, is a folk troupe and it is the successor of "Jiang Bei School" of Leather-silhouette Show in Heilongjiang province.

## 望奎厢白乡皮影协会

黑龙江望奎县厢白乡皮影协会,是民间剧社,也是黑龙江"江北派"皮影艺术的传承者。

### 7. Festival of Aurora Borealis in Mohe County

Mohe County lies in the northernmost part of China. Bestowed with its high latitude, it has the natural sight of "Polar Day" around the Summer Solstice (June $15^{th} \sim 25^{th}$) when there sometimes occurs Aurora Borealis. Thus Mohe County is known as "Nightless City in China" and the "Aurora City".

Although Aurora Borealis occurs four seasons around, it is more easily observed within some 9 days before or after the Summer Solstice every year, because at this time of the year in Mohe, it is, more often than not, sunny and bright during the day, while at night without the block from the solar beam and clouds, the sky tends to be as bright as daytime. The magnificent and spectacular astronomical phenomenon of Aurora Borealis is clearly visible at this time. While enjoying the wonders of "Aurora Borealis" and the "White Night", one can simultaneously admire the splendid view of the kindled sky mantled jointly by the afterglow and the morning glow.

The Summer Solstice (the highest point of sunshine is at the Tropic of Cancer) has been authorized to be Festival of Aurora Borealis by the Mohe County government since 1989 and it is mainly held inthe Greater Khingan Mountain, Xilinji and the Arctic-Pole Village annually. With the coming of Summer Solstice, thousands of people get together in Mohe County for celebration, during which period of time the Arctic Village on the verge of Heilongjiang River has become a tourist resort where over-night bonfire parties along the riverbank are held as well as full-length special performances, local product fairs, farmyard-visiting, and other recreational activities, etc.

## 北极光节

漠河县是中国纬度最高的县份,由于纬度高,使漠河地区在夏至前后(6月15日~25日)产生极昼现象,此时人们有时会看到北极光的出现,因此人们称漠河县为"中国的不夜城"、"极光城"。

北极光虽然一年四季都出现,但在漠河唯有每年夏至前后9天左右的时间内容易看到。这是因为此时漠河多是万里晴空的天气,夜晚没有太阳光线和云层阻隔,又如同白昼一般,就可以看到壮观至极的北极光了。人们在观赏"北极光"和"白夜"奇观的同时,又可看到晚霞与朝晖连成一片的红彤天宇。

自1989年以来,漠河县把夏至(太阳直射点在北回归线上)这一天定为北极光节,一年一次,主要在大兴安岭、西林吉镇及北极村进行。每当夏至到来,数万人集聚到漠河县北极村欢度北极光节。节日中,在黑龙江边的北极村成了旅游观光胜地。这里要举办大型专场文艺演出、地方产品展销会、探访北陲农家、江边通宵篝火晚会及其他游艺活动等。

# II. Ethnic Culture

## 1. Manchu Ethnic Group

Manchu ethnic group, one of Chinese ethnic minorities, mainly live in the northeast China-Heilongjiang, Jilin and Liaoning provinces, and some of them are scattered in the major cities of the country. In ancient times Manchu is known as Sushen, Wuji, Mohe and Jurchen. In the 2 000-year census, the population of Manchu is 10.68 million, ranking second among China's 55 ethnic minorities, just after the Zhuang ethnic group.

### Language

The Manchu language is a member of the Tungusic language group, Altaic language family. Due to a large number of Manchu people moving to Central Plains, and a large number of Han moving outside Shanhai Pass since Qing Dynasty, Manchu people and Han people have close contacts in the economic, cultural and social aspects, and Manchu people have been gradually accustomed to using Chinese language. Now the Manchu language is only spoken among a small number of elderly in Aihui and Fuyu County in Heilongjiang province, while the vast majority of Manchu people in elsewhere uses Mandarin Chinese.

### History

Manchu has a long history. About 3 000 years ago, the Sushen people may be their ancestors and their descendants have been living in the north of Changbai Mountain, the upper and middle reaches of the Heilongjiang and Wusuli river basin. One of the tribes of the Mohe, the Heishui (Black Water) Tribe, eventually becomes the ancestors of the Jurchen. In 1115, Wanyan Aguda established the Jin dynasty. In 1583 Nur Hachi dispatched troops and then gradually unified the Jurchen groups, and finally established a militarily and politically unified system of eight banners. On October 13, 1635, Hong taiji became Emperor, changed the national title to Qing, and changed the clan name to Manchou. In 1644, the Qing military got through the pass and gradually conquered the entire country.

### Costumes

Historically Manchu men like to weardeep-blue long gowns and mandarin jackets with chaps under it, braided hair tied on the back of head, wearing dome hats. Women like to wear dresses straight cheongsams, coil their hair in high tufts on top of their heads and wear earrings and embroidered shoes, no foot bound. Greatly different from Manchu women's costumes, today's "cheongsams" is not the Manchu woman's clothing in the history, but the fashion clothes absorbing western garment cutting methods.

### Houses

As for Manchu housing, in the past, there was a shadow screen wall in the yard, erecting a "Solo Pole" used for worshipping. The traditional Manchu dwellings are made up of three quarters in the west, middle and east. The main gate is toward south, the room in the west is called the upper west room, the middle one is called the hall, and the east room is called the down east room. In the upper west room there are three "kang" (traditional heated brick bed), respectively lying in the west, north and south. The "kang" in the west is for guests and friends, that in the north is for elderly and that in the south is for the younger.

## 满族

满族,中国少数民族之一。主要分布在东北的黑龙江省、吉林省、辽宁省,少部分散居于全国各大中城市。满族古称肃慎、勿吉、靺鞨、女真。2000年人口普查时,满族人口为1 068万。在中国55个少数民族中仅次于壮族居第二位。

### 语言文字

满语属阿尔泰语系满-通古斯语族满语支。由于清代以来大量满族迁入中原地区和大量汉族移居山海关外,在经济、文化、生活上交往密切,满族人民逐渐习用汉语文。现在,只有黑龙江瑷珲镇和富裕县,还有少数老年人会说满语,其他地方绝大多数满族人民已通用汉语文。

### 历史渊源：

满族历史悠久,可追溯到3 000多年前的肃慎人,其后裔一直生活在长白山以北、黑龙江中上游、乌苏里江流域。黑水靺鞨是满族的直系祖先,后发展为女真。1115年,由完颜阿骨打建立了金国。1583年,努尔哈赤起兵,逐步统一了女真各部,建立了军政合一的八旗制度。1635年10月13日,皇太极称皇帝,改国号清,改族名为满洲。1644年,清军入关,逐步领有中国全境。

### 服饰

历史上满族男子喜穿青蓝色的长袍马褂,头顶后部留发梳辫留于脑后,戴圆顶帽,下穿套裤。妇女则喜欢穿直筒旗袍,梳京头或"盘髻儿",戴耳环,腰间挂手帕,天足,着花鞋。但现今的"旗袍"并非历史上满族女子的服装,而是吸收了西方服装裁减方法的时装,和过去满族女子的服装大不相同。

### 民居

满族的住房,过去一般院内有一影壁,立有供神用的"索罗杆"。满族传统住房一般为西、中、东三间,大门朝南开,西间称西上屋,中间称堂屋,东间称东下屋。西上屋设南、西、北三面炕,西炕为贵,北炕为大,南炕为小,来客住西炕,长辈多住北炕,晚辈住南炕。

## 2. Manchu Eight Banners

The Eight Banners, a social organization, was established by Nur Hachi in 1601 and became perfected in 1615. Each organization set up one flat, and eight organizations had Eight Banners. These eight banners are: Plain Yellow Banner, Bordered Yellow Banner, Plain White Banner, Bordered White Banner, Plain Red Banner, Bordered Red Banner, Plain Blue Banner and Bordered Blue Banner.

The Eight Banners is a social organization system, as well as an important political and military system of the Qing Dynasty. At the beginning of its establishment, it embodies military, administrative and productive functions. All the members of Banners are in the charge of each Banner, and they work at the peacetime, and go to war at the wartime. All this takes place in the unit of Banner both for command and as the name of the troop. In the meantime, it is also the name of the administrative organization. In 1644 Emperor Shunzhi entered into the Shanhai Pass and unified the entire country, the Eight Banners' production function was weakened and its political and military functions were gradually enforced and finally turned into a mainly military organization. But with the Eight Banners stationing in each area, the Eight Banners' administrative units coexisted with the local governments of districts and counties, and the Eight Banners still had certain administrative functions.

## 满族八旗

八旗是清太祖努尔哈赤于1601年开始组建到1615年完善起来的八旗组织。每个组织打出一面旗帜，八个组织八面旗帜。这八面旗帜分别是：正黄旗、镶黄旗、正白旗、镶白旗、正红旗、镶红旗、正蓝旗、镶蓝旗。

八旗是一种社会组织制度，也是清代重要的政治、军事制度。建立之初，它兼有军事、行政、生产三方面职能。凡是满旗成员皆分隶各旗，平时生产，战时出征，都是以旗为单位，既是指挥的一面旗帜，也是部队的番号，同时也是行政组织的名称。1644年顺治挥师入关，统一了全国，其生产职能逐渐淡化，政治、军事职能逐渐增强，主要变成军事组织。但又用八旗驻防地区，各级八旗衙署与州县并存，仍兼有一定的行政职能。

### 3. The Ancestor Worship Ceremony of the Manchu people

Among many religious ceremonies, Manchu people think very high of the worship ceremony for ancestors. Through worshiping ancestors, the Manchu people can maintain the relationship of the family and clan, improve the family cohesion and harmony and praise the traditional clan traditions.

**Categories of Sacrificial Rituals**

The sacrificial rituals can be divided into ritual of happiness and ritual for funerals. The ritual for funerals is the clan funeral rites for the just-dead relatives according to the Manchu funeral ceremony; the ritual of happiness is for celebrating the normal festival order and some special dates, and people hold this ceremony for the first ancestors and the ancestors in every other generation

According to the time sequence, there are the Chinese New Year, the Lantern Festival, Tomb Sweeping Festival, Dragon Boat Festival, July 15 (in the lunar calendar), and the Mid-Autumn Festival. And in these festivals the ceremony may not be all necessarily held, but in the Lunar New Year festival it will.

According to the categorization of sites, there are indoor and outdoor ceremonies. The indoor ceremony is relatively simple, and in the Spring Festival, Lantern Festival, the Dragon Boat Festival, Mid-Autumn Festival, small families can hold their own indoor worship; the outdoor ceremony has tomb and garden ceremony. The tomb ceremony is generally held in Tomb Sweeping Festival, on July 15th (in lunar calendar), and in days before and after the twenty-third of the twelfth lunar month, and the garden ceremony is generally the large clan activities held by big families. Some large clans have memorial temple, where the major clan ceremony can be held.

There are also options for ceremonies like the ancestors' birthday, funeral, or big family events.

### Regulations of the Ancestor Worship Ceremony

Ancestor worship ceremony is a big ritual, and is also a solemn event. Things should be done according to a certain system of regulation and the most fundamental one is the "respect". There are strict requirements to the number of the ceremony, sacrificial utensils and sacrificial offering.

(1) Requirements for order. The ritual frequency embodies the "festival does not require quantity, which may result in annoyance and annoyance shows disrespect; the memorial ceremony cannot afford a long-time break, which causes laziness and finally forgetfulness". Clan ceremony will be generally held every five years.

(2) Requirements for sacrificial utensils. Sacrificial utensils are important props for traditional ceremonies; it should demonstrate respect, nobility, cleanness and specialty. Based on the different social status of people, there's strict distinction for sacrificial utensils. The commonly used utensils are: tripod, censers, incense boxes, casket, plates, bowls, candle environments of (digs), glasses, etc. The ordinary family should not set up tripods for they embodies respect and nobility. Sacrificial utensils dedicated to sacrifice should be special, clean, and once used. They need a careful cleaning and classifying, should be well preserved and exclusively used.

(3) Requirements for sacrificial offerings. The sacrificial offerings should reflect the novelty and harvest. According to the family living condition, there should be four or six samples. The ceremony's offerings should be the main food of that festival and should be put on the altar before meals. Sacrificial offerings in the Spring Festival are mainly sticky rice cakes and steamed buns. Large-clan ancestor worship ceremony should offer grazing animals (such as killing a black pig).

(4) Requirements for dresses. People should be dressed solemnly, avoiding dressing any casual and untidy clothes. In large ceremony activities, people should wear new, clean and pretty ethnic costumes (cheongsam long unlined gown); the woman should wear a flower in head

### Procedures of Worshiping

Due tothe differences in scale, location and time, the ceremony procedures are not necessarily identical. Common and small family's ritual activities during festivals have relatively simple procedures. The families who have the genealogy should firstly clean up the altar, then light incense, hang the genealogy (inviting God), display offerings, and kowtow to pray; the families without the genealogy could arrange an place in the west of the room and set an altar to display sacrificial offerings, light incense and kowtow to pray.

Largeclan's ceremony has rather complex procedures, which is equivalent to the formation of a complex and large-scale conference. At the early Qing Dynasty, the Shamanistic God was invited as a deacon to preside over the pray as well as incantations. But during the reign of the Emperor Jiaqing, the Shamanism went to decline, and people rarely invite the Shamanistic God. The family would choose the prestigious and learned seniors of the tribe to preside over the whole ceremony, including inviting god, reading prayers and guiding offerings.

## 满族人的祭礼

满族人在诸多的祭礼仪式中最重视祭祖活动。满族人通过祭祖活动来维系家庭、宗族关系,促进家族团结和睦,弘扬宗族传统家风。

**祭祀种类**

祭祖之礼可分为凶礼和吉礼。凶礼祭是丧礼中的祭祖之礼,其对象是新丧的亲人,按满族丧葬礼法进行;吉礼中的祭祀即平时岁节序和其他特殊时日进行的祭礼,对象是始祖以及其他各代祖先。

依时间节序分类,有春节、元宵节、清明、端午节、七月十五、中秋节等,这些节不一定都祭,但春节必祭。

依地点分类,有户内祭和户外祭。户内祭比较简单,小家门户逢春节、元宵、端午、中秋节在自家室内即可祭祀;户外祭有墓祭和庭院祭,墓祭一般都在清明节、七月十五、腊月二十三前后几日,庭院祭一般是宗族大户大型祭祖活动。有些宗族大户设有家庙的(祖宗祠堂),大型祭祖仪式要到家庙举行。

除时节岁序祭外,还有选择祖先生日、殡日、授功日祭祀的,家族中发生重大事件也可择日祭。

**祭祖的规制**

祭祖仪式是一项大礼,是件庄重的大事,要按一定的规制办事,最根本的一条是"敬",祭数、祭器、祭品都要有严格要求。

(1)祭次要求。在祭祀的疏密程度上体现"祭不欲数、数则烦、烦则不敬,祭不欲疏、疏则怠、怠则忘"。宗族大祭一般五年一次。

(2)祭器要求。祭器是传统祭典的重要道具,要体现尊、贵、洁、专。祭器依据人们社会地位不同而有严格的区别。祭礼一般常用的祭器有:鼎、香炉、香盒、楔、盘、碗、烛檠(蜡台)、酒杯等。鼎即体现尊又体现贵,一般家庭不能设鼎。祭器要专用、要清洁,用过一次要仔细清洗、整理,专门收藏起来,不挪作他用。

(3)祭品要求。祭品要体现新、丰,根据家庭条件设四或六样。祭品以当时节日食品为主,家人没吃前先放入祭台。春节祭品主要有年糕、馒头。宗族大户的型祭祖仪式要献牧牲(杀黑色猪一口)。

(4)着装要求。不能穿家常便服,更不能衣冠不整,而要郑重其事,大型祭祖活动族人穿戴要新、洁、美,着民族服装(旗袍大褂),女子头上要戴一朵花。

**祭祖程序**

由于祭祀规模、地点时间不同,其程序也不求一致。一般家庭小户年节祭祀活动程序比较简单,有家谱的先将祭台清扫干净。然后焚香,悬谱(请神),再摆放供品,叩头祈告;无家谱的可在室内设一位置(西侧),设祭台摆放供品、焚香叩头祈告。

宗族大户祭祖程序和仪式比较复杂,相当于组成一个复杂的大型会议。清朝前期都要请萨满神主祭,主持祈告、颂祭文等,清嘉庆以后,萨满教走向衰落,请萨满神的逐渐减少,家族多选本族中长辈有威望有文化的族长主持。请神、领牲、颂祭文、献供品等重要角色均选族中长辈进行。

### 4. The Brief Introduction to the Original Culture of Jin Dynast

Acheng is the starting point of the Jurchen (Nüzhen) nationality in the history of China, and the first capital of the Jin Dynast (1115–1153). From then on, four emperors of the Jin Dynasty ruled here: the Emperor of Taizu, the Emperor of Taizong, the Emperor of Xizong and Emperor Hailing. Acheng remained the political, military, economic and cultural center for 38 years. The Jurchen People, together with other peoples created the distinguishing cultural of the Jin Dynasty.

Based on the traditional culture of the Jurchen nationality, the original culture of Jin Dynasty extensively absorbed and mixed the culture of the Central Plains and the essential parts of other nationalities and tribes, and formed its culture with features of special time and terrain. The original culture of Jin dynasty started from the beginning of Jin dynasty to the end of it (1115–1232). The terrain of the dynasty centered on the Ashi River Valley and the civilization of the upper capital of Jin Dynasty, including the present Lalin River Valley, Hulan River Valley and the both banks of the middle of Songhua River. The scope was from Mudan River in the east to the right bank of the second Songhua River and from the upper reach of Hulan River in the north to the area of Jilin City in the south. It was equivalent to the terrain governed by Huiningfu, the upper capital of the Jin Dynasty.

### 金源文化简介

阿城是中国历史上女真族的肇兴之地,是金朝的开国都城(1115—1153)。金朝政权在此历四帝:太祖、太宗、熙宗和海陵王。这里作为金朝的政治、军事、经济、文化中心长达38年之久,女真族同其他民族一道在这里创造了独具特色的金源文化。

金源文化是以女真族传统文化为底蕴,广泛吸纳和融会了中原文化及其他民族、部落文化中的优秀部分,从而形成了自己独具时代和特定地域特点的文化。金源文化应从金代建国开始算起,直到金朝灭亡(1115—1232)。地域是以阿什河流域金上京城都市为核心,包括今拉林河流域、呼兰河流域、松花江中游左右两岸。其范围大致是:东至牡丹江,西至第二松花江右岸,北至呼兰河上游,南至吉林市地区,为当时金代上京会宁府行政区划所辖地域大体相当。

## 5. The Culture of Jin Dynasty

After the founding of the Jin Dynasty, it conquered Liao Kingdom and the Northern Song Dynasty swiftly. The Jurchen nationality soon adopted the culture of the Han nationality and even the language since they moved southward. Though the Jin culture retained and adopted some cultural tradition of the Jurchen nationality, the main part of it was from the Han culture of Liao Kingdom and Song Dynasty.

**The Jurchen Script**

The Jurchen people had no script before the Jin Dynasty was founded. In the third year of Tianpu Peiord (A. D. 1119) Wanyan Xiyin and Yelu created Jurchen script, which were called the big Jurchen script. After that in the first year of Tianjuan Period (A. D. 1138), Emperor Xizong created another set of Jurchen script, which were called the small Jurchen script. The above two sets of Jurchen scripts were all based on the Chinese and Qidan (Khitan) script. The big and small Jurchen script became the official script since they were created and issued for enforcement, and they were used together with the Chinese and Qidan script in the Jin Dynasty. The Jurchen scripts were used in writing credentials, orders and proclamations, and schools were set up to teach them.

**Confucianism and Historiography**

The Jurchen people had only the primitive Shamanism at the very beginning. After they conquered the Liao Kingdom, Buddhism which was once flourishing in the Liao Kingdom continued to evolve in areas such as the main capital of the Jin Dynasty. After the Northern Song Dynasty was conquered by the Jin Dynasty, the Confucianism of the Northern Song Dynasty began to dominate in the culture of the Jin Dynasty. The imperial examination system was held in the early Jin Dynasty, in which the talents were selected according to their grasp of the Confucian classics. Emperor Xizong built Confucian temples in the upper capital and ordered that the Confucian classics should be translated into the Jurchen script and *The Analects of Confucius* and *The Book of Filial Piety* should be read as required reading.

Historiography in the Jin Dynasty was not very advanced. After the Liao Kingdom was conquered, Xiao Yongqi from Qimiao carried on his teacher's career and compiled seven hundred and fifteen volumes of *History of Liao*, which was basically adapted from *The Veritable Records* written by

Yelv Yan, a writer of Liao Kingdom.

## Literature and Art

The Jurchen people at the early Jin Dynasty were mostly vulgar and illiterate, till Emperor Xizong and Emperor Hailing, the nobles of upper class adopted the culture of the Han nationality and, under the influence of the Confucian scholar, began to create literature works. The typical representatives were Emperor Xizong, Emperor Hailing and Wanyan Liang.

From the nobles to the common people, the Jurchen people all liked dancing and singing. Before the founding of the Jin Dynasty, the Jurchen people found their partners through singing songs. Their lives of fishing and hunting were also reflected through their dances and songs. The Jurchen people believe in the Shamanism and songs and dances of the Shamanism were recorded in many historical books.

## Science and Technology

Though superstitions were flourishing in Beijing area during the Jin Dynasty, science was still evolving gradually. Some scientific inventions appeared, firstly in the areas of astronomy and calendar system.

Astronomy: The Jin Dynasty set up astronomical observatories for the purpose of divining the good or ill luck of the dynasty.

Calendar system: In the fifth year of the Tianhui period in the Jin Dynasty (A. D. 1127), Yangji, officer of the authority that administer the affairs about the sky and calendar, began to compose *the Ming Dynasty Calendar*. In the eleventh year of the Dading period (A. D. 1171), *the Revised Ming Dynasty Calendar*, composed by Zhao Zhiwei, an officer from the same authority, was successful. Soon after the capital was moved to Mingchang, another officer of the authority composed another calendar. Unfortunately, the downfall of the Jin Dynasty brought an end to the new calendar when it was waiting for proofreading.

Because they had no calendar at the early stages of the Jin Dynasty, the Jurchen people didn't know their ages. They only knew that a year was passed when they saw the grass was green again. In the fifteenth year of the Tianhui period the first calendar was put into force, which was a big step forward in the development of the Jurchen society.

## Education

The upper capital of the Jin Dynasty was always the center of education and examination for the Jurchen people. During the time of Emperor Taizong, Yelv Gu, Head of Guangning was ordered to translate classic books to be used as textbooks. The appearance of the teachers such as Yelu who had a good command of the Jurchen script prepared for the establishment of the Jurchen schools.

In the third year of Tiande period during Emperor Hailing's reign, the Imperial College, the first national institution of higher education in the Jin Dynasty, was set up, which later became the administrative institution governing the Imperial Colleges and Taixue (the highest seat of learning in ancient China).

**Shamanism**

The Jurchen people showed their respect to the natural power and natural objects, which was one form of animistic religion—shamanism.

"Shaman" was originally a word from Tungusic, meaning people dancing crazily with excitement. Shamanism is also called "Shanman". In Shamans' dance ceremony to exorcize evil spirits they danced crazily and so were regarded as witches or wizards. It is said that shamans were the intermediary between the gods and the human being. They organized religious rites, addressed on behalf of the gods and convey the blessing from the gods.

Most ancient minorities in northeast believed in the heavenly laws, which advocated that everything had its soul, and from which Shamanism originated.

After the founding of the Jin Dynasty, Shamanism still spread in the upper capital area instead of disappearing. The etiquette and custom of worshiping heaven had developed thoroughly to the emperor etiquette.

The belief in Shamanism by the Jurchen people is demonstrated in the following five aspects:

(1) The Jurchen people believe that shamans can address people on behalf of the gods and predict the future events.

(2) According to the teaching of Shamanism, Shamans can let the soul leave the body and fly to the sky or the hell. They can communicate directly with the gods or spirits. When the shamans were possessed by the gods, they were worshiped by people as gods.

(3) The Jurchen people believed that shamans can cure illnesses and exorcize evil spirits.

(4) The Jurchen people used shamans to revenge and rob properties. They believed that shamans could cause death to people by imprecating.

(5) Shamans could pray for blessing for people.

Besides, shamans had their special clothing in religious activities: sacred hat, scared clothes, sacred shoes, lumbar bell. The instruments included sacred drum, sacred knife, sacred stick, and sacred soil.

After the Liao Kingdom and the Northern Song Dynasty were conquered by the Jin Dynasty, the integration of nationalities boosted the integration of the cultures. The Jurchen people adopted Taoism, Buddhism and Confucianism, and finally reached a religious state with the above three religions as integral part of the whole.

## Buddhism

After the founding of the Jin Dynasty, the Jurchen people, under the influence of refugees and Qidan people, soon adopted Buddhism, and believed it sincerely. Buddhism soon developed.

The flourishing period of Buddhism in the Jin Dynasty started from Emperor Taizong after the Jurchen people passed the Great Wall and moved southwards. During the period of Emperor Taizong, there were temples being built and activities of monks in the upper capital. But it developed slowly since the ruler did not attach too much importance to it. In October of the first year of Tianhui period of the Emperor Tai Zong (A.D. 1123), the first temple in the main capital was set up which was named Qingyuan Temple. Soon after, Emperor Taizong was converted to Buddhism. Till the period of Emperor Xizong, Buddhism was gradually viewed highly by the rulers of Jurchen people. Buddhism temples were widely built within and out of the upper capital. Buddhism preaching activities were on the increase. The Jurchen people, from nobles to the common people, all believed Buddhism. During the period of Emperor Xizong, Buddhism further developed and kept a close relationship with the royal family. The mother of Emperor Hailing, Empress Dowager Tushan, actively supported the Buddhist activities.

## 金上京文化

金朝建国后,较快地占领了辽和北宋地区,女真人南下后较快地接受了汉文化,甚至通用汉族的语言。金文化虽然保留和吸收了女真族的某些文化传统,但基本上是继承辽、宋的汉族文化。

### 道教

金的道教发达,道观各地陆续兴修。金上京地区兴起的教派主要有太一教、大道教(亦称真大道教)。

太一教是金初在北方兴起新道派之一,创立于金熙宗天眷元年(1138—1140),创始人为萧抱珍。

真大道是金朝初年北方出现的三大新道派之一,真大道的创始人是刘德仁,创教于金熙宗皇统年间(1140—1149)。

道教起于民间,早期具有强烈的人民性,倡平等思想,能以行医治病救人,深得民众的拥护。

### 女真文字

在金朝建立以前,女真人没有文字,天辅三年(1119年)完颜希尹和叶鲁创制了女真字,称作女真大字,在这之后,天眷元年(1138年)金熙宗又创造了女真字,称作女真小字。以上两种女真字都是仿汉字和契丹字创制。造出、颁行后的女真大小字,成为金朝官方文字,与契丹字和汉字在金朝境内通用。金朝用女真字撰写国书、谕令和文告,并设学校教女真字。

### 儒学和史学

女真族原来只有原始的萨满教。灭辽后,辽代兴盛的佛教在上京等地继续发展,灭北宋后,北宋的儒学逐渐在金代文化思想中占统治地位。金初行科举,即以"经义"取士。金熙宗在上京建孔庙,以女真字翻译儒家经书,学校以《论语》和《孝经》为必读课本。

金代史学,不是很发达,金灭辽后,契庙人萧永棋继承其师编修《辽史》七一五卷,但大抵是依据辽耶律严《实录》改编。

### 文学与艺术

金初的女真人,多粗俗不文。到了金熙宗和海陵王时代,女真上层贵族接受了汉族文化,在汉族儒士的影响下,开始出现文学创作活动。其中最有代表性的人物,是金熙宗和海陵王完颜亮。

女真人从贵族到平民,都喜欢舞蹈、歌唱。在金建立政权以前,女真人以歌声寻配偶,渔猎生活也以歌舞形式反映出来。女真人信奉萨满教,萨满教乐舞在史书上多有记载。

### 科学与技术

金代迷信盛行于北京地区,但是科学仍然缓慢地向前发展,也出现了一些科学上的创造发明,这首先表现在天文、历法上。

天文:金设天文观测之台,目的是占卜政权的吉凶。

历法:金天会五年(1127年)开始由司天杨级制造《大明历》。大定十一年(1171年)世宗司天监赵知微所制的《重修大明历》成功。在迁都北平至明昌初,司天监又制新历,但是,在等待复核校对中,未及用而金亡。

金初无历法,女真人也不知生年,唯见草复青,谓之一岁。在天会十五年始行历法,这是女真社会发展中的一大进步。

### 教育

金上京一直是女真教育和考试中心。太宗时,曾命广宁户耶律固翻译经书,以提供教材。叶鲁等精通女真文教师的出现,为女真学校的创立提供了条件。

海陵天德三年,设养士之所国子监,这是金朝第一所国立高等学府,后成为教育管理机构,管理国子学和太学。

### 萨满教

女真人初期表现出对自然力和自然物的崇拜,是为多神教的表达形式萨满教。

"萨满",原是通古斯语,其意是"固兴奋激动而手舞足蹈"。萨满亦称"珊蛮",行巫法时,舞姿癫狂,属于"巫师"、"巫婆"一类的人物。据说,萨满是沟通人神之间关系的使者,他们主持宗教仪式,代神发言,传达神的吉意。

活动于东北一带的古代少数民族多信天道,主张万物有灵,此为萨满教产生的由来。

金政权建立以后,萨满教并没有消失,仍然继续在上京一带流传。由女真风俗而流传下来拜天之礼俗,发展为帝王之礼,更趋完备。

女真人信仰萨满教主要体现在五个方面：
(1)女真人相信萨满能道神语,预知未来。
(2)按萨满教的说法,萨满能使灵魂脱离肉体而升天入地,说萨满能与鬼神直接交谈,而当神灵附于萨满身上时,萨满就被人当作神来崇拜,意思是萨满等于神灵。
(3)女真相信萨满能为人驱邪治病。
(4)女真人利用萨满,直接为氏族复仇和掠财服务,他们深信萨满能够借诅咒而置人于死地,给人带来灾难。
(5)萨满能为人祈福。

此外萨满从事宗教的活动有其特殊服饰:神帽、神衣、神鞋、腰铃,法具有神鼓、神刀、神杆、档土等。

在灭辽和北宁之后,民族融合促进了文化融合,女真人吸纳了道教、佛教和儒教;最终形成了"儒佛道三教合一"的宗教格局。

**佛教**

金政权建立之后,女真人在流人和契丹人的影响之下,很快地接受了佛教思想,信之甚笃,奉之虔诚,佛教遂发展起来。

金代女真佛教兴盛之时,应在统一女真诸部进入关内之后,始于金太宗统治之时。在金太宗时,上京已有佛寺的建筑和僧人的活动,但统治者并不注重佛教,后来方得发展。在金太宗天会元年(1123年)10月,就已经有了金上京最早的寺庙庆元寺,在不久之后,金太宗即皈依佛门。到了金熙宗时,佛教逐渐受到女真统治者的重视,金上京城内外广修佛寺,讲经活动日益增多,女真上层贵族以及平民百姓都信仰佛教。

熙宗时期,佛教的势力继续发展。皇室与寺院的关系依然十分密切。海陵王的嫡母徒单皇太后,积极支持佛教活动。

## 6. "Lurigele" Dance of the Daur

"Lurigele" Dance is a traditional hunting dance form of the Daur ethnic group, taking a circle formation and imitating animal and bird calls. There are three parts of the dance. Part one is for singing competition, singing primarily and dancing secondly. Part two is for dancing competition, dancing primarily and singing secondly. Part three is for fighting, shouting with arms up and fighting to win. This folk dance is a "living fossil" to study and explore the evolution of dance from hunting experiences in the Northern ethnic groups.

## 达斡尔族"鲁日格勒"舞

"鲁日格勒"舞是达斡尔族传统狩猎歌舞形式。有走圆圈队形,模仿走兽飞禽呼号等;还有"三段式"表演,一段:比歌,歌为主舞为副;二段:赛舞,舞为主歌为副;三段:打斗,振臂高呼彼此盘旋打斗决出胜负。"鲁日格勒"舞是研究和探索北方民族原始狩猎歌舞沿革轨迹的"活化石"。

### 7. "Wuqin" of the Daur Ethnic Group

"Wuqin" is an art form created in Manchu language by Daur writers in the Qing dynasty. The poems in chanting are termed as "Wuqin". The content is about national history, heroic deeds and stories from classic novels such as "Three Kingdoms" and "Outlaws of the Marsh" and so it is very popular with the Daur people. The genres of the tunes are chanting, narrative and short songs. The elderly people who sing "Wuqin" repertoire could sing for as long as several days and nights, or as short as a few minutes or hours.

The figure shows Bo Yue (1909-1887), a singer of "Wuqin" is performing Mukulan (Khomuz or Koxianqin in Chinese pinyin, the Mongolian jaw harp with one or two metal reeds).

### 达斡尔族"乌钦"

"乌钦"说唱,是在清朝年间由达斡尔族文人用满文创作,并以吟诵调朗读的叙事体诗歌,称作"乌钦"。作品题材中既有反映民族历史、莫日根和英雄事迹的,又有古典名著《三国演义》《水浒传》故事,深受达斡尔族民众欢迎。曲调有吟诵调、叙事歌曲调和小段小唱调。乌钦曲目长者可唱几天几夜,短者几分钟到数小时不等。

### 8. Gulunmuda Festival of Oroqen Nationality

Gulunmuda means showing respect to the God of Fire in Oroqen language. The festival is rich and colorful in form and content and it is hold in spring each year. Many activities are put on in the daytime such as horse racing, arrow shooting, gun shooting, wrestling, dance, story telling, chess and wood card playing; At night, people gathers around the fire and invite Shaman to dance to offer a sacrifice to the ancestor. The ancient Gulunmuda Festival contains rich cultural connotation. As a result of all sorts of reasons, the ceremony basically stops, but in recent years this custom was resumed spontaneously. However, the form and content have gone through dramatic changes and it is in imminent danger.

The figure shows Shaman Guan Kuoni is dancing to show respect to the mountain spirit "Bai Naqia".

### 鄂伦春族"古伦木沓"节

"古伦木沓"为鄂伦春语,意为祭祀火神。每年春季举行,内容丰富多彩。白天举行赛马、射箭、射击、摔跤、歌舞、讲故事、下棋及玩木牌等活动;夜间拢上篝火请萨满跳神,祭神祭祖。"古伦木沓"节蕴涵着丰富的文化内涵。由于种种原因,节日活动基本停止,近几年在民间有自发性的恢复,但活动方式和内容变异很大,已濒临消亡。

## 9. The Art of "Yimakan" of Hezhen Nationality

"Yimakan" is a unique art mainly consisted of talking and singing which is passed by mouth and ear from generation to generation of Hezhen Nationality. The tune Yimakan adopted is termed Yimakan tune, and the form is the combination of a person's talking and singing without instrumental accompaniment. It vividly displays their experiences of hunting and fishing, life and fight, marriage, dance show and other ceremonies, and it is a song and talk show of the customs of ancient Hezhen Nationality. Now, the way of life and production methods of Hezhen people have undergone tremendous changes and the traditional hunting and fishing culture has gradually lost the original color. Particularly, Yimakan singing and talking art, which represents the traditional hunting and fishing culture of Hezhen people, is in imminent danger.

## 赫哲族"伊玛堪"

"伊玛堪"是赫哲族独有的一种口耳相授、世代传承的民间说唱艺术。"伊玛堪"所用曲调称伊玛堪调。表现形式是说唱结合,一人说唱,无乐器伴奏。说唱将赫哲族的渔猎生产、生活、征战、婚姻、跳神及礼俗等展现得栩栩如生,是古代赫哲族的风俗画卷。当代,赫哲族的生活方式和生产方式发生巨大变化,传统渔猎文化渐渐失去了原有的色彩,代表赫哲族传统渔猎文化之一的伊玛堪说唱艺术正面临着一片贫瘠的尴尬。

## 10. The Craft of Fish-skin Clothing Making by the Hezhen Ethnic Group

The people of Hezhen Ethnic Group have their ancestral home in Heilongjiang province and fishing and hunting have long been their major source of livelihood. Fishing dominates their daily activities whereas fish remains the food on the table and fish-skin functions as their clothing. Thus they were famous for "Fish-skin Tribe" in history. Traditional crafts of fish-skin clothing making involves a whole procedure of complicated fish skin processing which can be subdivided into several steps, namely skinning the fish, drying the fish skin, softening the dried skin, cutting and sewing the skin, and artistically embellishing the finished handicrafts. Unfortunately, older generations with the mastery of this traditional craft have passed away successively nowadays. At present, the only craftsman alive is nearly 80-year-old You Cuiyu residing in Jiejunkou Hezhen Township. On the verge of extinction is this ancient and traditional craft of fish-skin clothing making which is in urgent need of succeeding and protecting.

## 赫哲族鱼皮制作技艺

赫哲族世居黑龙江,他们长期以渔猎为生,捕鱼、食鱼、穿鱼皮,在历史上以"鱼皮部落"闻名于世。传统的鱼皮制作技艺是一整套复杂的鱼皮加工过程,分为剥鱼皮、干燥、熟软、拼剪缝合、艺术修饰几个步骤。如今,掌握传统技艺的老人相继离世,仅有街津口赫哲乡的尤翠玉老人尚在,且已年近八十,古老的传统制作技艺濒临消亡,亟待抢救与保护。

# REFERENCES

[1]安福勇,毛春州,徐丽娜. 实用导游英语[M]. 武汉:华中科技大学出版社,2011.

[2]安静. 背包旅游英语[M]. 北京:旅游教育出版社,2007.

[3]安小可. 旅游英语实物教程[M]. 武汉:华中科技大学出版社,2010.

[4]薄喜如. 黑龙江导游词[M]. 北京:中国旅游出版社,2010.

[5]曹长波. 新编旅游英语[M]. 上海:复旦大学出版社,2011.

[6]曹明红. 全国导游基础知识[M]. 天津:天津大学出版社,2012.

[7]陈融. 英语的礼貌语言[J]. 现代英语,1989,3:14.

[8]陈巍. 导游实务[M]. 北京:北京理工大学出版社,2010.

[9]陈欣. 导游英语情景口语[M]. 2版. 北京:北京大学出版社,2012.

[10]陈欣. 导游英语情景口语[M]. 北京:北京大学出版社,2009.

[11]戴宗显. 全国导游人员资格考试培训系列教材.英语[M]. 北京:旅游教育出版社,1990.

[12]丁大刚. 旅游英语的语言特点与翻译[M]. 上海:上海交通大学出版社,2008.

[13]丁树德. 实用旅游英语口语[M]. 天津:天津大学出版社,2011.

[14]段开成. 旅游英语(高级)[M]. 天津:南开大学出版社,2004.

[15]高中山. 涉外旅游英语[M]. 上海:上海交通大学出版社,2005.

[16]关肇远. 导游英语口语[M]. 2版. 北京:高等教育出版社,2009.

[17]郭晓斌,尚季玲. 旅游英语[M]. 北京:中国人民大学出版社,2013.

[18]郭兆康,等. 宾馆英语[M]. 北京:高等教育出版社,2003.

[19]国家旅游局人事劳动教育司. 导游基础知识[M]. 5版. 北京:旅游教育出版社,2010.

[20]哈拉尔德·巴特尔. 合格导游[M]. 胡永震,译. 北京:旅游教育出版社,1988.

[21]何道宽. 英语·创意导游[M]. 重庆:重庆出版社,1995.

[22]黑龙江省旅游局. 自然神奇黑龙江——黑龙江省优秀导游词精选[M]. 北京:中国旅游出版社,2002.

[23]胡朝慧. 酒店英语[M]. 北京:北京大学出版社,2011.

[24]黄金葵. 经典旅游景观导游词赏析与口译[M]. 北京:北京交通大学出版社,2012.

[25]黄中军,刘爱服,曲琳娜. 实用旅游英语[M]. 北京:清华大学出版社,2010.

[26]贾柱立. 英语翻译与导游英语[M]. 天津:天津大学出版社,2012.

[27]孔永生. 导游细微服务[M]. 北京:中国旅游出版社,2007.

[28]李洪涛. 酒店英语口语话题王[M]. 天津:天津外语音像出版社,2012.

[29]李娌. 导游服务案例精选解析[M]. 北京:旅游教育出版社,2007.
[30]李亚妮. 导游业务[M]. 北京:清华大学出版社,北京交通大学出版社,2009.
[31]李燕,徐静. 旅游英语口语[M]. 北京:对外经贸大学出版社,2011.
[32]刘丽莉. 导游英语实用教程[M]. 天津:天津大学出版社,2010.
[33]刘爽. 旅游英语口语大全[M]. 北京:机械工业出版社,2012.
[34]卢春华. 导游英语口语[M]. 武汉:武汉大学出版社,2011.
[35]陆志宝. 导游英语[M]. 北京:旅游教育出版社,2003.
[36]陆志宝. 全国导游人员资格等级考试系列教材. 英语[M]. 北京:旅游教育出版社,1995.
[37]栾丽君,老青. 新航标职业英语·英语写作实训教程:旅游专业[M]. 北京:北京语言大学出版社,2011.
[38]南凡,刘素花. 旅游英语[M]. 北京:高等教育出版社,2011.
[39]彭华. 旅游专业英语[M]. 大连:大连理工大学出版社,2006.
[40]彭萍. 实用旅游英语翻译(英汉双向)[M]. 北京:对外经济贸易大学出版社,2010.
[41]钱炜,林珍珍. 旅游英语[M]. 天津:天津人民出版社,1991.
[42]邱立志. 导游英语900句[M]. 广州:广东旅游出版社,2008.
[43]任孝珍. 旅游应用文写作[M]. 北京:对外经济贸易大学出版社,2011.
[44]沈行华. 导游英语口语化的探索[J]. 职教论坛,2002,20:57.
[45]盛丹丹. 导游英语[M]. 北京:中国水利水电出版社,2010.
[46]舒伯阳. 旅游市场营销[M]. 北京:清华大学出版社,2009.
[47]孙喜林,荣晓华. 旅游心理学[M]. 大连:东北财经大学出版社,2002.
[48]谭荣璋,温建新. 旅游英语口语[M]. 北京:北京师范大学出版社,2012.
[49]陶汉军. 旅游经济(旅行社)专业知识与业务(初级)[M]. 北京:中国人事出版社,1997.
[50]田夕伟,唐晓云. 旅游英语实训教程[M]. 北京:北京师范大学出版社,2011.
[51]王堃. 导游英语[M]. 北京:北京大学出版社,2011.
[52]王浪. 中国著名旅游景区导游词精选(英汉对照·全新版)[M]. 北京:旅游教育出版社,2010.
[53]王连义. 怎样做好导游工作[M]. 北京:中国旅游出版社,1992.
[54]王琳,关铁山. 旅游英语应用教程[M]. 北京:高等教育出版社,2011.
[55]王世瑛. 旅游政策与法规[M]. 北京:旅游教育出版社,2011.
[56]王向宁. 实用导游英语(社会与文化)[M]. 北京:北京大学出版社,2011.
[57]王哲. 导游英语[M]. 北京:北京大学出版社,2008.
[58]修月祯. 旅游英语教程[M]. 北京:清华大学出版社,2010.
[59]徐坤耿. 导游业务(资格考试)[M]. 北京:旅游教育出版社,1995.
[60]巽一朗. 即学即用旅游英语会话词典[M]. 上海:外语教学与研究出版社,2006.

[61] 杨厚松. 旅游应用文写作[M]. 北京:北京师范大学出版社,2011.

[62] 杨华. 实用旅游英语[M]. 北京:中国人民大学出版社,2012.

[63] 杨天庆. 和老外聊文化中国:沿途英语导游话题[M]. 成都:天地出版社,2005.

[64] 姚嘉五,秦美娟,等. 最新英文公文写作大全[M]. 广州:广东旅游出版社,2005.

[65] 袁智敏,余益辉,丁志明. 旅游英语[M]. 北京:北京大学出版社,2005.

[66] 袁智敏. 导游英语实务教程[M]. 北京:北京大学出版社,2012.

[67] 张靖,余宝珠. 英语导游基础教程[M]. 北京:清华大学出版社,2009.

[68] 张靖. 英语导游基础教程[M]. 北京:清华大学出版社,2009.

[69] 张琼霓. 导游业务[M]. 北京:旅游教育出版社,2011.

[70] 赵冉冉. 导游应急处理一本通[M]. 北京:旅游教育出版社,2008.

[71] 周幼华,周志浩,姜萍. 导游英语实务教程[M]. 苏州:苏州大学出版社,2011.

[72] 朱葆琛,朱锡炎. 实用旅游英语(英文版)[M]. 北京:旅游教育出版社,1991.

[73] 朱葆琛. 导游业务[M]. 北京:旅游教育出版社,1990.

[74] 朱华,朱红. 旅游英语口语教程[M]. 北京:高等教育出版社,2010.

[75] 朱华. 旅游英语教程[M]. 北京:高等教育出版社,2006.

[76] 朱华. 旅游英语口语教程[M]. 北京:高等教育出版社,2010.

[77] 朱智. 旅行社运营管理实务[M]. 北京:国防工业出版社,2011.

[78] 邹晓燕,马飞,司爱侠. 旅游专业英语实用教程[M]. 北京:清华大学出版社,2011.

[79] COOK, VIVIAN. Second language learning an language teaching[M]. Beijing:Foreign Language Teaching and Research Press, 2000.

[80] ERVIN S M, OSGOOD C E. Second language learning and bilingualism in C. E. Osgood and T. A. sebeok(eds). Psycholinguistics: a survey of theory an research problems[M]. Blooington and London: Indiana University Press, 1965.

[81] JOHNSON, KAREN E. Understanding communication in second language classrooms [M]. Cambridge:Cambridge University Press, 1995.

[82] LEECH, GEOFFREY. Semantics[M]. London:Penguin Books UK, 1983.

[83] NIDA, EUGENEA. Language, culture and translating[M]. Shanghai:Shanghai Foreign Language Education Press, 1993.

[84] TYLER, ALEXANDER FRASER. Essay on the principles of translation[M]. Beijing:Foreign Language Teaching and Research Press, 2007.

# 读者反馈表

**尊敬的读者：**

您好！感谢您多年来对哈尔滨工业大学出版社的支持与厚爱！为了更好地满足您的需要，提供更好的服务，希望您对本书提出宝贵意见，将下表填好后，寄回我社或登录我社网站（http://hitpress.hit.edu.cn）进行填写。谢谢！您可享有的权益：

☆ 免费获得我社的最新图书书目　　　　☆ 可参加不定期的促销活动
☆ 解答阅读中遇到的问题　　　　　　　☆ 购买此系列图书可优惠

**读者信息**

姓名_____　□先生　□女士　　年龄_____　学历_____
工作单位_____　职务_____
E-mail_____　邮编_____
通讯地址_____
购书名称_____　购书地点_____

1. 您对本书的评价

   内容质量　□很好　　　□较好　　　□一般　　　□较差
   封面设计　□很好　　　□一般　　　□较差
   编排　　　□利于阅读　□一般　　　□较差
   本书定价　□偏高　　　□合适　　　□偏低

2. 在您获取专业知识和专业信息的主要渠道中，排在前三位的是：
   ①_____　　②_____　　③_____
   A. 网络　B. 期刊　C. 图书　D. 报纸　E. 电视　F. 会议　G. 内部交流　H. 其他：_____

3. 您认为编写最好的专业图书（国内外）

| 书名 | 著作者 | 出版社 | 出版日期 | 定价 |
|---|---|---|---|---|
|  |  |  |  |  |
|  |  |  |  |  |
|  |  |  |  |  |
|  |  |  |  |  |

4. 您是否愿意与我们合作，参与编写、编译、翻译图书？
_____

5. 您还需要阅读哪些图书？
_____

网址：http://hitpress.hit.edu.cn
技术支持与课件下载：网站课件下载区
服务邮箱　wenbinzh@hit.edu.cn　　duyanwell@163.com
邮购电话　0451-86281013　　0451-86418760
组稿编辑及联系方式　赵文斌（0451-86281226）　杜燕（0451-86281408）
回寄地址：黑龙江省哈尔滨市南岗区复华四道街10号　哈尔滨工业大学出版社
邮编：150006　传真　0451-86414049